# SOFTWARS

## The Legal Battles for Control
## OF THE Global Software Industry

## ANTHONY LAWRENCE CLAPES

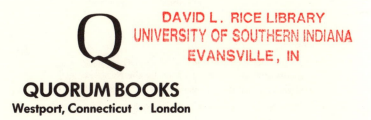

**QUORUM BOOKS**
**Westport, Connecticut • London**

**Library of Congress Cataloging-in-Publication Data**

Clapes, Anthony Lawrence.
    Softwars : the legal battles for control of the global software
industry / Anthony Lawrence Clapes.
      p.  cm.
    Includes index.
    ISBN 0–89930–597–0 (alk. paper)
    1. Copyright—Computer programs. 2. Computer software industry—
Law and legislation. 3. Computer software—Economic aspects.
I. Title.
K1443.C6C56  1993
338.4′70053—dc20          92–24223

British Library Cataloguing in Publication Data is available.

Library of Congress Catalog Card Number: 92–24223
ISBN: 0–89930–597–0

First published in 1993

Quorum Books, 88 Post Road West, Westport, CT 06881
An imprint of Greenwood Publishing Group, Inc.

Printed in the United States of America

The paper used in this book complies with the
Permanent Paper Standard issued by the National
Information Standards Organization (Z39.48–1984).

10 9 8 7 6 5 4 3 2 1

# SOFTWARS

# Contents

# Preface

For a thousand years in Europe the principal mode of determining guilt or innocence was trial by ordeal. There were several forms of ordeal, all of them possessed of a grisly medieval cruelty and having little to do with promoting justice. One ordeal entailed carrying a heavy weight for some distance over burning coals. Barefoot, of course. Another required the accused to plunge a hand (or sometimes more; say, a forearm up to the elbow) into boiling water and extract a stone or a metal object. The most perversely poetic of the ordeals, however, was trial by immersion. Here the accused was flung, dropped, or lowered into a river, lake, or pond. Culpability was determined on the basis of what is now known as specific gravity. If the subject floated to the surface, guilt was "proved" and the sentence was usually execution, almost irrespective of the severity of the crime.

There were certain obvious shortcomings with this approach to dispute resolution, and so an alternative methodology developed. It was called trial by battle. In its most refined form, trial by battle consisted of combat *mano a mano* between two "champions" specially hired for the purpose by the disputants. This form of dispute resolution had the advantage that the accused was spared some amount of agony, but the disadvantage that one or both of the champions probably suffered considerable agony, and that in the end there might be two deaths—the mortal defeat of the accused's champion and the consequent execution of the accused. In addition, of course, the process still bore no resemblance at all to a search for truth or justice.

In the thirteenth century, trial by ordeal and trial by battle succumbed to a more modern and certainly more humane form of settling altercations: litigation. It is that system, substantially evolved, that we use today. Litigation has certain similarities to trial by battle, of course: the use of surrogates and a battle (of wits, in the litigation context) between the surrogates. Some would say that litigation also retains certain attributes of trial by ordeal. Be that as it may, most commercial disputes that cannot be resolved consensually between parties today are submitted to the courts for resolution, and it can at least be said without fear of contradiction that litigation bears *more* of a resemblance to a search for truth and justice than did the two earlier forms of trial.

The software industry is the source of an increasing number of lawsuits. People who have no experience with other industries say that the software industry is "litigious," but that is not so. The number of lawsuits per industry participant in the software industry is still relatively low. The software industry *is* very competitive, however, and if we focus not on the number of lawsuits but on the nature of those lawsuits, we find that something very dramatic is going on. Moreso than in most other industries, litigation is determining the direction of competition in the software industry, and, derivatively, in the computer industry as a whole. That realization is what gave birth to the book you are now holding. I know of no other bit of industrial history that is so dependent on the outcome of "thematic" litigation; that is, litigation dealing with fundamental paradigms. What I have attempted to do herein is to explore those evolving paradigms, to explain why they are so determinative of the course of the software industry, and to give the reader a somewhat closer view of the processes by which these thematic cases are being decided.

Finally a brief word on scholarship. As in my previous book, *Software, Copyright, and Competition* (Quorum 1989), footnotes do not intrude on the text. The sources for the material presented in each chapter are cited at the end of the book, with an indication of the textual point to which each source relates.

# Part I

## At the War College

Wherein we study the nature of the property over which the softwars are being fought and survey the first two decades of those wars.

# 1

# A Brief Discourse on the Spoils of War: The Nature of That Which Is Being Contested

Fere libenter homines id quod volunt credunt.
—Julius Caesar, *Commentarii de bello Gallico*

*People readily believe what they want to believe*. The softwars—the clashes over ownership of the creative and inventive aspects of computer programs—comprise a global economic conflict, but over what is that conflict being fought? What kind of prize awaits the victors, and does the prize warrant the expenditures of money and resources on the battlefield? As is often the case with warfare, not all the combatants know.

In February 1990, the trial of the *Lotus v. Paperback Software* case was underway in federal court in Boston. Dan Bricklin, co-author of VisiCalc and one of this author's favorite figures in the software industry, was on the witness stand. He was appearing on behalf of the defendants, and was being cross-examined by Hank Gutman, Lotus' outside counsel. VisiCalc, as many readers know, was the progenitor of all electronic spreadsheet programs. The proceedings were interrupted by the arrival of a weekend, causing Bricklin's testimony to be suspended until the following Monday. By happenstance, it was the same weekend during which the Copyright Society of the United States had scheduled its annual meeting. Also by happenstance, that meeting had been sited at Harvard Law School in nearby Cambridge. Moreover, either by surreal coincidence or by diabolically prescient planning, Mr. Bricklin had been invited some time earlier to appear on a panel at that meeting. So had I. For obvious reasons, Hank Gutman and Lotus' general counsel, Tom Lemberg, decided to come over and sit in the audience.

Thus it came to pass that on a chilly Saturday afternoon in Cambridge I had the opportunity to participate in a tableau of most unusual construction. In one of those pseudo-amphitheatric classrooms that one now finds at university, a witness for the defense whose testimony would resume in court two days later (along with the lawyer for the defense, Dan Gupta, who was also on the panel) debated with me and others in a highly unstructured and unpredictable environment the very issues that were at the heart of the witness' ongoing testimony. Meanwhile, in the audience, the plaintiff's lawyer sat silently and cheerfully filling yellow legal pads with notes from which to conduct cross-examination on the following Monday. It was a scene characteristic of the clash between law and technology in the computer industry: a mélange of naivete, conviction, strategic advantage, conflict, and philosophic difference that made for a lively, dramatic, and occasionally tense afternoon. That same liveliness, drama, and tension infuses the software protection debate generally, and it is those qualities, rather than simply the recording of events, that I have sought to capture in this book.

There is a reason for the depth of feeling that permeates the international debate over intellectual property protection for computer programs; a reason only dimly perceived by many participants in that debate. As Bricklin sat in that lecture hall full of copyright lawyers, he knew that there was something fundamental at stake in the argument we were having, but he didn't seem to see clearly what it was. In the time that has passed since that day in Cambridge, what is at stake has become evident. The prize in the law school debate, in the *Lotus v. Paperback* case itself, as well as in numerous other courtrooms, lecture halls, and legislative chambers around the world—not as individual battles but collectively as a far-ranging war of words over intellectual property rights—is the computer industry itself.

The computer industry is, increasingly, a software industry. Indeed, an article in the *Harvard Business Review* in 1991 suggested that Western computer manufacturers should give up the hardware business altogether and become software companies. That such an article could appear in a serious business publication is eloquent proof of the central thesis of this book: that the outcome of the legal battles over software will determine the nature of the industry for the foreseeable future, and the nature of the industry will dictate the identities of the firms that will be most successful in competing in that industry. The softwars, in other words, will be a major determinant along with business and technological factors of the course of evolution in the computer industry. Assigning relative importance to the legal factor as compared to more traditional determinative economic factors such as access to skilled labor, availability of natural resources, suitability of industrial infrastructure, ability to obtain capital, and so forth, is an exercise in judgment. Judgment, in turn, calls on belief to give shape to the facts under consideration by the person doing the judging. When one asserts, as I do, that legal battles will have a disproportionately profound effect on the course of history in the computer industry, it is fair to inquire into the beliefs that underlay that judgment.

*People readily believe what they want to believe.* It is perhaps not immediately evident why a debate over intellectual property protection for computer programs should be a critical aspect of the larger competitive conflict over what the essence of the computer industry—including not only software but also hardware—will be in the next century. As we shall see, however, that larger conflict is being fought out on many fronts, among which are the research lab, the marketplace, the press, the halls of government—*and* the courtroom. It is a war of epic proportions in economic terms, the outcome of which will affect computer programmers, hardware engineers, salespeople, manufacturing personnel, and others employed in the computer industry directly and personally, profoundly influencing not only the nature of their work but also the very opportunity to do that work.

The legal aspects of this conflict, some of which were at issue in the *Lotus v. Paperback* case, are often regarded as theoretical debates, as matters of personal philosophy or of academic interest. They are not. The personal interests of those employed in the industry, and the interests of the institutions of which they are a part, are at stake. That the implications of the legal issues have not yet been widely appreciated was illustrated a few years ago, at an annual conference on "computer-human interfaces" held by the Association of Computing Machinery (ACM), the largest professional society for computer programmers. The conference was largely devoted to the technical and aesthetic aspects of "user interfaces" (the imagery on the monitor screen, the sound effects from the computer's loudspeaker, and the other modes of communication between humans and computers), but one of the sessions dealt with the legal protection available for these important aspects of computer programs. In connection with the debate, the moderator, a law professor with well-known antiprotectionist views, circulated a multiple choice questionnaire. Filling out the questionnaire with the same degree of reflection that they would have exercised had they been voting for their favorite TV shows, the majority of respondents at the conference indicated that they preferred to have neither patent protection nor copyright protection for user interfaces. That assemblage collectively took its eye off the ball, allowing the legal scholar to obtain "evidence," which she publicized widely thereafter, that the industry favored disestablishment of legal protection for the very intellectual property on which the popularity of commercial computer programs from which most of those assembled were earning their livelihoods critically depends.

Writing a book about intellectual property protection for computer programs that is designed to reach—and satisfy—a diverse audience of computer programmers, lawyers, judges, policymakers, and interested users is a daunting task. Intellectual property law is not generally known to be stimulating subject matter for readers other than specialists in the field. Neither is computer programming. And yet, just as the confluence of waters of the Rio Negro and the Solimoes produce the world's mightiest river, the confluence of computer programming issues and intellectual property law issues has produced a roiling, muddy Amazon of economic potential that is carving a broad channel through the landscape of the computer industry. Momentous events quite outside the computer industry have made it clear that, as far as we can see into the future, military confrontations will be taking a back seat to economic confrontations as a form of international conflict among major nations. The global economic conflict to which I have alluded is one such confrontation, and the scale of the conflict is grand enough to demand attention. The softwars represent the collision of two fundamentally different paradigms of industrial competition: innovation and imitation. These two paradigms define the terms of the struggle for international dominance of the computer industry. In industries marked by innovative competition, firms rely heavily on development of advanced products to gain competitive advantage. In industries marked by imitative competition, firms rely primarily on achieving lower prices for similar goods in order to gain competitive advantage. Under innovative competition, firms with skills in research development and creative arts have a comparative edge. Under imitative competition, firms with skills in low-cost manufacturing and the art of copying have a comparative edge.

Though both forms of competition have long existed in the computer industry, until now the industry's driving force has been innovative competition, with the result that the overarching characteristic of the computer industry has been technological progress. That progress has occurred under the existing rules of patent, copyright, and trade secret law. Since it is software, not hardware, that brings computers to life and allows them to serve their users in ways that those users find desirable, and since the ability to make a business out of software depends heavily on the existence of intellectual property rights in that software, it is becoming clear that the extent of software protection offered in the developed world will determine the outcome of what may be the last great competitive war of the current international industrial economy. One does not have to be an MBA to be able to see that if software were deprived of all legal protection, money to fund the development of new commercial software products would dry up. The reason? It is a matter of economic fact that throughout the developed world, capital to fund commercial research and development is largely in private hands. Private investors seeking to put their capital at risk by investing in development of software expect to achieve, on balance, repayment of the principal amount of the capital expended on the development of successful products, plus a surplus representing both a return of the capital invested in failed projects and a profit out of which to fund future research and development. As we shall soon see, such a return simply cannot be achieved in the case of software in the absence of intellectual property protection. That realization has deepened the interest of industry partici- pants and industry watchers in the modalities of asset protection available for software investments.

This book, *Softwars*, describes the interplay between economics, law, and business strategy in the struggle over the future of the computer industry. The title connotes the sublimated nature of the conflict we will examine and suggests the central role of software protection in that conflict. I mean to deliver to the reader a series of reports on what is happening on the front lines. The war, as we shall see, is at once a global conflict and a series of local firefights; at once a guerrilla campaign and a Wild West shoot-out. It is a religious war, too—or at least it is like a religious war—in that underlying the struggle is a collision between two belief systems, each with its mullahs in their mosques, its preachers in their pulpits, urging the pro- tagonists on to greater glory for the cause. It is a technological contest, a legal contest, an economic contest, and a political contest.

Facing off around the world in this deadly serious game are suppliers in North America, Europe, Japan, and other countries of the Far East. The larger companies, those with interests in computer hardware as well as software, are major players, as are industry associations, government agen- cies, and even legislatures and heads of state. The battlefronts on which their action takes place range from individual customer accounts to inter- national fora such as the gloves-off negotiations of the General Agreement on Tariffs and Trade (GATT) and the more decorous debates of the World Intellectual Property Organization. The weapons in the arsenals of the big firms are diverse. They include, on the one hand, new product introduction and pricing strategy, and on the other, lobbying efforts by individual firms and the formation of industry associations to shape public opinion on the legal issues. In Europe in 1989, for example, two industry associations were formed for the express purpose of promoting diametrically opposing out- comes in a major European Community software copyright debate that consumed the succeeding two years. IBM was active in one association; Fujitsu in another. Through those associations, the archetypal software dis- pute between the two big firms slipped the moorings of their multiyear arbitration and spread itself on the world stage. Of this, more later.

At the same time, like industrious ants going about their business on the battlefield at Gettysburg, oblivious to the Union and Confederate troops shooting one another down in the larger frame of reference, tens of thou- sands of software suppliers were, and still are, busily designing, writing, testing, and shipping programs of all kinds to a voracious customer set. Those software suppliers range in size from single programmers working alone to groups composed of many hundreds of programmers. The works they produce cover the gamut from computer games to operating systems. All but the largest of these suppliers have been either unaware or only dimly aware of the clashes over software protection that are taking place in the international arena. Yet at the level of those software suppliers, too, there are firefights and skirmishes that themselves affect the course of the broader war. The practices of individual software authors, if sufficiently similar across a broad enough cross section, influence the law, because the law is always struggling to catch up with technology. For example, the realities of retail marketing of programs for personal computers led software authors to offer their works to customers pursuant to the terms of "shrink-wrap" licenses rather than signed license agreements. The shrink-wrap license, which said in essence "read these terms before opening the package, and by opening the package you agree to these terms," was of dubious validity when introduced, but because of its widespread adoption by industry, numerous legislatures have now legitimized such forms of unsigned agreement by passing new statutes. Thus, the practices and views of software providers small and large, because they come to affect the legal norms that govern the extent of protection for computer programs, can alter the fortunes of war.

Grossly simplified, the war described between these covers consists of conflicts between software originators and software copiers. I use the term "copiers" here in a generic sense, not a copyright sense, to refer to those industry participants whose business is based on cloning, or imitating as closely as possible, the functioning and appearance of an originator's program. The competition between originators and copiers has significant international ramifications. At this writing, and for some time before, American software suppliers have dominated the world market. Attempting to catch up, the governmental-industrial combination known familiarity as Japan, Inc., sent its principal computer suppliers forth in the 1970s to clone American hardware and software. That strategy has colored the development of the Japanese software industry ever since. In Europe, the compatibility thrust has taken a somewhat different shape, influenced largely by the chauvenistic but quite natural practice of governmental and quasi-governmental users of computers of reserving substantial portions of their data-processing budgets for indigenous suppliers. The result of that practice was to create a need for connectivity and commonality between the hardware and software of European suppliers and the corresponding products of non-European—primarily American—suppliers. The advent of the personal computer in the United States over a decade ago increased the activity we now call cloning in Japan and Europe, and brought the "Little Tigers" of the Far East—Korea, Taiwan, Singapore, and Thailand—into the game of copying American hardware and software as well. It would not be correct to say, however, that the software protection issue is a matter of America against the rest of the world. In truth, much of the most innovative software available today has been written outside the United States, and at the same time much of the software cloning activity in the world today is undertaken by American companies. In effect, the battles between software originators and software clones are both international and intranational. Victory for one side will mean a continuation of the historical connection between innovation and economic success in the computer industry. Victory for the other side will convert the computer industry—over time, not overnight—into a commodity industry in which competition in hardware and software is based primarily on price, and in which little profit is available from which to fund innovation.

People readily believe what they want to believe about the softwars, but there are beliefs and there are *beliefs*. A homely hypothetical will illustrate the differences. Imagine that you are standing in a bowling alley. Depending on your leisure time preferences, this may or may not be difficult for you to visualize. You are holding a bowling ball against your chest. Now imagine that you release your grip. Doubtless, you *believe* the ball will fall to the floor, and that unless you jump back, it will strike your foot, and that if it does strike your foot it will inflict pain and perhaps serious physical harm as well. That sort of belief is nothing more than using your confidence in the regularity of physical laws to predict the outcome of physical acts. Suppose, however, that instead of releasing the ball, you turn it over and find a label etched into its surface: "Kawasaki." As a result of seeing that label, you believe that the bowling ball was made in Japan. That belief is the result not of using inexorable physical laws as predictors but of applying a (potentially faulty) logical syllogism to fill in a gap in knowledge. It would appear that you do not have either facts or inexorable connectors sufficient to justify the conclusion you have reached. Beliefs often fill in such gaps in our knowledge, and indeed that gap-filling function is both the greatest value and the greatest danger of belief systems.

Now, imagine that when you see that label, you immediately put the ball back on the rack in favor of a ball with an AMF label, on the belief that AMF has had far longer and deeper experience in designing and manufacturing bowling balls, and therefore the AMF ball is likely to be better suited to the purpose of knocking down tenpins. You might in fact have been better advised instead to try each of the balls in order to decide which is better, but if you don't, you will have made a judgment, based on belief, that is at a rather higher level of abstraction than the previous two. Whereas the earlier judgments were direct and rectilinear, this one is indirect and multistranded. It entails beliefs born of a jambalaya of knowledge, logic, and intuition. My judgment that the course of litigation and legislation affecting intellectual property rights in software will materially affect the course of evolution of the computer industry is that sort of judgment. Before we set foot on the battlefield, we should examine the beliefs on which that judgment rests.

Paramount among the factors elevating the importance of the legal system to the computer industry is the belief that computer programs are, in essence, exercises in imagination. Professor Frederick T. Brooks of the Computer Science Department at the University of North Carolina expounded most elegantly on this thought in his 1975 book, *The Mythical Man-Month*:

The programmer, like the poet, works only slightly removed from pure thought-stuff. He builds his castles in the air, from air, creating by exertion of the imagination. Few media of creation are so flexible, so easy to polish and rework, so readily capable of realizing grand conceptual structures.

Programming then is fun because it gratifies creative longings built deep within us and delights sensibilities we have in common with all men.

Amplifying on that theme, Professor Randall Davis of MIT told a forum of the National Research Counsel in 1990 that computer programs are "the ultimate creative medium" and "a tangible form of dreams and imagination." To readers who have not themselves written programs, these characterizations may come as something of a surprise. Readers may have seen flowcharts for programs, for example, that put them in mind of blueprints or circuit diagrams, and therefore come to think of writing software as a mechanistic process the result of which is inexorably dictated by the objective to be achieved. However, as Professor Davis points out,

There is almost no way to visualize software [in advance]. Sure, we have flow charts, we have data-flow diagrams, we have control flow diagrams, and everybody knows how basically useless those are. Flow charts are documentation you write afterward—because management requires them, not because they are a useful tool.

Just as the fact that a sentence can be diagrammed does not mean that it is unimaginative or uncreative, the fact that a program can be flowcharted does not mean that it is unimaginative or uncreative.

A few years ago, the magazine *PC World* published an article that examined the nature of computer programming. The article described a series of interviews conducted by the author, Susan Lammers, in the course of preparing a book-length study of the same subject. Lammers endeavored to get beyond the "magic and mystery" of software development, in order to determine

What did it feel like to develop a major program? Is programming an art or a science, a craft or a skill? What does it take to be a successful programmer?

For her study, Lammers interviewed a number of luminaries in the software profession. One of them, Gary Kildall, the author of the personal computer operating system CP/M, described the products of software development in artistic terms.

When a program is clean and neat, nicely structured and consistent, it can be beautiful. I guess I wouldn't compare a program to the Mona Lisa, but a good program does have a simplicity and elegance. . . . Stylistic distinctions . . . are intriguing, very much like the differences art critics might see between Leonardo's work and a Van Gogh. I like the LISP programming language because it's so pleasing. There's a concise form of LISP called the M expressions. When you write an algorithm using M expressions, it's so beautiful you could frame it and hang it on the wall.

Bob Frankston, co-author with Dan Bricklin, of the program Visicalc, gave Lammers the following comparison of the traditional arts and the software arts:

In music, and in various forms of art, we try to operate within rules, but you have to know when to break the rules and when to follow them, just as in programming. In art, you also ask yourself how people will perceive your work—you're trying to create a perceptual impression. When you communicate, whether in writing or in a program, what you say must be understood. . . . If you cannot explain a program to yourself, the chance of the computer getting it right is pretty small.

Lammers asked Robert Carr, who wrote the program Framework, whether programming was an art or a science. His answer?

It's really a combination of both. . . . Certainly, some very scientific, well-grounded principles are tremendously important for software development, but good software goes beyond. . . . Looking at the sketch of the decision-tree that led to the design of Framework, you'll see that I spent a lot of time thinking, scribbling—a lot of sub-conscious activity. That's where the art is. In art, you can't explicate how the end results were achieved. The best software comes from the realm of intuition.

*Almost pure thought-stuff. Castles in air. Gratifies creative longings. The ultimate creative medium. A tangible forms of dreams and imagination. Magic and mystery. Simplicity and elegance. So beautiful you could hang it on the wall. Trying to create a perceptual impression. A combination of both art and science. A lot of subconscious activity. The best software comes from the realm of intuition.* That is the kind of property we call computer programs. Writing software, according to J. F. Leathrum, author of *Foundations of Software Design*, is like writing a novel or a poem. "In both software and the literary analog," he says, "we are dealing with a highly creative activity." Not surprisingly, then, the task of supervising people who write software reflects the creative nature of programming. Noting that good programmers are often compared to artists and musicians, Patricia Keefe of *Computerworld* describes the task of managing these "often unconventional or egocentric types" as posing unique challenges. She quotes one software manager as saying that "People program because they love the intellectual challenge," and another manager as observing that because programming is a creative process, people tend to be more possessive of their work. A third suggested that programmers need a greater degree of freedom than other employees in order to "look around and explore different ideas." "A good programmer," the president of a small software company told Keefe, "is definitely a prima donna."

A good computer program, one may fairly conclude, is an expression of intellectual creativity. In point of fact—and this is why the softwars are so critical to the future of the industry—a program is nothing more than an expression of intellectual creativity. Like a novel, and unlike, say, an automobile, the physical medium in which that creativity is delivered to customers is insignificant. The intellectual content, not the package, is what is important and valuable about a computer program. Moreover, the intellectual content, not the package, is what costs money to create.

Another important aspect of computer programs is that the creativity they embody may have both scientific and artistic elements. Those elements are not necessarily separable. Just as the works of Lewis Thomas, John McPhee, and Claude Levi-Strauss can intermingle scientific principles and highly creative, expressive writing, so can computer programs. The important thing to keep in mind is that computer programming is *an exercise in writing*. In major part, a computer program is an imagined conversation between the programmer and a user (or all users) of the program being written. The programmer imagines the user sitting down at a computer or a terminal, accessing the program, and beginning an activity. What sorts of things will the user want to do? How should the user convey those desires to the programmer's creation (the program) as it exists dynamically in the computer's memory? How should the program convey through the computer to the user what to do next? What kinds of errors might the user make in conveying her or his desires to the program's dynamic embodiment? If the user begins to flounder and becomes irrational in communicating with the program, what sorts of messages or help should the program provide? If the user communicates clearly, what form should the output produced by the computer under control of the program take? If the user writes a program to work with the programmer's program, what things should the user say in that second program to invoke the services of the first program? The programmer-as-playwright imagines the range of conversations that should take place with the program being created and writes code that will facilitate those conversations.

Having decided what the *play* (as in "play of the game," and also as in "the play's the thing") of the program will be, the programmer confronts a complicated set of puzzles. The program is being written to direct the behavior of a computer. A computer is really an integrated set of machines that provides facilities for processing, storage, input, output, communication, and control of information. The "thinking machine," or processor, has a very limited vocabulary at its disposal, consisting of perhaps as many as a few hundred instructions that it can follow, and a highly structured syntax for identifying the information on which those instructions should operate. Just as an alphabet of only twenty-six letters is sufficient to permit a seemingly infinite range of expression in the English language, though, the "machine language" of a computer's instruction set is sufficient to allow the programmer to do virtually anything with information that can be conceived. One puzzle for the programmer, then, is how to string together the instructions understood by the computer so as to have a successful conversation with the user. What constitutes "successful" for the program is up to the programmer to decide. A successful conversation with a user may be one that meets all the user's desires (i.e, provides a broad range of possibilities from which the user may select), or one in which the user cannot fail (i.e., provides an extensive "help" function), or one in which many parties may participate (i.e., provides for communication with other users or other programs), or one which is over as quickly as possible (i.e., the program is blindingly fast). The programmer must juggle all those considerations and more into the limited syntax and semantics of the language in which the program is being written.

Another puzzle for the programmer is when to write directly in the language of the computer's instruction set (machine language) and when to write in a higher-level language. The computer's *operating system* is a program that provides a series of shorthand conventions for giving instructions to the computer, and in addition there are numerous *higher-level language compilers* that allow programmers to write programs in languages that are said to be more "natural" than machine language. Programs are often written in a mix of machine language, operating systems conventions, and higher-level languages, depending on how the programmer chooses to solve still further puzzles, such as how large the program should be, how it should utilize the computer's memory (and how much of that memory it should commandeer), how frequently it should cause the processor to retrieve from the computer's permanent storage devices either items of information or elements of other programs or elements of the program itself, or how much processing should be expended on creating screen displays. The programmer-as-problem-solver must find a path through the maze of such considerations. It is a maze through which there are usually a large number of acceptable paths, none of which is clearly better than any other (as well as an even larger number of false paths), and a maze in which whether the programmer has chosen the "best" path or not is ultimately a matter for people other than the programmer—that is, the program's users—to decide.

Next, there is the puzzle of organizing the ideas and concepts of the program into a particular concrete expression. This exercise consists of designing the detailed structure, logic, and flow of the program and writing the code. As in the case of other forms of writing, the design phase and the coding phase are not always separate or even separable. The programmer creates the following elements in the course of designing and writing a program.

—*Data structures*, the parts of the program that will cause the computer to allocate specific areas of memory to hold the information relevant to the program. In a static sense, data structures are somewhat like the tables of characters and their relationships that one finds at the front or back of a lengthy novel to help the reader keep track of the action. In a dynamic sense, data structures can be thought of as characters in a novel; they are the subjects to which things happen. The definition of data structures, the selection of the information to be stored in them, and the reservation in those structures of segments of memory of particular sizes for particular types of information are all discretionary decisions the program author makes based on the basis of training, experience, and writing style, as well as the objectives of speed, memory utilization, and functionality that are sought to be achieved.

—*Logic structures*, the programming analog to chapters, subchapters, scenes, paragraphs, and sentences in a book. The manipulation of the data relevant to the program is accomplished by processing the program's instructions, which direct the manipulation of that data, through the computer's processing circuitry. Those instructions are like imperative sentences (Do this, do that, add this to that, go there, etc.). The instructions that cause the computer to provide a particular capability are usually collected into a single chapter, or *module*, of a program. Within a given module, related instructions that together define an identifiable subset of the steps necessary to provide that capability are usually collected into blocks of code called *routines, subroutines*, or *macros*. These blocks of code typically have the attribute that they may be invoked from anywhere else in the program simply by referring to, or "calling," them. A call to a routine, subroutine, or macro causes the computer to jump or "branch" from whatever instruction of the program it is processing to an instruction in the logic structure that is called. Like data structures, logic structures are matters of personal choice of the programmer.

—*Logic*, the orderly sequencing of instructions within the program's logic structures. A novel or play must have logical development, or what the author John Gardner called "profluence, a requirement best satisfied by a sequence of causally related events." A program must also have profluence. Its instructions must be causally related to one another in order that the computer may be directed to produce a result. (A classic type of sequencing in many programming languages, for example, is "if-then-else" logic. The sequence of events called for by that logic consists of testing to determine if a described state of affairs exists, and if so, then to take one sort of action, but if not, to take another sort of action.) The logic sequences written by a programmer are a highly personal form of expression. In the hands of a talented programmer, sequences of great elegance and complexity can be created, just as in the hands of a talented composer, musical notes, chords, and rests may be organized into sequences of great elegance and complexity.

—*Control flow*, the aspect of a program that answers the question, "What happens next?" A computer does not typically process a program in the order in which instructions were written by the programmer. As just noted, at any point the program may call for a branch to some other part of itself. It may also call for looping through a particular subroutine numerous times before moving on. The extent to which a programmer uses seriatim, or "in-line," coding as opposed to nonlinear coding such as branches or loops again depends on factors personal to the programmer as well as factors extrinsic to the programmer such as efficiency, comprehensibility, and reliability.

—*Data flow*, the movement of data into and out of data structures as the program is being processed. Analyzing a program's data flow, one computer scientist has said, is like observing the way gossip is propagated among people. A tracing of the flow of data in a program identifies the relationships among all the characters (data structures) in the literary work that is the computer program.

Using programming structure, logic, and flow to create software is an exercise in creative writing. The programmer experiences writer's block, inspiration, manic productivity, creative construction, and creative exhaustion. The following first-hand description of the experience of writing code (in this case microcode, the highly machine-dependent programming that defines a computer's instruction set), taken from Tracy Kidder's *The Soul of a New Machine*, exhibits all of those emotional states:

Writing microcode is like nothing else in my life. For days, there's nothing coming out. The empty yellow pad sits there in front of me, reminding me of my inadequacy. Finally, it starts to come. I feel good. That feeds it, and finally I get into a state where I'm a microcode writing machine . . . You have to understand the problem thoroughly and you have to have thought of all the myriad ways in which you can put your microverbs together. You have a hundred L-shaped blocks to build a building. You take all the pieces, put them together, pull them apart, put them together again. After a while, you're like a kid on a jungle gym. There are all these constructs in your mind and you can swing from one to another with ease.

I've done this in short intervals for short periods each year. There's low intensity before it and a letdown at the end. There's a big section where you come down off it, and sometimes you do it awkwardly and feel a little strange, wobbly and tired, and you want to say to your friends, "Hey, I'm back."

Finally, in addition to these static and dynamic internal characteristics, software can transform the real world when it is processed through hardware. The system of which software is a part as well as the process that the software causes the computer to perform may therefore embody a technological innovation. Software has a dualistic nature thought by many to be unique. On the one hand, it is a highly expressive medium of creation. On the other hand, it can cause things to happen—not by itself, but as part of a system—and is in that sense functional, useful, and in some cases inventive.

Certain partisans in the softwars argue that the expressive nature of software should be ignored in deciding what elements of computer programs should be protected; others argue that the inventive elements of computer programs should be ignored. As we move deeper into the contested territory, we will learn which combatants champion which arguments, and why. However, at the outset of this exercise in battlefield journalism, it is advisable for the reader to have in mind the world view of the reporter. Having described my belief as to the nature of the craft of programming, I will now recapitulate the premises that shape my observations about activities on the front lines. Here is my credo:

1. Computer programs are written works. The languages in which they are written are somewhat arcane, to be sure, and at present more strictly disciplined than the languages humans use in everyday life. Nonetheless, programming languages have familiar parts of speech—nouns, verbs, prepositions, conjunctions, adjectives, adverbs—and the works written in programming languages have attributes familiar in other forms of writing: structure, flow, logical development, naming conventions, and even style. It would be saying too much to call computer programs literature, but it would be saying too little to call them purely utilitarian works. Protecting computer programs by *copyright*, and protecting them as literary works, is quite appropriate to the nature of intellectual property inherent in them. In addition to their written-down nature, computer programs allow computers to perform useful functions, and sometimes that enabling can constitute a novel and nonobvious advance over the preexisting technology. Protecting the utilitarian aspects of software by *patent* or *trade secret* law is therefore also appropriate, as we shall see herein.

2. In the form in which it is written by the programmer ("source code"), software is readable by people who have the requisite amount of training in reading programming languages. Source code contains readily recognized words and symbols. The BASIC programming language, for example, contains such ordinary words as "if", "then", "next", "read", "restore", "print", and "end", as well as the ordinary mathematical symbols "=", "+", "−", "*", and "/". In order for software to be read by a computer, however, these ordinary words and symbols must be translated into strings of ones and zeros, the "object code" or "machine language" understood by the computer's processing circuitry. That translation does not change the software's essentially textual nature. Although far fewer people can read the ones and zeros of object code, in fact software in object code form continues to have

the attributes of structure, flow, and logical development common to literary works generally.

3. As demonstrated above, it is also true that writing software can be a highly creative activity. Some programs are works of profound imagination and invention. Others, of course, are mechanistic extensions of obvious algorithms (methods for solving logical or mathematical problems). For books in which the range of available expression is great, the copyright law affords substantial protection for their structure, flow, and logical development (normally called "plot"), while for books in which the range of available expression is modest, the copyright law affords less protection for those nonliteral elements. So, too, programs in which the range of available expression is great should—and do—receive broader protection for their nonliteral elements than those in which the range of available expression is modest.

4. Like most industries based on the creation and distribution of intellectual property, as opposed to physical goods, the software industry is characterised by the need for front-end investment and by low production costs. The medium on which software is distributed is very inexpensive in comparison to the value of the material stored on that medium. Such industries are prone to the predation of pirates, and the software industry is no exception. In order to justify the investment in development of new programs, software authors must be assured that they will have a fair opportunity to achieve a return on that investment, and that pirates will not engage in the distribution of unauthorized copies.

5. The software industry is also highly competitive, and that competition is responsible for the rapid progress and consequent rapid growth that the industry has experienced. It is an industry that easily accommodates firms both large and small, and allows both large and small firms to prosper.

6. Further, the software industry is a worldwide industry. Participants in the software industry benefit from the fact that throughout the developed world software comes within the protection of copyright and patent, legal regimes that are themselves international as a result of multilaterial treaties. They are also fully articulated legal regimes, as a result of the long history of copyright and patent statutes, case law, and commentary. The availability of regimes of protection that are (1) available in all the important markets of the world, (2) predictable, and (3) reasonably consistently applied in those markets, has been critical to the ability of software developers to offer their products successfully on an international basis. If protection were substantially weaker (or stronger) in one country than in another, rights holders would find their expectations of return on investment varying widely from country to country, which fortunately has not been the case to date.

That is my point of view, based on two decades' association with the computer industry. Not everyone shares that view. (Indeed, not everyone at IBM agrees with me, and this is as good a place as any to assure the reader that the views expressed between these covers are my own, not those of IBM.) One reviewer of an earlier writing of mine on this subject said:

I confess at the outset that this book made me angry. I . . . disagree with the author's fundamental thesis concerning program copyrights.

The reason given by the reviewer for his disagreement with my viewpoint was that he felt the law was "unsettled" rather than predictable, and that the seminal American legal opinion explaining the applicability of copyright to the nonliteral elements of computer programs such as structure, logic, and flow (also called *structure, sequence*, and *organization* in the legal literature) "is far from the model of clarity of expression and logic."

Those objections are addressed to a fairly narrow aspect of the credo that I have just expressed. I think the reviewer and I would agree, for example, that computer programs are written works; that they have structure, logic, and flow; that they can be quite creative; that the software industry is highly competitive; that the economics of the industry make it prone to pirates; that copyright and patent laws protect against pirates; and that copyright and patent laws in general are stable, predictable, and international. If we could agree on that much, then it wouldn't particularly matter, for instance, whether a particular case was a model of clarity or not. The principles of law applicable to software protection do not leap from an individual case, full-blown and motherless like Athena from the head of Zeus. They derive from a legal tradition that dates back almost to Gutenberg. Does that legal tradition produce results that are predictable in the case of computer programs? It is an important question, with which we will deal in Chapters 2 and 3.

Unstated by the reviewer in question was his own strong personal bias. Elsewhere, he has passionately argued that computer programs should not be protected by copyright law at all. Although his review suggested otherwise—"No one doubts that software is copyrightable"—he was in fact on record at the time as saying that Congress was wrong over a decade ago when it extended copyright protection to computer programs. It is important for readers of reports about the softwars to keep in mind that unstated personal biases abound in this field of writing, and turn most reportage into editorials before they are done. My reviewer's philosophy, for example, aligns him with a small but vociferous coterie of law professors who were and still are striving to limit or reverse the scope of intellectual property protection for computer programs. The views of that particular group have little to do with the real world of computer programming and in my view would, if adopted, greatly injure the software industry. Yet they are hidden in articles that adopt a mantle of neutrality and academic authority. One of the most important lessons to learn while we are at the war college is to suspect claims of neutrality. I do not claim to be neutral either, and that is why I have disclosed my beliefs as to the nature of software at the outset, so that readers can form their own judgments and perspectives as we tour the battlefield.

This book does not take a "strong-protectionist" viewpoint, but rather a "traditional-protectionist" point of view. Its observations about the softwars are all made through the following thematic lens: (1) the software industry and the public benefit enormously from the application of traditional intellectual property law principles in disputes between innovators and copiers, and (2) such confusion as may exist over what those traditional principles are can readily by dispelled by clear and straightforward exposition. Since the traditional principles of patent, copyright, and trade secret law reflect a balance that society seems to find agreeable between the interests of innovators and the interests of copiers in all other fields of endeavor, allowing those principles to serve as the "rules of war," the Geneva convention of the softwars, makes sense. Attempts either to weaken or to strengthen those principles by partisans or their hired guns should therefore be viewed askance.

With that understanding, let's review the history of the softwars prior to the 1990s.

# 2

# Aerial Reconnaissance: The First Two Decades of the Softwars

"[T]he one who controls the software controls the war."
—Katsuhide Hirai, Fujitsu Ltd., quoted in
*Northeast International Business*
(November 1989)

Why does humankind make war? It is a question repeatedly brought to mind, in recent times as a result of the Persian Gulf crisis, the sad spectacle of a Yugoslavia bent on self-destruction, and the population-destroying civil war in Ethiopia. Is bellicosity innate to the species, so that we might say that humans make war for the same reason that they make love, to wit, because they are human? Or is warfare a desperate response of a society threatened—or perceiving itself threatened—by destructive external (or internal) forces, in which case we might conclude that war is not a state arising spontaneously, but rather a collective defense mechanism that could lie dormant forever if society were only able to avoid the dire circumstances that awaken it? Do nations sink into physical conflict because of irreconcilable differences of religious or secular principle? Is war the result of massive and uncontrolled ego, emotion, or accident? Or do we fight simply because we have armies?

I am no military analyst, but as a litigation lawyer I have observed that—litigation being a kind of sublimated warfare—enterprises sue one another for all of the reasons just set out. There are companies that are aggressive by nature and that use litigation aggressively. There are firms, beset by the negative fortunes that ravage markets now and again, that sue their suppliers, competitors, or customers as a way of transferring blame, or perhaps just surviving. In some cases, irreconcilable principles prevent resolution of a dispute between two enterprises through negotiation, and resort is had to the courts to settle the issue. In other cases, ego or emotion underlies the actions of enterprises, which after all are merely groupings of individuals, in suing one another. Not many lawsuits are filed by accident, but it does happen that companies accidently get themselves into positions from which only a lawsuit can extricate them. Finally, it is almost tautological that firms that have lawyers are more likely to litigate than are firms without lawyers.

The softwars are legal battles, but there is a dimensionality to them that is not found in most litigation. They arise in the context of competition among suppliers of commercial computer programs, and they establish the rules of that competition. Since competition is also a form of warfare, bloodless though it may be, the softwars can be seen as conflicts over conflict itself. And since the conflict that is the subject of the softwars is a worldwide struggle for leadership of the computer industry, the jewel in the crown of industrial enterprise in the "Information Age," the legal battles we are going to consider herein have a significance to the developed world that extends far beyond the interests of the combatants in individual cases. For example, one of the great software legal battles of the 1980s involved a tiny software house in Pennsylvania and one of its customers. At issue was whether the customer, a dental laboratory, had unlawfully copied a lab accounting package written for it by the software house. A prosaic, narrow question, it would seem, of little interest in the vast arena in which the world's great computer companies compete. Yet that case, *Whelan Associates, Inc. v. Jaslow Dental Laboratories, Inc.*, has generated more debate, lobbying activity, and legal commentary than any other software intellectual property case, and the world's great computer companies have participated energetically in that debate, activity, and commentary. Why? Because the *Whelan* case, as we shall see momentarily, extends to computer programs the kind of protection traditionally afforded to novels, plays, essays, and other works in which there is a broad range of expressive possibility, and that kind of protection limits the ability of others to copy original computer programs. The ability freely to copy other authors' software works to the advantage of certain classes of competitors in the computer industry; the ability to protect original software against copying works to the advantage of other classes of competitors. The *Whelan* case tilted the competitive balance in the computer industry in favor of original authorship and against the copiers.

The leverage that court cases have over the fortunes of war in the computer industry arises precisely because, as we saw in the last chapter, software is "soft." As pure intellectual property, its existence is fragile indeed. Computer programs suffer from an essential vulnerability: they are easy to copy. In contradistinction to the case of hardware products, copying of computer programs requires no research laboratories, no factories, no chemical formulas, no strategic materials. Copying a computer program is no more difficult than duping an audio tape or plagiarizing a story. What can be freely copied cannot form the basis of a business if the copying can be done with impunity. Thus, the nature and extent of society's rules against such copying actually dictate the boundaries of the software business. Further, because buyers of computers make their hardware purchases in large measure because of the software available for such computers, the rules against copying of software strongly influence competition for computer hardware. Hirai-san was right: *the one who controls the software controls the war.*

The issue is not so much the control of the development of individual software products. That form of control is evanescent and not very interesting. Apple Computer Company controlled—and still controls, for whatever it's worth—the operating system for the Apple IIe. Yet Microsoft's MS-DOS was able to become the preeminent operating system for personal computers, and personal computers running MS-DOS came to outnumber the Apple IIe overwhelmingly. Microsoft, in turn, controls MS-DOS, yet its chairman, Bill Gates, know that MS-DOS will before long be replaced as the preeminent PC operating system, and fears that the replacing product will not come from Microsoft. Lotus Development Corporation controls the spreadsheet software known as Lotus 1–2–3, yet newer products such as Borland's Quattro Pro and Microsoft's Excel are bidding fair to displace Lotus 1–2–3 from its leadership position. Ashton-Tate controlled dBase, the dominant data base program for personal computers, but lost its lead—and ultimately its independent identity—due to quality problems. The sort of control that matters for the future of the computer industry, then, is not control over the development of software but control over the copying of software. If copying is controlled by the author, the future will unfold in one way. If copying is controlled by the copyist, the future will unfold in a completely different way.

As you read these words, the softwars have been underway for the better part of two decades. The conflicts taking place across the face of the globe during the 1990s build on the position gained during the 1970s and 1980s. What was the relative posture of the combatants at the end of the 1980s? Understanding the answer to that question requires an appreciation of legal principles established centuries ago. (We will concentrate in this chapter on the American theater because, until recently, the progress of the legal campaigns for control of the software industry was faster in the United States than in other countries. As we shall see, the world has now caught up with, and in some respects got ahead of, the United States with regard to software protection issues.) The following reconnaissance report is in the nature of a synopsis of "the story thus far" for the benefit of readers who may have missed the first few episodes.

The Constitution of the United States provides the basis for American patent and copyright law. It provides, in Article I, Section 8, that "The Congress shall have power.... To promote the Progress of Science and the useful Arts, by securing for limited Times to authors and inventors the exclusive Right to their respective Writings and Inventions." Patent and copyright laws had existed in Europe since the Renaissance, but the revolutionists who were crafting their new society were writing on a blank slate, having erased the existing legal order in the war with England. They concluded, without any controversy during the dramatic convention that established the American republic, that the central government ought to extend the privilege of government-enforced exclusivity to authors and inventors as a means of inducing the creation of writings and inventions that lead to progress in science and the useful arts. Writing for the *Independent Journal* in 1788, James Madison observed that

The utility of this power will scarcely be questioned. The copyright of authors has been solemnly adjudged, in Great Britain, to be a right of common law. The right to useful inventions seems with equal reason to belong to the inventors. The public good fully coincides in both cases with the claims of individuals.

*The public good fully coincides in both cases with the claims of individuals.* With that conclusion, the stage was set, the basic rules of war drawn up for the American theater. While the constitutional *purpose* was to promote progress in science and the useful arts, the only constitutional *power* given to the legislature in order to achieve that purpose was the power to grant exclusive rights. One could imagine an entirely different mandate, one which attempted to promote progress by depriving authors and inventors of exclusive rights and instead placing their writings and inventions in the public domain. That is not what the framers of the constitution did, however. Article I, Section 8, and consequently the patent law and copyright law that have devolved from it, favor the creator of original works, not the copyist. That favoritism was meant to be limited in time, of course, and limited only to the subject matter actually created by the author or inventor. Otherwise, though, the framers intended for Congress to allow authors and inventors to exploit their writings and discoveries to the *exclusion* of others. As we shall see, much of the argument against software protection is based on the premise that the public good—including, but not limited to progress in the software arts—is best served by giving copyists free rights in writings (i.e., programs) or inventions (i.e., software implementations) created by others. While those arguments may or may not have some theoretical merit, they have no legal merit. American law simply does not proceed from that premise.

Another important bit of ground ceded to creators in the Constitution but contested in recent years by many proponents of weak exclusive rights for software was the principle that exclusive rights should be granted to writings in order to promote progress in the "useful arts." A principle argument of the commentators, principally academics, who attack the notion of applying traditional copyright principles to computer programs is that programs are "functional" in that they actually cause tangible results to be achieved by a computer. (Some of these commentators seem to believe that programs themselves "function," while others accept that programs are written instruction that cause a computer to "function.") In this quality, it is said, they differ from works historically accorded protection by copyright, which are not "functional" but rather are "aesthetic." At this point in writing, I have paused to open the closest reference works at hand, to wit, *Roget's II: The New Thesaurus* and *Webster's New International Dictionary*. I find that the former defines "functional" as "serving or capable of serving a *useful* purpose," while the latter gives as a principal definition of "functional" the following: "designed or developed chiefly from the point of view of *use*" (emphasis mine). While it must be conceded that the founding fathers did not have either of those reference works available to them when they were choosing the language of Article I, Section 8, it seems well beyond question that, had they intended to confine the benefit of copyright privileges only to aesthetic works, they would have chosen words different from *"useful* arts" to convey that intent. Indeed, the very first American copyright statute, enacted a year after the Constitution was adopted, protected three types of works—books, maps, and charts—of which the latter two were wholly functional in nature and the former may include functional items such as instruction manuals or cookbooks. The question of the "functional" or "util-itarian" nature of software and its implications for copyright protection was extensively argued in the *Lotus* case, the first softwar of the 1990s and the subject of Chapter 3.

Our aerial reconnaissance of the software protection battlefield now swoops from the eighteenth century well into the twentieth century, after the stored program computer, and therefore the computer program, first appear as the technological offspring of World War II. Commercialization of stored program computers proved to be completely dependent on the availability, quality, and diversity of programs available for those computers. Although the first copyright registration was issued for a computer program in 1964, the head of the United States Copyright Office at that time was not sure that programs were actually within the scope of existing copyright law, and issued the registration and subsequent software registrations under the Office's "rule of doubt." The first lawsuits involving computer programs were not filed until the 1970s. Those skirmishes largely involved video games. The judges who decided those cases tended to exhibit much less doubt than had the Copyright Office about the protectability of computer programs. Generally, the video game cases held that numerous aspects of the games in suit, including the code of the underlying programs, were protected. In 1976, Congress appointed a blue ribbon commission (the

Commission on New Technological Uses of Copyrighted Materials, or
"CONTU") to study, among other things, the question of copyright protection for computer programs. Despite the curmudgeonly dissent of CONTU
member and author John Hersey, who labored under the misapprehension
that copyright was intended to protect only works of aesthetic merit such
as his own, CONTU recommended adding language to the copyright statute
to make it clear that computer programs were copyrightable subject matter.
Those recommendations were adopted in 1980, and set the stage for the
first pitched battles in the softwars. Shortly before the CONTU recommendations were issued, however, in a case called *Synercom Technology, Inc.
v. University Computing Co.*, a federal trial court in Texas ruled that input
formats to a computer program were not protected by copyright. The formats in question were forms filled out by users of a computer-aided design
program. The information on the forms was then entered into the computer.
The trial judge found that the formats contained no expression distinct from
their ideas. Since ideas are not protected by copyright, and since the input
formats were a kind of user interface, the *Synercom* case gave a temporal
victory to suppliers of compatible software.

Meantime, on the patent front, fortunes had also swung temporarily
against the innovators. Until 1972, the courts had tended to find software-
related patents valid. In that year, however, the case of *Gottschalk v. Benson*
was decided by the United States Supreme Court, and the direction of the
law changed abruptly. Benson's patent was perhaps not the best software-
related patent on which the Supreme Court could have cut its teeth. It was
almost pure mathematics, as it attempted to protect a method for converting
numbers from Arabic representation to binary representation. Arguably, it
was not even clear from the patent whether the "method" Benson sought
to protect had to involve a computer at all, or whether it was a method
that could equally be accomplished using pencil and paper. Uncomfortable
with the prospect of allowing mathematics to be patented, the Court ruled
that mathematical formulas, or algorithms, were ideas, and ideas alone cannot be patented. Since any software-related patent must involve a "method,"
"means," or "process" for accomplishing something in the physical world,
and since that method, means, or process must entail the use of algorithms,
*Benson* did not bode well for software patentability.

At about the same time as it undercut software patent protection, though,
the Supreme Court reaffirmed, in a case called *Kewanee Oil v. Bicron*, that
the federal patent law did not supercede the common law of trade secrets.
Innovators who did not wish to disclose their inventions to the public
(which disclosure is required in order to obtain a patent) could continue
to obtain the protection of state trade secret laws. Trade secret protection
also has a long history, and by the time of the Supreme Court's ruling on
this subject, each of the states provided some substantial form of protection
for proprietary information.

We should pause here, before turning to the 1980s, a decade in which greed infected the software industry as it did many other walks of life, to consider what the essence of copyright protection, patent protection, and trade secret protection really is. Both patent and copyright provide exclusive rights, but those rights are quite different. Copyright is the right to copy, distribute, display, perform, or create derivative works of an original work of authorship, and to prevent others from doing any of those things with that work of authorship. Any computer program containing original work can be copyrighted. Copyright protects an author against plagiarism. It does not protect against another author *independently* coming up with a highly similar, or even identical, text. Nor does it protect against the use of ideas or facts described in a copyrighted work. Anyone can copy these in another work dealing with the same subject matter, so long as the result is not a copy of the "expression" of the original work. We will spend a significant amount of time in later chapters considering what is "expression" and what isn't. One limitation on copyright protection, though, is that in cases where there is only one way to express an idea, the expression of that idea is not protected. Another limitation on copyright is that it does not protect systems, processes, or methods of operation. A third limitation is that copying for purposes of "fair use," such as academic research or criticism is permitted by law. The reader can appreciate, therefore, that the exclusive rights of a copyright holder are fairly weak.

In contrast, the exclusive rights of a patent holder are fairly strong. Patent holders have the exclusive right to their patented inventions. They may prevent anyone—even persons who come up with the same invention independently—from reproducing or using their inventions. If the invention is a device, no one may make the device without license from the patent holder. If the invention is a process, no one may implement the process without license from the patent holder. A patent, in other words, is a right to exclude. Fortunately, not every computer program is patentable. Far from it. It is not enough that the subject matter of a patent application be original; it must also be novel and not an obvious extension of existing technology. The applicant must disclose the "prior art" (i.e., the relevant existing technology) to the Patent Office, so that the government's patent examiners may make determinations as to novelty and nonobviousness before issuing the patent. A program is "original" for *copyright* purposes to the extent it originated with the author, but it may not be novel or nonobvious for *patent* purposes, in light of the body of software extant when the patent is applied for. Though thousands of software patents have been filed, millions of programs have been written. Patent protection is thus a strong form of protection, but is not applicable to most computer programs.

Trade secret, like copyright, is available to protect any computer program, but the effectiveness of trade secret protection is fairly limited. In general, any information that provides a competitive advantage and is energetically kept secret is a trade secret, and is protected against theft. In other words, one who steals a trade secret may be sued to be restrained from using it or for damages. That which is published, however, is by definition not secret. Is commercially available software, delivered to customers as magnetic blips on a diskette, "published"? And what if one who lawfully acquires a copy of an original program can figure out by some process what those blips are and what they mean? Has the trade secret been "stolen"? Questions like those, to which we'll return in Part Two, limn the fuzzy boundaries of trade secret protection.

The Reagan decade, the yuppie years, that long slow stretch of time in which America seemed to prosper while it was approaching bankruptcy and opportunists proliferated in the software industry as in others, was also the period in which the software industry discovered the intellectual property laws. All across the spectrum of programming endeavor during the 1980s, from the monumental epics of mainframe software to the staccato haiku of microcomputer microcode, the value of commercially successful software was being sapped by the activities of blatant plagiarists. Lawyers for software authors spanned the globe to combat those who threatened the investments made in writing original computer programs. Of the thousands of lawsuits filed around the world during the 1980s, the vast majority were settled, concluded summarily, or otherwise disposed of in ways that were not of great interest to posterity. Only a handful of cases had any lasting meaning in terms of the fortunes of war, and most of those were decided in the United States. To those, we now turn briefly.

The first, and arguably still the most important, of these was the case called *Apple Computer, Inc. v. Franklin Computer Corp*. For a brief moment in history, a computer called the Franklin Ace had challenged the popularity of the wildly successful Apple II, the personal computer that had captured the imagination of a generation. The Franklin challenge was fueled by the system software inside Franklin's machine. It was identical to the system software inside the Apple II, with the result that all of the computer games, all the word processing programs, all the accounting packages, indeed all the software that an Apple II user had bought or could buy in a computer store, would run on the Franklin Ace. The Ace was a totally compatible, cheap replacement for the little khaki machine with the striped, bitten apple logo on its carapace. In the inevitable lawsuit that followed on Franklin's commercialization of the Ace, Franklin conceded that its software was a complete knockoff of the Apple software, but argued that without copying that software, Franklin could not have produced a product that would have run all the application programs written for the Apple II. Without copying, in other words, Franklin's business strategy of compatible replacement would not have been possible. Franklin also argued that the copyright law was not intended to protect either object code (the magnetic-blip, non-human-readable form of computer programs), or to protect computer programs embodied in a hardware device (a read-only memory, or ROM, in this case) or to protect operating systems software as opposed to application software, or to protect utilitarian software. Although some of those arguments achieved success with the trial judge, the appellate court that issued the ultimate ruling was not much moved by any of them. In inverse order, the court held that the copyright law did not distinguish, in terms of protectability, between those works that produced useful results and those that didn't, or between operating systems and application programs. It held further that copyright applies to works "fixed in a tangible medium of expression," and ROM is in fact a tangible medium of expression. It held that Congress had amended the copyright law in 1980 to make clear that the law protected computer programs "used directly or indirectly in a computer," and that the only form in which a program could be used directly in a computer was object code form; therefore Congress must have intended that object code be protected. Finally, as to the alleged necessity to copy in order to achieve compatibility (a theme that—as we shall see—haunts the success of original computer programs like the ghost of Banquo haunted Macbeth's feast), the court laid down a pattern of reasoning that set the stage for the outcome of the other major software legal clashes of the decade.

Seizing on the principle that the copyright law protects expression but not ideas, Franklin's lawyers argued that the idea of Apple's operating system was to "run the vast body of Apple-compatible software." (To such ends are lawyers driven when their clients admit copying.) The court did not find that argument satisfactory. The idea of a program, it said, was simply the subject matter of its expression. For example, one of the Apple programs translated source code (i.e., human language) programs into object code (machine language) form. The idea of that program was how to translate human-intelligible programs into machine-intelligible programs. So long as other ways of expressing that idea were available, the particular expression chosen by Apple was protected. Franklin's desire to offer replacement software for the Apple operating system was held to be completely irrelevant to the determination whether that operating system contained expression separate from its ideas. In so holding, the court of appeals did more than simply hand Apple a victory over an aggressive clone; it laid down the principle that a "compatible replacement" business strategy is entitled to no greater sympathy in the context of computer programs than it is in the context of traditional copyrighted works. That principle, though not particularly surprising, was important to software innovators in the struggle for control of the computer industry. It assured that suppliers of proprietary software would have the opportunity to obtain a return on their investments. (The *opportunity* to obtain a return on investment is not, of course, the same as the *achievement* of that return, which can only materialize if the proprietary software is attractive to a sufficient number of customers.) The *Apple* case signalled to clones that they were living under a cloud; that risk would dog their paths as they sought to duplicate the operating environments provided by proprietary software.

That risk was heightened in 1986, when the same court that decided the *Apple* case addressed a situation in which one company had adapted another company's program without authorization so that it operated on a different computer, and marketed the resulting product as its own. In that case, the *Whelan* case mentioned above, a small software house had written an accounting program for a dental laboratory. The program ran on the IBM Series/1 minicomputer, and was the property of the software house. For each copy sold to any other dental laboratory, Jaslow, the customer for whom the work was originally written, received a 10 percent royalty. With the advent of the personal computer, Jaslow realized that there would be a much broader market for dental lab accounting programs. Without so much as a "by your leave," Jaslow obtained a purloined copy of Whelan's source code, rewrote Whelan's software so that it ran on the IBM personal computer, and began to sell the product as its own. In the lawsuit that resulted, Whelan demonstrated that in many respects the structure, sequence, and organization of the Jaslow program was identical to that of the Whelan program, even though the individual lines of code were different. In effect, Jaslow had paraphrased Whelan's program, duplicating the logic and data structures of the original program in several areas. Thus, whereas in the *Apple* case the copying was literal and slavish, in *Whelan* the copying was somewhat more abstract. Jaslow argued that a program's sequence, structure, and organization is entirely part of its idea, not its expression. Why should this be so for computer software, when it is not so generally under the copyright law except where—as in the case of phone directory white pages—structure, sequence, and organization is dictated by the purpose of the work? Jaslow could offer no good reason. The court concluded that the idea of a utilitarian work is its purpose or function, together with everything necessary to that purpose or function. In the case at hand, Jaslow was held to have copied elements of Whelan's program not necessary to the purpose of automating dental laboratories. The fact that much of the nonliteral similarity between the two programs was unnecessary, the court said, was demonstrated by the existence of other dental lab programs that differed in sequence, structure, and organization from Whelan's program.

Although the *Whelan* case was highly controversial because of some of the language used by the court (which we'll have the opportunity to examine in Chapter 14), in fact the decision represented nothing more than an application of traditional copyright principles to a case involving computer programs. Copying by creating a work having "comprehensive nonliteral similarity" to an original work had long been considered copyright infringement. *Whelan* simply confirmed to those enterprises whose business strategies were based on reproducing, as closely as the law would allow, the work of other software authors that paraphrasing instead of literal copying would not insulate them from liability. The amount of original work they would have to do, in other words, was higher than they might have expected.

Another victory, some conclude, for purveyors of proprietary software. The *Whelan* case is sometimes called a defeat for supporters of "open systems," that is, software of a type that can lawfully be offered by many different suppliers, but that suggestion is a form of newspeak. A clone supplier is not a supporter of an "open system"; a clone supplier is a copier of someone else's system. Some of that copying is lawful, but some of it may not be. To the extent the copying is not lawful, the system copied was not "open." "Open systems" are programs designed to specifications lawfully available to multiple suppliers, just as the music of Mozart is lawfully available to any orchestra wishing to record it or any tunesmith who wants to borrow a melody. Mozart's copyrights have long since expired, obviously, and that is what makes his music "open." What makes software specifications "open" is the fact that they are generally promulgated by public or quasi-public standards bodies, or the fact that the author's rights are not reserved, or the fact that, if rights are reserved, a license is available at a low price. We will look more closely at open systems and standardization later on, as they are powerful trends that tend to shift the balance of power among competitors in the computer industry, but for now it is enough to note that *Whelan* did not reduce the ability of industry standards bodies to do their work. What it did reduce was the ability of Company B to convert Company A's program into a "standard" simply by copying it.

In a series of lawsuits that followed *Whelan*, the notion that creating comprehensive nonliteral similarity can constitute copyright infringement was extended to the aesthetic or arbitrary elements of screen displays. The march toward protectionism was tempered, however, by other cases placing limits on the rights of software copyright owners. The *Plains Cotton* case held that similarities in structure, sequence, and organization that result from attempts to produce output of a type already standard to users in a particular industry (in that case, a cotton industry "recap report") do not constitute copyright infringement. The *Softklone* case established that common mnemonics (in particular, the use of the first two characters of what would be, to a modem mavin, obvious commands relating to the use of modems, such as "duplex", "emulate", or "speed") are not protected, although the particular arrangement of such mnemonics on a screen may be protected. The *Frybarger* and *Data East* cases, both relating to computer games, taught that similarities in appearance arising from the rules or conventions of the game in question—a simple maze chase game in the first-named case, and a karate match in the latter—are similarities in idea rather than expression. The natural extention of copyright principles to computer programs during the course of the 1980s thus tended to affirm that while the law would not permit plagiarism, neither would it permit the suppression of functional similarity.

Turning to the world of patents, we find that there was a sea change in the rules on availability of patent protection for computer programs in the 1980s. In 1981, the U.S. Supreme Court had the opportunity to revisit the scene of the carnage it had wreaked in *Gottschalk v. Benson*. The 1981 case, *Diamond v. Diehr*, involved not pure mathematics but rubber curing. Diehr and his co-inventor claimed to have discovered a way of overcoming the chronic problem of either overcuring or undercuring in the process of molding synthetic rubber. Their solution was to measure the mold temperature continuously, and to feed the temperature data into a computer that continuously recalculated the cure time using the Arrhenius equation and, at the appropriate time, signalled the press containing the mold to open. (Those readers who are not chemical engineers may not find the phrase "the Arrhenius equation" particularly resonant. Svante Arrhenius was a Swedish scientist of the nineteenth century who left us, among other things, a formula for determining the effect of temperature on the length of time required for chemical reactions to take place. According to the Arrhenius equation, small changes in temperature can have quite dramatic effects on reaction rate, if logarithms may be considered dramatic.) It does not take a chemical engineer to observe that at the heart of Diehr's invention lies mathematics, pure and simple. What salvaged his patent from the *Benson* wreckage, though, was the fact that the process claimed to have been invented was not a mathematical process but an industrial process: the application of computers to curing rubber in a particular way. The significance of that distinction has not been lost on patent lawyers. Thousands of software-related patents have been filed since *Diehr*, all based on methods of accomplishing a real-world result by using a computer under the control of a program.

In the trade secret arena, numerous cases were decided during the 1980s involving computer programs. Since trade secret protection attaches to any information having commercial value that is kept secret, it is not surprising that those cases have extended that protection to confidential information consisting of computer programs. The question whether the source code for a program for which the object code is widely distributed may be eligible for trade secret protection has not been settled, but certain things are clear. For example, customers for Microsoft's MS-DOS, or IBM's versions of the same program, PC DOS, do not receive source code. (Source code is the text of a program as written down by its author. Compared to the zeroes and ones of object code, it is eminently readable and comprehensible.) Tens of millions of copies of the object code for those programs have been installed. Yet despite the wide distribution of DOS no one has the right to break into Microsoft's development laboratory and steal a copy of the source code. No Microsoft employee has the right to secrete diskettes containing the source code in his or her briefcase, remove them from Microsoft's premises, and sell them to the highest bidder. No Microsoft competitor has the right to hire away Microsoft programmers for purposes of having them reconstruct the DOS source code from memory.

A more interesting question, as of this writing, is whether a licensee of a copy of DOS can lawfully reconstruct the source code of that program by deciphering its object code. The law of trade secrets typically stops at the point of sale. What customers acquire on the open market they can normally analyze, test, measure, and reverse engineer freely if they wish. (Reverse engineering is the process of attempting to determine how a product was made.) Thus, trade secret law places no necessary constraints on the ability of Microsoft's competitors to translate the DOS object code into source code. In order to close that gap in protection, though, Microsoft, like most other software suppliers, includes terms in its license agreements that prohibit reconstruction of the source code. Leaving to one side the issue of the enforceability of such contracts if they are not actually signed by the customer (as they are not in the case of the so-called "shrink-wrap" licenses that accompany most personal computer software), a customer who agrees not to reconstruct source code has probably agreed to protect it against disclosure in sufficient measure to preserve its trade secrecy.

Expanding the ambit of our surveillance beyond the United States, we find that although the nature of trade secret protection varies from country to country, patent law and copyright law are more reliable. At the end of the 1980s copyright protection was available for computer programs either by statute or by case law, as was patent protection for a system composed in part of software, in almost every country in which a thriving software business is done. (The U.K. was less accommodating than other countries in respect of software patents.) Given the global nature of the software business, these well-understood regimes of protection, available on a reasonably consistent basis around the world, stood as the rules of engagement in the softwars. As the reader will appreciate, those rules tended to favor persons or firms who were contributing original works or inventions to society. That bias, in the case of American law, at least, sprang from the Constitutional vision that granting exclusive rights to authors and inventors was the way to promote progress. At a more altruistic level, the bias toward creativity is part of human nature. Entertainers whose *shticks* consist of impersonating others are generally less beloved than the successful personalities they impersonate. The movie *Battlestar Galactica* has not become the cultural place marker, or the financial success, that *Star Wars* has. Lots of writers produce westerns, but there is only one Louis L'Amour. The citizen whose gift is the ability to recognize, "Hey, I can do that, too," may achieve wealth and prominence, but usually only by accepting the depreciated price that a copycat product is able to attract, and only by taking care not to violate laws that society has seen fit to lay in place to protect originators.

It has always seemed odd to me that in the software industry and among academic and press observers of that industry, there should exist large numbers of people who claim surprise or disappointment that intellectual property laws apply to computer programs. Yet there are. The notion of "cloning" has in fact acquired a singular acceptability in the computer industry. In the developed world, one understands that cloning a Rolex watch without permission from Rolex might land a manufacturer in jail, or at least subject that manufacturer to an injunction and damages. Similar results are to be expected in a case of cloning a successful sound recording, book, movie, automobile, compact disc player, or any product protected by copyright or patent. When it comes to computers, however, or computer programs, those expectations are somehow suspended in the minds of many. Cloning of those high-tech products, portrayed by those who engage in it as a legally neutral activity, a process of "studying a product" to "extract its unprotected elements" and offer "an independently created competitive product," is defended as a way of assuring customers cheaper "second sources" for original software. There is, though, something very wrong-headed about that notion. Fundamentally, the purpose of intellectual property laws is to *deprive* customers of cheap second sources of the very same original products, for limited times and within subject-matter bounds, unless the copyright or patent holder licenses such second sourcing. There are no exceptions from that purpose for computer programs.

The status report from the situation room, then, at the opening of the 1990s, which Lotus Development Corporation's Jim Manzi has called "the decade of software," was that the nations of the developed world had recognized the need to protect software against copying, had looked in most cases to existing regimes of intellectual property law for such protection, and had applied those regimes, sometimes modified, sometimes not, to cases of software infringement in a small but growing number of cases. The high ground, by and large, was held by writers and publishers of original computer programs. As is the case with motion pictures and popular music, in the present era America is the predominant source of writers and publishers of successful original computer programs. Because in part of the effect of software on hardware sales, computers designed by American firms also predominated on the world market. (Inside, those computers may have been full of Far Eastern components, and they may have been entirely assembled in Europe, but the flag flying over the corporate headquarters of the principal suppliers—which is all that many foreign trade bureaucrats care about—was in most cases American.) All around the high ground, however, the forces of opposition were gathering for a pitched battle that would soon rage from Tokyo to Brussels, from Melbourne to Mountain View: a global conflict with the aim of changing the very rules of war themselves. In September, 1989, at the Stuart Alsop's Agenda 90 conference, Jim Manzi spoke about the "wars on the verandah," the industry convocations at which speakers talk publicly "about the future of the industry, the good of the industry, the need for standards, the need for open systems, and, first and foremost, the supremacy of the end-user." "But," he said,

then there's the cocktail hour, or a coffee break, and we all converge on the verandah. Rarified talk about the good of the industry, or the supremacy of the end-user, quickly evaporates, and the air becomes thick with plots, conspiracy and intrigue. Feverish negotiations begin, deals are cut, alliances formed, and we get down to the essential task of eviscerating our competitors.

Even more important than the wars on the verandah to the future of the industry, however, are the wars in the courtroom and in the corridors of government power. The decade of software is also the decade of the softwars, and it happens that Manzi's company was a combatant in one of the most significant of these. Let us turn now to the first softwar we will examine closely, the case of *Lotus Development Corporation v. Paperback Software International*.

# Part II

## Fear and Loathing, Look and Feel

Being a consideration of the nuclear (or is it "unclear"?) wars over user interfaces, and the fallout therefrom.

# 3

# Gaining Enlightenment from the *Lotus Sutra*: *Lotus Development Corporation v. Paperback Software International*

Even though you can say something about it, I will give you thirty blows of the stick. And if you can't say anything about it, I will also give you thirty blows of the stick.

—Zen *koan*

Not long (historically speaking) after the death of the Buddha, his followers began to divide into two schools of thought, a schism that eventually became formalized into the Mahayana (Greater Vehicle) and Theravada (Way of the Elders) movements. The Theravadins believed that the ideal Buddhists were ascetics who achieved Nirvana through their own efforts. The Mahayanists, on the other hand, believed that the ideal Buddhists postpone their own enjoyment of Nirvana in order to help others achieve enlightenment. One of the great early texts of Mahayanist literature is the *Saddharmapundarika-sutra* ("Lotus of the Good Law" or, more popularly, *"Lotus Sutra"*). Students of the *Lotus Sutra* find in its text encouragement to copy that very text and propagate it to others.

In that deep philosophical difference between these two great divisions of Buddhism, there is an analogue to the deep philosophical difference between those who favor traditional copyright protection for computer software and those who favor weaker copyright protection for computer programs than for traditional works of authorship. The former believe that the state of economic Nirvana should be pursued by independent creation of innovative software products. The latter believe that economic Nirvana should equally be achievable by copying and propagating the innovative software of others. If the literal code of original programs may not be copied, the weak protectionists argue, then at least the "look and feel" of the great works should be available for duplication by those seeking balance-sheet bliss. The phrase "look and feel" is an imprecise construction that refers generally to those aspects of an interactive program most readily observable to a user when the program is running in a computer and the user is interacting with that computer.

For three years before June 1990, the software industry had been awaiting enlightenment as to those philosophical issues. The question whether the "look and feel" of a computer program could be copied had been thrown into the courts in 1987, putting the softwars onto the front pages of the trade press. Suspense deepened as the press bombarded subscribers with articles and letters to the editor, heating up the debate but shedding little light on its substance. At seminars across the country, software clones paraded their technical experts to declare that user interfaces were simply functional articles, like toasters, designed by engineers, and their legal experts to opine that therefore copyright protection was inappropriate for such interfaces. Software innovators, in turn, brought forward technical experts to declare that user interfaces were arbitrary and imaginative ways of communicating with users, and legal experts to opine that therefore such interfaces were eligible for copyright protection. By June of 1990, however, the federal courthouse in Boston had become the focus of industry attention, since it was there that the first "look and feel" decision would be rendered.

In 1989, before any of the major "look and feel" cases had been decided, I had hazarded certain predictions as to the likely outcome of those cases, predictions that may now be measured by the unforgiving ruler of history, since the most important of those cases has now been tried and decision rendered. Briefly, the predictions were

—the user interfaces, or what Alan Kay has aptly called the "user illusions," generated by the original programs in those cases would be found to be the result of the application of considerable thought and effort;

—the structure, logic, and flow of the suites of screen displays in those programs would be found to be copyright-protected subject matter to the extent that such structure, logic, and flow had not been dictated solely by functional considerations;

—conventional elements common to programs having the same idea as the plaintiffs' programs would not be held to be protected subject matter; and

—the courts would protect the original elements in the user interfaces where the expressive content of such interfaces rises above the level of "blank forms" such as accounting worksheets, but would not protect either the ideas as to how to convey information on a screen or the expression necessary to convey those ideas.

Those predictions may now be taken as a kind of litmus test. If they have proven accurate, the reader should take the result as a demonstration not of the prescience of the author but of the fact that applying copyright law to computer programs produces predictable results rather than uncertainty. That conclusion in itself would be of considerable significance, because, as suggested in Chapter 1, many journalists and commentators have been trying their level best to convince both the public and the government that the law in this area is terribly uncertain.

On June 28, 1990, the industry got its answer to the "look and feel" question from the judiciary. On that date, the decision in *Lotus Development Corporation v. Paperback Software International* was rendered. Some liked it, some didn't. Some congratulated Lotus; others picketed Lotus. Those whose only knowledge of the decision came from reading the newspapers (which includes virtually all of the programming community) got a short-hand notion of what was decided, on the basis of which many predicted dire consequences and raged against false demons. The case deserves a closer and more thoughtful look than the press has given it. Possessed now of a Lotus Sutra for software protection, in the form of a comprehensive and careful analysis of user interface copyright issues by federal judge Robert Keeton, we are in a position to assess the reliability of the legal advice available to software developers who wish to adopt the user interfaces of other developers' programs.

The *Lotus* case involves what has become known as "electronic spreadsheets." A spreadsheet is an accounting worksheet consisting of rows and columns of related numbers. An electronic spreadsheet is a computer program that not only displays rows and columns of related numbers like a paper spreadsheet, but also automatically changes the values in those rows and columns. This highly popular concept is the brainchild of Dan Bricklin, one of the most outspoken and yet endearing figures in the pantheon of software industry deities. Whereas the Buddha achieved spiritual enlightenment at age 35 under a *bodhi* tree, Bricklin gained software enlightenment at a much younger age in a graduate school classroom, in one of those flashes of insight that can arrive when someone is daydreaming about ways of being lifted out of a frustrating or painful situation. The situation in question was Harvard Business School, and the frustration was the welter of accounting and forecasting figures that Bricklin had to juggle as a student in the late 1970s. Often, because of the relationships between those figures, a mistake in one variable would cascade throughout a table he was creating, requiring extensive recalculation. Bricklin imagined a magical blackboard that would perform those recalculations for him. In his mind, he visualized himself changing a number in one cell of a spreadsheet, and he watched as all the other figures on the spreadsheet that were dependent on the changed number simply transformed themselves without any work on his part. Out of that daydream, the computer program called VisiCalc was born. For a while, its corporate parent, Visicorp, grew and prospered.

In your own mind's eye, take an upper-case L, rotate it clockwise 90 degrees and expand it until it almost fills the monitor screen of a personal computer. Now add alphabetical column headings along the horizontal axis (say, A through H) and numerical row headings along the vertical axis (say, 1 through 20). Above the matrix thus suggested, place a line of text (the "command line") consisting of the commands you will give the program. You have just recreated the essential screen display of VisiCalc. It happens that you have also recreated, subject to certain refinements, the essential screen display of Lotus 1–2–3. (Fortunately, the copyright law does not protect against copies that exist only in the mind's eye, and you needn't be concerned that Lotus will sue you for infringement.) The two screen displays correspond because Bricklin the creative genius was far better at what he did than Bricklin the industrialist. Despite—or perhaps in part because of—the success of VisiCalc, its corporate owner, Software Arts, was unable to sustain itself as a going enterprise. Initially written to run on the Apple II, VisiCalc was rewritten to run on the IBM personal computer, but the rewrite did not take advantage of the greater capacity of the IBM machine. There came a terrible moment in which Bricklin realized that the additional external investment he was seeking in order to pump cash into the business was not going to materialize, and that the business of Software Arts would have to be liquidated. At that fateful moment, Mitch Kapor and his company, Lotus Development Corporation, were around to pick up the pieces. Lotus Development Corporation had improved on the electronic spreadsheet concept expressed in VisiCalc, and written their program in a way that exploited the larger memory and more versatile keyboard and screen display capabilities of the IBM PC. They now stepped in and bought all rights to VisiCalc and went on to become one of the most prominent software houses in the world.

After Bricklin put the idea of an electronic spreadsheet into play, a number of other software developers concluded that they could also write such a program, and indeed perhaps do it better than Software Arts had. One of those developers was James Stephenson. In January 1982, Stephenson set out to write a better spreadsheet program. By April 1983, an operational version of that program was installed with a customer. In December 1983, Stephenson entered into a letter of intent with Adam Osborne, noted personal computer commentator and entrepreneur, regarding the publication of the program, which Stephenson had named VP-Planner. Osborne then organized Paperback Software International. (Unless the context requires otherwise, I will refer to the defendants in the *Lotus* case collectively as "Paperback" from now on.) Improvement of VP-Planner continued during 1984, but in the fall a decision of grave consequence was made. The market lead and acceptance of Lotus 1–2–3 was by then considerable. Stephenson and Osborne concluded that because of the position of 1–2–3, VP-Planner should be "compatible" with the Lotus program. What that meant, in their view, was that the menu structure and command names of VP-Planner would have to be the same as those of Lotus 1–2–3. With such "compatibility," users of 1–2–3 would be able to switch to VP-Planner without retraining, and they would also be able to manipulate, using VP-Planner, spreadsheets created using Lotus 1–2–3 without rewriting any macros that might be imbedded in those spreadsheets. (Macros, in this context, are sequences of instructions written by users using the command terms of Lotus 1–2–3. The menu structure of VP-Planner was converted into a menu structure that mimicked that of Lotus 1–2–3. (The term "menu," in this context, refers to the lists of words or symbols used to designate the operations that users of Lotus 1–2–3 could choose to have the computer perform under the control of Lotus' program.) All VP-Planner commands were rewritten to begin with the same first letter as those of 1–2–3, and were restructured to appear in the same position in the menu hierarchy as those in 1–2–3. Functions available in the Lotus program but not in VP-Planner were added to the Stephenson program, and certain functions of VP-Planner that 1–2–3 did not contain were discarded even though they would have been useful to customers. VP-Planner also reproduced the rotated L format, the lettered columns and numbered rows and the two-line menu bar of Lotus 1–2–3, though the latter was placed at the bottom of the screen rather than at the top. The user manual for VP-Planner, written after all the changes were made, reported that "VP-Planner is designed to work like Lotus 1–2–3, keystroke for keystroke.... VP-Planner's worksheet is a feature-for-feature workalike for 1–2–3. It does macros. It has the same command tree. It allows the same kinds of calculations, the same kind of numerical information. Everything 1–2–3 does, VP-Planner does."

In retrospect, such pointed comparisons may seem to Messrs. Stephenson and Osborne to have been somewhat improvident. In any case, Paperback commenced actively to market VP-Planner and in due course, that is to say, in 1987, the company was served with a summons and complaint by attorneys for Lotus Development Corporation. The trial did not take place until 1990, and judgment was rendered in the same year.

Although the case is widely known as a "look and feel" case, Judge Keeton did not find the term "look and feel" particularly helpful and did not use it. Indeed, even Lotus ultimately decided that the term "look and feel" was not a useful way of describing the elements of 1–2–3 that it claimed Paperback had infringed, and ended up referring to those elements as the "user interface" of its program. What is a user interface? It is the perceived relationship between a person and a physical article. The user interface between you and this book is the page and the printing on the page. The user interface between you and the compact disk to which you listen as you read these words is the music you are hearing, as well as the buttons and knobs on your stereo system that you must push or turn in order to hear the music. The user interface between you and your car is the steering wheel, the dashboard, and the pedals.

The elements of the user interface of Lotus 1–2–3 were:

a) the menus and their structure and organization;
b) the "long prompts," a series of expressions that elaborated on the menu items;
c) the screen layouts or formats;
d) the assignment of function keys; and
e) the macro commands and macro language.

These are traditional elements of a user interface. Other user interface aspects, not involved in the *Lotus* case, include the selection of audio input or response, the particular use of color, the specific iconography, and the use of motion and animation sequences. Because the case involved less than all conceivable elements of user interfaces, some have argued that, for example, the *Lotus* case does not determine the protectability of screen icons such as file folders or trash cans. Such arguments are the intellectual equivalent of the ostrich sinking its head into the sand to avoid danger. *Lotus v. Paperback*, itself a natural extension of *Apple/Franklin* and other cases mentioned in Chapter 2, is a lodestar. Judge Keeton applied traditional copyright reasoning to the question of protectability and infringement of each of the elements listed as "a)" through "e)" above, and described his thought process in elaborate detail. The detailed analysis assured that there would be no mistaking how he arrived at his judgment, so that the appellate court—if the case were appealed—would be satisfied that he had done his job. On this author's reading of the case, Judge Keeton was also attempting to settle once and for all the argument over protectability of user interfaces, to unburden the federal courts of frivolous litigation or frivolous defenses thenceforward.

The jurist began his analysis by noting the agreement by both parties that the source code and object code of Lotus 1–2–3 were protected by copyright. The differences between the parties related to the extent of protection available for the nonliteral elements of Lotus' program. Paperback had asserted that for a number of different reasons, which we will consider momentarily, copyright did not extend to any nonliteral elements of a computer program. Lotus, obviously, argued that all expressive elements of a program, literal and nonliteral, were protected. Judge Keeton pointed out that the answer to the question of scope of protection must come from the statute itself: its language, history, context, and "object and policy." The language and history of the Copyright Act make it clear, he said, that computer programs are protected under the law as literary works. That is not because Congress was deluded into believing that computer programs were literature. It is because the statutory definition of "literary works" is not limited to works that we would consider literature:

"Literary works" are works, other than audiovisual works, expressed in words, numbers, or other verbal or numerical symbols or indicia, regardless of the nature of the material objects such as books, periodicals, manuscripts, phonorecords, film, tapes, disks, or cards, in which they are embodied.

For literary works of a more traditional nature (plays, novels, or greeting cards, for example), the context of the law makes crystal clear that infringement may occur without literal reproduction of the words or pictures. Copying of the work's plot, characters, sequence of events, or setting may be a sufficient appropriation to violate the law. "This type of copying," the judge noted, "has never been upheld as permissible copying; rather, it has always been viewed as copying of elements of expression of creative originality."

Did Congress intend that the same rule be applied to computer programs? Judge Keeton found the legislative record and history to be less than explicit on the point, and therefore felt it necessary to consider at length the "objects and policies" of the copyright law in order to answer the question. Paramount among those objects and policies was the principle that the advancement of public welfare was best accomplished by extending the prospect of private reward ("personal gain" or a "fair return for an 'author's' creative labor") to program authors. Accordingly, the line between protectability and nonprotectability could not be drawn either so broadly as to harm public welfare or so narrowly as to discourage programmers from creating original works. The line drawn by Congress, the judge concluded, was the idea-expression dichotomy. Long a part of American common law, the rule that ideas are not protected by copyright, while the expression of those ideas is protected, was codified into the Copyright Act in 1976, at a time when Congress had begun to consider the extent of protection for computer programs. Moreover, the Commission on New Technological Uses of Copyrighted Works (CONTU), which recommended the modest changes to the 1976 act that Congress adopted in 1980, had concluded that the idea-expression distinction should be used to determine which aspects of computer programs were protectable.

Of course, computer programs are not primarily aesthetic works; they are useful works, and it is also a tenet of copyright law that the functional aspects of "useful articles" are not protected by that law. In the case of a Mickey Mouse watch, to take a simple example not used by Judge Keeton, the two-handedness of the device, the fact that the hands move in a circle, the fact that the hands are distinguishable from the background, and the fact that the background has the numerals 1 through 12 arrayed around its periphery are all functional elements free for the taking. The image of the beloved rodent, however, is not. The judge's conclusion as to Congress's intent was that, despite the functional character of software, where computer programs include literal and nonliteral elements that can be identified separately from and can exist independently of the utilitarian aspects of the programs, those elements may be protected. (Actually, in rejecting copy-right protection for functional elements of computer programs, Judge Kee-ton seems to have misapplied the "useful article" exception. Under the Copyright Act, the unavailability of protection for the functional aspects of "useful articles" is specified only in the case of "pictorial, graphic or sculp-tural works." Computer programs, including their user interfaces, are not protected as pictorial, graphic, or sculptural works, but rather as "literary works" or as "audio-visual displays." For the latter two categories, there is reason to believe that functionality capable of being expressed in a variety of ways is protected by copyright.)

Both Lotus and Paperback urged on the court numerous policy reasons why the Lotus 1–2–3 user interface should (in Lotus' view) or shouldn't (in Paperback's view) be considered protected by copyright. These served as the basis for the court's extended exposition of the "object and policy" of the statute. Observing first that the purpose of copyright was to advance the public welfare, not to reward authors, he noted that, even so, the method adopted for serving the public good was to secure a fair return for authors' creative efforts. He quoted the Supreme Court opinion in the case of *Mazer v. Stein*: "encouragement of individual effort by personal gain is the best way to advance public welfare through talents of authors and inventors." Thus, the question of what is protected and what is not protected in a copyrighted work turns on the balance between, on the one hand, en-couraging individual effort by allowing personal gain to authors and, on the other, bestowing strong monopolies that would discourage other authors from offering still better products. In the judge's view, the way Congress handled that balancing act was to toss all the canes and hats to the courts, in the form of the idea-expression dichotomy. In each copyright infringe-ment case, the courts are to juggle the canes and hats to assure that the expression in a copyrighted work is protected, but that the ideas are not. How then to apply that dichotomy to the case at hand?

The first significant factor for Judge Keeton was that Congress had not cre-ated a new formulation of the distinction between protectability and non-protectability for computer programs. The idea-expression dichotomy was the standard that applied to all other literary works, as well as motion pic-tures, musical and dramatic works, and even "useful articles." The judge therefore was compelled to reject Paperback's argument that the 1–2–3 user interface was not entitled to copyright protection at all because it was simply a "functional, useful article." The centerpiece of Paperback's argument had been the *Synercom* case, which, as mentioned in Chapter 2, predated the 1980 amendments to the Copyright Act, and predated as well most of the development of the case law on software copyrightability. *Synercom* put for-ward a curious analogy: the data inputs of a program, the court opined, were like the H pattern of an automobile gearshift. To Judge Keeton, *Synercom* was ancient history. (To the automobile industry, it was ancient history, too.

When was the last time you used a gear shift with an H pattern? At the moment, there are four cars in my driveway. The shift pattern on one of them is basically a straight line. Another has a Wn pattern, where the right leg of the n is reverse gear. A third has a uW pattern, where the left leg of the u is reverse. The fourth, a faithful reconstruction of a 1955 Porsche Spyder, utilizes a nH shifting pattern.) Under the current state of the law, *Synercom*'s central proposition—that expression of a nonliteral sequence and order of program elements is inseparable from idea and therefore not protected—was no longer viable. Noting that designing a suitable user interface is a more difficult intellectual task than writing the code that implements that interface, Judge Keeton concluded that the *Synercom* proposition would deny protection for the more significant creative elements of a program.

Now the jurist turned to the critical but ultimately inexplicable process: that of determining what is protected expression and what is unprotected idea in the particular case. Here, I will apply a modest amount of literary license (call it "analytic interpretation," if you wish) to the court's exposition, which becomes somewhat cryptic at this point, reflecting the surpassing difficulty of putting into words the subjective and intuitive judgments by which idea is parsed from expression. Four factors, Judge Keeton said, guided his analysis. First, the work must have originated with the author, a test that measures the content of the work against history and may disclose that what seems to be expression is really just an idea that has appeared before, or conversely what seems to be an idea is really a particular expression of an idea that has been expressed differently before. Second, if the work is functional, its utilitarian aspects are part of its idea(s), not its expression. Take the case of a decorative switchplate. While the decorative elements are protectable, the little rectangular hole at the center, cut to standard size so that the wall switch can protrude through, is not. Third, elements that are obvious, such as the "push" sign next to a door handle, do not merit protection. (The "obviousness" factor, by the way, is new to copyright law, at least by that name. While there might be a theoretical objection that Judge Keeton has erected a hurdle to achieving copyright protection that didn't exist before, I think it more likely that the term "obvious" is just the judge's personal shorthand for what is, in effect, an aspect of the fourth factor.) The fourth factor is the matter of merger. Where there is only one way, or where there are only a few ways, of expressing an idea, the expression merges with the idea for legal purposes and loses protection. An example would be helpful here, but to be honest with you, I can't think of an example with which I'm comfortable that cannot also be described either as "functional" or as "obvious." The difficulty is that if a work's idea(s) are defined narrowly enough (which is what copyright defendants try to get courts to do), there may never be more than one way of expressing them. Conversely, if "idea" is defined broadly enough (a tendency of copyright plaintiffs), alternate expressions can always be concocted. A famous case involves a piece of jewelry shaped like a bee. The owner of the copyright sued a second jewelry designer who had also made a bee pin. In deciding that there was no infringement, the court held that the idea was that of a lifelike, jewel-encrusted bee pin, that there were not many ways of expressing that idea, and therefore that the particular expression chosen by the original designer was not protectable.

There is something unsatisfying about that holding. For one thing, there are about 12,000 species of bees: honey bees, bumble bees, carpenter bees, leaf-cutter bees, and cuckoo bees, to name just a few. For another, bees are capable of more than one posture. Still further, while the selection of jewels that would produce a "lifelike" image of a bee (if one can imagine a lifelike image made from jewels) may not be infinite, neither is it unique. And finally, what is the difference between a lifelike, jewel-encrusted bee pin and, say, a lifelike bust of John Kennedy that would render the former unprotected and the latter protected?

In truth, the idea-expression dichotomy is a license to the trial court to make a subjective determination based on the inherent qualities of the works in question. In other words, "you had to be there" in order to understand why the cases dealing with that dichotomy come out the way they do. In Judge Keeton's words, "to speak as if it were ever possible completely to disentangle an idea from an expression of that idea is to speak abstract fiction rather than real-life fact." In a given case, the court must define "idea" somewhere along the scale between the most abstract and the most specific of conceptions. If the case involves computer programs, the judge concluded that one must also distinguish between elements essential to all expressions of the same idea and elements not essential to all such expressions. In addition, one must consider whether the nonessential elements are a substantial part of the copyrighted work, qualitatively as well as quantitatively, for if they are not, the work may not be protected. If the parameters of this analysis sound more than a little metaphysical, it's because the question "Is it plagiarized?" is—like the question, "Is it pornographic?"—one that can only be answered by assessing the material in question as a whole, intuitively as well as analytically.

Once he had set out the legal framework on the basis of which his intuitive/analytic assessment of the evidence would be based, the next step for Judge Keeton was to determine what aspects of the Lotus 1–2–3 user interface were protected. Many readers are already conversant with that user interface as it existed in 1987, but a brief description may be helpful for those who are not. Above the earlier-mentioned rotated "L," there is a two-line menu that gives the user a choice of actions that the program (or more accurately, the computer under control of the program) may be commanded to take. Examples of those commands are "file", "graph", "copy", and "quit". Selection is made either by shifting the cursor right or left on the command line to the desired command and pressing the "Enter" key, or by entering the first letter of the desired command. The top command line consists of single-word commands such as those just quoted. The second command line contains the long prompts, some of which describe in greater detail the single-word commands on the first line, others of which offer subcommands for those single-word commands. When a command having subcommands is selected, the subcommands take over the top line and a new series of long prompts appears on the second line. Further commands may be communicated to the computer by pressing the function keys ("F1," "F2," etc.).

Performing operations using 1–2–3 consists of selecting sequences of commands. Numerical values in a column or a cell within a column, for example, may be created by performing a series of transformations on the contents of another column or cell. Because pressing function keys and moving cursors in order to construct complex operations is a boring, error prone, and inefficient activity, Lotus 1–2–3 provides the capability to store sequences that may be used repetitively. These stored sequences are called "macros," and they are themselves computer programs. Lotus macros are inherently dependent on the structure, logic, and flow of the 1–2–3 menu hierarchy.

Lotus' suggestion as to what aspects of the 1–2–3 user interface were protectable, as already mentioned, included the menus and their structure, the long prompts, the screen displays, the function key assignments, and the macro commands and languages. The judge did not altogether agree. As a first principle, he held that "electronic spreadsheet" was an idea not in itself protectable. He then ruled that the two-linedness of the cursor menu was both functional and obvious; therefore, it was idea and not expression. Next, he observed that the rotated "L" format was common to most spreadsheet programs and seemed to be intrinsic to paper spreadsheets, which the screen displays of such programs were designed to mimic; accordingly, this aspect of 1–2–3 was not protected either. Continuing to weed the garden, the judge ruled that the use of " + ", " – ", "*", and "/" to indicate mathematical operations was not protectable due to obviousness and further that the choice of the "/" key to invoke the menu command system was not protectable because it was one of a very few keys that were both easily accessible and not also used to indicate a value that could be entered in a cell. So far, Paperback was "on a roll," but as we know Paperback's story does not end happily.

The principal reason for the downturn in the clone's fortunes was the menu hierarchy of 1–2–3. It was clear to the judge that the structure and organization of the menus, the order of the commands, the way each command was expressed on the screen, and the long prompts were susceptible of a wide range of alternate choices and, indeed, that other spreadsheet programs—notably Excel and Supercalc—were quite different from 1–2–3 in those respects. This was true even though many of the individual Lotus commands were either obvious or merged with the idea underlying them, because under the law an original selection of elements each of which is individually unprotected may in fact be protected. (For example, the words "thee," "I," "day," "shall," "a," "summer's," "to," and "compare" are not individually copyrightable, but "Shall I compare thee to a summer's day" would be copyrightable, had the Bard not written that line before there was a copyright law.) Judge Keeton thus rejected Paperback's invitation to dissect the menu structure into its element and rule on the protectability of each element individually. As a whole, he concluded, the menu structure of 1–2–3 was an original and nonobvious (i.e., nonmerged) way of express- ing a command structure. From a legal point of view, that conclusion was no great surprise in light of the long and consistent string of precedents holding that it is infringement to copy nonliteral but expressive elements of a program, particularly the structure, logic, and flow of the program, including the structure, logic, and flow of its user interface.

Judge Keeton also concluded that the menu structure was indeed a sub- stantial part of 1–2–3, because of its uniqueness and popularity, and it is worth pausing a moment to consider the implications of that conclusion. The clones and their (intellectually and sometimes financially) allied aca- demic supporters had for years been urging that precisely because of their popularity, the user interfaces of the best-selling programs should be ren- dered unprotected, else competition would be stifled. Users become "locked in" to (i.e., familiar with) a particular screen illusion, so the argument goes, and are not willing to switch to a different illusion. Now, the factual premise of the argument is demonstrably untrue, given (1) the rapid pace of tech- nological change in the industry and (2) the presence of successful, com- petitive nonclone programs on the market. The interesting thing about the *Lotus* opinion, however, is the clarity with which it states the principle that the popularity of a particular program element is grounds for holding that element protectable as a matter of copyright doctrine, rather than grounds for depriving it of protection. As Judge Keeton put it:

[O]ne of the objects of copyright law is to protect expression in order to encourage innovation. It follows, then, that the more innovative the expression of an idea is, the more important is copyright protection for that expression. By arguing that 1– 2–3 was so innovative that it occupied the field and set a *de facto* industry standard, and that, therefore, defendants were free to copy plaintiff's expression, defendants have flipped copyright on its head. Copyright protection would be perverse if it only protected mundane increments while leaving unprotected as part of the public domain those advancements that are more strikingly innovative.

With this language, the judge deflated a hot-air balloon that had been floating across the landscape of computer law for several years, thereby leaving a gaggle of commentators stranded in the infertile desert of unsub- stantiated arguments. (Many of those commentators returned to Judge Keeton's courtroom, by affidavit if not in person, during the *Lotus v. Borland* case as members of the "gang of ten," a group of law professors who were seeking to limit the aspect of the *Lotus v. Paperback* case just quoted.) Articles in the legal literature and guest editorials in the programming trade press had too long misled practicing lawyers and programmers into believing that somehow the copyright law stopped applying, or applied with only reduced vigor, to works of authorship that became exceedingly popular, leaving those works especially vulnerable to cloning. Although the *Lotus* case is simply a natural extension of existing precedent, one of Judge Keeton's great contributions to the advancement of public understanding of copyright law was his puncturing of the dangerously misleading legal theories that many in the industry had been taking as gospel.

Having established that the user interface of Lotus 1–2–3 contained protected expression, Judge Keeton had next to decide whether Paperback's clone program had copied that expression. Here, there was no substantial question. The copying of the 1–2–3 user interface was "overwhelming and pervasive." In fact, Paperback had essentially admitted copying, and rested its defense on a series of philosophical arguments. One of these was that copyright law is properly seen as protecting only the source code and object code of a program, not the user interfaces. That argument was rejected by the court as being inconsistent with existing precedent and with the nature of copyright analysis. A second version of the same argument was that applying traditional copyright principles to user interfaces would stifle progress in computer programs generally in the United States. Lotus, of course, countered with the philosophical argument that failure to protect user interfaces would destroy the incentive to innovate. The judge swept aside these policy arguments, pointing out that his job was not legislating, but rather interpreting legislation passed by Congress. He observed that Congress had long ago faced academic criticism of the proposal to extend copyright to computer programs, had received expert testimony that copyright protection for software might have "disastrous consequences...on standardization" in the industry, and had heard proposals that copyright for programs be limited to protecting only the instructions themselves. Nonetheless, Congress had decided simply to extend traditional copyright protection to computer programs. Traditional copyright protection prevents copying of nonliteral expressive elements of a copyrighted work. Accordingly, "this legal issue must be resolved in such a way as to extend copyright protection, clearly and unequivocally, to those nonliteral elements of computer programs that embody original expression."

A related argument advanced by Paperback was that the purpose of the copyright law, as stated in the U.S. Constitution, is to advance "progress of science and the useful arts," and that since such progress occurs incrementally by improving on the progress already made, copyright law should not preclude incremental advancements on existing user interfaces. The judge responded to this argument in two ways. Copyright law, he wrote, does promote incremental advances. It does so by ensuring that ideas in a protected work are free for the taking. Even more, he wrote, if an idea is capable of only a limited range of expression, such as the rotated "L" format or—in the context of spreadsheet programs—the use of the "/" key to invoke the menu command, then the expression itself is free for the taking. To the assertion that customers would not have accepted Paperback's incremental improvements on Lotus' ideas unless Paperback offered them with the same underlying user interface as that offered by Lotus, the judge replied that

1. others have achieved success in offering improved spreadsheet programs without cloning Lotus 1–2–3;

2. if in fact a second-comer spreadsheet program might not succeed unless it could execute the many macros already written by customers to run on Lotus 1–2–3, Paperback could have written a conversion program, as Microsoft had done for its Excel spreadsheet program;

3. Paperback could have offered its improvements as add-in software to run with Lotus 1–2–3, as others had done; and

4. there is no authority, statutory or case law, for the proposition that once a program has become so popular as to set the standard for programs of that kind, it should be treated as public property.

One final argument made by the defendant deserves particular attention. Paperback contended that in copying the 1–2–3 user interface, it had copied only a "language." Although expression is protected, the argument went, the language in which that expression is written is not protectable. The Lotus 1–2–3 macro capability allows users to write computer programs (called "macros") in a programming language that consists of the Lotus macro commands. In copying those commands, therefore, Paperback had copied only a "macro processing language." That argument, and Judge Keeton's treatment of it, take the *Lotus* case across a frontier into legal territory that many commentators claim to be uncharted. *Lotus* is generally read as a "look and feel" case, and of course it is a "look and feel" case; but the "programming language" argument transcends look and feel. Suppliers of compatible software usually try to copy not only as much of the end-user screen display interface of a target program as they can, but also as much of the programming interface of the target program as they can. Whereas the user interface is the means by which users communicate with a program interactively, the programming interface is the means by which programs written by users communicate with other programs. An operating system clone, for example, would want to be able to run as many as possible of the application programs designed to run on the target program. To do so, the clone would have to copy the "application programming interface" of the target program. In the Great European Copyright Debate, which we will consider in Chapters 8 and 19, the lobbyists favoring weak copyright protection asserted that application programming interfaces uniformly consist of ideas and never contain expression. They cited in that regard the conclusions of a group of ten American law professors—most of whom would readily admit that they could not read a computer program to save their own lives—that the "creation of a different program" that "recreate[s] or reimplement[s] the same interface" as the target program was "legal." That conclusion, uttered by the conferees at the LaST (Law, Science, and Technology) conference held at Arizona State University in February 1989, was wrong as a matter of law at the time it was rendered, but until the *Lotus* decision there was no clear articulation of the reasons why programming interfaces, like other nonliteral elements of computer programs, may be protected by copyright. Where a programming interface is sufficiently specific to contain expressive elements as well as ideas, *and* those expressive elements are not essential to convey the ideas in the interface (as may be evidenced by the existence of incompatible programs with interfaces expressing the same ideas) *and* those expressive elements are a substantial part of the program (either quantitatively or qualitatively), the programming interface is eligible for copyright protection.

One computer lawyer whose company sells PC clones told me that the programming language aspect of the *Lotus* case makes the compatibility business much harder. I replied that the compatibility business was always hard, and the problem actually was that the clones and their lawyers had been fooling themselves into thinking it was easier than it was. *Lotus* makes that self-deception impossible and, in the lawyers' case, malpractice. At the same time, it illustrates how to determine which elements of user interfaces and programming interfaces are not protected, and in that sense makes it easier for would-be clones to follow the eight Principles for Software Clones which I first articulated in 1989 in a slightly different form:

1. Questions about the conflict between software compatibility objectives and intellectual property rights should be decided on the basis of existing laws (copyright, patent, and trade secret), rather than by making up a separate set of rules.

2. The mere fact that a supplier adopts a compatibility strategy does not give that supplier carte blanche to copy whatever it wants from the target program of another supplier.

3. The compatible supplier may copy the ideas in the target program and any expression essential to implementing those ideas.

4. Compatibility achieved completely independently of the target program does not constitute copyright infringement.

5. The exclusive rights of the copyright owner do not constitute a grant of monopoly over the information in the copyrighted work.

6. Clean room strategies are only as good as what is put into the clean room.

7. There is no special dispensation to copy interfaces, since they are a part of the program's design.

8. Less is more.

Those principles, written before the *Lotus* decision, also illustrate how predictable the law is, which is one of the great benefits of traditional copyright law over special new legislation for software protection. There is no real uncertainty about copyright protection for software. Don't let anyone tell you differently. The *Lotus* case is a long *sutra* that allows those with interests in the computer industry to achieve *satori*, the inner enlightenment that comes—in this case—from realizing that which was already within one's capacity to know.

The dominant metaphor in this book is military, however, not religious. The *Lotus v. Paperback* contest was a loss for the clones, and even though the outcome of the case was predictable, it shifted the advantage in the conflict for control over the computer industry decidedly toward the innovators. Judge Keeton's *Lotus* decision brings us the conscious awareness of what we already knew: to be a leader, one must stop following.

## Endnote: The Augury of the Dismal Scientists—An Introduction to the Economics of Intellectual Property

> There is a common element to all decision problems which is expressible in the apparently trivial question, "Is it worthwhile?"
> —William J. Baumol, *Economic Theory and Decision Analysis* (1965)

*(I'd like to offer you at this point the first installment in a seven-part correspondence course in the economics of software protection that we'll be taking in endnote form as we tour the battlefield. In the original draft of this book, the economics course occupied two full, contiguous chapters in the middle of the tour, and my test-market readers reported that they found the change of pace noticeable and not felicitous. The seven endnotes that comprise our correspondence course should be easier to digest, and you may even find them a welcome respite from the rigors of the front.)*

One side in the softwars vigorously avers that without strong legal protection for computer programs, the industry will stagnate. The other side swears that unless legal protection for computer programs is weakened, a few large monopolists will inherit the entire business. Which side is right (if either)?

Would you like an empirical answer to that question, or a theoretical answer? Empirically, one can observe that in the first decade after the U.S. copyright law was explicitly amended to accommodate computer programs and the U.S. patent law was extended to computer programs, the number of software companies active in the United States roughly doubled. Since 1980, the leading software houses have therefore had to share their success with vast numbers of newcomers. Some leaders, indeed, have stumbled rather badly. Ashton-Tate, the premiere supplier of database software for PCs, had terminal difficulties in enhancing its product to stay ahead of the competition. Lotus Development Corporation, despite its success in court, lost market share to other spreadsheet suppliers. Microsoft, the company that has supplied more operating systems for more computers than any other company in the world, is facing the struggle of its corporate life for the hearts and minds of the microprocessors of the future, with other DOS suppliers, a broad range of suppliers of UNIX programs, IBM's OS/2, and the IBM/Apple joint venture arrayed against it. Sun Microsystems, the most successful supplier of workstations, has been forced to offer its version of a UNIX operating system on Intel-based systems as well as on its own workstation hardware in order to stem potential losses to Microsoft and to the Apple/IBM venture. And of course, personal computer and workstation software realizes much of its market growth by competing successfully against mainframe and midrange software solutions. The software industry appears to have the hallmarks of a highly competitive, dynamic sector of commerce.

Perhaps, though, you would prefer a theoretical answer. If so, this correspondence course may interest you. In seven endnotes interspersed with our reviews of major battles in the softwars, we will consider the economic theory of intellectual property protection. I have a vision here of the reader quickly performing Baumol's "Is it worthwhile?" analysis with the thought perhaps of skipping the correspondence course. Economics is generally considered a dry subject; some consider it a soporific. The fault for this negative public attitude toward economics must be laid at the feet of economists themselves, who tend to portray their field as a science, suffusing it with the off-putting symbolic embroidery of quantitative analysis. In fact, economics is not a science. If it were, the world would be full of flannel-shirted millionaires. Rather, economics is a series of vain attempts to apply the scientific method to the herd behavior of the multitudes, to human nature itself. At bottom, economics is fiction. Even the sobriquet "dismal science" with which economics is stuck derives from a fiction: the Malthusian conceit that population grows geometrically while food supplies grow arithmetically. To assert that economics is fiction is not to detract from the value of economic theory as a way of assessing the worth of human institutions or human behavior. Great economics, like great literature, can give us the profoundest of insights into such matters. Our excursion into economic theory will hopefully deliver profound insights without loading the reader down with scientific pretense.

Let us begin then not with Adam Smith, but with a more universally recognized fictionalist, Émile Zola. We turn to Zola not because he believed that the novel could and should be an exposition of scientific theories, which he did; nor because he believed that by experimenting on his characters he could provide as much useful, practical information on human behavior and human nature as economists could provide, which he did as well. Rather, we turn to Zola because he understood the profound importance of intellectual property laws on creativity. Until Zola's time, writers in France, like painters, were dependent on patronage for their existence. Their writings were distorted by the predispositions of their benefactors. By the latter half of the nineteenth century, however, the copyright laws that were swept in with the Revolution had taken hold and allowed authors to obtain a personal return on their investment of time and brainpower. "It is money," Zola wrote, "it is the legitimate gain realized from his works that has freed [the writer] from all humiliating patronage. . . . Money has emancipated the writer, money has created modern letters." Before Baumol's question had been asked, Zola had answered it insofar as it related to authorship. The hard work of translating inspiration into text is made worthwhile by the opportunity for personal profit that the intellectual property laws provide.

There is an opposing perspective, of course. Those who wish to compete with the patent holder or the copyright owner must also ask themselves, "Is it worthwhile?" From the perspective of such a competitor, the intellectual property laws can appear to be an impediment, not an incentive. An impassioned statement of that perspective comes from T. J. Rodgers, the chief executive officer of Cypress Semiconductors. Cypress has been the target of twenty-three intellectual property lawsuits, some of them the result of having hired away employees of their competitors. In an interview with the magazine *Upside*, Rodgers described in the following terms the effects of the intellectual property laws on his ability to manage Cypress:

Today is Friday, and not an atypical one. At 8 A.M. I was at Wilson, Sonsini [a prominent Silicon Valley law firm] meeting with [representatives of three other semiconductor firms] and six expensive lawyers, and we spent three hours hashing over the TI suit. Then I came back here and spent a half-hour instructing my people on our planned defense.

After that, I had an interview with the *Wall Street Journal*, and the reporter got really interested in litigation, so I spent an hour on that with him. Now I'm talking to you. Meanwhile, over in Tokyo, Mr. Yasafuku-san of Hitachi has spent the entire day figuring out how better to kick U.S. butt.

Are Cypress' problems the result of predatory practices on the part of larger competitors who are misusing their intellectual property rights in order to suppress competition? Are they the result of Cypress' own business strategies, which lead the company to imitate reasonably closely the products of others? Whatever the cause, there is no doubt that companies in Cypress' position can find themselves spending more time and money defending themselves in infringement or misappropriation lawsuits than they would like. Settlements are forced on them, or in cases that cannot be settled they are forced to endure courtroom trials that further drain their financial and executive resources. "So," Rodgers told *Upside* in an epigram as cutting as it is indelicate, "when I hear orators out there defending intellectual property, I want to throw up. Sleazeballs."

These opposing perspectives cannot be reconciled, so it is reasonable to inquire instead whether the legal regime that gives rise to such differences is really necessary. It is a legitimate question for the economists, since economic activity is what gives rise to the differences of opinion. The literature of economics is vast, and against it this correspondence course is of modest proportion indeed. Fortunately or unfortunately, the area of greatest interest to us is territory not extensively explored by economists. In 1964, a United Nations study lamented that "[i]t is painfully clear that in relation to these problems which lie in the borderland of law, technology and economics, very little concrete research and analysis of specific situations is available." The state of affairs has not improved in the intervening decades. "Intellectual property," business consultant Robert Sherwood observed in 1990, "has not been a mainstream subject for economic theory." Even so, there has been enough writing on the subject that we will need to structure our inquiry so that we can tap efficiently into the literature, get what we need, and not get mired down. I propose that we consider first what the effects of technological change on a country's economy are; then decide whether those effects are desirable; if so, assess whether legal regimes are required in order to produce those effects; and finally, to determine whether the existing regimes are reasonably designed to produce the desired effects without generating undesirable side effects. Hearing no dissents, that is how the endnotes that follow the next six chapters will be organized.

# 4

# After the Fall: The Weak Protectionists Regroup

The following day, the Southlanders set fires around the hill. Liu Pei's troops scurried away in disorder, leaving him in extremity. Then through the glare of the blaze, a group of men cut its way through to the hilltop. The leader was Kuan Hsing, son of Lord Kuan. "The flames press closer; we must move on," he said. "My lord, make haste to Pai Ti, where we can again regroup our forces." And they moved out.
— Lo Kuan-chung, *Three Kingdoms* (Fourteenth century)

Do you have a trash can on top of your desk? No? How about a window? A clipboard, perhaps? A scrapbook? One of those puzzles with fifteen numbered squares and a null square to rearrange in sequence? My work has taken me into thousands of offices of businesspeople, teachers, government officials, and professionals around the world, and—based admittedly on casual observation and anecdotal experience—it is my deeply held belief that not one of the listed objects is a typical occupant of the surface of a desk. Yet it is argued straight-facedly, by persons whose imaginations seem to fall rather short of their ambitions, that those objects are not only a natural part of the "desktop metaphor" but are in fact so necessary to the "desktop metaphor" that representations of them on computer screens should not be protected by copyright.

My desktop is messy. Does that mean that I not only want but must have a "messy desk" metaphor for a user interface to my computer? The truth is, I don't want my desktop to be messy. I don't want my user interface to be messy, either. Maybe the reader does. If so, be of good cheer. There are user interfaces that will give you the impression that you have piled windows, trash cans, alarm clocks, puzzles, scrapbooks, file folders, loose papers, rulers, and other objects all over the working surface of the imaginary desk on your computer screen. For me, such impressions are not felicitous.

Why, indeed, should I be bound to a desktop metaphor at all? A graphical interface is just an illusion. It is not a realistic depiction of what is actually inside the computer. Who says that the desktop illusion is the best one for users? Why not an "office metaphor" or a "secretary metaphor" or an "accounting department metaphor," or a wide variety of metaphors from which we could choose depending on what we were trying to accomplish? Or no metaphor at all, but just a graphic representation of the machine's innards? In point of fact, the nature of user interfaces is highly arbitrary. Though one can speak of the design of user interfaces as "interface technology" and "human factors engineering," those are merely catchwords for a highly subjective and creative process, just as the phrase "software engineering" is a catchword for what court after court has found to be a highly subjective and creative process: writing computer programs.

In the aftermath of the *Lotus* decision, the combatants in the softwars adjusted their positions in light of the outcome of that case. Lotus consolidated its victory by pursuing Borland and Santa Cruz Operations, the authors of two other spreadsheet programs. (Actually, Borland attempted a preemptive strike by filing a suit of its own in California, asking that its spreadsheet program be declared noninfringing of Lotus 1–2–3. The sole purpose of the preemptive attack was to give Borland leadership of the case and its choice of the courthouse in which the infringement issue would be decided. The strategem didn't work. The California court, recognizing the similarities of the issues raised by Borland to the issues involved in the *Lotus* case, dismissed Borland's lawsuit, with the result that *Lotus v. Borland* went forward before Judge Keeton.) Lotus argued that the basic issues in the case had already been resolved in the *Paperback* opinion. Borland submitted the opinions of ten copyright law teachers advising Judge Keeton that his *Lotus v. Paperback* decision was wrong. (See note 3.3 for subsequent developments in *Lotus v. Borland*.) Meanwhile, Santa Cruz Operations capitulated, withdrawing the offending program from the market and recommending that its customers switch to Lotus 1–2–3. Lotus also successfully completed the prosecution of its look-and-feel lawsuit against another clone, Mosaic Software.

Opponents of software copyright displayed their displeasure, each in the fashion to which he or she was best suited. A law professor advised readers of a computer professional journal not to worry, because the judgment would be appealed by Paperback. (By the time her advice was published, the case had in fact been settled, so that there would be no appeal.) A group at MIT called the League for Programming Freedom (up with whom we shall meet momentarily) organized a protest down the street from the campus, at Lotus Development Corporation headquarters. Law firms with clientele at risk as a result of the decision salted the legal literature and the trade press with articles critical of Judge Keeton's handiwork. For the most part, these tactics were ineffectual. The *Lotus* decision has been sewn into the warp and weft of American law. The only way to counter it now, if it should be countered, is to change the law through legislation or further case law precedent.

Or to shout really loud. Here are the words of a Silicon Valley lawyer with clients whose interests Judge Keeton had just disadvantaged, writing in the trade paper *Computerworld* shortly after the *Lotus* decision:

The recent court decision in *Lotus Development v. Paperback Software* is wrong for so many legal and technical reasons that it is difficult to know where to start discussing it. It is living proof that the adversarial jungle of a trial court is an unsatisfactory place to present highly technical concepts to a judge, who rarely has time to develop a clear understanding of the complex subject.

Hard cases like this are seldom resolved correctly until they reach the U.S. Supreme Court, and not always then. Unfortunately, this case will probably never get there for economic reasons. Paperback Software is effectively out of business, and appeals can take years, even if an insurance company pays for them. The public and the computer industry may be stuck with the many fallacies of the decision.

The pen is a mightier weapon than the sword, and if the pen is dipped in vitriol of sufficient concentration, it can powerfully influence public opinion. Judges do read the headlines, and if a public groundswell against the *Lotus* decision could be created, perhaps the ground lost to the innovators in *Lotus* could be retaken in subsequent cases.

One great advantage that guest editorials written for the press have over legal briefs and legal opinions is that the former are not at risk of failure if they depart from the facts. Thus, the writer of the *Computerworld* article was free to assert, and did assert, that Judge Keeton, intoxicated by Lotus' emotional arguments, ignored the legal requirement that he find that VP-Planner was *substantially* similar to Lotus 1–2–3 in order to hold it infringing. He could also assert that, as a result of what he referred to as "intellectual foreplay," the court granted Lotus "the exclusive right to the use of a set of common English words," and the exclusive right to "use the F1 key for a Help function." He could also warn, without mentioning Judge Keeton's careful delineation of the difference between copying expression and copying idea, that the *Lotus* rationale would make it impossible to develop industry standards using *concepts* from a copyright program. Since the vast majority of *Computerworld* readers have not read Judge Keeton's opinion—or even an extended description of it such as is contained in the last chapter—the lawyer's strident critique was an opportunity to sow seeds of insurrection in the programming community.

Another successful propagandist in the psychological war for the hearts and minds of the American software community writes a regular column on legal issues relating to computers in the *Communications of the ACM*. Her message about the *Lotus* case to readers of *Communications* was that Judge Keeton's opinion was indecipherable, and that the world would have to wait for the appeal or for subsequent cases to clarify the status of user interfaces under the copyright law.

I have read Judge Keeton's opinion carefully and I have worked very hard to figure out what it means. I would tell you what it means if I could understand it, but I cannot. And neither can anybody else.

For now, all we can do is hope that the First Circuit Court of Appeals will clarify what interpretation should be given to the Lotus case.

So that she would not be seen by her readership to be advocating that they simply ignore Judge Keeton's decision, the columnist inserted a tentative, if not altogether consistent, call to arms at the conclusion of her article:

If people in the software industry do not think the outcome in the Lotus v. Paperback case was the right outcome, or are worried about the broader implications of what Judge Keeton said in his opinion, or want a fast rather than litigation's tediously slow method of resolution of the issues about what copyright law should protect about program interfaces, they might want to think about supporting legislative initiatives.

*Might* want to *think about* supporting...? The hesitant tone of the author's call may have been occasioned by the realization that she couldn't consistently suggest both that no one can understand the *Lotus* decision and that her readers should be able to figure out for themselves that the decision needed to be corrected by legislation. Consistency, however, is another constraint with which propagandists need not be concerned. Thus, in her *Communications* article, the legal commentator reminded her readers that

I have always thought *Lotus v. Paperback* was a close case.... It is very difficult for a lawyer to look at a set of screen displays like those that present Lotus' commands and not see a protectable compilation of words.

Eighteen months earlier, however, the same commentator had expressed a rather different view of the strength of Lotus' case:

[L]ook and feel has virtually no standing in copyright law as to any category of protected work. Although there are a couple of cases involving copyrighted fabric design which contain some discussion of similarities in the look and feel of fabrics, look and feel has no precedent as a copyright standard.

Lotus may have a tougher time winning its lawsuit not only because its user interface is more functional, and less pictorial and graphical, than the Apple interface, but the Lotus lawsuit is also taking place in Massachusetts where a total concept and feel approach has not been endorsed in any case, let alone in a software user interface case.

And a year after telling her readers that it was difficult to look at Lotus' screen display and not see protected subject matter, this ACM commentator had reversed field again, appearing as one of ten academics who told Judge Keeton that the test of copyrightability employed in *Lotus v. Paperback* was "inconsistent with the copyright statute, the copyright caselaw and traditional principles of copyright."

Another challenge to the *Lotus* decision was issued by a New York lawyer in an article proposing new software protection legislation in the wake of *Lotus* which appeared in the periodical *The Computer Lawyer* for August 1990. Written too soon after the June 28 *Lotus* decision to be regarded as a rigorous critique, the New York piece nonetheless focuses on the single consistent theme in the criticism of Judge Keeton's opinion: the fact that user interfaces of computer programs are not merely aesthetic elements of a program, but are also useful, makes it difficult to differentiate the idea of a program from its expression. The author asserted that Judge Keeton's analysis didn't take into account the need to differentiate the expressive aspects of the Lotus interface from its utilitarian aspects. (Curiously, he also argued that programs are more complex and layered than most traditional literature. He did not conclude from this that programs were therefore at least as deserving of copyright protection as traditional literature. Rather, he said, because of the complexity and layering the normal process of separating idea from expression is not really workable in the case of computer programs.) The consequences of Judge Keeton's supposed error, the author asserted, are that cloning the instruction set of a personal computer such as the IBM PC or writing a compiler to translate a programming language created by someone else into machine language may be copyright infringement. Thus, he warned, *Lotus* runs the risk of spawning a line of cases that create unwarranted monopolies.

There is an obvious difficulty with this analysis: its premise is false. Judge Keeton did not ignore the fact that the Lotus 1–2–3 interface was utilitarian. As we saw in Chapter 3, Judge Keeton explicitly recognized that fact, and held only the elements of a program not essential to its utilitarian purposes to be protected by copyright. As to the assertion that the copying of a machine instruction set or the writing of a compiler might constitute infringement under Judge Keeton's formulation, the *Lotus* case does not address either act. Clearly, either act may be either legal or illegal as a matter of copyright law. The result would depend on whether the structure, sequence, organization, or text of a substantial portion of a program, including its user interface or programming interface, contain expressive elements not necessary to the program's purpose, and whether those expressive elements have been copied.

Is the distinction between the idea-expression dichotomy in utilitarian works and aesthetic works as clear as the weak protectionists would have us think? You climb the porch of my house and ring the doorbell. The chimes play a few bars of Little Richard's "Keep a-Knockin'." Is the music aesthetic or utilitarian? (Some might say "neither." Would Clapton's rendition of "Knockin' on Heaven's Door" be a more aesthetic piece? How about "The Great Gate of Kiev" from Moussorgsky's *Pictures at an Exhibition*? Suit yourself. My job here is to impart to you a sense of the law, not of artistic merit. It is only important to the exercise that you choose a work that you consider to have artistic merit.) The music, *aesthetically* pleasing as it may be, also has the desired *utilitarian* effect: my wife comes to the door. She tells you that I'm at the supermarket. You chase me down, and our conversation about the *Lotus* case takes place between the arugula and the tomatillos. From loudspeakers hidden in the ceiling, an endless stream of high-energy, bouncy music accompanies our debate. The music has been carefully selected by behavioral scientists to stimulate buying. It serves no other purpose insofar as the grocer is concerned. Is the music aesthetic, or is it utilitarian? Is it protected when you hear it on the radio but not when you hear it in the grocery store?

These questions suggest a thought experiment. Imagine that Lotus Development Corp. had licensed the rights to employ Beatles songs in the user interface of Lotus 1–2–3. (Because of the advantage taken of the Liverpudlians when they "was fab," the license would have to have been acquired from Michael Jackson, who bought majority interest in the copyrights some time ago, but fear not: Jackson is more liberal in licensing the songs than the Beatles would be.) Then, suppose that instead of using terms like "file", "copy", and "quit" for the Lotus macro commands, the designers implement the lyrics of the Lennon-McCartney tune "Yesterday" as the names of those commands. For example, users would select "yesterday" when they wanted to file something, "all" when they wanted to copy something, "my" when they wanted to print, "troubles" when they were ready to quit, and so on until each word of the Beatles' lyrics was assigned to a Lotus command. Should "Yesterday" lose protection because of this utilitarian incarnation? Should the "Yesterday" Lotus macro command set gain protection because the macro calls are now different words? Is it any easier to determine what the ideas of that command set are and what its expression is if we overlay "Yesterday" on the Lotus user interface? The answer to all three questions would seem to be no. (It could be argued that the answer to the middle question might be yes. The assignment of names to the macro command set by using words from popular songs results in greater arbitrariness or creativity. Greater arbitrariness or creativity is thought to warrant greater protection. In fact, though, that argument misses the mark. If

there were only one way to structure a spreadsheet user interface, trying
to paper over the merger of idea and expression in that interface by giving
the macro calls musical pseudonyms would not cure the essential nonprotectability of the interface. Indeed, if there were only one way to structure
the interface, one could not, by definition, substitute musical pseudonyms.
On the other hand, if there were numerous ways to structure such an
interface, copyright protection would already extend to the expressive elements of logic, structure, and flow in the interface, and using musical pseudonyms would not enhance the essential protectability of the interface.)

The most virulent antiprotection propaganda in the wake of *Lotus* came
not from lawyers or law professors, but from the radical fringe of the programming community: those who believe that the way to end the softwars
is to deprive software of virtually all legal protection. The organization with
the distinctly Orwellian appellation "The League for Programming Freedom"—One imagines their motto to be something like "We know what's
good for you."—began a pamphleteering and protest-marching campaign
designed to subvert the software protection establishment by direct action.
In an article published also in the *Communications of the ACM*, the League's
principal spokespersons set out the group's political agenda in the wake of
the *Lotus* decision. The agenda was preceded by an energetically distorted
presentation of the facts and law underlying the look and feel issue. It is a
time-honored tradition in military propaganda, of course, to present distorted factual and legal arguments. Paul Fussell describes the phenomenon
in his introduction to the *Norton Book of Modern Warfare*:

"Force and fraud," said Thomas Hobbes, "are in war the two cardinal virtues." From
the days of the Trojan horse, war has necessitated ruses, espionage, deceptions,
misrepresentations, and other elements of fiction, and a modern war can be distin-
guished from others by the extent depth, sophistication and technological expertise
of these operations.

The League should therefore not be singled out for criticism on the ground
of manipulating the facts. But readers interested in understanding what the
laws provide, and why, should be wary of obtaining that understanding from
groups with extreme political agendas.

For example, a user interface, in the League's form of newspeak, is what
you have to learn to operate a machine, and a computer program is just a
kind of machine. Therefore, the League article suggested, protecting user
interfaces for computer programs by copyright is like protecting a steering
wheel or a gas pedal by copyright. The League's use of that analogy was
equivalent to suggesting that protecting movies by copyright is like protecting the buttons on a VCR by copyright. Turning from technical to policy
considerations, the League asserted that the constitutional purpose of copy-

right is to "promote the progress of science and the useful arts." "Conspic-
uously absent," the League announced, "is any hint of intention to enrich
copyright holders to the detriment of users of copyrighted works." Yet the
only reason that such a "hint" was absent was that the League omitted to
quote the rest of the relevant sentence in the Constitution: "by securing
for limited times to authors and inventors the exclusive right of their respective writings and discoveries."

Swinging their cannon from policy to history, the League said that copyright protection for user interfaces was "unheard of" until 1986, and the
software industry had developed successfully without such protection. One
can only take that view of history by ignoring a long string of cases stretching
well back into the 1970s (the first decade in which copyrighted, priced
software was made widely available) that held the user interfaces of software
video games to be copyrightable subject matter. The extension of the "front
of screen" principles of those cases to software that was not entertainment
oriented was as natural and expected as a baby's burp after feeding.

From history, the League paper leapt to prognostication. "The monopoly
on the established interface," it predicted somberly, "will yield in practice
a monopoly on the functionality accessed by it." Further, "interface copyright will actually retard progress." The League's article was published in
November 1990. At the same time, in the real world, the trade press was
reporting that because of its lack of a graphical user interface, Lotus 1–2–
3, the imagined copyright monopolist of spreadsheet user interfaces, was
losing ground to Miscrosoft's Excel. *Sic transit* monopoly.

Another assertion in the League article was that protecting user interfaces
does not help small software houses, but only large software houses. It is
an inescapable fact of life in the industry, however, that most large software
houses today were either small software houses ten years ago or not even
in existence at that time. While small software houses that want to remain
small might not care if the user interfaces to their programs are protected
against plagiarism, small software houses that want to grow and prosper
tend to have the opposite view.

Buried deep in the League article was the real reason for the organization's
show of emotion: the concern that copyright protection for user interfaces
would reduce the demand for "freeware," "shareware," and other forms of
software distributed without attempting to recover the development expenditures therefor. We will deal more extensively with these New Age
software concepts later. For now, let it be said simply that to the extent
the purveyors of low-cost or no-cost software had intended to act as black
marketeers of illicit copies of someone else's work, then they should not
expect a great deal of sympathy if demand for their "products" is reduced.
To the extent they had no such intent, the concern voiced by the League
should not arise.

The League reported that "resentment of these lawsuits has led to boycotts by programmers and users who stop buying from the plaintiffs, stop developing software for their systems, or refuse job offers." In fact, the described actions were nothing more than the program of guerrilla warfare that the League itself was trying to organize. A flyer distributed by League members after the *Lotus* ruling advocated the following acts of subversion against companies trying to preserve their intellectual property rights in user interfaces:

Don't buy from Xerox, Lotus, Apple or Ashton-Tate. Buy from their competitors or from the defendants.

Don't develop software to work with the systems made by these companies.

Port your existing software to competing systems.

Join the League for Programming Freedom and help organize further activities.

Above all, don't work for the "look and feel" plaintiffs, and don't accept contracts from them.

Tell your friends and colleagues about this issue and how it threatens to ruin the computer industry.

Duplicate this handout and distribute it at shows and meetings.

Write to or phone your elected representatives to show them how important this issue is.

For programmers engaged in writing programs for profit, much of the League's agenda was a sure-fire formula for bankruptcy, and the movement has not caught fire. The League persists, however. Its members are still in the streets, and stalking the halls of academe, proselytizing at every opportunity, trying to convince the workers of the software world to rise up against their capitalist masters and give away the fruits of their labors for the good of society. Meanwhile, the copyright law moves forward. In a case reminiscent of our doorbell hypothetical, a New York court held that a rap musician's digital sampling and inclusion in his own recording of three words and associated musical notes from someone else's recording constituted infringement. (Afficionados of rap music may wish to know that the infringer was a singer by the name of Biz Markie, the offending song was called "Alone Again" and the infringed work was "Alone Again (Naturally)" by Raymond "Gilbert" O'Sullivan.) Surely the user interface of a complex computer program warrants at least as much protection as three words and six musical notes from a popular song of some considerable age.

# Endnote: Public Goods—
# Resources That Are Never
# Used Up

Student: "Why do economists ask so many questions?"

Professor: "Why shouldn't economists ask so many questions?"
                                    —Adapted from John Allen Paulos,
                                    *Mathematics and Humor* (1980)

The *Lotus* case raises the question whether the creator of software intellectual property, like the Lotus user interface, that causes a technological
change has contributed something of value to society for which society
should reward the creator. That specific question has not been the subject
of rigorous economic study; but the question whether technological change
in general is of value to society has been answered by the economists.
Beginning in the late 1950s, a series of studies, notably those by Nobel Prize
winner Robert Solow, strongly suggested that technological change was an
important factor in the long-term economic growth of the United States.
Solow's study related to the growth of the nonagricultural sectors of the
American economy in the latter four decades of the first half of the twentieth
century. He determined that during the period in question, the average rate
of technological change was 1.5 percent per year; that is, the amount of
output that could be derived from a fixed amount of input (capital and
labor) increased by 1.5 percent per year. Comparing that rate to the rate
of increase of per capita output over the same period, he concluded that
nine tenths of the increase in per capita *output* during that period was
accounted for by technological change. Other economists built on Solow's
work. Edward Denison examined the period 1929–1957, and identified 40
percent of the increase in per capita *income* as having derived from technological advances. He also found that 1.4 percentage points of the annual
growth in income per person during the years 1948–1969 and 1.6 percent
of the annual growth rate in the years 1969–1973 was attributable to "advances in knowledge." Edwin Mansfield selected specific innovations in
various American industries (including primary metals, machine tools, electronics, chemicals, construction, paper and, that all-important sector—for
television advertisers, anyway—household cleaners) and showed that the
median *social rate of return* (the quantifiable profit to society as a whole)
on investments in those innovations was 56 percent. Mansfield concluded
that "technological change seems to have been a very important factor,
perhaps the most important factor, responsible for our economic growth."
While the casual observer might wonder why these economists did not
stick to the same unit of measure in their various studies, the message of

their work is clear, and indeed is consistent with intuition. New technologies tend to expand economic activity.

In our interdependent world, economic growth entails foreign trade. It seems that intellectual property is a very important ingredient in the success of a nation's export program. Taking the United States as an example, we find that although the country's balance of trade has been substantially negative over the past decade, American exports of high technology products has been consistently positive through most of the period. The authors of a report of the Congressional Economic Leadership Institute entitled "Intellectual Property at the Crossroads" observe that

In 1950, products rich with intellectual property (computers, books, electronics, semiconductors, motion pictures, biotechnicals and pharmaceuticals) accounted for seven percent of total U.S. exports. In 1988, goods from these industries alone made up more than 23 percent of total U.S. exports.

More to our point,

American software producers control approximately 60 percent of the world software market, and virtually no computer programs are imported into the United States. [The latter assertion indicates a modest lapse of research on the authors' part.] According to the Department of Commerce, U.S. software producers earned some $33 billion in sales in 1988, of which foreign software sales yielded approximately $11 billion. With world software sales predicted to reach $1 trillion by the year 2000, software firms could be one of the biggest manufacturing sectors in the United States by the end of the decade.

Further study by Mansfield and others of the economic effects of technological change leads to the conclusion that the private rate of return, or in other words the profit rate of a firm investing in new technology, tends to be substantially lower than the social rate of return. In other words, society as a whole seems to profit from introduction of new technology to a far greater extent than do the individuals or corporations responsible for the innovations themselves. The innovators, for various reasons, are not able to appropriate to themselves all the economic advantage of their original work. This is in large measure because intellectual property is what economists call a "public good." That unfortunate term has nothing whatever to do with who owns the property in question, but rather with an inherent quality of the good, to wit, that in theory it is susceptible of being freely used over and over without being used up. One person's consumption of a public good does not affect the ability of another person to consume the same good. Software certainly has that characteristic, and it is also true that the social return from software development seems to be far larger than the private return. Even absent the freedom to create exact clones, the dissemination of ideas and concepts as to what software can cause a computer to do has led to a grand smorgasbord of consumer choice. In our next installment, we will take a closer look at the economic effects of technological change.

# 5

# "You Could Look It Up": Why Copyright Law Protects the Yellow Pages but not the White Pages

Toward the end of his life, when "Dr. Livingstone, I presume" had passed into the common culture, and Stanley himself had passed into legend, there were those who wondered whether he really had uttered the phrase. A young curate named Tovey who came to tea when the prematurely aged Sir Henry Stanley was living in Surrey, dared to put the question to him: "You didn't really say it, did you?" Stanley fixed the clergyman with his disconcertingly steady gaze and remained silent for what seemed like minutes. Finally he answered.

"Yes," he said. "I couldn't think what else to say."
—John Bierman, *Dark Safari: The Life Behind the Legend of Henry Morton Stanley* (1990)

In saying that most lawyers would expect software user interfaces to be protected by copyright because they are compilations, the ACM legal columnist was right, but for the wrong reason. User interfaces are not compilations. Compilations are collections of facts. User interfaces are more or less imaginative means of communicating. The compilation analogy used to be applied to computer programs both by those theorists who favor weak intellectual property protection, and also—in the early days of the softwares, when it was not clear that courts would accept the notion of copyrightability of software—by theorists who favored extending traditional protection to the new form of expression. That practice had fallen into desuetude as it has become clearer and clearer that the courts, which have to deal with questions of copying the text of a computer program, will treat those questions within the framework of the law applicable to literary works generally.

In recent years, the compilation argument had arisen most frequently in the context of data bases, which *are* in fact compilations.

In March 1991, the United States Supreme Court decided a case involving certain types of compilations—telephone books—that the weak protectionists, whose combat tactics commonly include the vigorous use of creative analogy, have trumpeted as a major turn in the tide of battle. The case, *Feist Publications, Inc. v. Rural Telephone Service Company, Inc.*, involved copyright protection for telephone white pages. The issue was straightforward. Feist had simply copied 1,309 listings from Rural's phone directory white pages without permission. The trial court didn't even feel it necessary to give Feist the benefit of a full trial. Finding that there were no material questions of fact that required trial, it granted summary judgment for the phone company. The court of appeals affirmed, in an opinion it considered insufficiently interesting to warrant publication. Feist asked the Supreme Court to hear its case, and the court consented. After hearing arguments on both sides and from interested observers, the court reversed the judgment and held Rural's white pages, and white pages generally, to be unprotectable by copyright. Almost immediately, the weak protectionists began bootstrapping the arguments against protectability of white pages into arguments against protectability of computer programs. Though, as we'll see in Chapter 14, the weak protectionists' argument has proven seductive to courts less interested in assessing the facts for themselves, the analogy is unconvincing, for the simple reason that white pages are alphabetical listings of extrinsic facts while computer programs are in large measure complex works of imagination, as we have seen.

Like most phone companies, Rural distributed phone directories to its subscribers. It was a monopoly, chartered by the state of Kansas to offer telephone service in a specified part of the state. One condition of its franchise was that it publish a telephone directory, which it did by accumulating information from applications for phone service submitted by residents of its service area. The information—name, town, and telephone number—was then arranged alphabetically and printed in the white pages of the directory. The yellow pages, as is usual, were organized alphabetically by supplier within type of service or product and contained advertising material as well.

Feist was a publishing company that specialized in producing phone directories covering broader calling areas than those within a particular phone company's service region. Its directories also contained yellow pages, and as a result, Feist competed with the telephone utilities for advertising revenue. The phone companies had an advantage over Feist, though, by virtue of their phone service business, which gave them ready access to the information necessary to create white pages for their service areas. The enterprising publisher took a direct approach to neutralizing that advantage. In the case in question, it approached the eleven different phone companies operating in northwestern Kansas, and simply asked to buy the right to copy their white page listings. Ten of the companies consented. Rural did not.

Feist, however, needed a list of Rural's subscribers to complete its directory. Without such a list, its phone book would lack substantial value, and advertisers would lose interest in paying for space in its yellow pages. It seems as though Feist was aware that simply copying Rural's listings would lead to an infringement suit, because in large measure it did not simply copy. Instead, it hired people to verify the data in Rural's directory. In addition, Feist's canvassers attempted to obtain street address information, which was not part of most of Rural's listings. Further, Feist removed several thousand names from Rural's list because they belonged to inhabitants of areas that Feist did not intend to cover in the regional directory in question. It is axiomatic that one may use a copyrighted work as a basis for another original work, so long as the copyright is not infringed, and it appears that Feist was intent both on demonstrating that it had undertaken substantial "independent" work and on adding information that would differentiate its listings from Rural's. Unfortunately, Feist's canvassers were not able to do a complete job for various reasons. Consequently, Feist had to cheat a little. Some 1,309, or just under 3 percent, of the listings in Feist's 1983 white pages were identical to those in Rural's white pages. Even more unfortunately, four of those listings were completely fictitious, traps that Rural had inserted in its directory to snare the unwary copyist.

The phone company sued. In the suit, it asserted that the only way Feist could lawfully have produced a white pages directory was to do either a door-to-door survey or a telephone survey. The reader will immediately recognize that in making that assertion, Rural was emphasizing an argument that was, psychologically, unfavorable to its cause. Because of its privileged position as the sole supplier of telephone service in its service area, the cost to Rural of collecting the information necessary to assemble a white pages directory was essentially zero, while the cost to anyone else, if Rural's argument was correct, was substantial. That cost difference, while of no theoretical import for copyright purposes, was emotionally a point in Feist's favor. Rural could be seen as leveraging its lawful monopoly of phone service into an area where it had no monopoly: phone directories. Feist, indeed, argued that it should be allowed to copy from Rural's directories because preparing a phone directory in any other way would be economically impractical. The argument was reminiscent of Paperback's arguments as to why it had to copy the user interface of Lotus 1–2–3, and fared about as well. None of the three courts that heard Feist's case, including the Supreme Court, thought that economic impracticality justified copyright infringement. Still, one can see that the dramatic advantage Rural had in data collection, and the fact that that advantage derived from a unique privilege granted by the state, would weigh on the minds of the judicial decision makers. It was perhaps for such reason that the other ten phone companies approached by Feist agreed to license their listings. Better to take the royalties and suffer the competition than to risk losing the copyright altogether. One major thematic difference between the *Feist* case, then, and virtually every software copyright case that has arisen, or will arise, is that the latter cases do not involve situations where the original author has a vast cost advantage conferred as a result of a state franchise of some sort. Instead, the copyright holder is usually just another joe trying to compete in the marketplace. Sometimes, it's a fairly sizable joe and sometimes it's a little joe, but almost never does a computer program derive from privileges available only to those with a government franchise. Instead, it is the software copyist who typically has a cost advantage, since such activities as market research, product design, coding, testing, and market development have already been done by the original author.

Feist fared much better with a second argument, which was that the information it copied was not protected by copyright. In 1985, the Supreme Court had summarized a basic principle of copyright law as follows: "[n]o author may copyright his ideas or the facts he narrates." The case involved President Ford's memoirs, and the copying by the magazine *The Nation* of a passage of less than 500 words from the then-unpublished version of those memoirs. Though the passage dealt with *facts*, in particular, the facts surrounding the pardon of former President Nixon, *The Nation* was held to have infringed the copyright in the way those facts were expressed. However, the principle that facts are not protected by copyright has a special resonance when it comes to phone directory white pages. These linear, nonimaginative works are simply alphabetic lists of names, addresses, and phone numbers. They are not even selective lists. The attempt of the directory compiler is to provide an entry for each telephone user in the service area covered by the directory. What is it in such a work that could possibly be protected by copyright?

One answer is sweat equity, or "sweat of the brow," as it is called in copyright tradition. Prior to *Feist*, some courts had held that a compilation of unprotected facts was protectable if it was the product of "industrious collection."

The man who goes through the streets of a town and puts down the names of each of the inhabitants, with their occupations and their street number, acquires material of which he is the author.

Now, in fact there would be nothing wrong with such a rule. Though not all federal courts followed it, it had been the law in some federal circuits for over half a century, without any disastrous effect on commerce or society within the geography of those circuits. Protecting industrious collection would provide incentive for people to engage in industrious collection. In *Feist*, however, the Supreme Court skewered the "sweat of the brow" rule and consigned it to the ash heap of legal history. It was not necessary for the court to do so, as the phone company hadn't really dampened its corporate brow in the first place in assembling the information contained in its white pages. Nonetheless, the "industrious collection" rule is gone. Compilers of white page phone directories no longer have the shelter of the copyright law to protect their handiwork. Before entrepreneurial readers rush off to the photocopiers with their local phone directories, however, they would be well advised to read on.

The Supreme Court struck down the sweat principle on the grounds that it ignored a basic tenet of copyright law, to wit, that the work be *original* with the author. Facts, the court said, are not original but rather are within the public domain. Thus, when a news service was hauled into court early in this century for lifting the facts from dispatches of a rival service and publishing them in its own articles, the Supreme Court had held the information lifted by the enterprising paraphraser to be free for the taking, even though the dispatches themselves were protected. Though the case was not a copyright infringement case, the principle was the same: the facts could be copied, but not the particular expression of those facts, the latter being the original contribution of the first reporter. Originality is a statutory prerequisite to copyright protection. The Copyright Act applies in terms only to "original works of authorship." Although "the requisite level of creativity is very low," according to the court, and "the vast majority of works make the grade quite easily, as they possess some creative spark, 'no matter how crude, humble or obvious,'" white pages lack originality.

Why? Because, in the court's view (and in reality) the raw facts in Rural's white pages did not originate with Rural. "[T]hey existed before Rural reported them and would have continued to exist if Rural had never published a telephone directory." That, of course, is true of all compilations. Yet compilations are specifically protected by the Copyright Act. What, the reader may well ask, is protected about a compilation of facts if the facts themselves are not protected? What is protected is the selection, arrangement, and coordination of the pre-existing facts. The "selection" made by Rural was rudimentary. It listed all subscribers. It only published certain information about those subscribers, of course, but the information it selected for publication—name, town, and telephone number—was not creative or original. In addition, the court noted that the selection was not really chosen by Rural, but rather imposed by Kansas law as a condition of Rural's monopoly franchise. As to "coordination" and "arrangement," the court could find nothing original in an alphabetical arrangement of telephone subscribers, and it is hard to quarrel with that conclusion.

On the other hand, there *are* complete listings of names in mundane order that have high drama and tragic power. I have seen such a list bring mature adults to their knees, causing them to weep openly and depriving them of the faculty of speech. You can see it, too. Just stop for a while at the Vietnam Memorial the next time you are in Washington, and watch what goes on there. No work of fiction or imaginative art affects people more profoundly than does that list. No Greek play propels its audience through greater catharsis. Is the sad majesty of that work conveyed in the facts it displays, or in the aesthetics of the medium on which they are displayed? Would a simple paperback listing printed on white pages have the same effect? If it did, should it be protected by copyright? Why do I ask more questions that I answer?

(The answer to the last question is that intellectual property law, like all areas of law, is full of unanswered questions. The law cannot anticipate every circumstance that may arise. It can only provide guidelines for future behavior. Like all guidelines, the intellectual property laws are a little gray when it comes to suggesting how to behave in unanticipated circumstances. Asking questions is one way to bounce around in the gray areas of those laws without getting hurt.)

The *Feist* decision does not invalidate all copyrights in lists or compilations. The Supreme Court observed, however, that the architects of the Copyright Act, in providing protection only for "original works of authorship," must have intended that some works would not meet the modest statutory test of originality. "Given that some works must fail," the court said, "we cannot imagine a more likely candidate." Where a compilation consists entirely of unprotected facts, but those facts are selected, coordinated, and arranged in ways that are original with the compiler, the work is eligible for copyright protection. Thus, though the court did not say so, phone directory yellow pages are likely, in the usual case, to be protectable subject matter. Computer data bases are also likely to be protectable subject matter, unless they are the equivalent of white pages. Normally, they are not, either because the entries in the data base contain certain elements added by its creator to enhance searchability or because the choice of entries is more selective than that of the white pages. In addition, even Rural's listings may be protected against mechanical reproduction, to the extent that choice of font, placement on page, column width, and other visual factors meet the minimum test of originality.

What does all of this have to do with user interfaces? Nothing, really. Indeed, to the extent that *Feist* speaks at all to the issues involved in the "look and feel" cases, it is consistent with protection for user interfaces, because the essence of *Feist* is that such elements of a copyrighted work as selection, arrangement, and coordination—abstract, nonliteral elements such as those held to be protected in the *Lotus* case—are protected by copyright.

Shortly after the Supreme Court handed down its opinion in *Feist*, the United States Court of Appeals for the Second Circuit, formerly a bastion of "industrious collection" theory, decided a case involving copyright protection for baseball rating forms. The case, *Kregos v. The Associated Press*, dealt with a form consisting of nine items of information concerning a pitcher's past performance; items such as won/lost record, earned run average, and innings pitched. The items were grouped in three categories: season record, season record against upcoming opponent at the site of the upcoming game, and last three outings. Kregos had sued AP to protect his right to the exclusive use of that particular set of items. Kregos asserted copyright not in the underlying statistics, but only in his selection of items. The principal issue was whether that selection was sufficiently original to warrant copyright protection. (The *arrangement* of the data was considered to be too obvious to warrant protection.) The three-judge court held that the copyright law did not preclude such protection, if as a matter of fact the selection was original. In the opinion, written by Judge Jon Newman, the court also observed that the fact that most of the statistical items Kregos had selected had previously been published elsewhere did not preclude a finding of originality. What was at issue was the originality of Kregos' selection, not the originality of the statistics. Protection of that selection did not depend on Kregos discovering facts that had not been published before, but only on the extent of creativity exercised in selecting the facts to include in the form. Finding that no previous form was identical to Kregos', nor different only in trivial degree from Kregos', the court held that the validity of his copyright could not be challenged on originality grounds. (The court went on to consider whether there was a merger of idea and expression in Kregos' form. Two of the judges thought the idea of the form was "an outcome predictive pitching form." One thought the idea was "the nine most significant statistics in attempting to predict the outcome of a baseball game." If the dissenting judge had been right, there would have been merger, as the selection of "most significant statistics" would have been an idea and the arrangement was unprotectably obvious. The majority felt, however, that Kregos' form did not provide a system for predicting outcomes, but only useful data from which readers would have to make their own predictions; and further that there was room for substantial variation in selecting relevant facts for such purposes. The court pointed out, however, that Kregos' copyright would not prevent AP or another from offering forms that differed from his in more than trivial degree.)

Some user interfaces are no more complex than Kregos' pitching forms. Most are far more complicated. Some are just categories into which to put data. Most include means for interacting with the program other than merely filling in a blank. Elements of a user interface may of course be listed—and often are, in the manual that accompanies the program providing the interface, for example— but that does not make the user interface a compilation, any more than a listing of *dramatis personae* makes a play a compilation. Simply put, the elements of a user interface are in general not facts, but rather are the words, phrases, pictures, or sounds of a conversation between a program author and a program user. As such, unless they spring from a source other than the program author, they can be expected to meet the statutory test of originality. It comes as something of a surprise, then, to learn that the issue of originality featured prominently in two of the leading look and feel cases that followed *Lotus*. After the next installment in our economics course, we will grapple with *Apple v. Microsoft* and *Ashton-Tate v. Fox*.

## Endnote: Trickle-Down Theory—The Leakage of Intellectual Property

> God wants to intervene in the world, and how is he to do it except through man? I think the Devil is in the same predicament.
> —Robertson Davies, *World of Wonders* (1975)

Although intellectual property partakes of the attributes of what economists call "public goods" that can be used over and over again without exhaustion, it will be obvious to the reader that in the real world overuse of certain kinds of intellectual property can in fact use up its value to society altogether. Jokes and television reruns are examples that immediately spring to mind. Products subject to piracy and widespread illicit distribution are also vulnerable to dissipation of their value to society, to the extent that part of their value is that they encourage creation of new products. Speaking at a conference on capital formation and intellectual property rights held in Washington, D.C., in 1987, Robert Benko put it this way:

Ordinarily, society maximizes its welfare through not charging for the use of a free good. Since the marginal cost of supplying an additional unit of [the same] knowledge is near zero, static efficiency standards suggest that a zero price achieves the optimal allocation of resources.

Social welfare, however, has a dynamic dimension that must be considered in the case of intellectual goods. Although these goods once created may be used at no additional economic cost, to create them may be an expensive proposition. Invention or artistic creation often involve considerable cost that cannot be recovered at a zero selling price. Therefore investors have no incentive to invest in inventive or creative activity.... Thus a zero price maximizes welfare in the static sense at the expense of dynamic efficiency or future innovation and creative advance.

The "leakage" of intellectual property rate of return away from the creator of the property tends to redound to the benefit of imitators. Mansfield found that imitators are "able to obtain information quickly concerning the detailed nature and operation of the new products and processes developed by a firm." Federal Judge Frank Easterbrook, writing in the *Harvard Journal of Law and Public Policy*, pointed out a couple of advantages that the imitator has, even where intellectual property laws prohibit reproduction. First, he observed, the imitator does not bear the cost of design. The creator has traveled the false trails, tried the alternatives, and perfected the design. The end-point of those preproduction efforts is the start of the imitator's preproduction efforts. Second, the imitator can "cherry-pick," selecting for imitation only those innovations that have been successful, while the innovator pays for all research and development, successful or not. The phenomenon was recognized by John Dryden over three centuries ago, in his "Prologue to *The Tempest*":

> As, when a tree's cut down, the secret root
> Lives underground, and then new branches shoot;
> So from old Shakespeare's honored dust, this day
> Springs up and buds a new reviving play:
> Shakespeare, who (taught by none) did first impart
> to Fletcher wit, to laboring Johnson art.
> He, monarch-like, gave those, his subjects, law;
> And is that nature which they paint and draw.
> Fletcher reached that which on his heights did grow,
> Whilst Johnson crept, and gathered all below.
> This did his love, and this his mirth digest:
> One imitates him most, the other best.
> If they have since outwrit all other man,
> 'Tis with the drops which fell from Shakespeare's pen.
> The storm which vanished on the neighboring shore,
> was taught by Shakespeare's *Tempest* first to roar.
> That innocence and beauty which did smile
> in Fletcher, grew on this *Enchanted Isle*.
> But Shakespeare's magic could not copied be;
> within that circle none durst walk but he.

The imitator can also concentrate on improving the technology copied. At certain points in history, that ability has been highly prized, as Waldemar Januszczak describes in his book, *Sayonara Michelangelo*:

I once visited a nightclub in Tokyo where every single act on the bill attempted an imitation of the Beatles: the same songs, the same clothes, the same hairstyles, the same harmonies, all learned with note-perfect Japanese precision. Of course, the differences were more significant than the similarities, and by the end of the night the Beatles imitations had metamorphosed into a peculiarly Japanese hybrids of Moptop Pop. In the same way, the early Toyota cars built in imitation of American models were significantly different from the originals, smaller, more practical, with better fuel consumption. And Japanese baseball, which NTV covers so well, is significantly different from the American version, which was itself a corruption of the English game of rounders. Since the whole of the Japanese economic miracle is built on imitation, it is worth noting that the modern Japanese are therefore closer relatives of Renaissance men than modern Italians are. Imitation meant something positive to the Renaissance that it does not mean to the modern West. Not only was it an accepted way of learning and of paying homage to a worthy subject, it was also more than that, more than a fashion: it was an attitude that underpinned the entire economic and social development of the Renaissance.

The two major economic effects of technological change, then, are that it is a major stimulus to economic growth and that it brings profit both to the persons responsible for the change and to their imitative competitors. Are these effects desirable?

To economists, economic growth is generally accepted as a desirable goal. The benefits of economic expansion, particularly when population is expanding, are fairly obvious. On a microscopic level, readers who are either college graduates living with their parents for want of employment sufficient to fund economic independence or the parents of such graduates can appreciate that economic growth offers substantial social benefit as compared with economic contraction. Although noneconomists, in this time of belated environmental consciousness, challenge the notion that economic growth is a universal good, few of us are willing to advocate economic decline in its place, particularly when other nations' economies are growing in relation to ours. An additional reason for the general reluctance to accept economic status or decline as an objective of public policy is that economic growth has a qualitative dimension as well as a quantitative dimension. Not only does output of goods and services increase during expansionary times, but (largely through technological innovation) new types of products are produced that enhance the quality of life in general. Without presuming to speak for any individual reader, it is consistent with history, politics, and consumption patterns to conclude that most readers will accept, with whatever internal limits on rate of change seem comfortable to them, the economists' view of the desirability of economic growth.

What do we make of the second economic effect of technological change, the fact that the agents of change are not able, by a wide margin, to keep for themselves the full economic advantage that accrues from their creativity? Professor Mansfield tells us that the private rate of return from new technologies is on the order of thirty percentage points lower than the social rate of return. Where the former seems to be on the order of 25 percent, the latter seems to be on the order of 56 percent, or even higher. Is this goodness? In fact, it is better than goodness. Investors in innovation are rewarded handsomely for taking risks. A 25 percent rate of return over a sustained period is more than sufficient to attract capital to projects involving the creation of intellectual property. (That is not to say, of course, that every investor in every such project will earn 25 percent per annum, but that the promise of such returns from successful projects is sufficient to entice capital.) The surplus return earned by the rest of us is like manna from heaven, or what has been called "the lever of riches"; a gratuitous enhancement of our well-being the further production of which we, like ants stroking the mandibles of their honey-collecting fellows, should encourage. Certainly those competitors in industry whose business strategy is one of imitating rather than creating, and whose livelihood therefore depends on the creativity of others, find the surplus social rate of return desirable, for in it is the basis for their own rates for return.

In sum, though not all new technology works to the advantage of humankind, in aggregate a nation's research and development activities, when they result in the proliferation of new products and services, improve its citizens' economic well-being and are therefore to be encouraged from an economic viewpoint. That conclusion, I trust, is not terribly controversial. After examining the *Apple v. Microsoft* and *Ashton-Tate v. Fox* cases, we will consider the question whether protective legal regimes are necessary in order to encourage the desired proliferation of new technologies, or whether other forms of incentive might be sufficient.

# 6

## Never-Ending Stories: *Ashton-Tate v. Fox, Apple v. Microsoft*, and the Future of User Interfaces

The eyes delight in beautiful shapes of different sorts and bright and attractive colours. I would not have these things take possession of my soul. Let God possess it, he who made them all. He made them all very good, but it is he who is my Good, not they. All day and every day, while I am awake, they are there before my eyes. They allow me no respite such as I am granted in moments of silence when there is no singing and sometimes no sound at all to be heard. For light, the queen of colours, pervades all that I see, wherever I am throughout the day, and by the ever-changing pattern of its rays it entices me even when I am occupied with something else and take no special notice of it. It wins so firm a hold on me that, if I am suddenly deprived of it, I long to have it back, and if I am left for long without it, I grow dispirited.

—Saint Augustine, *Confessions* (397–98)
(R. S. Pine-Coffin, Tr.)

Poor Saint Augustine would not fare well were he, as in Dylan's dream, "alive as you and me" today. The very stimuli that tormented him and distracted him from contemplating the Almighty have become ubiquitous trappings of modern culture. Light and color. Movies, TV, neon, fireworks. User interfaces.

User interfaces? Indeed, light and color are key aspects of modern user interfaces. According to Penny Bauersfeld of Apple and Jodi Slater of Letraset, "Color is important in interface because the appropriate use of color can make interfaces easier to understand and use." Bauersfeld and Slater recommend that user interface designers come to understand how artists and

graphic designers are trained to think about color. In particular, they suggest
that user interface designers study Josef Albers' color theory, as elaborated
in his book, *Interaction of Color*. Albers was a painter, poet, and teacher
whose classroom exercises for art students demonstrated the instability and
relativity of color. In their paper prepared for the 1991 ACM Computer-
Human Interaction (CHI) conference, Bauersfeld and Slater state that

Albers' primary principles of color theory include the role of perceptual memory
in color recollection, the relativity of color, the importance of form in color perception, the significance of lightness, and the exploration of multiple solutions to a
problem. Each of these principles has ramifications on the design of interactive color
tools [for use in user-oriented color interface design].

Color and light are one important respect in which user interfaces are
evolving in the direction of the arts. Provided that the law does not evolve
in the directions advocated by the antiprotectionists, the arts both high and
low will increasingly invade the domain of the computer interface designer.
The United States clearly has a comparative advantage in the production of
low art at the moment, as the global proliferation of American movies, TV
shows, and popular music amply demonstrates, and since very little high
art is being produced anywhere in the world, one might expect American
software suppliers to maintain their edge on the world market if there is
no change in the current state of legal protection for user interfaces. One
might do so, that is, if it were not for Super Mario Brothers, the signature
Nintendo user interface that is seducing children worldwide.

Of the future of user interfaces, both technological and strategic, there
will be more to say as soon as we have stepped (lightly) through the mine
fields of two confrontations that, with the *Lotus* cases, comprise the tri-
umverate of "look and feel" archetypal conflicts: *Ashton-Tate v. Fox Software* and *Apple v. Microsoft*. Whereas the *Lotus* cases proceeded in
reasonably orderly fashion from complaint through pretrial motion practice
and discovery to trial, the other two paradigmatic user interface cases were
distinctly nonlinear in evolution. The *Apple* case tended to shuck off judges.
Its first assigned judge, Robert Aguilar, left the bench in the wake of alleged
improprieties on unrelated matters. The second, William Schwarzer, was
asked by the federal judiciary to accept a full-time assignment aimed at
improving the administration of justice, and gave up the case. The third
judge, Vaughan Walker, picked up the pieces in 1990 and did his best to
bring structure, logic, and flow to the litigation. Apple had sued both Microsoft and Hewlett-Packard (H-P) for copying the "fanciful displays and
images appearing on the computer screen" of the Apple Macintosh. The
Cupertino Company asserted in its complaint that those displays and images
were "artistic, aesthetically pleasing" creations that were "widely recognized as a hallmark of the Macintosh computer system." Apple had certainly

studied the copyright case law before filing its complaint in 1987. The terminology of its complaint, and the decision to confine the lawsuit to the screen display aspects of the Macintosh user interface, attempted to put its case squarely in the mainstream of copyright tradition.

Microsoft was alleged to have copied substantial elements of the Macintosh user interface into its Windows software product. Windows is a program that runs in conjunction with Microsoft's DOS operating system and provides a user interface rather more forthcoming than the infamous, intimidating DOS C prompt. (To be greeted by nothing more than "C>" and a flashing cursor on booting up DOS is the microcomputer equivalent of a college math professor conducting each class by saying something like, "OK, ask me any question about differential equations. Come on, ask me a question.") Hewlett-Packard's allegedly infringing product was New Wave, a program that runs together with DOS and Windows and offers an enhanced graphical user interface built on a Windows base. The lawsuit was not susceptible of resolution on the basis of a simple comparison of the Apple user interface with the Windows and New Wave interfaces, because Microsoft was licensed to reproduce certain aspects of the Macintosh interface and H-P was a licensee of Microsoft's Windows. Microsoft's license from Apple had arisen out of an earlier dispute between the two companies as to whether Microsoft had appropriated to itself certain work that it had done for Apple on the Macintosh operating system. In settling that dispute, Apple gave Microsoft the right to reproduce certain Macintosh similarities that had already been embodied in Windows and in certain Microsoft application programs that ran in a DOS/Windows environment. In exchange, Microsoft acknowledged that the visual displays in Windows Version 1.0 and in five of its application programs were derivative works of the visual displays in the Macintosh and Apple Lisa operating systems. The gist of Apple's complaint was that Microsoft created Macintosh similarities in Windows 2.03 that went beyond those existing at the time the license was granted. Hewlett-Packard, not being licensed at all by Apple to reproduce aspects of the Mac user interface was simply sued for overall infringement. (Ironically, at the same time as Apple was pursuing Microsoft for violating the 1985 license agreement, the Beatles were pursuing Apple, not for using Beatles' tunes in Apple's user interface, but for violating a license agreement that allowed Apple to use the name "Apple" on devices, i.e., Apple computers, so long as they were not designed to play music. "Apple" was the trademark of the Beatles' record company.)

Just as a separation agreement complicates a couple's lives, the license agreement complicated Apple's prosecution of its case. Normally, a copyright plaintiff, particularly one who is asserting copyright in graphical images, is entitled to have an infringing work evaluated against the original work on the basis of the *gestalt* of the two works: the overall impression or "total concept and feel" that they convey. If the later work copies the total concept and feel of the earlier work, infringement may be found. Apple attempted to convince the court that, despite the existence of the license, the Mac and Windows user interfaces should be compared on the basis of their total concept and feel, because the license did not give Microsoft the right to create works with a total concept and feel more like that of the Mac user interface than those that existed on the date of the license. Microsoft and Hewlett-Packard argued that what was licensed cannot be part of a claim of infringement, and that the court must subtract out of its infringement analysis every licensed element. The case law cited by the parties made it clear that sometimes the rule for which Apple was arguing is appropriate and sometimes the rule that the defendants had propounded is appropriate. Under the circumstances of the litigation at hand, Judge Schwarzer found that the defendants' rule should prevail. That decision resulted in the subtraction exercise described above and, as a result, in the limitation of the case against Microsoft to a short list of discrete screen display attributes. These were

—overlapping windows in front of a muted background;
—windows appearing partly on and partly off the screen;
—top overlapping window displayed as the active window;
—window brought to the top of stack when mouse clicked;
—gray outline of window dragged along with cursor when mouse pressed on window's title bar;
—window dragged to a new position when mouse released after dragging the window's outline;
—newly exposed areas on screen are redisplayed after the window is moved;
—icon may be moved to any part of the screen by dragging along with cursor when user presses mouse on icon;
—display of icons on screen behind any open windows; and
—icon's title displayed beneath icon.

As to Hewlett-Packard, the list of remaining similarities was on the order of a few dozen, since New Wave allegedly went beyond Windows 2.03 in providing a Macintosh-like user environment.

Judge Schwarzer's decision, to which Judge Walker felt constrained to adhere when he took over the case, was a blow to Apple, because the elements on which it could proceed against Microsoft and Hewlett-Packard were not all closely connected with one another, and therefore infringement of each would likely be analyzed separately. Whenever copyright infringement is analyzed atomistically, there is a greater propensity that defenses like idea-expression merger will succeed. Readers familiar with the Mac, Windows, or New Wave user interfaces will appreciate just how vulnerable each individual element on the foregoing list of ten is to the argument that it is not original expression. Indeed, subsequent to that ruling, both defendants moved for summary judgment that none of the nonlicensed similarities was protectable expression. That motion was denied, but not because Judge Walker concluded that the unlicensed elements were in fact protected expression. Rather, the judge felt that the motion was premature, in that insufficient information had been put before him on which to base a decision.

The defendants' initial tactical success was tempered by a ruling in March 1990 in Apple's favor. At the same time at which he ruled that it would be premature to adjudge the idea-expression question, Judge Walker ruled on a motion by Apple that its copyrights in the Macintosh user interface be declared valid and that the defendants' attacks on their validity be dismissed. The court again found much of what Apple was seeking to be premature, but agreed to decide whether two of the attacks—the argument that Apple had committed a fraud on the copyright office and the argument that the Macintosh user interface did not originate with Apple—should be dismissed. In the process of deciding those issues, Judge Walker made a number of revealing statements about his own view of the case. For example:

In developing the Macintosh computer operating system software, Apple made one of the major commercial breakthroughs of the 1980s. The graphic user interface generated by the Macintosh system software consisted of windows, icons, pull-down menus, and other images or visual displays projected on the computer screen. The Macintosh user interface proved so intuitive that users were able fairly quickly to learn how to manipulate the screen displays and mouse and thus accomplish what had theretofore been the daunting task of learning to operate a computer. This breakthrough vaulted Apple to the top of the personal computer industry. [Footnote omitted.]

The obvious difference between a stage play and a computer interface is that in the latter, the user directs the action. The "user friendliness" of the Macintosh interface gave Apple a competitive edge over other personal computer manufacturers.

H-P's assertion that Apple had committed fraud on the copyright office was based on one of the enduring bits of Silicon Valley folklore: that the Macintosh user interface was copied wholesale by Steve Jobs, then head of Apple, from Smalltalk and Star, two projects he had been invited to observe at the Xerox Palo Alto Research Center (PARC). There is no question that Jobs and others at Apple saw the icon-based Star system at Xerox PARC, as well as the mouse-based Smalltalk software which, among other things, provided overlapping windows, and that the Xerox projects heavily influenced the Macintosh. As put to the court by H-P, however, the issue was whether Apple defrauded the copyright office in order to obtain a copyright certificate by failing to disclose that the Mac user interface was based on those preexisting works. Judge Walker held that H-P would have to prove two things in order to succeed on that issue: that Apple's work copied the expression of Xerox's work, and that Apple intended to deceive the copyright office. As to the latter element, the judge found that H-P had offered no evidence at all of intentional deception. As to the former, the judge took another analogy from the aesthetic arts:

To require a designer of a computer graphic user interface to acknowledge sources of artistic influence would be similar to expecting Roy Lichtenstein to declare in a copyright registration that a particular work is derivative of a named comic strip.

Unlike the requirements for obtaining a patent (which include the necessity for patentees to list on their applications all "prior art," or relevant preexisting technology, known to them so that the patent office can assess whether the patentee has in fact invented something), the requirements for copyright do not require a listing of relevant preexisting works and the copyright office does not attempt to compare the registrant's work with works from which it may have been derived.

A derivative work, the judge rule, is "one which is substantially copied from a prior work." If a second work would not be deemed infringing of the first, it is not derivative. H-P had introduced no proof that the Mac user interface substantially copied the expression of the ideas of Smalltalk or Star, despite the depositions, exhibits, and published articles offered into evidence, and the court concluded that there was no triable issue as to the copying of the Xerox programs. Accordingly, he ruled that H-P's defense of fraud on the copyright office was "meritless."

Both H-P and Microsoft had also claimed that Apple's work lacked originality, either because they were derivative of the PARC programs or because they were no more than compilations of preexisting, uncopyrightable material. The judge found no merit in that argument, either. He observed that the statutory requirement of originality required only "minimal" originality. All that was necessary was that the work be independently created by the author and that it embody a very modest amount of intellectual labor. So long as the work was not produced by copying someone else's expression, it is original for copyright purposes, and "photocopies of visual displays from the Smalltalk and Star programs within the parties' exhibits reveal scant similarity of expression between Xerox's and Apple's visual displays." The result of the court's ruling on originality seemed to have been to take the critical issue of the genesis of the Macintosh in Xerox PARC out of the case at an early stage.

Accordingly, Microsoft and H-P asked Judge Walker to reconsider. Their briefs argued that the copyright law does not prevent the copying of unoriginal elements in a protected work. The result of the defendant's request was an illustration of the maxim, "Be careful what you ask for; you just might get it." Judge Walker agreed to reconsider, and did reconsider, despite having read in a *Wall Street Journal* article that Microsoft's counsel did not think the motion was very important. The upshot of his revisiting the issue of preexisting public domain works was a ruling that confirmed, as the defendants had requested, the relevance of lack of original expression both to the question of what is protected expression and to the question of what similarities between two works can establish copyright infringement. But the judge did not stop there. The opportunity to reflect further on these matters had given him the opportunity to consider two related matters. One of these was the extent of original material that must be added to preexisting public domain works in order to render the combination protectable. The result of the jurist's rumination was the following conclusion:

If a plaintiff directly copied the expressive elements of his work from preexisting works, he has no right to preclude others from using those same "unoriginal" elements. The defendant may not, of course, take any original expressive elements from plaintiff's work and use them in a substantially similar manner simply because plaintiff used "unoriginal" elements and this remains true even if all but one of the expressive elements of the plaintiff's work are unoriginal. The addition of even one original expressive element may so alter a work otherwise wholly comprised of unoriginal elements that copyright protection is appropriate.

Defendants must show that the component features of Apple's work which are allegedly "unoriginal" have been directly copied from prior works. In other words, if Apple's expression of those component features is different from the expression of similar features in preexisting programs, then defendants have failed to establish that Apple's expression is "unoriginal."

More significantly, the second matter that reconsideration had "awakened" in the mind of the judge was his "concern with the apparent state of the law . . . suggesting that elements of an allegedly infringing work which are found to be unprotectable must be eliminated from consideration" in comparing defendants' works to plaintiffs' works to establish whether they are substantially similar. That notion, it seemed to the judge, could only be taken so far. He gave three examples. First, a compilation of preexisting facts. Remove all the facts because they are unprotected, and what is left to compare? Second, a musical composition. Individual musical notes are unprotected, but take them out of plaintiff's and defendant's compositions before the substantial similarity test is performed, and infringement would never be found. Third, an abstract painting comprised entirely of standard geometrical forms arranged in an original pattern. (This third example obviously comes very close to the case of the Macintosh user interface.) If the geometrical forms are excluded from the infringement analysis, nothing would be left on which to base a substantial similarity determination. The jurist concluded that he should not exclude the unprotected elements of the Macintosh interface from his determination whether Windows and New Wave infringe the listed elements of that interface. (But see note 6.4 in Notes and References.)

Instead, if it is determined that the defendant used the unprotectable elements in an arrangement which is not substantially similar to the plaintiff's work, then no copyright infringement can be found.

If, on the other hand, the works are deemed substantially similar, then copyright infringement will be established even though the copyrighted work is composed of unprotectable elements. There is simply no other logical way of protecting an innovative arrangement or "look and feel" of certain works.

If you were a lawyer for Microsoft or H-P, would you ask for further reconsideration after receiving such a ruling?

The case was scheduled to begin trial while this book was in the process of publication. Its outcome is of critical importance to the combatants, given Apple's multibillion dollar damage theory. The outcome of the case, however, is less important to the evolution of the rules of combat in the softwars than are the principles on the basis of which it was decided, most of which have now been articulated. Although one could quarrel with Judge Walker's choice of words, or to some extent with the conclusions he has reached, the important thing to note is that he was applying traditional, long-standing principles of copyright law to the works at issue, not creating a new legal regime specific to software. Applying existing legal principles to cases before them is what judges do for a living, and it is what makes for stable, consistent, and predictable regimes of intellectual property protection.

Parenthetically, one of the side shows to the Apple/Microsoft/H-P litigation was a lawsuit filed by Xerox against Apple over some of the very same issues. Seeming to awaken like Rip van Winkle after a long slumber to find a world not altogether to its liking, Xerox claimed that Apple had unfairly appropriated the Xerox PARC work. The suit was not a copyright infringement suit, however, because Xerox had let the right to bring a copyright suit slip through its fingers by waiting too long to bring its lawsuit. (Another bit of enduring Silicon Valley folklore is the extent to which Xerox let the benefit of the PARC projects of the 1970s slip through its fingers.) There are, unfortunately, severe legal problems with bringing a lawsuit for copying that is grounded in legal principles other than copyright. One problem is that the copyright statute explicitly provides that it preempts all other laws that attempt to protect against copying expression. Another problem is that the nature of the suit that Xerox did bring—basically a petition to have its copyrights declared to be Xerox property and Apple's copyrights declared to be invalid—did not result from an actual dispute between Xerox and Apple. It is a basic tenet of American jurisprudence that courts will not render advisory opinions, but will only deal with real and substantial disputes between two parties. Apple had not challenged Xerox's copyrights in any way, and consequently Xerox's lawsuit was handily dismissed on Apple's motion.

Emboldened by Judge Walker's initial decision on originality, Apple attempted to turn up the heat. It filed a motion to amend its complaint by adding a claim that Microsoft defrauded Apple into settling by license the original dispute between the parties, by pretending to believe that the terms of the license prohibited Microsoft from creating a more Mac-like interface. Apple also moved to supplement its complaint in order to bring Windows 3.0, Microsoft's hot new release, into the lawsuit. Windows 3.0, Apple said, indicated "a steady progression toward making the similarities of the visual displays of the Windows products more like the Macintosh visual displays." Judge Walker denied the motion to amend by adding a fraud claim, but granted the motion to supplement by adding Windows 3.0, thereby enhancing the newsworthiness of the lawsuit, because Windows 3.0 was a substantial enhancement to Microsoft's DOS-oriented graphical user interface.

Behind the Apple lawsuit, behind the theoretical arguments over whether ideas or expression had been copied from Xerox, lay a critical business issue for Apple. The Macintosh user environment had been its principal software asset. Apple had kept that asset "closed," not licensing others to reproduce it. That strategy had led to a highly profitable, if not high volume, product line of personal computers. Windows and New Wave, on the other hand, ran on IBM and IBM-compatible personal computers, which collectively represented the lion's share of personal computer installations. If the salient attributes of the Macintosh environment could be freely reproduced on IBM and IBM-compatible computers, Apple might be swamped in the wake of the Intel-based systems' success. The lawsuit was an attempt to stem that tide, or at least to add substantial cost in the way of damages to Microsoft's and H-P's business equations. The principal question in the lawsuit was whether those salient attributes, to the extent not already licensed to Microsoft, constituted idea or expression. That is a question that does not often arise in a cloning context, because clones are typically not licensed to do what they do. Therefore, although the outcome of the case will have a significant effect on the course of the softwars, it will not be because the case is significant as a legal precedent. Since the 1985 license agreement gives Microsoft significant rights to copy the Mac interface, it is impossible for the court to write a definitive opinion on the scope of copyright protection for graphical use interfaces. Rather, the outcome of the case will be significant because of its effects on the parties themselves and their relative competitive positions.

In an odd way, events may have overtaken the litigation, rendering its strategic underpinnings obsolete. In October, 1991, Apple, Motorola, and IBM entered into a significant collaboration. One aspect of that collaboration was the proposition that Apple would develop a version of the Macintosh operating system that would run on IBM computers. Another was that Apple and IBM would form a joint venture to develop an advanced, easy-to-use operating system that would run on a variety of hardware platforms. Apple's willingness to join the brave new world of open systems seems to have reflected a dramatic "paradigm shift" at the company. Paradigm shifts—in plain English, new ways of looking at things—are much discussed in the computer industry as a means for stimulating growth, profit, employee morale and motivation, and other desirable ends. In Apple's case, the shift seems to have entailed a realization that in order to infiltrate a broader base of customers, Apple had to put its own base at risk by making its operating systems available on non-Apple computers.

Whereas the *Apple v. Microsoft* litigation comes close to presenting as-yet undecided issues in software copyright law, Ashton-Tate's lawsuit against Fox Software was virtually a replay of the *Lotus* case. Fox stood accused of copying "the novel and highly successful application development and data management environment of the dBase programs and duplicat[ing] their unique look and feel to the program user." The version said to have been copied was dBase III, a program with a character-oriented user interface, not a graphical user interface. The "unique look and feel" of dBase III therefore consisted of the selection, organization, and arrangement of words, numbers, or other typographic symbols on the screen; the structure, sequence, and organization of the screen displays; and the macro interface used by customers to write dBase application programs. There was no question that the developers of FoxBase targeted dBase III as the principal competition for their program, and that they sought to compete with dBase III in part by closely duplicating its operating environment. The principal substantive issue in the case was whether the duplicated elements were protected or not. Federal courts in California approach that issue in an analytical fashion somewhat different from that employed by their brethren in Massachusetts. Nonetheless, Judge Keeton's opinion was a reasonably good predictor of the thought process on which the outcome of the *Ashton-Tate* case would turn. Original expressive elements of the dBase III user interface would be held protected; ideas or functional elements of that interface will not be protected.

In December 1990, the *Ashton-Tate* litigation had nonetheless taken a surprising turn, however, on procedural grounds. Fox Software had moved for summary judgment on the grounds that Ashton-Tate had engaged in inequitable conduct in its dealings with the copyright office. As H-P had done in the *Apple* case, Fox alleged that Ashton-Tate had committed fraud on the copyright office by failing to disclose, in its original applications to register its dBase III copyrights, that dBase III was based on preexisting public domain programs. Without any explanation at all, Judge Hatter granted the motion. The decision, which was completely unexpected, voided Ashton-Tate's copyright registrations, a result with ramifications reaching far beyond the infringement case and a mortal blow to the company. If the copyright were void, Ashton-Tate would be barred from bringing any future infringement suits against anyone, leaving dBase III exposed to unrestrained copying and destroying its value to Ashton-Tate as a business asset.

News of Judge Hatter's ruling spread through the software industry like word of the fall of Richmond through the American south. Some exulted, others despaired, but almost everyone was stunned by the dramatic force of the result. Though Judge Hatter had provided no explanatory opinion, the powerful irony of a copyright plaintiff being deprived of the very rights it was seeking to enforce spoke volumes.

The surprises were not over, however. As soon as it could catch its corporate breath, Ashton-Tate moved for reconsideration, it being clear that Judge Hatter could do no greater damage than he had already done. In connection with its motion, the company obtained a sworn declaration from Ralph Oman, United States Register of Copyrights. Mr. Oman pointed out that copyrights, unlike patents, arise automatically as soon as a work is created. No government act is necessary to make them effective. In that respect, copyrights differed markedly from patents, which do not come into existence until a thorough inspection has been undertaken by a government agent. Registration of copyrights with the copyright office simply recognizes and records rights that have already arisen, and memorializes certain basic facts about the copyrighted work.

Among these facts, Oman observed, is a brief, general description of preexisting works that have been "recast, transformed or adapted" by the copyrighted work. The copyright office does not conduct a search to compare the copyrighted work with preexisting works, and is normally not even in a position to evaluate the copyrighted work standing alone, since program authors are not required to deposit complete copies of their programs with the office, but only identifying portions—for example, the first and last twenty-five pages of source code.

Ashton-Tate had in fact filed "Supplemental Copyright Registrations" which "corrected and amplified certain items with respect to the registration of" dBase II, dBase III, dBase III Plus, and dBase IV. I have not checked with the copyright office to determine when those supplements were filed, but it would be neither surprising nor unusual if they were filed as a result of Fox's motion. Initial registrations are often not even filed until the eve of lawsuit, since they are not necessary in order to perfect a copyright but by law are a necessary precondition to enforcing a copyright. Supplements to initial filings, in such circumstances, would naturally find their way to the copyright office during the course of—and perhaps because of—the litigation. In any case, Registrar Oman examined the Ashton-Tate supplementary registration certificate and concluded that even if the information they contained—including information about the preexisting works—had been disclosed in Ashton-Tate's initial filings, the copyright office would have issued registration certificates anyway. Further, he said, where a copyrightable work is "merely influenced or inspired by," not substantially copied from, a preexisting work, there is no requirement that the earlier work be disclosed on an application for registration. "The Copyright Office," he observed, "recognizes that the authors of computer programs and other works borrow ideas from many different sources."

According to the *Computer Industry Litigation Reporter*, Oman's declaration is believed to have had a material influence on the thinking of Judge Hatter. On April 18, 1991, he issued an order every bit as sweeping and unexpected as the order he had issued the previous December. In a brief ruling, and once again without any explanation, the judge rescinded his earlier order, thereby reinstating Ashton-Tate's copyright registrations. In addition, he denied Fox's motion for summary judgment based on the defense of fraud on the copyright office. Thereafter, the case resumed its march toward trial. Meanwhile, however, dBase was losing popularity in the marketplace due to Ashton-Tate's inability to deliver a reliable version of the latest release. Sales volumes were insufficient to support the company's size, and this supposed "monopolist" of the data base sector became vulnerable to acquisition. Borland International's CEO Philippe Kahn seized the opportunity to expand his company's presence in that sector. Given Borland's experience as a defendant in the "look and feel" lawsuit brought by Lotus, and the prospect that the dBase user interface would change as that product was melded with Borland's own data base products, speculation immediately arose that Borland would not be interested in vigorous prosecution of the lawsuit against Fox. The final surprise in *Ashton-Tate v. Fox*, though, resulted from the Justice Department's antitrust review of the acquisition of Ashton-Tate by Borland. Apparently, the department felt, in the face of unequivocal evidence that Ashton-Tate had lost any market power that it might have had and despite the substantial competition among personal computer data base programs and between such programs and data base programs on midrange and mainframe computers, that there was a risk of monopolization of some segment of demand for data base software as a result of the acquisition, and that it would make things easier for Borland's competitors if they could freely copy the dBase user interface. Of course, while those competitors who chose to do so were developing dBase-compatible software, Borland would be developing a merged product with a new interface. One can hear Philippe Kahn protesting, "Don't throw me in that briar patch," as he allowed his firm to be subjected to a consent judgment requiring Borland to settle the Fox litigation and to refrain from suing anyone else for copying the dBase user interface. Given the commercial senselessness of the Justice Department consent decree, one has to wonder what its real purpose was. Were the antitrust authorities trying to send the industry a message about user interfaces, and if so, what was that message? The general counsel of a small software house told me not long after the Justice Department announcement that her firm viewed the decree as an indication of the Department's opting to join the side of the clones in the softwars. As we shall see in one of our economics endnotes, though, that is probably an overly pessimistic reading of Justice Department policy toward innovation.

Regardless of the outcome of the *Apple* and *Ashton-Tate* cases, there can be no doubt that user interfaces are fast becoming the most expressive attributes of computer programs. In addition to color and light, papers presented at the 1991 CHI conference described the use of animation, aural cues, interactive speech, video, three-dimensional representation, virtual reality, and adventure game interactive techniques in user interface design. Those presentations served to confirm that user interfaces are illusions. One marvelous panel discussion treated the topic "Interface and the Narrative Arts: Contributions from Narrative, Drama and Film." "In recent years," the written introduction to that panel reported,

there has been growing interest in the use of insights and techniques from narrative literature, storytelling, film, and theatre in the design of human-computer activity.... As we move from the notion of computers as computational devices to a notion of them as representation-making machines, it is natural to begin to draw upon other representational arts.

One of the panelists, Joseph Bates from Carnegie Mellon University, described a project concerned with developing the technology necessary to create "virtual worlds," in which users interact with computers through "agents," software constructs that appear to have not only intelligence but emotions; worlds in which the interactions take on certain dramatic characteristics. His work, he feels, may have application to data base query systems, simulation software, and educational software.

As time passes, user interfaces will become more expressive, not less so. "The Moving Finger writes," said the poet Edward Fitzgerald, "and, having writ, moves on: nor all your Piety nor Wit shall lure it back to cancel half a Line, nor all your tears wash out a Word of it." The Moving Finger has writ that computer programs are protected by copyright. Although some might think of that circumstance not as the inexorable evolution of history but as the result of what 1960s comedians Rowan and Martin called the Fickle Finger of Fate, in fact copyright protection for computer programs has won virtually universal acceptance around the globe. It is the essence of copyright that expressive elements in a work may not be substantially copied, and that rule will doubtless be extended to user interfaces, either as parts of the computer programs from which they spring or as separate audiovisual works.

I had the pleasure to participate in a debate at CHI '91 on the subject of the "look and feel" cases. One of the other participants was Michael Jacobs, a San Francisco lawyer whom I had come to know well as a result of his representation of Fujitsu in the arbitration action initiated by IBM in 1985 and still going on. Mike is an advocate of considerable talent, and he did an excellent job of pointing out that what was to his way of thinking new, different, and troublesome about the *Lotus* case was its protection not just of the organization and arrangement of menu prompts, but of the suite of menu commands themselves. That, he felt, was a substantial blow to compatible software developers. (The same point had been made to me in private, as I mentioned in Chapter 3, by a lawyer for another supplier of clone software.) He illustrated his thesis with slides of sample screen displays from various character-based user interfaces. What Jacobs had not realized—nor had I until I prowled the booths at the New Orleans conference—was that to the audience of forward-thinking interface designers whom he was addressing, the slides that he was showing were only of archaeological interest. Compared to what they had been seeing in the other sessions and in the demo rooms at the conference, and what they were doing in their own development laboratories, the character-based user interface of Lotus 1–2–3 was a clunky, obsolete means of expression. Moreover, the protectability of that obsolete means of expression didn't really affect their ability to design modern user interfaces.

Since American suppliers are presently the principal sources of innovation in such interfaces, it is easy to conclude that the manifest future direction of user interfaces and the manifest future direction of legal protection for user interfaces will work to the advantage of American suppliers. That conclusion is too facile, however. It must be tempered by the knowledge that communicative arts are not the monopoly of any particular country. Although the bulk of the CHI '91 activity consisted of exposition of the work of researchers in the United States, other presenters at CHI '91 hailed from Canada, the U.K., Denmark, France, Italy, Switzerland, the Netherlands, and of course Japan. Once again, I remind readers that a generation of the world's children is being raised on Nintendo's Super Mario Brothers. Lest there be any doubt that Super Mario Brothers constitutes a user interface, I draw your attention to the fact that in Japan the moustachioed Mario introduces users to a service jointly developed by Nintendo and Nomura Securities, through which consumers can use their television sets and Nintendo's video game controller to trade stocks. Nintendo is working with Fidelity Investments of Boston to offer software for similar purposes in the United States. Nor is Nintendo the only multinational with its eye on the connection between play and work in selling software. In what seemed a wry contrast to the lineup in the legal debate, Professor Bates reported that the Carnegie Mellon computerized drama project was being supported by none other than Mike Jacobs' client, Fujitsu.

## Endnote: Lotto Isn't Enough— Why We Need Intellectual Property Laws

> Most readers will have heard of Heisenberg's *uncertainty principle*. According to this principle, it is not possible to measure ... both the position and the momentum of a particle accurately at the same time.... [T]he more accurately the position $x$ is measured, the less accurately can the momentum $p$ be determined, and *vice versa*. If the position were measured to *infinite* precision, then the momentum would become *completely* uncertain; on the other hand, if the momentum is measured exactly, then the particle's location becomes completely uncertain. To get some feeling for the size of the limit given by Heisenberg's relation, suppose that the position of an electron is measured to the accuracy of one nanometer ($10–9$); then the momentum would become so uncertain that one could not expect that, one second later, the electron would be closer than 100 kilometers away!
>
> —Robert Penrose, *The Emperor's New Mind* (1991)

Clearly, the grant of exclusive rights is not the only incentive to creative endeavor that one can imagine. In his book *The Lever of Riches: Technological Creativity and Economic Progress*, Joel Mokyr chronicles twenty-five centuries of technological advance prior to the year 1914, during only a small portion of which period private intellectual property rights have been recognized. Indeed, during most of that period, no private rights of any kind were much regarded. Over the long course of history, the mother of Invention has been Necessity, not Venture Capital. Yet recent times (i.e., the last two centuries) have seen the outbreak of liberal democracy and the rise of free market economies across the globe. We are no longer in a world where benevolent despots or government departments control the bulk of the resources that might be applied to producing new technology. Those resources are overwhelmingly under the control of private capital, and the question for us is how to promote research and development in that world, not in nineteenth century England, fifteenth century China, or twelfth century Islam. The economic historian David Landes, who has studied the relationship between technological change and economic development in Europe between 1750 and 1968, has said that protection of intellectual property was a vital precondition to much of the technological progress in that region during the last two centuries.

In modern democracies, we certainly find that private intellectual property rights are not the only means that governments use to stimulate technological advance. Others include prizes or subsidies, recognition, tax breaks, and even war or the threat of war. If I may, I'd like to leave aside the proposition that warfare (other than the sublimated warfare of economic competition) should be encouraged on grounds that it promotes progress; but what about the other stimuli just mentioned? Might they be sufficient? It seems a fairly academic question, since all countries of the developed world have long provided for private property rights in creative contributions to society. However, that academic question is pertinent because—particularly as regards computer programs—there are some who argue vocally that creative contributions should not be treated as property at all. Let us imagine their world, then, and let us see how motivated the innovators are. In this ideal world, the creator of a new product would receive a significant prize—perhaps cash, or a new Mercedes, or maybe a Hawaiian vacation for two. If I ask the reader to imagine further that the prize is bestowed on national TV by a popular, if superannuated, master of ceremonies, I might be accused of belittling the proposition, and yet an instructive point lies in this "publisher's sweepstakes" analogy. When those envelopes arrive in the mail, announcing that the recipients have won ten million dollars (if they return the winning number), a large proportion of recipients conclude that it is worth the price of a stamp to find out whether one of the numbers allotted to them is the winner. Many, indeed, apparently believe it is even worth the price of a magazine subscription, so that they can use the "yes" envelope, which is believed to win them favor with the sweepstakes operator. If, in order to contend for the prize, however, recipients had to invest ten dollars, the envelope return rate would be much lower. If the price of playing were ten thousand dollars, only people with money to burn would participate. And if the price were two million dollars, only wealthy lunatics would play.

Similarly with research and development funds. Given the double uncertainty that confronts the originator of new products—whether the product can in fact be designed and manufactured, and whether consumers will buy it—if the rule were that innovators could not count on building a business out of their creations (which they could not if they were not permitted to assert proprietary interests in those creations), then the financial calculus of investment in research and development would become nothing more than that which precedes the purchase of a very expensive lottery ticket. That is not the kind of investment which will attract responsible venture capital, and therefore the outcome of such a financial calculus is not likely to be satisfactory to policymakers wishing to encourage research and development. Further, if a government were to lower the odds in order to encourage participation, for example by awarding subsidies rather than prizes, the cost of the incentive program would rise substantially, burdening the government budget with private sector risks.

Tax incentives are another non-rights-oriented tool that has in fact been widely employed in developed countries to encourage investment in new technologies. In those countries, however, legal protection for intellectual property is also available. Without such protection, tax incentives serve no purpose other than to reduce the cost of the R&D lottery ticket. As Robert Sherwood puts it, "[s]ince corporate planners realize that the results of research and development are likely to be lost if there are no adequate safeguards, even a double or triple incentive is unlikely to draw much water to the R&D budget." Amplifying on the point, Dr. Mansfield asks, "who would be willing to pay for a commodity [new intellectual property] that, once produced, becomes available to all in unlimited quantity? Why not let someone else pay for it, since then it will be available for nothing?"

As to public recognition, for example, knighthood, as a form of incentive, it is a solution that satisfies egos, but satisfying egos is not sufficient, except in extreme cases, to encourage commercialization of products. Moreover, if *every* author or inventor were to achieve public recognition, the ego satisfaction quotient appurtaining to such awards would not be very great.

The League for Programming Freedom (LPF) and the Free Software Foundation (FSF) propose a different form of reward: distributors of free software should be permitted to earn money not from the software itself but from the provision of support and service for that software. Unfortunately, support can be provided by anyone, so the revenues from that activity are not likely to pay for the livelihoods of the programmers who wrote the program initially. Service usually consists of reissuing portions of the initial software with corrections, and it is not clear whether the LPF or the FSF feel that the service charges may, in their utopian world, be permitted to recover the cost of writing those portions of the initial software as well as the cost of correcting it.

In point of fact, in market economies an efficient system of property rights has been closely associated with economic development. By "efficient," economists mean a system of property rights in which the net social gain and the net private gain are the same. As we have seen, even where comprehensive intellectual property laws exist, net private gain does not approach net social gain, but it is still high enough to attract risk capital. Where there were no intellectual property rights, but only the nonproprietary incentives described above, the net private gain from innovation would be minuscule in comparison with the net social gain, but there would be little innovation and therefore limited economic growth. In their paper on "Benefits and Costs of Intellectual Property Protection in Developing Countries," Richard Rapp and Richard Rozek draw an analogy between nonproprietary incentives to innovation and the economics of commonly owned resources such as land and water. When property rights to such resources are not clearly defined, they suggest, individuals have a "perverse incentive," which results in pollution. "The precarious state of the world's common-pool resources (like ocean fisheries, rain forests and the ozone layer) has its origins in decades of neglect for the institutional arrangements governing activities affecting those resources."

Let us return momentarily to Zola's exclamation, "Money has emancipated the writer." The ability for the writer (of computer programs as well as books) to earn money derives from the intellectual property rights that the author has in his or her work. Economist William Landes and Judge Richard Posner explain that, absent such rights, anyone could buy a single copy of the work, reproduce it many times and sell the copies. The price of the work would eventually drop, because of such competition, to the cost of producing a single new copy. In consequence, the author and publisher would not be able to recover the cost of developing the work in the first place, and therefore that development would most likely not take place.

Reinforcing this point, D. North and R. Thomas, authors of *The Rise of the Western World: A New Economic History*, explain the centuries of delay attendant on the invention of an accurate marine chronometer:

The benefits to society of accurately determining a ship's position were immense in terms of reducing ship losses and lowering the costs of trade. How much sooner might the breakthrough have occurred, had there been property rights to assure an inventor some of the increased income resultant on the saving of ships and time? (He would also, of course, have had to bear the high costs of research and the uncertainty of finding a solution.) The payments to mathematicians and the proferred prizes were artificial devices to stimulate effort, whereas a more general incentive could have been provided by a law assigning exclusive rights to intellectual property including new ideas, inventions, and innovations. In the absence of such property rights, few would risk private resources for social gains.

Treating the products of intellectual exertion as property has the singular advantage, it is submitted, of creating a market for them, thereby allowing the populace to "vote with their wallets" on which creations should be rewarded, permitting originators of intellectual products to create businesses around those products and reducing the need for government manipulation of private behavior. A venture capitalist made that point to a committee of the U.S. National Research Council:

Eliminate the financial incentive for making software, suggested John F. Shoch, general partner at the Asset Management Co., and today's intellectual property disputes would disappear, but so would the pipeline of products that add new capability after new capability to the computer. "If software had no value and nobody wanted to buy it, this would be a very academic discussion," Shoch maintained. "It would be a wonderful hobby. It wouldn't be a business, and nobody would care where intellectual property boundaries are drawn because no one would be making any money."

In order that the ethereal products of the mind can be treated as property, there must be laws on the books prescribing the property rights that may exist in such products. That conclusion has the happy attribute of being consistent with the collective legislative behavior of the developed world, which tends to validate its reasonableness.

It remains to us, then, to consider whether the existing legal regimes provide an appropriate balance of the interests of authors and inventors with the interests of society. The principle protective mechanisms for products of the mind, as already discussed, are patents, copyrights, and trade secrets. There are other mechanisms as well, principal among them being trademark and unfair competition, but these create a penumbra of rights around the core triad. This book deals only with the core intellectual property laws. In the next three endnotes, we'll examine them with the economist's eye.

# 7

# Heavy Artillery: The Patent Laws as Armaments in the Softwars

During the great slaughters of 1916, men lived, made ready to kill, and prepared to die below ground, with the slit of sky that hung over their trenches the only proof that they had not already crossed into the world beyond the grave.... No longer heroic, no longer glorious, war and death thus had become the depersonalized products of the same great technological age that, in a touch of supreme irony, had provided man with the means to preserve life through the wonders of immunology and sterile surgery at the very moment it had given him the means to destroy it on an unprecedented scale. "Man, as it were, is shoved into the background [in modern war]," one critic wrote, "even though it is ultimately his destruction which is at stake."

Nowhere was that truth more certain than on Europe's eastern front, where thousands of unarmed Russian soldiers stood defenseless in trenches awaiting the moment when they could charge forth to seize the rifles of their fallen comrades and continue their attack. While they waited "until casualties in the firing-line should make rifles available," Britain's General Sir Alfred Knox reported in outraged amazement, they were "churned into gruel" by the Germans' heavy guns.

—W. Bruce Lincoln, *Red Victory: A History of the Russian Civil War* (1989)

There are those who claim that patenting computer programs is the economic equivalent of training the heavy guns on unarmed opponents. "Software patents," says the League for Programming Freedom, "threaten to devastate the American computer industry." An article in the April 1990

issue of the MIT journal *Technology Review* reports that "[s]oftware developers who understand the impact of patents are demoralized" and that
"[n]early 40 percent of the software patents that the U.S. Patent Office now
issued go to Japanese hardware companies." Writing in the *Emory Law
Journal*, Professor Pamela Samuelson observed "substantial opposition to
patenting program innovations from within the computer science community and the software industry." Mitch Kapor, formerly of the head of
Lotus Development Corporation and now the head of tiny ON Technologies,
calls software patents the "toxic waste" of the software industry, lying un-
detected below the surface of development activities, insidiously poisoning
the freedom to create.

Is there a new cause for concern, or is the handwringing over software
patents just another manifestation of the disputes that have underlain the
softwars for some years now? After all, the patent system has been part of
the fabric of technological progress in the United States for over two centuries, and has been applied to new technologies one after another without
any apparent long-term social or economic dislocations. In the computer
industry in particular, competitors have been patenting their inventions for
the past forty years, and numerous software-related patents were issued
even during the dry spell in apparent protectability that followed the *Gottschalk v. Benson* decision discussed in Chapter 2. Because of the equivalency
of software and logic hardware (i.e., most processor functions can be implemented either in hardware or software), large numbers of hardware
patents that are, in their "look and feel," very much analogous to software
patents have been on the books for quite a while. Yet, as a major article on
patent law in the *Columbia Law Review* notes, "patents have played only
a very minor role in the computer industry, and where patents are concerned, cross licensing is common. As a result, the pace of technical change
has been rapid." Patents involving software have been sought by inventors
throughout the history of the computer industry. It seems to be the case
that the rate of issuance of software-related patents increased dramatically
in the 1980s, but then so did the rate of increase in the number of computer
programs being written. It would be natural for the number of software
patent *lawsuits* to have increased dramatically during that period as well,
but that did not happen. By and large, it appears that competitors in the
computer industry have used patents not to carve out an exclusive territory
but to protect themselves against aggressive use of patents by others. Such
behavior would make sense where the rate of innovation is high, the barriers
to new innovation are not great and the sources of innovation are numerous.
In an economic environment of that sort, a willingness to license one's
patent portfolio in exchange for cross-licenses from others, to pay royalties
for technology of others that one wishes to use, and to allow others to use
technology for a fee gives a firm freedom of access to a broader base of
technology than its own development laboratories can generate.

What, then, is the source of concern over software-related patents? After all, as noted earlier, fully a decade after *Diamond v. Diehr* legitimated patents involving computer programs the number of software-related patents issued is on the order of thousands, while the number of computer programs written is on the order of millions. A search for software-related patent infringement decisions by American courts produces only a few dozen cases. Clearly, there is no great problem today.

But will there be one tomorrow? Perhaps. The patent grant depends on government review of the claimed invention. It is not automatic, like copyright, or self-executing, like trade secret. A government agency reads the invention claimed in the patent against preexisting technology to determine whether there has indeed been an invention. The U.S. Patent and Trademark Office (PTO), however, has not placed itself in a position to be able to evaluate software-related patents against the "prior art." Its examiners are in general neither trained in computer science nor experienced in computer programming. Moreover, there are problems in knowing what the prior art is. The Office's collection of prior art is modest, reflecting the fact that there has not been much software-related patent activity to date. In addition, since much software is unpublished, the prior art is hidden in the trade secrets of software suppliers, computer users, and others. One result of these imperfections in PTO readiness to assess the novelty and nonobviousness of software-related patents is likely to be the issuance of some number of patents that should not have been issued.

If so, software-related patents would be following a long tradition. Until a few years ago, roughly two-thirds of all patents that were challenged in court were held to be invalid. American industry has survived for several generations the missteps of overworked or underequipped patent examiners. The court system serves as a snare in which to catch patents that should not have been issued and take away their sting. That is not to say, of course, that the present state of affairs in the PTO should be allowed to persist. The PTO should recruit patent examiners with computer science backgrounds. It should have better access to the prior art. To the latter end, Professor Bernard Galler of the University of Michigan, a teacher of great wisdom, moderation, and vision, has spearheaded an effort to set up an institute that would serve as a repository of prior art and a source of education for patent examiners. It is an effort to which all industry participants and university computer science departments should contribute, and which can't help but improve the accuracy of PTO determinations. In addition to the Michigan initiative, the Commissioner of Patents in 1991 convened a commission to study, among other things, the shortcomings in the patent process as they relate to computer programs. The recommendations of that commission, if implemented, should help to improve the situation markedly.

In order to allay fears about the possibility that patents on pure mental or mathematical processes would be issued as a matter of course, the PTO

published an article "for the benefit of the public" in August 1989 that
provides insight into the standards that the courts have applied in reviewing
software-related patents. Though the article does not address the problems
of finding the prior art and hiring more examiners trained in computer
science, it is a valuable introduction to what are, in effect, the property pass
procedures of one of the principal armories in the softwars: the patent
office.

An inventor cannot obtain a patent, those property pass procedures state,
no matter how useful, novel, and nonobvious the claimed invention, unless
it is a discovery that comprises a process, machine, manufacture, or composition of matter. This standard *must* be met. If an invention does not fit
within one of the four categories, it is not "statutory subject matter," and
can't be patented. (Note that patent protection is available only for "useful,"
or utilitarian, inventions.) A "process" consists of acts, and is equivalent to
a "method." A "machine" is an "apparatus." Clearly, software, standing alone,
is not an apparatus, manufacture, or composition of matter; but is it a
process?

According to the rules the courts have laid down for issuance of software
patents, mathematical algorithms, like laws of nature, are not the sorts of
processes to which the patent law refers. Now, all processes are in a broad
sense algorithmic, in that they are step-by-step procedures for arriving at a
given result using given inputs. However, stretching the term that broadly
on the rack of interpretation tortures its meaning to the point of breaking.
One of the arguments made against software-related patents is that they
protect "nonmathematical algorithms," and "nonmathematical algorithms"
are no different in essence from mathematical algorithms. Can that argument
be valid? Do I use an algorithm in deciding which route to take to work?
Is the Bessemer process algorithmic? Are the pull-down menus on your
word processor algorithms? What about your mother's recipe for apple pie?
What about Ravel's *Bolero*? Give me a break. "Nonmathematical algorithms"
are not algorithms; the term is a kind of malapropism imported into computer science lexicography, akin to the creeping (some would say, "gallop-
ing") use in journalism of the term "reticent" to mean "reluctant."

Mohammed ibn-Musa Al-Khwarismi, from whose name the word algorithm derives (and who also gave us the word algebra), was an early con-
tributor to the intense period of Islamic mathematical and scientific
contribution that stretched from the ninth century to the fourteenth century. His book, *Kitab al-jabr wa al-maqabalah*, connected Baghdad with
the roots of mathematics in ancient Mesopotamian and Greek culture and
helped trigger a revival of mathematical study that produced impressive
advances in trigonometry and geometry. In the Middle Ages, an *algorist*
was a mathematician who used Arabic numerals and arithmetic as tools of
mathematics. The other school of mathematical computation used abaci and
were called abacists. Thus, algorithm has come to mean a mathematical

procedure, and to speak of "mathematical algorithms" is to speak a redundancy. In the *Gottschalk v. Benson* opinion, the Supreme Court defined "algorithm" as "a procedure for solving a given type of mathematical problem." Recipes, steel-making processes, pull-down menus, and rules for driving to work are not algorithms, though they are like algorithms in that they often proceed in a step-by-step fashion. Computer programs also proceed in step-by-step fashion, as do instruction manuals, history texts, murder mysteries, Ravel's *Bolero*, and other products of mental activity. Let us suppose that a scientist—call her Dr. Ruth—invents a process for increasing the prospects of conception in infertile couples that relies heavily on the use of Ravel's *Bolero* in certain of its steps. (Leave aside for the moment, please, the substantial prior art questions that arise in connection with such an invention.) If the PTO issues a patent to Dr. Ruth, has it engaged in patenting an algorithm? Or, if you've decided that *Bolero* is not an algorithm, then has the PTO engaged in patenting music?

The reader senses, I imagine, that we have strayed slightly from the exposition in the PTO article. I will now unite that exposition with my excursion, which began with the discussion of the term "nonmathematical algorithms." The courts approach the question whether a software-related patent is valid or not in two steps. First, they determine whether the claims in the patent recite a Benson-type (i.e., mathematical) algorithm. If so, then the courts assesses whether those claims have the effect of preempting that algorithm. The "claims" of a patent are the paragraphs that assert precisely what the proposed invention is. These paragraphs bound the statutory grant of an issued patent. If, within those paragraphs, no algorithm is recited, then the granted patent does not encompass an algorithm. If within those paragraphs an algorithm is recited, then no patent will be granted unless the claimed invention is something other than the algorithm itself. In particular, the role of the algorithm in the claim must be one of implementation, such that either an apparatus that is claimed to have been invented has the structural relationship of its physical elements defined by the algorithm, or a process that is claimed to have been invented has its steps refined or limited by the algorithm. It is not sufficient, in other words, that claims reciting an algorithm also merely recite processes or apparatuses.

If the patent application claims only an improved method of calculation, then it claims unpatentable subject matter and it will not be allowed. On the other hand, the mere fact that a claim contains direct or indirect reference to an algorithm does not defeat patentability, so long as what is patented is an apparatus or a process. Naturally, clever patent lawyers have attempted to circumvent the limitations on patentability of algorithms by making algorithmic claims look like apparatus claims or process claims. While a program, standing alone, is not an apparatus, it may be an element of a patentable apparatus. Lawyers have taken advantage of that circumstance by putting vague references to hardware elements of an apparatus into patent claims that fundamentally recite nothing but software. Thus, for example, "What is claimed is a *means* for computing the square root of an irrational number." (The word "means" is a patentspeak synonym for "apparatus.") The courts are alert to such attempts to "exalt form over substance," as one court described that sort of draftsmanship. Judges put the burden on patent applicants to demonstrate that their claims recite a *specific* apparatus, rather than a generic apparatus; otherwise the claims will be treated as process claims. For example, if Dr. Ruth's patent application recited only a "means for playing *Bolero* to infertile couples," it would be regarded as essentially a claim that the playing of *Bolero* was patentable.

Similarly, some patent lawyers attempt to render algorithmic claims as patentable process claims by simply tacking onto the solution of the algorithm some sort of post-solution activity. Pursuant to this stratagem, Dr. Ruth might claim as a process step "the decoding of a digital representation of Bolero followed by the audible output of that decoding." The addition of the "audible output" activity does nothing to enhance the patentability of the decoding algorithm, since patent examiners do not regard the transmission of output as a step that transforms an algorithmic claim into a protectable process that merely uses an algorithm. Other drafting techniques that do not suffice to create protection for an algorithm (or a piece of music) arc "field of use" limitations (e.g., "*in sex therapy*, a means for increasing fertility....") or gratuitous structural (apparatus) limitations in process claims (e.g., "playing *Bolero* through a system consistently of a CD player, an amplifier and loudspeakers").

The federal courts, then, attempt to prevent the patenting of algorithms, but not to prevent the patenting of useful, novel and nonobvious machines or processes in which one or more essential elements or steps are algorithmic. What does that judicial approach mean in the case of computer programs?

When the invention is a process in which some (or all) of the steps are directed by software, what is protected is not the text of the software, but the steps that the software directs the computer to perform. Here, we must revert momentarily to a usage just criticized: "mathematical algorithm." Where the claimed invention involves a computer program, if the claimed invention is nothing more than the solution of a "mathematical algorithm" through the use of a computer program, the claim will not be sustained. If the claimed invention is more than just a solution of a mathematical algorithm—for example, if the invention is a process for curing rubber—then so long as the standard tests for patentability are met, process claims that include steps directed by a computer program will probably be sustained. When the invention is an apparatus including hardware and software elements, if the hardware elements are specific and the apparatus otherwise meets the standard tests for patentability, the apparatus will probably be held patentable. A current question is whether a computer program on a diskette can be patented not as an apparatus or process, which it is not, but as an "article of manufacture." If so, the question continues, what subject matter would be protected by such a patent? The PTO has issued a number of patents of this sort, but seems to have concluded that there is little difference between treating programs on diskette as patentable subject matter and treating Jane Fonda's workout tapes as patentable subject matter.

Let's look at a few actual cases, both within and outside the software context, to get a feel for how "heavy" the heavy artillery of a patent is. What we will want to know in that connection is what the range of the projectiles is (i.e., what is the *scope* of patent protection for software), and what the destructive capacity of the projectiles is (i.e., what *power* does the patent give patent holders over their competitors).

In terms of the scope of patent protection, it is necessary to differentiate between the scope of protection represented by patents granted by the PTO and the scope of patents upheld by the courts. If we were to focus on the former, we would find—as suggested above—that a number of elementary and arguably obvious techniques, as well as algorithmic steps, are being patented. That problem will be solved as the PTO's ability to assess software patent applications improves and as questionable software patents are challenged in court and new court decisions feed back into the PTO procedures, establishing a more stable equilibrium between issued patents and valid patents. The real scope of patent protection for software is defined by the courts, not the PTO, and the following abstracts will impart a sense of what the courts are doing.

Let us look first at the case called *In re Abele*. (Who or what, the non-lawyer-reader may ask, is *In re*. The answer is that the In re cases are "In the matter of..." suits brought by a patent applicant against the patent office, usually because of an adverse decision on the patent in question.) *In re Abele* was a case in which the inventor had attempted to patent a method of displaying data by way of a gray scale. The gray scale was created from the underlying data through the use of an algorithm. In general, the court concluded that the algorithmic conversion of data into a gray scale chart was not a step that "refined or limited" the underlying data, and was therefore not the kind of process step that was in itself patentable. However, in order to determine whether what the inventor had described was patentable, the court "subtracted" the algorithm from the patent claims, then sought to determine whether what remained in the claims was patentable subject matter, on the theory that if the remainder of the claim was patentable, the addition of an algorithm to the claims did not vitiate that eligibility. On performing that intellectual exercise, the court concluded that the inventor's broad algorithmic claims, though phrased in terms of "process" or "apparatus," did not qualify, but that a narrower claim did, because it limited the application of the algorithm to display of "x-ray attenuation data produced in a two dimensional field by a computed tomography scanner," and required data-gathering steps not dictated by the algorithm, which steps were in themselves patentable subject matter. The *Abele* case suggests that patents claiming no invention other than an algorithm for displaying data graphically, together with the data collection steps necessary to provide input for the algorithm, will not be upheld.

*In re Meyer* tested the boundaries of the theory that mental processes in themselves are not patentable. *Meyer* involved a patent that the applicants characterized as "replacing, in part, the thinking processes of a neurologist with a computer," or more grammatically, replacing with a computer the thought processes of a neurologist. The claimed invention was embodied in the Cadeseus program, which gave the computer the ability to receive from a doctor data relating to symptoms or test results, to query the doctor if further data is needed, and then to produce a list of potential ailments, as well as suggestions for further tests. The court perused the inventor's claims in search of process steps or apparatus elements that went beyond the description of what the applicants conceded were "a mental process that a neurologist should follow," and found none. Accordingly, the court agreed with the patent examiner who found that the claimed invention was not patentable. This was true even though the patent application recited that the steps required a "general purpose data processor of known type operating under the control of a stored program." That language was insufficient to convert the claimed invention into an apparatus, because no specific apparatus was described, only a generic stored-program computer. *Meyers* limns the boundary of patent protection for expert systems, and illustrates the principle that mental steps are not patentable.

The *Merrill Lynch* case caused a fibrillation in the heartbeat of the industry when it was decided, but does not seem to have had lasting significance. Merrill Lynch owned a patent on an apparatus that provided cash management services for clients with multiple types of accounts. The apparatus was not described in physical detail, but certainly sounded like a computer operating under the control of a program. There is no doubt that the essence of the claim—the automatic management of funds as between brokerage accounts, money market accounts, checking accounts, and credit card accounts—was best effectuated by a program. As is well known, Merrill Lynch was not the only brokerage house to offer computerized cash management services; among others, Paine Webber did so. Indeed, Paine, Webber did so according to the method described in the Merrill Lynch patent, a fact which the latter firm did not hesitate to bring to the attention of the former. In a Borland-like attempt to seize the initiative in the ensuing dispute, Paine, Webber sued in federal court in Delaware for a declaration that the patent was invalid because, among other things, the cash management method it covered was not patentable subject matter. Merrill Lynch naturally counterclaimed for infringement, but its competitor had sited the litigation in a court of its choice and had managed to make invalidity, not infringement, the centerpiece of the litigation. Pressing its advantage, Paine, Webber filed a motion for summary judgment that the patent was invalid for lack of patentable subject matter. In lay terms, Paine, Webber asserted that the claimed invention was either (or both) an algorithm or a business method, and neither algorithms nor business methods are protected by the patent laws.

The strategy did not work. Summary judgment motions are filed before there has been a full trial on the merits. The courts may not entertain them unless, among other conditions, there are no material questions of fact requiring trial on the merits. Accordingly, in order to press its motion Paine, Webber had to refrain from asserting other, more fact-intensive reasons for invalidating the patent, such as lack of novelty or obviousness in light of the prior act, which Merrill Lynch might dispute. The motion was therefore entirely focused on the question whether the cash management system claimed by Merrill Lynch was either an algorithm or a business method.

Here is the first invention claimed in the patent. The convoluted language of the claim is typical of patent applications. I have taken the liberty of adding punctuation and formatting that does not exist in the original, in order to enhance readability.

In combination,

in a system for processing and supervising a plurality of composite subscriber accounts—each comprising

  (1) a margin brokerage account,
  (2) a charge card and checks administered by a financial institution, and
  (3) participation in at least one short term investment, administered by a second institution,

—said system including

  (a) brokerage account data file means for storing current information characterizing each subscriber margin brokerage account of the second institution,
  (b) manual entry means for entering short term investment orders in the second institution,
  (c) data receiving and verifying means for receiving and verifying charge card and check transactions from said first institution and short term investment orders from said manual entry means,
  (d) means responsive to said brokerage account data file means and said data receiving and verifying means for generating an updated credit limit for each account,
  (e) short term investment updating means responsive to said brokerage account data file means and said data receiving and verifying means for selectively generating short term investment transactions as required to generate and invest proceeds for subscribers' accounts, wherein said system includes plural such short term investments,

—said system further comprising

> (f) means responsive to said short term updating means for allocating said
> short term investment transactions among said plural short term invest-
> ments,
>
> (g) communicating means to communicate said updated credit limit for each
> account to said first institution.

(Grammatical errors should be attributed to Merrill Lynch's patent attorney
or to the case reporting service, not to this author.)

The tenor and content of the foregoing claim may be taken as typical of
those in the patent. It will be evident to the reader that the claim does not
describe an algorithm, in the sense of the usage of that term in *Benson*. No
algorithm is disclosed in the claim and therefore none was sought to be
protected by the issued patent. So the court found. As to whether or not
the patent claimed a business method, the court observed that the *product*
of the patent is indeed a highly effective business method, which would be
unpatentable if done by hand. However, where a computer program is
involved, the inquiry is not as to the *product* of the operation of the program
on the computer, which may often be unpatentable. Rather, so long as a
*Benson*-type algorithm is not involved, the question is whether the patent
teaches a *method of operating* the computer. If so, the patent is claiming
statutory subject matter.

The trade press tended to report the *Merrill Lynch* case as a decision
that Merrill Lynch's patent was valid. Similarly, Professor Samuelson, in her
lengthy article in the *Emory Law Journal* setting out "the case against patent
protection for algorithms and other computer-program-related inventions,"
described the decision as "upholding the validity" of the patent. As can be
seen from the nature of the motion made by Paine, Webber, those characterizations are entirely erroneous. The decision had only turned aside
one possible argument as to why the patent might be invalid: lack of statutory
subject matter. Several others, for instance obviousness or lack of novelty,
could have been made at trial, had there been a trial. Regrettably for posterity, though perhaps best for the brokerage industry, the case was settled
after the decision on the summary judgment motion.

*In re Pardo* left less of a mark on the industry when it was decided, but
has attracted a lot of attention since. The patent application, filed by Canadian co-inventors Rene Pardo and Remy Landau claimed both process
and apparatus inventions relating to converting a sequential processor into
a processor that rearranges the order of execution of instructions. For example, one of the apparatus claims (again, reformatted and repunctuated
for clarity) reads as follows:

A *general purpose data processor* of known type, operating under the control of a
*stored program* containing a set of instructions for enabling the data processor to

execute formulas in an object program comprising a plurality of formulas, such that the same results will be produced when using the same given data, regardless of the sequence in which said formulas are presented in said object programs, said data processor performing the following functions:

(a) examining each of said formulas in a storage area of the data processor to determine which formulas can be executed as defined;

(b) executing, in the sequence in which each formula is designated as defined, said formulas designated as defined;

as required until all said formulas have been designated as defined and have been executed;

whereby to produce the same results upon execution of the formulas in the sequence recited in step (b) when using the same given data, regardless of the order in which said formulas were presented in the object program prior to such functions.

Other claims in the patent presented variations on this theme. In some cases, however, the reordering of execution was claimed to be accomplished by other means.

The patent application was filed in 1970, and after two years a patent seemed about to issue from the patent office, when the Supreme Court decided *Gottschalk v. Benson*. On the basis of the high court decision, the patent office reopened its prosecution and rejected the claimed inventions on the grounds that they were not patentable subject matter. All the claims in the application were directed to what was explicitly referred to as an "algorithm." The term "algorithm" had been used, somewhat shortsightedly, by the applicants to describe the process of reordering formulas for execution, and *Benson*, the patent office concluded, held that algorithms were not patentable. Bad luck for the Canadian duo, 'ey? Adding insult to injury, the patent office thereafter also rejected numerous claims of the applications on the grounds that the "algorithm" in question would have been obvious to an "artisan" facing the problem of solving multiple formulae where the data needed for some of the formulae depended on the solution to others, since it involved nothing more than solving first those formulae that could be solved first.

Pardo and his co-inventor appealed. In 1982, twelve years after their application was filed, the Court of Customs and Patent Appeals reversed the action of the patent office. In its decision, the court explained its two-step methodology for analyzing algorithmic cases: first, ascertain whether a "mathematical algorithm" is recited, either directly or indirectly; then determine whether the algorithm is applied to a physical process or physical elements. Not all algorithms are "mathematical algorithms," the court observed, and the applicants' use of the term "algorithm" in describing the key process of their invention was not fatal. The applicants' claims did not directly recite a "mathematical algorithm," but the patent office had argued that since the key process was a set of operations on programs that did embody mathematical formulae, the claims indirectly recited "mathematical algorithms." The court did not accept that argument, noting that a calculating machine that operated on mathematical formulae would nonetheless be patentable subject matter. Concluding that the application did not recite a *Benson* algorithm at all, the court held that the invention constituted patentable subject matter.

The patent office's obvious rejection was addressed only to those claims that achieved nonsequential processing by rearranging instructions. No citation of prior art had been made by the PTO in support of that rejection. Rather, the PTO simply put forward the proposition that, in essence, it was obvious that the algorithm was obvious. The court felt that the patent office had not followed the procedures established by the Supreme Court for determining obviousness: establish the scope and content of the prior art, ascertain the differences between the prior art and the claimed invention, and ascertain the level of ordinary skill in the art at the time the invention was made. That omission was the patent law equivalent of failure by the police to give a Miranda warning, and just as criminals known by many to have been guilty have in the past been freed because of lapses in police procedures, so the Pardo patent claims, known by many to have been obvious, were sustained because of a lapse in patent office procedures.

In due course, then, a patent was issued to the two inventors. Seeking to exploit their patent by licensing it to suppliers of computers and programs, the inventors assigned it to a company called Refac, the sole business of which is to license patents and pursue infringers. Depending on one's point of view, Refac is either the salvation of the small inventor, equalizing the inventor's bargaining power with that of the large companies that would otherwise ignore demands for royalties, or a predatory parasite, gathering up questionable patents from dubious sources and blackmailing leading innovative firms with threats of jury trials over complex issues of patent validity and infringement, potentially leading to runaway verdicts in favor of the "little guy" inventor and against the "deep pocket" industry leaders. Refac took up the Pardo patent and came to what was, for it and the patentees, a stimulating conclusion. If the reader hasn't already done so, then please consider the following question: What popular types of software reorder mathematical formulae presented to them by other programs before processing them?

Right! Spreadsheets! Big bucks, 'ey? Refac filed infringement suits against a number of suppliers of spreadsheet programs, ultimately dismissing all except Lotus Development Corp. There are two popular theories within the patent bar as to the best strategy for signing up an entire industry for licenses to a patent. One theory holds that it is best to start at the periphery, pursuing small, undercapitalized companies that cannot afford a strong defense to an infringement suit. In that fashion, a patent holder can either obtain a number of licensees relatively quickly or, if forced to litigate, have a better chance of prevailing. Having a large number of licensees can have a snowballing effect on other potential licensees. Prevailing, for a patent holder in an infringement suit, will usually result in a ruling that the patent is valid; a ruling that can then be used to induce others, including the larger firms, to take licenses.

The second theory holds that one should go for the jugular: take on the industry leader, the firm that has most to lose if it is found to have infringed, and either wrest a license from that firm or take it to court. The litigation will generate a lot of publicity and demonstrate that the patent holder is aggressive and confident. If and when it settles (and these cases usually do settle), the settlement terms will generally be confidential, so even if the patent holder accepts a far more modest royalty from the industry leader than had been sought, the difference can probably be made up from all the other potential licensees who are by then lined up with their checkbooks open. Refac seems to have adhered to the second theory.

There are those who say that Lotus was getting a taste of its own medicine. There are those who decry the spectre of a patent applied for in 1970 still haunting the industry in the 1990s. There are those who are sure that the technique claimed to have been invented by Pardo and Lamey was well-known in the industry in 1970. And there are those who argue that the essence of the invention is in fact mathematics, and elementary mathematics at that. (It is with the latter that I find myself most in harmony. Solving simultaneous equations in logical sequence is in itself a mathematical exercise.) But the last word on the validity of the Pardo patent is likely to come from Lotus, which is again represented by Hank Gutman, the architect of Lotus' victories over Paperback Software and Borland.

Though all that Refac wants from spreadsheet licensees is a "reasonable" royalty of 5 percent of revenues from all spreadsheet sales, infringing a patent can in some instances have terminal consequences. The most extreme consequences tend to arise not in Refac-like situations but in cases where one competitor is suing another. In such cases, the successful patent holder can often enjoin further sales of the infringing goods. That is what happened to Kodak which, when it was found to have infringed Polaroid's instant photography patents, was forced to shut down its instant camera and film factories, thereby incurring a nine-figure writeoff. In addition, the successful patent holder may recover damages for sales of the infringing goods up to the date of the injunction. In the *Polaroid* case, Kodak had sold instant film and cameras from 1976 to 1985. In the damages phase of the case, the judge determined that Polaroid would have made most of the sales that Kodak had made, and was therefore entitled to damages from Kodak in the amount of the profits it (Polaroid) would have made on those sales. In total and with interest, the judge found, the amount of those profits was just over $900,000,000. What is most interesting about that figure is that it was not the product of a runaway jury, but rather the product of an economic analysis by a federal judge.

What we can conclude from the foregoing is that the patent office intends not to issue software-related patents to applicants claiming only algorithms, mental steps, or business methods as inventions; and if they do issue such patents, they will likely be invalidated. Patent law will protect computerization of processes that could be performed by hand, but only if the other tests for patentability (novelty, utility, and nonobviousness) are met. Though some questionable patents have issued as a result of weaknesses in patent office staffing and procedures (questionable in light of the prior art or questionable as algorithms or mental steps), the law provides the necessary defenses against assertion of those patents. Unquestionably, however, there is the possibility for software patents broad in scope to issue. Moreover, patent law provides for strong remedies in cases of infringement. In that sense, patents can indeed be considered "heavy artillery" in the softwars. On the other hand, the value of that artillery depends very much on the extent to which a patent precludes competition. The broader the scope of competition precluded, the wider the range of the artillery. Appropriately, the next installment in our correspondence course deals with the merits of the patent law from the point of view of economic effects.

## Endnote: A Leaky Monopoly—The Economics of the Patent Grant

Over the centuries the islanders—attractive, slightly feckless—have developed a stable, conservative society, largely based on intermediate technology. They still have access to all man's accumulated knowledge, but they have added little to it. Their boats, aircraft, and cars are built to last a lifetime, and they never throw anything away they can use again. Since there is no other habitable planet in the system, they have no spaceships, but they can still launch the (rather primitive) satellites essential for their scattered islands' communications and meteorological services.

Though they have had no physical contact with outsiders for centuries, they still inject their records and news, such as it is, into the local stellar network. The current update is long overdue, partly because of a mounting power crisis.

The Shaanans get most of their electrical power from OTEC (Ocean Thermal Energy Conversion), which employs the temperature difference between the warm surface water and the very cold water several kilometers down. . . . For some unknown reason, several of the factories

have failed, apparently owing to damage at the deep end. Typically the
Shaanans don't have the submersibles needed to investigate at such
depths; they are still arguing about what to do next.
—Arthur C. Clarke, "The Songs of Distant Earth," *The Sentinal* (1983)

Would the lot of the Shaanans have been improved by passage of a patent
law? From an economic perspective, it seems so. Patent laws are powerful
incentives to innovation. As opposed to trade secret and copyright, patent
is a strong form of protection. Patent holders can exclude everyone from
using their inventions, including those who independently come up with
the same inventions. While it would be overstatement to say that the patent
system can protect all the ideas in a computer program, for example, it is
certainly true that patents protect more than just expression. The level of
abstraction inherent in the rights of the patent holder is much higher than
that inherent in the rights of the copyright holder. A few decades ago,
economist Fritz Machlup told a congressional committee: "If we did not
have a patent system, it would be irresponsible, on the basis of our present
knowledge of its economic effects, to recommend instituting one." Closer
to us in time and focus, in 1989 a four-hour program was held at MIT,
hotbed of the "free software" movement, on the interrogative subject, "Software Patents: a Horrible Mistake?" And (writing as though the United States
were still on the threshold of according patent protection to software-based
systems rather than graced with two decades or more of experience with
such patents) Professor Samuelson reports that "the software industry has
grown tremendously under the regime of copyright and has exhibited an
astonishing capacity for creative innovation in the past two decades," but
warns that "[b]ecause of the stronger monopoly right that they convey,
patents do seem likely to increase barriers to entry in the software market."

Although patent rights are often spoken of as "monopolies," one is in fact
hard-pressed to identify any high-tech industry that has been monopolized
because of one firm's patents. Dr. Mansfield makes the point this way:

Without question, the patent system enables innovators to appropriate a larger
portion of the social benefits from their innovations than would be the case without
it, but this does not mean that patents are very effective in this regard. Contrary to
popular opinion, patent protection does not make entry impossible, or even unlikely.

Even where a patent system is in effect, private returns from innovation
are far lower than social returns, which means that by some mechanism
competitors are able to take advantage of an innovator's patented inventions.
How does this occur?

Licensing is one way. The general practice in the computer industry is
to license patents at reasonable royalty rates. The impetus for that practice
is not charity but enlightened self-interest. Computer technology evolves
particularly rapidly, and inventions can come from any quarter. No firm has

a monopoly on innovation, and all firms are at risk of having their growth blocked by other firms' (or individuals') patents. In such an environment, a policy of open licensing gives all players the freedom of action necessary to remain competitive. Even where licenses are not forthcoming, though, the patent system has a feature not shared by either trade secret or copyright: enforced publication. A patent is public information, available to be read by anyone. To obtain a patent, inventors must describe their inventions. A survey of 650 research and development executives rated patent disclosure close behind licensing as the most effective means of technology transfer. (Next in line were publications or technical meetings, conversations with employees of innovating companies, and hiring such employees.) Consequently, competitors have readily available the information that will allow them to "invent around" patented inventions, thereby developing noninfringing products. Moreover, competitors have the information they need to generate "blocking patents": patents that improve on an invention in ways that the original innovator would ultimately want to improve it. The generation of blocking patents, a strategy practiced widely and vigorously by Japanese computer companies, among others, is a way of forcing the original innovator to enter into cross-licensing arrangements. According to reporter Michael Malone,

It is known that many of the largest Japanese electronics corporations employ entire departments to systematically comb through U.S. patent filings in order to track individual American inventors and companies as they leave a patent trail toward some new breakthrough technology. The Japanese firm then tries to beat the opponent to the goal. Or, short of that, to surround that patent with a cloud of so many increments that the core patent owner is essentially "bracketed," unable to move, forced to negotiate licensing with the Japanese.

(Some small software firms worry that—unlike larger firms, which typically have substantial patent portfolios that can be used as bargaining chips in cross-license negotiations—they will be forced to pay for licenses from a number of different patent holders. Without patent portfolios of their own, they will, they fear, be forced out of business by the cost of obtaining licenses. This may in fact happen in a few cases. It has happened, after all, even to large companies such as Kodak, and is one cost of the patent system. The number of such situations should be low, however, because of the stringent requirements for patent validity. Moreover, if a sufficient number of small firms are worried about this phenomenon, nothing prevents them from pooling their own patents in a licensing consortium that would increase their bargaining power in licensing negotiations with their competitors.)

Rapp and Rozek, performing the statistical incantation known as regression analysis on the growth rate figures for national economies with varying degrees of patent protection, have found that the level of national economic development is closely aligned with the level of patent protection offered by a country's laws; further, that countries with the strongest patent systems have experienced the most rapid economic development. They offer three explanations for that correlation.

First, well-developed patent rights foster economic growth, so nations that upgrade their intellectual property rights system can expect improvements in the rate of innovation and investment in innovative activities. Second, inadequate property rights impede economic development, so weak patent regimes can be expected to correlate with economic backwardness. Third, as economic development occurs, it makes patents and other intellectual property rights more valuable because of enhanced prospects for sales and profits from their exploitation.

The view that patents impede, rather than advance, economic development was based on flawed economic analysis. Views such as Machlup's are now considered to be the economic equivalent of the wildly impractical, finned automobiles of the 1950s. The current thinking, and the reason for it, is reflected in a 1985 speech delivered in London to a large group of American intellectual property lawyers by Justice Department official Roger Andewelt. (How did it happen that an American government official had to travel to London to address an assembly of American intellectual property lawyers? Don't ask, just be thankful. Anything that can be done to get large numbers of lawyers out of the country, even for a few days, should be encouraged.) Andewelt explained that in earlier decades, Justice's Antitrust Division had been hostile to intellectual property protection, thinking that exclusive rights were inconsistent with the competitive environment that the antitrust laws are designed to promote. That hostility, he explained, was the result of the following "incomplete economic analysis":

Assumption number 1: the antitrust laws are intended to maintain vigorous competition in our economy. Assumption number 2: intellectual property protection inhibits one form of competition—competition through copying or using, without authorization, the creations of others. Conclusion from these two assumptions: intellectual property protection inhibits the goals of the antitrust laws.

Historically, the brunt of the enforcement policies that resulted from this now-dated economic thinking had been borne by patent holders, because patents were thought to create monopoly power. In his speech, Anderwelt went on to describe why evolution in economic thought had changed the attitudes of the antitrust enforcers:

When a more complete economic analysis is performed, it becomes apparent that intellectual property protection can promote competition. It can encourage firms to compete through the development of new technologies and thereby can result in additional choices for consumers; new and better products and services and cheaper prices. The key to understanding these procompetitive benefits is to understand the impact that intellectual property protection has on what economists call the "free rider" phenomenon.

"Free riding," in this context, is the process by which competitors appropriate the benefit of originators research and development activities without the need to pay for those activities. Andewelt said the Justice Department now understands that free-riding can result in the short-term dispersal of technology, so as to promote short-term competition at the expense of long-term competition, which is impeded by the undermining of investment in future R&D.

Monopoly power is the power to set prices and exclude competition. Patent holders certainly have the power to exclude competitors from making or using their inventions, and in theory have the power to set prices for their inventions wherever they wish. However, patents do not in themselves create monopoly power. Where there are close substitutes for a patented product, the power to exclude suppliers from the market and to set prices arbitrarily high cannot exist. The exclusive rights in a patent are granted only to the extent of the written claims of the patent, which have to be drawn narrowly enough not to include the "prior art." That is, claims that attempt to give a patent holder exclusive rights to preexisting, known technology are invalid. A patent cannot issue unless its claims demonstrate novel and nonobvious advances over what was already known. The requirements of novelty and nonobviousness force patent claims to be reasonably narrowly drafted. In turn, the claims limitations normally give competitors the opportunity to create competitive products without infringing patents. In addition, the requirements of novelty and nonobviousness assure that patents do not issue for anywhere near every new product. In particular, in the case of software, most programs will not be patentable because they do not contain patentable subject matter. William Holmes, author of the treatise, *Intellectual Property and Antitrust Laws*, tells us that "it is probably most accurate to avoid usage of the term monopoly altogether" in referring to patents, and instead to "refer to a patent simply as a legal right to 'exclude others' from exploitation of the patented item."

It is true that once in a while, particularly in the early days of a new technology, a seminal patent will issue to a single patent holder, which all other competitors will infringe if they are not licensed. The patents on xerography, invented by an individual, Chester Carlson, and assigned to a small company in Rochester, New York, are an example. Have those patents imparted an enduring monopoly of the copier business to Xerox? Judge Easterbrook (another eminent Chicago Schooler) deals with the issue of patent "monopoly" this way:

Patents give a right to exclude, just as the law of trespass does with real property. Intellectual property is intangible, but the right to exclude is no different in principle from General Motors' right to exclude Ford from using its assembly line, or an apple grower's right to its own crop. A patent *may* create a monopoly—just as an auto manufacturer *may* own all of the auto production facilities—but property and monopoly usually differ. That a patent covers an "entire" idea or product no more implies monopoly than the fact that USX Corporation owns the "entire" South Works in Chicago. Frequently, indeed almost always, different patented goods and processes compete with each other and with unpatented goods and processes.

The patent laws, Easterbrook concludes, represent a trade-off of short-term allocative loss (by which he means that in the short term, the patent holder may achieve profits from the patent) for long-term dynamic gain (i.e., the incentive to additional invention provided to competitors and to the original innovator by the existence of the patent).

"Economics," Walter Reuther is said to have observed, "is the only profession where you can be wrong every time and still have an outstanding reputation." There are academic views of the patent system diametrically opposed to those described above. For example, law professor Robert Merges and economist Richard Nelson argue that limitations should be placed on the permissible scope of patents such that there could be more direct competition *in the patented invention itself* by closer copying of the invention than the patent laws now permit. If we revert to empiricism, however (otherwise rendered as "a peek is worth two finesses"), and look to the real-world evidence for corroboration, it seems that existing patent laws have contributed materially to economic development without creating monopolies, and have rewarded innovation while dispersing most of the benefit of that innovation to the rest of society (including competing firms) rather than to the inventor. While any good law professor and any good economist can create an interesting alternative to the existing framework, it appears in fact that the existing social contract in respect of patents is a very reasonable bargain indeed.

# Part III

## Engineers of Monotony

Wherein we consider why it is nonsense to talk about "reverse engineering" software, and why people talk about it nonetheless.

# 8

# Beyond Arbitration: Fujitsu and IBM Take Their Show on the Road

I talked to several couples who had an awful moment in the first session: after going in hopefully, expecting to hear a reassuring lecture about getting over "this little bump in the road," what they actually heard was along the lines of, "Well, we can give therapy a try, but in your case I'm not sure it's worth it. This relationship sounds dead." But when they got over their shock, there was a feeling of relief—as terrible as the decision to break up might be, at least there was *someone else* there to help make it with them. One woman was so pleased with this idea that after breaking up with her boyfriend and starting a new relationship, she insisted that the man go into couples therapy with her right away.

"I will never," she announced, "be in an unsupervised relationship again."

—John Tierney, "Mind Health," *Vogue*, July 1990

The details of Fujitsu's supervised relationship with IBM are hidden from public view by order of the arbitrators who, by common consent of the two companies, had been given jurisdiction over intellectual property disputes between the largest Japanese computer maker and the largest American computer supplier until the year 2002. Or so they thought. In fact, Fujitsu and IBM are free to dispute intellectual property issues in public to their hearts' content, making the same arguments that they have made to the arbitrators if they wish, so long as they don't reveal anything about the arbitration and so long as they don't attempt to sue one another over intellectual property matters.

It was as a result of such freedom that before dawn one morning in the fall of 1989, a lawyer representing IBM climbed aboard the Trans-European Express (TEE) outbound from Paris. Less exotic than it sounds, the TEE is nonetheless a wonderful train ride for one accustomed to traveling the metropolitan commuter lines in the United States. Fast, smooth, and reliable, the dining car set with linen tablecloths and napkins, the TEE provides the early riser with a most civilized way of putting the day in motion. Ensconsed in an overstuffed armchair of a seat, with the French countryside brightening into view outside the window at the lawyer's left hand, the only annoyance—and a very gentle one it was, indeed—was the problem of keeping croissant crumbs off the notepad on which he was writing. As breakfast progressed, the sun crept above the tree line, bathing the table in glancing light. The American lawyer's three tablemates, all strangers to him, babbled on in French or buried their noses in the morning's *Le Figaro*, while our subject immersed himself in legal briefs that had been submitted to Eurobit, a European computer industry trade association, by Fujitsu, Ltd.

For those who understood the strategic importance of copyright protection to the software industry, the years 1989 and 1990 were a period of intense anxiety. As part of its drive toward "Europe 1992" and a unified European market, the European Community, or "EC," was undertaking an effort to bring into line, or "harmonize," the copyright laws of the twelve member states. Europe 1992 was a monumental undertaking, with myriad ramifications for the member states and the rest of the world, made more complicated still by the completely unforeseen disintegration of the Eastern bloc and even the Soviet Union itself after decades of mismanagement and repression, followed by a short, sharp taste of *glasnost* and *perestroyka* and then the cold-reality shower of joining a free market world economy with nothing to offer that market. In order to create a true monetary and economic union for Western (and, maybe someday, Eastern) Europe, hundreds of major directives had to be created through complex, twelve-party negotiations, and those directives had to be implemented in the laws of each member state by the 1992 deadline. One certainly would not have expected to find software copyright protection among the matters considered of paramount importance by EC leaders and *functionnaires* in achieving that goal. Yet, along with the questions of a common European currency, migration of workers among member states and management of European fisheries, the "eurocrats" had set for themselves the task of resolving the question of the scope of copyright protection for computer programs in what would become the largest single market in the world. A draft directive on software copyright protection was in circulation within the EC institutions, and public comment was being received. That the draft directive existed at all is eloquent testimony to the strategic importance of the computer industry to the developed countries, and the strategic role of software in the future of that industry.

In large measure, the resolution of the EC copyright question was destined to be achieved by persons who did not understand the question very well, who had many other matters of greater political significance with which to deal at the same time and who were working to a very tight deadline. In such an environment, it is no wonder that computer industry representatives on all sides of this arcane debate were descending in droves on Brussels, the main seat of the EC government and the destination of the TEE that fall morning.

In the EC member states (Belgium, Denmark, France, Germany, Greece, Italy, Ireland, Luxembourg, the Netherlands, Portugal, Spain, and the U.K.), copyright law as applied to software was not yet as broadly articulated as it was in the United States. The statutes, case law, and commentary were not as well developed, and certainly not as thematically consistent. The proposed copyright directive was intended to change that situation, by significantly shaping member state law in a uniform fashion. Inevitably, it would do so either to the advantage of the authors of original software or to the authors of nonoriginal software. In fact, the verbiage in circulation at the time of the voyage in question attempted to give something to each side. The innovators were pleased by the language making it clear that computer programs should be protected as "literary works" throughout the EC. That language placed software squarely within the mainstream of copyright doctrine, assuring that program authors would benefit from a traditional and well-understood regime of asset protection. The clones, in contrast, were pleased with the language providing or implying that "algorithms," "programming languages," "rules," and "interfaces" would be excluded from copyright protection.

The innovators spent much of the year 1989 and 1990 lobbying in Brussels and in the member states to narrow or eliminate those exclusions, while the imitators spent much of the same period lobbying to expand them. Officials of the EC received delegations from the opposing camps (many of whom were American or Japanese) with what may fairly be called a jaundiced eye, and with increasing impatience. Listening to the conflicting advice from the representatives of foreign software suppliers, the eurocrats were trying to decide what would be best for the European computer industry.

What the Fujitsu briefs made clear to the American as he rocked toward Brussels was that a new issue had been injected into the debate, an issue that did not appear at all in the draft EC directive. Fujitsu had advised the EC officials that in addition to strengthening the interface exceptions that already appeared in the directive, a new exception should be added: the directive should explicitly permit "reverse engineering" of software. Here was a notion worthy of the preeminent software clone. The proposition put forward by Fujitsu was stated with a fair degree of indirection, as is the Japanese way, but its intended consequences were quite easy to grasp. Fujitsu wanted to ensure that software imitators would be free to translate the computer programs of software innovators from the ones and zeroes of *object code* into a language more like that of *source code*, the original, easily readable form of the program as written by the program's author, which was readily understandable and manipulable by the imitator's programmers. Because computer languages are (currently) more formally structured than languages of everyday human communication, they are much more susceptible to being translated from one to another through the use of a computer. Translation from object code to a language as readable as source code, then, is usually a highly automated process called "reverse assembly" or "reverse compilation," depending on whether the language translated to is assembler language or a higher-level language such as COBOL or C. Reverse assembly or compilation are necessitated, say the followers, because software innovators have largely stopped publishing the source code to their programs.

Reverse assembly and reverse compilation, which I shall refer to collectively as reverse compilation unless the context requires otherwise, are useful to a software clone because the result of the process provides the clone's programmers with an easily readable base text on which to operate. In the European debate, the clones referred to their use of the reverse-compiled text as "research." Fujitsu and other software clones said that the only reason they produce that base text of source-like code is to study the original program more easily. In the extreme case, however—and although I do not here attribute this practice to Fujitsu's arbitrator-supervised development activities, I have seen it many times in the programs of other suppliers—the clone's programmers simply rename program elements, change the physical arrangement of modules or routines in ways that do not affect the "meaning" of the reverse-compiled text, and rewrite only those program elements on which they think they can improve or which must be modified to work in the clone's operating environment. The extreme case, obviously, is not research but rip-off. It produces extreme reactions on the part of software innovators, who tend to see such activity as a way of free-riding on their development efforts, a kind of free-riding that allows the clones to expend development efforts on enhancing the innovator's product as a prelude to marketing it under the clone logo.

Fujitsu's briefs had touted interface and reverse-compilation exceptions as being in the best interests of European software developers, particularly the smaller, more innovative developers. In truth, of course, the Fujitsu proposal was quite antithetical to the interests of such firms, for whom any weakening of traditional copyright protection would be particularly deleterious, for the reasons described in our correspondence course on economics, primarily the loss of the ability to attract capital with which to finance growth. Despite that incongruity, and despite the transparent self-interest inherent in Fujitsu's proposal, the Japanese computer supplier had managed to garner some considerable support in the Brussels eurocracy for its point of view. More surprisingly, it had managed to attract active support from influential European and American computer companies, most prominently Bull of France, Olivetti of Italy, and NCR and Unisys of the United States. It mattered not that two of the most active supporters, NCR and Tulip (the latter being a prominent Dutch supplier of personal computers), like Fujitsu, had had the unpleasant experience of being charged with infringing copyrights in computer programs. There is strength in numbers, and there are also clever ways to increase the apparent numbers of persons holding a common view. The companies aligned with Fujitsu formed a trade association, the European Committee for Interoperable Systems, or ECIS, and caused that association to commence lobbying in its own name, in order to create the appearance of a ground swell of industry support for an interface exclusion and a "reverse engineering" exception to European copyright law.

On the other side of the issue were arrayed a number of individual European and American companies, and a number of professional and industry associations. In the forefront of those opposed to the suggested weakening of traditional copyright protection were IBM, Siemens, Philips, DEC, Apple, and the Software Protection Association, the latter representing microcomputer software houses. Moreover, despite rather pointed differences of opinion over the look and feel of the Apple Macintosh user interface, all three participants in the Apple "look and feel" case (Apple, Microsoft, and Hewlett Packard) united to oppose the creation of an interface exclusion and a "reverse engineering" exception to copyright, their common participation underscoring the anathema with which authors of original software viewed these proposals. In reaction to the formation of ECIS, the companies who favored traditional copyright protection for software also formed a lobbying group, called the Software Action Group for Europe, or SAGE, to promote their views.

No health food is served on the TEE, or at least there was none served in the fall of 1989. The traveler instead could choose from among the following breakfast items: eggs, ham, cheese, coffee, tea, croissants, toast, hot chocolate, and a thimble-sized glass of orange juice. Settling for juice, croissants, and a pot of *chocolat chaud*, the lawyer from IBM poured himself a cup of the latter and reflected on Fujitsu's arguments.

There was a surface appeal to them—Why shouldn't competitors be able to "study" and do "research" on one another's programs?—but as the arguments Fujitsu propounded were directed rather explicitly at the copyrighted works of the lawyer's client, he uncapped a pen and began noting down counterarguments as he read.

Fujitsu's argument was that

It should be permissible... for a developer to study another vendor's programming material (including documentation), to document the program's interface specifications, and then to write new code embodying the interfaces necessary to develop a complementary or compatible hardware or software product. Replicating interfaces in new code is difficult, time-consuming, and expensive. It is this use of interface information—not as code, but as technical specifications—that Fujitsu believes must be clearly exempted from the monopoly otherwise conferred by copyright law.

*Counterarguments*: First, no definition of the term "interfaces" is offered, except to say that programs commonly contain a "myriad" of them. The definition given to that term can of course radically change the meaning of Fujitsu's argument. For example, read the foregoing quote substituting "macro, data area, screen display, and message" for "interface." Then read it again, this time substituting "published attachment protocol" for "interface."

Second, what difference does it make that the clone is using "interface information," by whatever definition, as "technical specifications" rather than code? If the screen displays of my program are used as the "technical specifications" for your program, does that mean your programmers are going to copy my screens, or doesn't it? If the structure, logic, and flow of my program are used as "technical specifications" for your program, are your programmers going to copy that structure, logic, and flow or aren't they?

Third, while "replicating interfaces in new code" may—depending in part on what the term "interfaces" means—be difficult, time-consuming, and expensive, it is inevitably cheaper than designing the interfaces and then implementing them in new code. The question is, why is a clone entitled to that cost saving, any more than it would be entitled to the cost saving that would result from the flat-out copying of the originator's code? Also, note the diversionary use at the outset of the neutral terms "study" and "documentation." No one can argue with the proposition that a clone should be able to study a program's manuals or object code, but that proposition has little to do with Fujitsu's actual proposal, which is to reverse compile the program.

Finally, the "monopoly" conferred by copyright is no monopoly at all. Anyone who has not had access to my program is free to market any program developed independently, no matter how similar, and even someone who has studied my program can market a program that performs the same functions, so long as my program has not been copied.

EC computers [sic] users will enjoy increased functionality, product variety, and competitive pricing only if it is clear that software interface information, like its hardware and telecommunications counterparts, is not within the artificial monopoly conferred by the copyright law.

*Counterarguments*: Increased functionality is the domain of the innovator, not the clone. The clone's ability to offer new function is severely restricted by the clone's desire to be compatible and to profit from the innovator's design. Moreover, the greater right the clone has to copy, the less incentive the innovator has to innovate.

Similarly, clones do not offer variety. The essence of their products is sameness. The copyright law promotes variety by prohibiting, not encouraging, copying.

While the clone may indeed offer a lower price, that price reduction results from free-riding on the innovator's work. Lower prices due to free-riding may not be legitimate competition, if the free-riding entails copying the expression in the original program. The EC needs to decide whether Europe's small- and medium-sized software houses, and also Europe's large but in most cases fragile systems suppliers, can survive even more intense clone competition than IBM and others have experienced in Japan and the United States, since Fujitsu's proposed changes in the Directive would result in more intense clone competition.

Article 4 of the Proposed Directive confers upon copyright holders the right to authorize:

The reproduction of the computer program....

The term "reproduction" as used here should not be defined or interpreted so broadly as to preclude such commonly accepted and widely used practices as machine analysis or reverse engineering.... If the term "reproduction" is construed to prohibit the means by which computer programs can be read or analyzed, copyright law will effectively become an exclusionary device more expansive than patent or trade secret protection—but without their requirements or restrictions....

We believe that a sentence should be added at the end of sub-paragraph a) stating:

The foregoing shall not apply, however, to any acts of reproduction by an owner or licensee of a program to the extent necessary to research, study or extract the unprotectable "ideas" or elements of a program.

*Counterarguments*: This is the heart of the matter. Once a program has been translated from object form to source form, "extraction" means nothing other than copying. This language says that a programmer can make as many copies or translations of another programmer's work as necessary in order to extract information from that work. Note that the nature of the information sought to be extracted is not limited to "interface information."

Note also that the information is not limited to "ideas," but also includes "elements of a program." Further that it is the clone programmer who decides, while he is developing the substitute and therefore similar program, what elements of the original work are "unprotectable" and therefore extractable.

Between copyright, trade secret, and patent, copyright is the least exclusionary. Second comers are not excluded by copyright from providing a functionally similar program, though they would be by patent. Second comers have access to substantial information about a copyrighted program, including the ability to read the program itself in the language in which it is distributed. A trade secret is, by definition, secret.

To the extent that the Directive can be read to preclude machine analysis or reverse-engineering techniques common in the industry, such as line traces or benchmarks, that shortcoming would be corrected by language much different than that proposed here.

In the succeeding months, the arguments and counterarguments about reverse compilation became louder and more insistent, leading the EC officials, as we shall see, to feel that they must do something that would recognize the interests of firms on both sides of the debate.

Europe 1992 was a powerful and profound initiative, the force of which is already being felt around the world. Even before unity was achieved, the EC drive had begun dramatically to alter the economic face of the planet. The prospect of a unified European market with a common currency and no internal trade barriers was one of the underlying motivations behind *perestroyka* in the Soviet Union and the sudden outbreak of democracy in the Warsaw Pact countries. No one wanted to be lying on the tracks when that gigantic economic engine came roaring through. To have within the EC a rule that an original computer program may be freely copied, adapted, or translated as a step in creating a competitive program could permanently skew the competitive balance in the computer industry in Europe. It would also inevitably lead to similar legislative initiatives in the United States and Japan. At the end of our tour of the software protection battleground, we will therefore return to the question of the EC copyright directive. By that time, we will have studied the other important aspects of the softwars, and we will have considered a number of interesting questions about reverse compilation and other activities undertaken in the name of "reverse engineering" of software. What is "reverse engineering" of software? What legal principals govern it? Will society be better off or worse off if people engage in it? Are there acceptable modes of reverse engineering and unacceptable modes? Is there a difference between "reverse engineering" and the normal competitive instinct to see whether the other guy's product is better and, if it is, to see what makes it better?

The train crept like a gentle Leviathan into Brussels' central station. The other passengers stood and gathered up their belongings. Outside, porters swung their carts into position along the *quai*. The American put away his pen and notepad, retrieved his jacket from the overhead rack, and set out to make such modest contribution as was within his means to the resolution of the great debate.

## Endnote: Author, Author! Programmer, Programmer!— The Economics of Copyright

> Suppose you came here from another planet. You have no eyes, no ears, just infrared sensors to help you get around. You notice that an object is thrown on your doorstep every morning. But you are not equipped with the concept *newspaper*. You subject this strange artifact to physical and chemical analysis. You weigh it everyday and see that it goes from thin to fat in seven-day cycles. You analyze the ratio of black to white and find that it is fairly constant. You note that the chemical composition of the paper sometimes changes. But in understanding what a newspaper is, much of that turns out to be irrelevant. Will you, the alien, ever make the leap and somehow realize that on the surface of the paper are rows and rows of tiny markings, that they cluster into patterns that carry information? And, if you are someday driven to make this radical hypothesis, is there any hope that you will learn to read the thing?
> —George Johnson, *In the Palaces of Memory* (1991)

The real question is, will the alien eventually decide to publish a competing newspaper and, if so, to what extent can the alien use the text of the terrestrial newspaper as the basis for the extraterrestrial newspaper? That is where the copyright law intercedes. Unlike the patent grant, a copyright is actually a rather weak form of protection. Although it protects both published and unpublished works, the nature of copyright protection is rather limited. Patent law prevents others from practicing the patented invention, whether they had known about the patent or not. Copyright, on the other hand, only prevents others from copying, distributing, performing, displaying, adapting, translating, or recasting the copyrighted work. Only the particular expression chosen by the creator of the work is protected, and an accused infringer must have had access to that expression. Reading the copyrighted work and using the ideas in it are obviously permitted under the copyright law. In addition, copyright, like trade secret, offers no protection whatever against independent creation of the same material by someone else.

Landes and Posner have written a paper entitled "An Economic Analysis of Copyright Law," on which this endnote is based. The reader should be forewarned that both authors of that paper are leading adherents to a belief system called "the Chicago School," of which economist Milton Friedman is the high priest. Adherents to the Chicago School believe fervently in the free-market system, and in a style of economic analysis that can best be described as Newtonian. I say "Newtonian" because it is a mathematically rigorous analysis in which the math is Newtonian calculus (or a subset thereof) and the conservation laws of Newton's physics are replaced by a motivation law that is said to drive all rational economic activity undertaken by private enterprise. That law is *profit maximization*. To Chicago School-ers, profit maximization is as sacred a tenet of human behavior as conservation of momentum is a sacred tenet of particle behavior to Newtonian physicists. Firms pursuing the objective of profit maximization (or loss minimization, in cases where costs unavoidably exceed revenues) will create an orderly and efficient allocation of a nation's resources and distribution of its private income.

Like Newtonian physics, Chicago School economics leaves little room for quantum effects and can for that reason be considered somewhat dated philosophically. The notion that matter behaves sometimes like particles and sometimes like waves struck at the heart of Newtonian physics. Similarly, the notion that people sometimes behave rationally and sometimes irrationally strikes at the heart of Chicago School economics. Nonetheless, just as Newton's laws of motion have proved to be pretty good predictors of the behavior of matter in the observable physical world, the Chicago School law of motivation has proved to be a pretty good predictor of enterprise behavior in the observable economic world. With that introduction under our belts, let us turn to the Landes and Posner analysis of copyright, which I think the reader will find cogent and persuasive despite its philosophical limitations.

The authors begin by noting the obvious feature that distinguishes intellectual property from other forms of property: the cost of creation is much, much higher than the cost of reproduction. If the price set on copies by the creator of the work is equal to, or almost equal to, marginal cost (i.e., the cost of reproduction), then others will be discouraged from making illicit copies because there will be little or no profit in doing so. However, if the price of copies is set in that fashion, the creator may never recover the up-front expense of creation. Further, in the absence of legal protection against unauthorized copying, no matter what price the creator initially set, others could freely reproduce the work and the market price would quickly be bid down to a point near marginal cost, with the result that the up-front expense of creation (in the case of software, research and development, testing, advertising, and a support system) would never be recovered. In addition, not every creative work will find a market. Some are duds, so that there is a risk of failure that must be factored into any rational decision process about whether to invest in creating intellectual property. Without protection against unauthorized copying, the additional return necessary to compensate for projects that fail would not be recovered either, since that return must come from the projects that succeed and those projects are precisely the ones on which the copyists will concentrate.

Looking more closely, one can discern a number of factors other than the copyright law that might deter copying. For example, if the creator's cost of reproduction is lower than the copyists' cost structure, there would be no economic incentive for copying because the creator could always underprice the copyist. Similarly, if the copyist had to incur *some* up-front expense (such as mold making), the incentive for copying would be reduced. An allied consideration is that timing is often important to the success of a new product. The first to market will often capture the bulk of the demand. Also, even absent copyright creators could protect the work of authorship by contractually obligating their customers not to copy (though that protection would not reach persons who came into possession of the work without being contractually bound). Ultimately, it can also be argued that general principles of morality should dissuade plagiarism. If one could rely only on such other factors, however, and not on copyright, the nature of commercial products based on intellectual property would undergo shifts. There would be emphasis, for example, on faddish products for which timing is everything in the market, on products that are hard to reproduce and on low-volume products where contractual protection would be more effective. Copyright law serves to neutralize such biases.

In the movie *All of Me*, actor Steve Martin plays a character whose body is invaded by the spirit of a dead woman, played largely off-screen by Lily Tomlin. In one scene, Martin walks down the street in an amazing display of physical coordination, one side of his body executing a macho strut while the other side performs an effeminate swish. In point of fact, authors of computer programs and other works of intellectual property are similarly schizophrenic when it comes to protection against copying. On the one hand, they want maximum protection for their own work, so that they they need share as little as possible of the social return with others. On the other hand, they want minimal protection for everyone else's work, so that they may freely borrow from the existing universe of human thought without incurring legal liability. In Chicago School terms, the cost of creation rises as the level of protection rises. As in life generally, the law does not usually allow for having one's cake and devouring it at the same time, and Posner and Landes find in the copyright law a balance between the competing interests of protection and use. The authors set up a mathematical model of copyright economics and discover that, as the level of copyright protection increases, the cost of creating new copyrighted works increases (because of the steps that must be taken to avoid infringement) and the profit earned from copyrighted works—by a firm that sets out to maximize profits—goes up (because of the reduced competition from copyists). In consequence of the increases in the cost of creation and also the costs of copying, they find, strengthening copyright protection is likely to reduce the welfare benefits—the sum of consumer surplus and producer surplus—generated by any one copyrighted work. The macho strut overpowers the effeminate swish. That effect, which is traditionally viewed as tending to reduce access by consumers and competitors to copyrighted works, is said to prove that strong copyright protection is inconsistent with the objective of broad dissemination of protected works.

The traditional view, though, ignores the question whether—although welfare benefits decrease for any individual work—total welfare generated by *all* copyrighted works increases as copyright protection increases. Working through their formulae, Posner and Landes find that there is an optimal level of protection below which total welfare increases and above which total welfare decreases. They also conclude that the higher the welfare benefits (i.e., value) of any particular work, the higher the optimal level of copyright protection. Providing higher levels of copyright protection for works that have greater social value, however, is a level of fine tuning that the law does not—and for various reasons, should not—attempt.

Turning to the copyright system in place in the United States today, Posner and Landes find that reasonable efforts have been made to optimize the scope of protection. First among those is the notion that independent creation is not prohibited by the law. The freedom thus provided to authors reduces the cost of preventing accidental copying and focuses the attention of the courts on the economic rationale for copyright, which is the prevention of free-riding. Next is the limitation that copyright does not protect ideas. Given that the cost of generating a new idea may be fairly low, and the cost of avoiding infringement of a new idea may be high, the protection of ideas through the copyright system—which automatically protects an item of intellectual property as soon as it is written down—would be likely to reduce total welfare as well as welfare per work. Taking up briefly the question whether the "look and feel" of software user interfaces constitutes idea or expression, the authors conclude only that the issue should be decided not by semantic legerdemain but by examining the economics of the problem: "specifically, by comparing the deadweight costs of allowing a firm to appropriate what has become an industry standard with the disincentive effects on originators if such appropriation is forbidden." (That, in a qualitative way, was what Judge Keeton did in the *Lotus* case.)

Other aspects of copyright protection that evince a search for the optimal level of protection include (1) the reservation to the original author of the right to create derivative works, such as translations—which increases the author's incentive to create such works and also reduces transaction costs for licensees because there is only a single source from which license is needed—and (2) the "fair use" doctrine. The fair use doctrine allows for limited copying that does not adversely affect either the supply of copies of the original work or the demand for such copies by creating unauthorized versions of that work. "Fair uses" include criticism, parody, teaching, and academic research.

The Posner-Landes analysis gives an aura of intellectual rigor to the conclusion that many have reached intuitively: copyright protection is a balanced form of protection against the sorts of acts that would tend to chill the economic interest in creating expressive works. The extension of copyright protection to computer programs can be seen, therefore, as a salutary step in the evolution of the industry.

# 9

# At Sea over Reverse Engineering: The *Bonito Boats* Case

The UAR uses a portable Swiss-built encrypting machine which is like a combination typewriter and adding machine. Inside it has a number of discs that are specially set every two or three months. The code clerk, in order to create a secret message, writes the message into the machine in clear text in five letter groups. Each time he completes five letters he pulls a crank which sets the inner discs whirling. When they stop the jumbled letters that appear represent the encrypted group....

The National Security Agency cannot break this code system mathematically but they can do so if sensitive recordings can be obtained of the vibrations of the encryption machine when the discs clack to a stop. The recordings are processed through an oscilloscope and other machines which reveal the disc settings. Knowing the settings, NSA can put the coded messages . . . into their own identical machines with identical settings, and the clear text message comes out.

—Philip Agee, *Inside the Company: CIA Diary* (1975)

A boatyard in South Florida. The summer sun beats down on a weathered shed, its windows blackened against prying eyes. An ancient air conditioner protrudes from one wall, whining in protest over the impossibility of its assignment. Inside, the figures of two men loom ominously in the light from a single dangling bulb. Between them, a hulking oblate object with skin rough and rippling sits elevated on two sawhorses.

Moving to opposite sides of the mysterious object, the men place their hands underneath the skin, take a secure grip and jerk upwards. The shell lifts easily, revealing underneath the sleek, upended hull of a small fiberglass fishing boat. The inner surface of the just-removed covering, now set on the floor, is revealed to be a mirror image of the hull. The two men are not codebreakers, but like codebreakers they are trying to reproduce someone else's original work. They have made an unauthorized mold of a boat's hull, and will now use that mold to manufacture cloned boats of their own.

The original hull had been produced after a complex development process that involved designing, model building, testing, creating engineering drawings, building a wooden prototype, and then spraying the prototype with fiberglass to create the manufacturing mold. The men in the shed have skipped all the steps except the last, saving themselves considerable development expense as compared to the originator. Since they have doubtless chosen a popular model to clone, they have saved themselves as well the cost of independent market research and the risk of unpopularity. The question is, should they be allowed to do so? Is it socially desirable to permit competition by rip-off? If so, to what extent? The answer given to those questions by the makers of public policy is obviously relevant to the softwars in the computer industry.

The Florida legislature thought that such behavior was not socially desirable. It passed a law in 1983 prohibiting the copying of boat hulls by the direct-molding process. Unfortunately, the Supreme Court of the United States disagreed. It ruled that the Florida statute was unconstitutional, and left our two direct molders in their shed free to profit from their cloning strategy. The high court's decision is interesting to us because, like the *Feist* case, it has been taken up as a weapon by software clones and their legal advisors, who view it as an anthem for reverse engineers. Naturally, the innovators and their lawyers argue that the case has no relevance whatever to reverse engineering of software. Let's look a little more closely at the Supreme Court opinion than the combatants usually do, and see for ourselves what it says.

The catalyst for the clash of viewpoints that reached the Supreme Court was the discovery by the Bonito Boat Company that a competitor, Thundercraft Boat Company, was selling a craft with the same hull as the Bonito 5VBR. The Thundercraft pleasure boat, it seemed, had been created in major part by direct molding of the hull of the 5VBR. Bonito filed suit in state court in Florida, and thereby embarked on a campaign of ignominious defeats. Thundercraft moved to dismiss Bonito's complaint. The motion was granted. Bonito appealed the dismissal. The dismissal was affirmed. Bonito appealed to the highest court in Florida. That court affirmed the dismissal, too. The end of the trail was in Washington, where the United States Supreme Court agreed to hear Bonito's petition. Having done so, however, the Supreme Court agreed with the three state courts, thereby sealing the fate of the 5VBR.

The reasoning of all four courts was the same. Once an article of commerce is put on the market without patent protection, it becomes part of the public domain. Thereafter, it would conflict with the patent laws to allow states to protect the article's design from being copied. Writing for an unanimous Supreme Court, Justice Sandra Day O'Connor put it this way:

From their inception, the federal patent laws have embodied a careful balance between the need to promote innovation and the recognition that imitation and refinement through imitation are both necessary to invention itself and the very lifeblood of a competitive economy. The novelty and nonobviousness requirements of patentability embody a congressional understanding, implicit in the patent clause itself, that free exploitation of ideas will be the rule, to which the protection of a federal patent is the exception.

Although

state protection of trade secrets did not operate to frustrate the achievement of the congressional objectives of the patent laws,

this was in part because

[t]he public at large remains free to discover and exploit the trade secret through reverse engineering of products in the public domain or by independent development.... Reverse engineering of chemical and mechanical articles in the public domain often leads to significant advances in technology.

The competitive reality of reverse engineering may act as a spur to the inventor, creating an incentive to develop inventions which meet the rigorous requirements of patentability.

End of anthem. Those readers who have doffed their caps and are standing at attention should resume their seats and read these passages again. You will note that they are a vigorous endorsement of reverse engineering of products that have been placed *in the public domain*. The phrase "public domain" means that the program becomes like Central Park in New York City. Anyone can have access to it, any time, for any lawful purpose and probably, as is the case with Central Park, for many unlawful purposes as well.

In most parts of the world, computer programs offered by commercial firms are not in the public domain, even if they have not been patented. In the usual case, nothing in the program rises to the level of invention that can be patented, and so the principal statutory protection available for the program is copyright. No formal acts need to be taken in order to obtain copyrights; they arise as soon as the program is written down, so if authors wish to put a program into the public domain, they must take some overt action to waive their copyrights. Companies that are trying to make money by marketing their programs don't normally waive those rights. Instead, they licence certain rights, such as the rights to reproduce, adapt, and perhaps further distribute to customers for limited purposes under some form of license agreement. Even "shareware," software distributed free or for no more than an administrative charge, is not public domain, in that authors usually rely in copyright in order to retain some rights in their handiwork. The software distributed by Richard Stallman's Free Software Foundation—which we'll discuss in Chapter 16—is distributed on what is called a "copyleft" basis: Stallman's copyrights are used to obtain agreement from his licensees that they will redistribute without charge any code into which FSF software has been incorporated. On the whole, however, most software that people acquire for use in their homes and businesses belongs to other people or enterprises who have shared their rights to that software in a limited way and for a fee. Therefore, one might think that the issue presented by the *Bonito Boats* opinion—whether state law can protect designs that are in the public domain—is not particularly apposite to the case of computer programs. And yet...

In addition to copyrights, authors of computer programs also rely on trade secret (or in some countries breach of trust) law to protect the asset value of their programs. Trade secret protection is obtained—or at least sought—through a two-part strategy. First, authors market their programs in machine-readable object-code form only. Customers do not receive source code either in the form of listings or in machine-readable form. The theoretical underpinning of this arm of the strategy is that the object code, while readable by the trained and diligent programmer, is something like a crossword puzzle. Its structure and form are readily discerned, but its content and meaning yield themselves only over time, by following clues and by trial-and-error analysis. The time it would take a competitor's programmers to solve the puzzle, however short or long, is the *lead time* that is the only benefit offered by trade secret protection.

Second, in order to ensure that competitors' programmers who seek to unlock the secrets of an original program do so by trying to solve the puzzle rather than by peeking at the answer book, authors of original programs typically license those programs pursuant to agreements under which the licensees promise not to engage in reverse compilation. Running an object-code program through a reverse compiler takes little time and produces a result that is much like the original source code. It is the computing equivalent of peeking. (As I've already mentioned, even without the contractual prohibition, reverse compilation is a transformation of the author's work from one language to another and therefore a copyright violation as well.)

To put our earlier question into context, is reverse compilation of software a socially desirable activity? Would Justice O'Connor have written a paean to the programmer who both infringes a copyright and breaches a contract by peeking at the answer? The answer to both questions must, we shall now see, be negative.

To understand why, the reader must appreciate that the Supreme Court has, in other cases, held the term "public domain" not to refer to material protected either by copyright or by contract. In *Compco Corp. v. Day-Brite Lighting, Inc.*, the court was faced with a situation in which the defendant had copied the functional aspects of the plaintiff's unpatented fluorescent lighting system. The elements that were copied, being unprotected by patent or copyright law and not being secret, were in the public domain. Nonetheless, the plaintiff had sued under the Illinois unfair competition law, and had obtained an injunction. In dissolving the injunction, the Supreme Court ruled that it "interfere[d] with the federal policy, found in Art. I, Sec. 8, cl. 8 of the Constitution and in the implementing federal statutes, of allowing free access to copy whatever the federal patent *and copyright* laws leave in the public domain." (Emphasis added.) The *Compco* case was not overruled in *Bonito Boats*, rather, it was cited with approval as foreshadowing the decision in the latter case. Thus, there is no question that if material is copyright protected, it is not in the public domain and the reasoning of *Bonito Boats* does not apply to that material. Since reverse compilation is simply an act of translation, and producing a translation is the exclusive right of the copyright holder, reverse compilation of copyrighted material has clearly not been given the green light by the Supreme Court.

As to contractual protection against reverse compilation, the Supreme Court had in earlier cases made abundantly clear that state trade secret laws are not unconstitutional invasions of the territory controlled by federal law. At first blush, it may seem inconsistent to rule on the one hand that public domain material not protected by federal law may not be protected *from copying* by state law, but on the other hand that states can pass laws protecting such materials from other kinds of appropriation. After all, isn't that just what the Florida legislature had done? The distinction that explains the apparent contradiction is secrecy. Justice O'Connor explained that distinction in *Bonito Boats*, writing that trade secret material, not being widely known to the public, can be said not to be in the public domain; further, that the "fundamental human right" to privacy is threatened when industrial espionage is condoned or made profitable; and finally that trade secret law is far weaker than patent law, as it leaves the public free to create the same product independently or even to reverse engineer the product protected by trade secret. Trade secret protection is therefore a legitimate increment to the protective mechanisms offered by federal law.

How are trade secrets kept secret? The fact is that no trade secret is secret from everyone. The people who developed it know it. Others around them have access to it. Contractors may be utilizing it. Competitors may even be licensed to practice it. What, then, does "secret" mean? In general, it means not known or readily knowable to the general public. Keeping the public away from the secret usually entails some kind of physical security. It usually also requires contractually binding those who have access to the secret not to reveal it to others or to act in such a way as to endanger its secrecy. The case in which the Supreme Court harmonized state trade secret law with federal patent law is *Kewanee Oil Co. v. Bicron Corp.* In that case, Kewanee had developed a process for manufacturing large crystals useful in the detection of ionizing radiation. Some of the steps in that process were secret. One way that they were kept secret was by Kewanee's managers making sure that the employees who worked on the process signed agreements requiring them not to disclose trade secrets they obtained during the course of their employment. Some of those employees later left Kewanee and formed or joined Bicron, which was created to compete with Kewanee in the production of large crystals. In producing crystals at Bicron, the former Kewanee employees used or disclosed Kewanee's trade secret in violation of their nondisclosure agreements. The Supreme Court noted that

The maintenance of standards of commercial ethics and the encouragement of invention are the broadly stated policies behind trade secret law. "The necessity of good faith and honest, fair dealing, is the very life and spirit of the commercial world." ... [E]ven though a discovery may not be patentable, that does not

"destroy the value of the discovery to one who makes it, or advantage the competitor who by unfair means, or as the beneficiary of a broken faith, obtains the desired knowledge without himself paying the price in labor, money or machines expended by the discoverer."

The Court noted that a developer of useful new information would be unwilling to share that information with others unless it could impose binding legal obligations requiring the payment of license fees and the protection of the secret. The *Kewanee* case was cited with approval and abstracted at length in *Bonito Boats.* It should not be expected, therefore, that the Supreme Court will hold the breach of contractual provisions designed to prevent the rendering into easily readable form the content of a computer program to be socially desirable activity.

Those who declaimed that *Bonito Boats* was a major victory for the clones were obviously playing to an audience sitting around the home fires, not to people who have observed the battle at close range. Still, one must put the episode in perspective. If reverse compilation has not been sanctioned by the Supreme Court, but reverse engineering has, what can we make of the state of the battle? Have both sides won some ground, or has neither side won anything?

In order to find out, we have to look behind the rhetoric. As a first order of business, we must recognize that "reverse engineering" is a term that makes no real sense when applied to software. The use of the term is a form of propaganda that obscures what is really going on. Take an example from another field of literary works. Someone gives you an audio tape containing a reading in French of Flaubert's *La Temtation de Saint Antoine*, which, from the abstract that you've read, you feel could be successfully turned into a great comedic novel set in Malibu. As you have not been able to find an English translation (and with good reason: before publication, Flaubert's best friend told him to burn the manuscript, it was so boring), and the only hard copy you've been able to find is in the *Bibliotheque Nationale* in Paris, where creating a translation is inconvenient at best, you are delighted to have received this *livre-sur-ruban*. You hire a French-speaking stenographer to transcribe the reading while the tape is playing, and a translator to render the transcription into English. Can the stenographer and the translator be said to have "reverse engineered" *Le Tentation de Saint Antoine* by creating *The Temptation of Saint Anthony*? Of course not. What they have done is simply to translate the text into a language you can more readily understand and mark up to create your hilarious sendup of Southern California. Had the book still been protected by copyright, translating it would have been an infringement.

For an even closer analogy, let us return to the world of espionage. Decompiling a computer program is essentially the same process as translating encrypted text, as the reverse engineering process we will encounter in Chapter 17 will illustrate. The following decryption examples are taken from Hamilton Nickel's book, *Codemaster: Secrets of Making and Breaking Codes*:

Hiding a message in a banana or in a shoe are examples of concealment systems, but in this manual, we are concerned with systems that conceal a message within another message. Consider the following:

I WILL DO IT. IF NOT TODAY, THEN TRUST ME. SIGNED,
SMITH.

Can you read it? Copy out every third word.

I WILL DO IT. IF NOT TODAY, THEN TRUST ME. SIGNED,
      DO       NOT               TRUST
SMITH.

SMITH.

The skilled codebuster would look at the slightly awkward style of the message and bells would ring. He would look for a set of words that made more sense than the apparent message.

Try the following cryptogram sent on December 13, 1944, during World War II. A key was used.

FANAB IASSO NADME ETSSH IPOWILLRNU NNLTO SOONK NIGIT NTTRE LONCE GCODE LNOTE AISAN SFOUR

Remember that the strict definition of a concealment cipher does not allow shifting symbols or making substitutions. The message is there for you to see, but some method has been used to draw attention away from it. Without the *key*, even a professional cryptanalyst would struggle with this for some hours, perhaps longer.

```
FANAB IASSO NADME ETSSH IPOWI LLNRU NNLTO SOONK
 A   BA   N D              OWI LLN      L O   O K
NIGIT NTTRE LONCE GCODE LNOTE AISAN SFOUR
   I  N          G        L     AS  S
```

At first, there doesn't seem to be any order in the arrangement of the nulls [i.e., blank or meaningless spaces], but if you change the date into all numbers, December 13, 1944, becomes 12 13 1944 or 12131944, and you can see that the number of nulls between the plaintext [i.e., letters that have significance] corresponds to the value of each succeeding digit in the date.

```
FANAB IASSO NADME ETSSH IPOWI LLNRU NNLTO SOONK
1A22B 1A333 N1D99 99999 99O44 44N44 44L1O 22O1K
NIGIT NTTRE LONCE GCODE LNOTE AISAN SFOUR
333I1 N9999 99999 G4444 L4444 A1S22 SXXXX.
```

The process of decompiling the binary form of a computer program is no different conceptually from the foregoing. Because computer programs are lists of elementary instructions, however, the task of decoding them can be substantially automated. Commercially available programs can take the object code of an original program as input and produce source-like listings. Other software tools can create flow charts and tables that explicate the structure, logic, and flow of that program. Then, by a series of simple transformations such as changing instruction sequences, using synonyms and "global replacement" of register or memory references, the original program can be transmuted into a program that, although it is a mechanically altered and completely equivalent derivative work, is difficult to recognize as such.

Those supporting a "reverse engineering" exception to copyright law have proposed that the protection against translation traditionally offered by copyright should be eliminated in the case of computer programs. In furtherance of that objective, they have argued that the confluence of trade secret and copyright protection is a kind of "double whammy" that creates a situation inconsistent with the purpose of copyright. Their assertion is that the purpose of copyright is to cause dissemination of ideas, and that if programs are published only as unreadable object code and translation is prohibited, the ideas in the program are not disseminated. That assertion is fundamentally wrong on all counts. The purpose of copyright is to encourage publication of original work. More specifically, in the United States, the purpose of copyright is to promote progress in science and the useful arts. In connection with that publication or progress, much unpublished material may be created. The unpublished work is also protected by copyright, whether or not anyone other than the author is meant ever to see it.

Copyright protection attaches automatically as soon as a work is written down. If the unpublished work has commercial value, it also qualifies for trade secret protection. There is no requirement, or even a suggestion, that for either copyright or trade secret protection the unpublished material—such as drafts, notes, outlines, storyboards, outtakes, sketches, concordances, design documentation, or indeed source code—must be published along with the work actually disseminated.

Moreover, programs published in object code are not unreadable. Some programmers can read object code. Many more can decipher it with effort. It is certainly not as easy to read as source code, or as easy to mark up on the way to creating a competitive program, and indeed what qualifies the source code of a program as a trade secret even when the object code is published is the fact that very few people in the world can sit down with dumps of object code and immediately absorb their meaning. Nonetheless, as is the case for *Finnegan's Wake* or for company books written in code for commercial reasons or books written in Laotian Tai for the tiny Lao community in America, protecting software despite the obscurity of the ideas in untranslated object code is in no wise inconsistent with the fundamental purpose of copyright.

In the end, of course, an object code rendition of a program can be loaded into a computer. The computer will then fall into the program's thrall and begin to do things in response to the program's instructions. A dynamic system is thus created, and that system can be reverse engineered in the traditional sense. Its functioning may be observed. The frequency of execution of individual machine instructions may be counted. The time required to accomplish particular tasks may be assessed. The user interface may be analyzed. The interactions between the processor and peripheral devices while the program is executing may be monitored. The communications between the computer in question and other computers or file servers may be traced. The contents of the computer's memory may be read. The manuals that accompany the program may be read. All of these procedures and more may be undertaken without infringing the program author's copyright; that is, without making a copy or adaptation of the program. They will disclose numerous ideas contained in the program, including—most importantly—all the ideas that customers of the program will ever care about.

There are limitations on such procedures, though. In rare instances, a system consisting of a computer under control of a program is protected by a process patent, which is a patent not on a product but on a particular way of doing something, in such a way that running the system may actually be an infringement of the patent. Holders of such patents would normally license customers under their process patent to the extent necessary to run the system, but might not license them to reverse engineer the system at all. Indeed, even absent a process patent, some software houses routinely attempt to prevent reverse engineering of a system under control of their programs by specifically including prohibitions against some of the above-listed activities in their license agreements. *Bonito Boats* does not speak to those situations at all.

The *Bonito Boats* case was not really a campaign in the softwars. Seized on as a weapon by those whose competitive position is advanced by weakening intellectual property protection for computer programs, it has proven to be a dud. They key to victory in warfare, according to Clausewitz, is battle, not theory, and *Bonito Boats* was not a battle between software suppliers. The case raises interesting questions about the relative strategic advantage of the opposing forces, but ultimately leaves both the innovators and the clones, the American, European, and Asian suppliers, in the same relative positions that they held before the case was decided. After finishing our correspondence course with a chapterlet on the economics of trade secret, however, we will turn to two lawsuits that really did alter the fortunes of war, in the all-important Pacific theater.

## Endnote: "Gentlemen Don't Read One Another's Mail"— The Economics of Trade Secret

> Yang had paid six yuan for the bird, a sizable sum. He planned to release it later in the afternoon.
>
> "For six yuan, I think I can enjoy him a little. Then he will fly away into the trees and eat insects until he is fat."
>
> Releasing birds was an old Buddhist tradition. In the past, clever vendors stationed themselves outside temples and sold worshipers birds that were trained to return home to their cages. The pious gained credit in heaven, the vendor retained his capital, and the hard-working bird was assured a permanent roof over his head.
> —Fergus M. Bordewich, *Cathay* (1990)

Yang's bird was, in a sense, a public good. His purchase did not deprive others in the community—except briefly—of the privilege of the same enjoyment. The bird could be bought every day by a different person without exhausting its utility. The bird vendor was happy to part with his property each day, knowing that it would return each night. The vendor would have been very upset, however, if someone had stolen his money-making charge and the cage that protected it.

Trade secrets are, by definition, not public goods (though they can become public goods when they are no longer secret). Generally speaking, any information that is kept secret and provides a competitive advantage is considered, in American law, to be a trade secret. Similar notions prevail in other developed countries. Although it is often said that Japanese law, for instance, does not recognize trade secrets, in fact laws in Japan protecting against abuses of relationships of trust provide cognate protection. Trade secrets are protected only against *misappropriation*. In other words, the only exclusive right that the holder of a trade secret has is that others may not lawfully steal the secret. That principle seems consonant with general notions of public order. It is difficult to accept, for example, that competitors should be allowed to break into one another's laboratories by night and purloin design documents or marketing plans. That is no more than an extension of the rule that the public order should preclude competitors from breaking into one another's buildings for any purpose. Trade secret protection, though, extends beyond the physical protection of the land and buildings in which the secret is kept. Competitors may not bribe employees of a firm to divulge the firm's secrets, or even hire them in order to obtain those secrets. (See note 9.E.1.) In general, competitors may not sit outside one another's laboratories in vans loaded with electronic listening gear, so as to absorb trade secrets that radiate invisibly from the laboratories as electronic or sonic waves. But can Ford engineers fly through the open airspace over GM's test track in order to photograph GM's experimental cars? Can Amdahl employees haunt the bars in Poughkeepsie, listening in on conversations of IBM engineers in the hopes of learning something about IBM's next mainframe product line? Can a contract programmer hired to assist in writing a new program for a software house use the knowledge of that program to write a similar program for his own account later? Such questions lie at the boundaries of trade secret law; they deal with matters such as the definition of "secret" and the definition of "misappropriation." The answers to these and other boundary questions vary from case to case and from place to place.

One thing is certain about trade secret law, however. It does not protect that which is available to the public. Thus, one who reproduces the secret from personal research or from public materials is not guilty of misappropriation. In particular, when a product is put on the market, anything that can be learned by examining the product, by "reverse engineering," in the vernacular, is free for the taking—so long as the learning process does not entail violation of some other legal regime, such as patent or copyright. (As noted earlier, the process of reverse engineering a patented product may in certain cases entail steps that in fact infringe the patent in the product or a patent in the process by which the product is produced, and therefore be illegal. Similarly, certain processes by which copyrighted products, such as computer programs or books written in foreign languages or the contents of compact disks, are analyzed may involve copyright infringement, and therefore be illegal.) In addition to permitting reverse engineering of publicly available products, trade secret law also contemplates that independent discovery—indeed the serendipitous creation down to the last detail—of the same information that constitutes another person's trade secret, should be lawful.

The rights provided by trade secret law, then, are not exclusionary, or even exclusive. They protect only against theft or abuse of relationships of trust and confidence, such as those of employer-employee or licensor-licensee. They are based in principles fundamental to the workings of a just society, such as the principle that one should keep one's promises, the principle that one should not profit from the benefits of a cooperative activity with others without also complying with the obligations imposed as a condition of undertaking that activity and the principle that Thou Shalt Not Steal. Robert Sherwood has surveyed business executives in countries where trade secret protection is nonexistent. He finds that even in those countries, companies do what they can to prevent the loss of valuable proprietary technologies. In two such countries, Brazil and Mexico, Sherwood discovered that enterprises have become very circumspect about giving employees access to their leading-edge technologies. In family run businesses, technologies are shared only with family members. In other businesses, access is confined to older, trusted employees. The loyalty of new employees is carefully weighed before such employees are entrusted with the firm's technological know-how. Generally, the number of employees given access to such know-how is kept very small.

These practices profoundly affect commercial product development activities in those countries. According to Sherwood:

The consequence of these training and employee use practices is loss of synergy among the skilled elements of the work force. The newer employees are less likely to learn from the experienced senior technicians, as happens in Europe and the United States. By the same token, the older technicians do less learning from the younger engineers who, fresh from the universities, bring with them the latest advances. There is less opportunity to expand the knowledge base within the firm and the accumulation of tacit knowledge proceeds slowly. Team building is impeded and group approaches to problem solving suffer.

It is as though there is an invisible barrier to acceleration of technological advance within firms. Precisely as more Brazilian and Mexican firms verge on greater technological prowess, their need to safeguard the results of their work is greater. At the same time, in the absence of adequate safeguards, their capability to rapidly generate in-house technology is impeded because of their need to limit technical interchange within the work force. This is a silent or invisible barrier, yet one with profound consequences for the speed and quality of industrial development.

Sherwood concludes that without legal recognition of trade secret rights, the value of proprietary information as a tool for economic development is substantially diminished. He then observes that, for the rights granted by trade secret law, the administrative costs are not material:

Trade secret protection involves no specific public administration and therefore creates no burden on public revenue. No registry is required. No bureaucracy is created. Once the law creates the rights and duties of protection, vindication of those rights is attained, when necessary, in private litigation. If the country elects to provide criminal sanctions against offenders, then the costs associated with prosecution by the public prosecutor will be an incremental public expense. To the extent that private litigation is the primary means of protection, the costs of the system will be borne by private parties.

It seems that in terms of (1) the moderate level of rights granted the innovator, (2) the lever of riches consequent on the ability of others to reverse engineer after commercialization, and (3) the "bang for the buck" derived from low administrative costs, that trade secret protection is a sensible and desirable component of a progressive intellectual property regime.

In terms of public good, the principal regimes of intellectual property protection appear to work well. That should be no surprise, since—at least in the United States—we have had over two centuries to refine, adapt and evolve them, or to toss them out if they did not fairly allocate the nation's resources. As I write these words, though, I hear the reader murmuring, "Ah, yes, Doctor Pangloss, but if this is the best of all possible intellectual property worlds, then why is T. J. Rodgers' digestive system so upset?" Fair question. The answer is that the state of T. J.'s digestive system is a quantum effect. Whereas an assessment of public good requires a macroscopic, Newtonian perspective, an assessment of what is good for T. J. Rodgers requires a microscopic perspective, a view of things on a level at which uncertainty and irrationality are important determinants of behavior. To judge whether the effects of the intellectual property laws on an individual company are desirable or undesirable, we would have to know a great deal about what business that company is in and how it goes about the process of designing its products. Even if those effects were undesirable in a particular case, though, it would be an unwarranted leap of faith to project a larger undesirability on intellectual property laws in general. The combatants in the softwars will use whatever weapons society provides them. Better that they should be armed with weapons the use of which serves the public interest, rather than those which serve only the private interests of some of them.

We have completed our correspondence course. Let us now leave the economists to their analytic musings and return to the give and take of the battlefield. Destination: Oz.

# 10

# Antipodean Logic: *Autodesk v. Martin Dyason*

Before the whites came, Flynn went on, no one in Australia was landless, since everyone inherited, as his or her private property, a stretch of the Ancestor's song and the stretch of country over which the song passed. A man's verses were his title deeds to territory. He could lend them to others. He could borrow other verses in return. The one thing he couldn't do was sell or get rid of them.

Supposing the Elders of a Carpet Snake clan decided it was time to sing their song cycle from beginning to end? Messages would be sent out, up and down the track, summoning song-owners to assemble at the Big Place. One after another, each "owner" would then sing his stretch of the Ancestor's footprints. Always in the correct sequence!

"To sing a verse out of order," Flynn said somberly, "was a crime. Usually meant the death penalty."

"I can see that," I said. "It'd be the musical equivalent of an earthquake."

"Worse," he scowled. "It would be to un-create the Creation."
                                    —Bruce Chatwin, *The Songlines* (1987)

On the morning of March 13, 1990, Martin and Christine Dyason walked into the wood-paneled courtroom of the Federal Court of Appeal in Melbourne, Australia. Martin Dyason, of slightly less than average height but sturdily built, with a trim moustache and neatly combed, prematurely white hair, wore a dark suit, a white shirt, and a quiet tie. His wife, frizzy-haired, possessed of a certain unsophisticated charm, wore a peach-colored cotton jacket over a cream-yellow silk top. Her skirt was black. In a week, summer would be over. High on the walls to either side of the chamber, the hinged windows were open, and the seasonal songs of birds wafted in. The Dyasons, a modest, middle-class couple, were here to listen as their lawyers appealed the judgment of an Australian trail court the winter before, in which they were branded as copyright infringers.

They took seats in the second row of pew-like benches, facing the podium whereon the three-judge court would shortly alight. Next to them sat Peter Kelly. Tall, gray-haired and balding, Kelly was co-appellant and the man who had created the infringing product and convinced the Dyasons to sell it. In front of the three appellants sat their barristers, in black robes and powdered horsehair wigs: one a Queen's Counsel, or "silk," and the other his assistant, or "junior." Next to those two barristers sat two other matched pairs of silks and juniors; one pair for the appellee and one for IBM Australia, which was seeking leave to intervene as *amicus curiae*, "friend of the court." Facing each silk, and therefore with his or her back to the podium, sat an "instructing solicitor," ready to pass notes, whisper advice, or retrieve documents as circumstances might require. Behind the Dyasons, in last place as befit a nonparty, hoping for an opportunity to give the court some useful assistance on an appeal of considerable importance to the industry, sat representatives of IBM. It occurred to me more than once during the day's proceedings that those who wrongly accused IBM of favoring extremely strong copyright protection for computer programs would be quite nonplussed by the *amicus* arguments being put forward by IBM in this case.

The judicial triumvirate entered, also berobed and bewigged. The bailiff directed the multitudes to "be upstanding," and we were, the audience rising as one and nodding deferentially to the court. The court nodded back, distinctly less deferentially, and the audience resumed their seats. The argument on appeal of the first major copyright case to be decided under Australia's new software copyright law had begun. As we shall see, the case against the Dyasons and Kelly raised tricky and multifaceted questions about the nature both of computer programs and of the practice of "reverse engineering" computer programs, and thus finds its place well within the intellectual combat zone that we are traversing.

The plaintiffs in the case were Autodesk, Inc. and its Australian subsidiary. Autodesk is the developer of AutoCAD, a drafting program for personal computers. The Autodesk companies had sued Martin and Christine Dyason and Peter Kelly because the threesome had put on the market a device that completely unhorsed a clever system of copy protection that Autodesk had employed for its drafting program. Copy protection—or rather, the phenomenon giving rise to the need for copy protection, software piracy—is one of the matters uppermost in the minds of suppliers of programs for personal computers, as is evidenced by the forethought Autodesk had given it.

A customer licensing the AutoCAD program in Australia received, along with a copy of the program, a device called an "AutoCAD lock." The AutoCAD lock was quite literally a little black box. On one end was a plug and on the other, a socket. Those two terminators allowed the lock to be inserted between the user's personal computer and the cable leading to the computer's printer. Communications between the computer and the printer were completely unaffected by the intrusion, the lock's purpose being in no way connected with such communications. The lock's purpose, in fact, was nothing more than—to borrow a phrase from Peter Sellers' last movie—"being there." If it was there, AutoCAD worked. If it wasn't, it didn't.

The human mind is a devilishly clever thing, and no field of endeavor gives freer rein to its cleverness than does computer programming. The developers of AutoCAD had coded into that program a routine that periodically distracted the computer's attention from the task of processing the user's drafting project in order to make certain that the AutoCAD lock was still "being there." That routine, called "Widget C" by its authors, caused the processor to generate a binary number and to transmit that number to the AutoCAD lock. Inside the lock was a simple electronic circuit consisting of an input line, a clock, a shift register containing an initial number known also to the AutoCAD program, an exclusive-OR gate, and a single-bit output line. Each time an appropriate binary salutation was received on the input line, the following things happened inside the lock. The clock ticked one notch. The shift register shifted its contents one position to the left (thereby dropping the leading, or leftmost, bit). The exclusive-OR gate received as inputs the two new leading bits in the register and provided the register a new trailing bit resulting from the "exclusive-ORing" of the inputs. And finally, the output line received the new second bit from the register and sent it on to the computer's memory.

Meanwhile, back in the processor, Widget C had caused the computer to simulate the operation of the lock, and to derive its own value for the second bit in the lock's register. When that bit was received from the lock, the two values were compared, and if they were the same the processing of the user's drafting project resumed. The entire process having taken place at computational speeds, the user never noticed that his or her drafting project had been interrupted, or indeed that it would continue to be interrupted from time to time so long as AutoCAD was running.

Unless, of course, the AutoCAD lock were removed. In that case, the user would notice something quite significant: the drafting project would terminate. If the lock were absent when AutoCAD was booted up, the program would not run at all. Through that mechanism, Autodesk frustrated the illegal practice of licensing a single copy of its program and then replicating free copies for friends or colleagues.

Unfortunately, the human mind is a cleverly devilish thing, and no field of endeavor gives freer rein to the deviltry than does computer programming. In the field of computer programming, no activity evinces that deviltry more strikingly than the activity known as "hacking." Hackers are people who "hack around" with other people's programs, usually in order to see if they can cause those programs to do something other than what they were intended to do. Peter Kelly was a hacker. His introduction to AutoCAD came while he was engaged in an abortive attempt to become a retailer of computer hardware and software in the western suburbs of Melbourne. For reasons that might, in the first instance, have been described as curiosity, Kelly developed a particular interest in learning how AutoCAD worked. Profiting from his training as a radio technician in the Royal Air Force, he hooked up a dual-channel oscilloscope to watch and record the stimuli passing from the computer to the lock and the responses passing from the lock to the computer. After several weeks of drudgery, which only an *intensely* curious person would have endured, he had deduced what the appropriate stimuli were. This enabled him to write a program that generated only those stimuli, thereby greatly accelerating his detective work.

In short order, Kelly had reverse engineered the external functionality of the AutoCAD lock. From that point forward, his motivation could no longer be described simply as curiosity. His efforts now turned to the development of a device that could replace the AutoCAD lock. Kelly's design diverged from that of the original lock, in that it contained neither a shift register nor an exclusive-OR gate. Instead, Kelly employed a read-only memory into which he placed a look-up table containing binary sequences that, when triggered, produced the same outputs as the AutoCAD lock. The sequences in Kelly's look-up table, it turned out, were the same as those in a state table in the AutoCAD program, although Kelly had not looked at the code of the AutoCAD program (or, for that matter, at the interior of the AutoCAD lock). His reverse-engineering techniques were confined to stimulating the AutoCAD lock, observing the responses, and analyzing that data.

Once he had a prototype of a replacement lock in hand, Kelly sought out a patent attorney and obtained a letter opinion assuring him that the device he had developed could be marketed "without any real substantive fear of a patent or copyright action being taken against you successfully." Clearly, Kelly had by now crossed the boundary between intellectual curiosity and commercial opportunism.

The Kellys and the Dyasons had been friendly for some years. At dinner one night, the subject of Kelly's research was broached. Kelly proposed that the Dyasons market his replacement lock. At the time, the Dyasons were down on their luck, having sunk all their capital, including the equity in their home, into a venture that failed. Living like gypsies in a series of rented or borrowed quarters, running a very modest antiques business, with Christine holding down a temporary job and taking care of the kids, the Dyasons were attracted to the idea of a product that could be marketed from home with no capital investment and the prospect of high profit. Although Kelly told them about the favorable legal advice he had received, the group decided that Kelly's device, which they dubbed the "Auto-Key Hardware Lock," would be marketed in such a way as to conceal the identities of its producer and sales representatives. Advertisements would contain only phone numbers and post office box numbers. Surnames would not be used in phone conversations. Signatures would be altered. These and other precautions were taken in the expectation that, no matter what the solicitor's advice was, AutoDesk would react fairly negatively to the availability on the market of the Auto-Key.

There was ample reason to expect such a reaction. The price of the Auto-CAD program was $5,000, Australian. The price of Kelly's Auto-Key Hardware Lock was set at $499, which included a $100 selling commission for the Dyasons. For a tenth of the price of the AutoCAD program, therefore, a customer could acquire a gadget that would allow a bootlegged copy of AutoCAD to run normally on a personal computer. Peter Kelly may have viewed himself as the Robin Hood of the computer-aided design business, but he anticipated that Autodesk would be siding with the Sheriff of Nottingham.

In the event, it did not take long for Autodesk to notice the anonymous marketing campaign, to call the advertised phone number, in due course to find the Dyasons, and then to obtain a court order causing their home to be searched for Auto-Keys and related materials, requiring them to identify Mr. Kelly and restraining them from marketing the Auto-Key.

Autodesk's lawsuit may not have worried the defendants at first. After all, they had an opinion letter, and Autodesk's allegations seemed particularly flimsy. The plaintiffs claimed, for example, that the AutoCAD lock—a hardwired electronic circuit—was a computer program, and was part of the AutoCAD program. They also claimed that the Auto-Key lock—developed without even looking at the code of the AutoCAD program—was a copy of part of that program. The lawsuit was exactly the kind of harassment they had been trying to avoid by their no-profile marketing approach, but given the far-fetched nature of the claims, the whole affair might blow over in short order. Obviously, the defendants' presence in the Court of Appeal in March 1990 indicates that matters did not unfold so felicitously; but before we review the outcome of the trial, let us examine Peter Kelly's reverse-engineering efforts in a little more detail.

The two arguments just mentioned, that is, that hardware can be software and that one can copy without peeking, were central to the case of *Autodesk v. Dyason*. At the heart of those arguments lies the central question in software protection today and for the foreseeable future: to what extent is a second comer free to appropriate elements of an original computer program. The first of the arguments is that a computer program may be embodied in a "hard-wired" electronic circuit. (Before the age of integrated circuits, "hard wiring" referred to the act of soldering transistors, capacitors, resistors, and wires together to create electronic circuits that performed a particular function. Today, hard wiring refers to the creation of electronic circuits by whatever means, and connotes the materiality and immutability of such circuits once created.) It is, at first blush, preposterous to suggest that a hardware device can be a computer program. A computer program is a set of instructions, a text. With what struck me, at least, as flawless and ineluctable logic, I described in Chapter 1 the similarities between computer programs and such works as novels, philosophical tracts, musical scores, and other works of authorship. One cannot reasonably consider replacing Sterne's *The Life and Opinions of Tristram Shandy, Gentleman* or Kierkegaard's *Fear and Trembling* or Bartok's String Quartet No. 3 with silicon logic chips. And, indeed, one cannot reasonably consider replacing IBM's MVS operating system or Microsoft's Excel spreadsheet program or Aldus' Pagemaker desktop publishing program with silicon logic circuits, either.

The reason that replacing such works of authorship with silicon cannot be considered, however, is not because it can't be done. It is possible to "hard wire" *Tristram Shandy* and Excel. It makes no sense to do so, though, for two reasons: cost and loss of flexibility. The cost of the enormous number of circuit elements required to hard wire a large, complex text—whether a work of fiction or a work of programming—is vastly higher than the cost of delivering the same text on storage media such as paper, magnetic tape, or magnetic diskette. More importantly, it is axiomatic that, just as a leopard cannot change its spots, a hard-wired circuit cannot change its function. The market for computers the only function of which is to print out *Tristram Shandy* or computers the only function of which is to calculate Excel spreadsheets, is exceedingly thin; so thin as to be commercially uninteresting. The genius of the computer is its ability to change function simply by changing the contents of its memory: to play an excerpt from Bartok's String Quartet No. 3 one minute, retrieve a quote from *Fear and Trembling* the next, and set up a brochure using Pagemaker the next. Escaping the constraints of hard wiring through the use of the stored program is the *sine qua non* of computer science and the computer industry.

At the same time, it must be recognized that there is an undeniable union between software and hardware. For example, in the mid-1960s, IBM introduced a family of computers called "System/360." The success of System/360 changed the course of the computer industry, but that is a story to be read elsewhere. What is pertinent here about System/360 is that the processors in the System/360 family, which ranged from very small mainframes to supercomputers, offered the same instruction set (the set of commands that the computer's processor can execute), so that programs written to run on the smallest machine would also run on the largest. That compatibility represented a novel and for its time daring product strategy, and it was achieved by interchanging hardware and software. In the larger System/ 360 models, the entire instruction set was hard wired: commands issued by the operating system or by application programs were acted on directly by the circuitry of the processors. In the smaller models, part of the instruction set was "microcoded" rather than hard wired. Microcode in these lesser processors translated the non-hard-wired commands issued by the operating systems or application programs into combinations of instructions that were in fact hard wired. The use of microcode to intermediate between programs on the one hand and hardware circuitry on the other predated System/360, but achieved spectacular success in that family, and has been in common use ever since.

Generally speaking, any function that can be hard wired can also be programmed, and computer designers are constantly making trade-offs between hardware and software implementations. Hard wiring assures speed of execution, but increases cost, size, and weight. Software implementations tend to be slower, cheaper, and easier to fix or to upgrade. Does this substitutability of hardware for software suggest that hardware should be protectable by copyright? Not really. The reader who has traveled abroad has no doubt viewed those supposedly helpful little films shown aboard commercial aircraft just before landing to familiarize passengers with the immigration, baggage retrieval, customs, and ground transportation procedures they are about to encounter. Those films, lacking though they may be in aesthetic appeal, are protected by copyright. As is the case with computer programs, the function of the films can also be performed by hardware. A series of hallways in the airport that channel arriving passengers inexorably from passport control to baggage claim to customs to ground transportation would be much more efficient than educational films, though much more costly and inflexible. The fact that hallways can substitute for movies, however, does not compel the conclusion that hallways are protected by copyright. Similarly, in a high-school shop class, an illustrated text explaining the design of a carburetor is a substitute for giving each student a carburetor to tinker with, but the fact that the text is a copyright-protected literary work does not mean that the carburetor is also a copyright-protected literary work.

Under what circumstances, if any, the reader may wonder, may an electronic device be considered a computer program protected by copyright? I would suggest that the question should not be framed that way. A computer program is a set of instructions. A set of instructions may be stored in any of several forms of media. Among those media are computer chips consisting of electronic circuits. When a computer chip stores a program, the program—not the chip—is protected. Chips that store programs and chips that substitute for programs are as different from one another as potato chips and buffalo chips. A storage chip is a repository, from which the text of a program issues in bursts to cause the logic circuitry of a processor to produce a desired result. The logic circuitry itself is also a chip, or a set of chips. It performs only the function inherent in its design. It does not consist of text or contain text. It is not a literary work.

In the *Autodesk* case, however, the trial judge (Northrop, J.) decided otherwise. He had no precedent to guide him, this being the first case of its kind to be decided under the 1984 amendments to the Australian copyright law, which extended clear and explicit protection to software. In particular, there was no prior interpretation of the term "computer program." Very much like the American statute, the Australian law defined "computer program" as "an expression, in a language, code or notation, of a set of instructions... intended... to cause a device having digital processing capabilities to perform a particular function." In trying to decide whether the law was meant to protect the AutoCAD lock, Judge Northrop could do nothing but parse the language of the statute. Mindful, no doubt, that that statute had been passed specifically to overturn a High Court ruling interpreting the prior copyright law as not protecting object code (the only significant defeat in Apple Computer Company's global legal offensive to protect the operating system of the Apple II), Judge Northrop decided to give the new statute a "wide construction." Working backward, the judge first found that the AutoCAD lock was clearly "a device having digital information processing capabilities," and that it was clearly devised to "perform a particular function." Further, he said, there was no disputing that the contents of the lock's shift register comprised a "language, code or notation." The difficult question, and the one about which the plaintiffs and defendants disagreed most vigorously, was whether the lock contained or constituted a "set of instructions." The defendants argued that the AutoCAD lock did not fetch, store, interpret, or execute instructions, but instead responded slavishly as dictated by its invariant circuitry to inputs received from the computer. Moreover, they argued, the "set of instructions" and the "device" referred to in the statute were intended to be separate entities, and even if the AutoCAD lock contained or comprised a "set of instructions," those instructions were not separate from the "device."

These arguments did not strike a responsive chord in Judge Northrop. In his view, the term "device" could reasonably be construed to mean the AutoCAD lock, and indeed the Auto-Key lock as well. One cannot really quarrel with the jurist's conclusion that each of these black boxes constituted a "device having digital information processing capabilities," and each was designed "to perform a particular function." However, the process of atomizing the statutory language and interpreting its individual elements on which he had embarked runs the risk that the decision maker will miss the forest for the trees, ending up with a Ptolemaic result—logical, but unrealistic. And indeed, the further into this thicket that Judge Northrop strayed, the more darkly obscure his opinion became. Using his *Oxford English Dictionary* (2d edition) as though it were a Baedeker to this un-

:harted territory, the judge found the following dictionary definitions il-
luminating:

*Instruction*: "Computers. An expression in a program or routine, or a sequence of
characters in a machine language, which specifies an operation (especially a basic
operation) and frequency also of one or more operands, and results in its performance by the computer."

*Code*: "Cybernetics. Any system of symbols and rules for expressing information or
instructions in a form usable by a computer or other machine for processing or
transmitting information."

*Notation*: "The process or method of representing numbers, quantities, etcetera by
a set or system of signs; hence, any set of symbols or characters used to denote
things or relations in order to facilitate the recording or considering of them."

*Expression*: "Manifestation."

Although they add little to the statutory language, those definitions
seemed to help the jurist to back his way through the underbrush. Based
on them, he held that AutoCAD was a computer program. (*A no-brainer.*)
He held that Widget C was a computer program. (*OK.*) He held that there
may be subsets of instructions within Widget C, themselves computer programs. (*Well, yes, but how far...* ) He held that, as Widget C transmits a
challenge to the AutoCAD lock, and the lock receives, processes, and re-
sponds to that challenge, the subset of instructions in the lock can be seen
to constitute the expression of a set of instructions. (*Whoa, there's a logical
leap here that we need to focus on.*) He held that as ROMs, EPROMS, and
disks are kinds of hardware on which computer programs were encoded,
there is no obstacle to finding electronic circuitry to be an encoding mechanism for computer programs. (*Wait! You see, Your Honor, the program
is read out of the EPROM for execution by the electronic circuitry...* ) As
a result, Judge Northrop ruled, the AutoCAD lock was a computer program.
(*Oh, dear.*)

Oh, dear. The holding of the trial court in *Autodesk* seems to have been
reached without regard to the consequences that it could have beyond the
resolution of the dispute between Autodesk and the defendants. Certainly,
some remedy seemed desirable for defendants' destruction of Autodesks's
copy-protection mechanism, but holding that electronic circuitry is protectable as a literary work was an unfortunate way to accomplish that end.
All computer circuitry has attributes found in the AutoCAD lock: registers
for storage of data or instructions, logic circuitry, clocks or interval timers,
input and output lines. There is thus no inhibition, under the rule in the
*Autodesk* trial court opinion, against finding all types of computer processors
protected as literary works. For that matter, certain circuitry inside CD
players, digital thermometers, ABS braking systems, and other devices having

digital information processing capabilities would be protectable literary works as well.

Computer programs are literary works: they are authorial intellectual property, the value of which normally exceeds the cost of reproduction by one or more orders of magnitude. Copyright is a natural mode of protection for such works. The first copyright laws were enacted in response to the invention of the printing press, the principal benefit of which invention was to precipitously reduce the ratio of the cost of reproduction of literary works to the value of those works. Electronic circuitry is not written down. It is constructed of physical elements. The value of the circuitry normally exceeds the cost of reproduction, but not by an order of magnitude. One who wishes to clone an electronic device must have a factory, must buy raw materials or parts, must have mastered the necessary and usually complex manufacturing processes. Copyright is neither a natural nor a necessary mode of legal protection for such devices. Unpredictable and undesirable shifts in the law can occur when legal norms invade alien territory.

For example, how does one infringe a copyright in a hardware device? According to Judge Northrop, by studying the function of the device and reproducing that function. He accepted that Peter Kelly had not actually seen Widget C, nor had he seen the internal circuitry of the AutoCAD lock. The sorts of study and analysis described as having been undertaken by Kelly did not in fact involve dismantling the AutoCAD lock, nor did they entail the production of an interim infringing work. (There are other sorts of study and analysis—of which reverse compilation is one—that do entail the production of an interim infringing work, since they consist of translating the ones and zeros of a program available only in machine language into a higher-level language more like that of the original source code. Kelly did not engage in reverse compilation.) The "black box" activities that Kelly undertook in order to decipher the AutoCAD lock's protocols are commonplace in the industry, and are useful as a form of competitive analysis. They result in a specification of the output that a device produces in response to particular inputs. In the case of a complex program, a complete listing of inputs and outputs in all their forms (e.g., communications protocols, displays on a computer screen, printout formats) certainly could be an interim infringing work, but the inputs to and outputs from the AutoCAD lock, because of their simplistic and mechanistic nature, did not in themselves constitute a protected work of authorship. (In Chapter 17, we will encounter protocols sufficiently complex to warrant copyright protection.)

The reverse engineering in which Kelly had engaged was designed simply to deduce the precise external functioning of the AutoCAD lock, and resulted in the creation of a device that exactly reproduced that function. In the judge's view, that reverse engineering was a *use* of Autodesk's work by which *reproduction* of that work, in the copyright sense, was achieved. Identity of function was sufficient similarity to constitute reproduction, according to Judge Northrop. Therein lies a further problem with the *Autodesk* opinion.

Protection of function is the province of patent law, not copyright law. That is as it should be, since in order to be patentable, a device must possess a degree of novelty and nonobviousness. Most electronic circuitry does not possess those characteristics, so that the functions of most electronic circuitry can be duplicated in competitive devices, provided that the competitor is willing to make the investment in plant, equipment, and time. The protection of function only when it is novel and nonobvious—which is what the patent law requires—is consistent with the fact that protection of function is a very broad sort of protection. It is also consistent with the fact that the patent grant is a strong grant of exclusive rights, protecting the right holder even against independent creation of the same invention. Copyright, on the other hand, has no requirement of novelty or nonobviousness. (Except, as we saw, in connection with the *Lotus* case, in the sense that an obvious way of expressing something may not be protected.) Any work that originates with the author, as opposed to being copied from somewhere else, qualifies for protection. A larger number of works by far is therefore eligible for copyright protection than is eligible for patent protection. That is consistent with the fact that copyright is a weaker form of protection than patent, since it does not preclude independent creation and also does not protect the higher levels of abstraction in a work such as function.

As we saw in Chapter 2, the seminal American case on protection of higher levels of abstraction is *Whelan v. Jaslow*. In that case, the court held that copyright protects the detailed design of a computer program, but not its function. While the question has not been addressed as directly in other countries, it is a general tenet of copyright the world over that ideas and principles are not protected. The function of a copyrighted work, being an abstraction at a high level from the implementation that constitutes the work, is generally viewed as part of the ideas and principles of the work. The lower court's decision in *Autodesk* in that sense stands outside the mainstream of international copyright philosophy.

There is a way of reading Judge Northrop's opinion, though, that redeems it from the netherworld of copyright aberrations. At a certain point in his opinion, the jurist writes that the information sent to the AutoCAD lock by the computer, and the responses sent to the computer by the lock, are instructions. While I disagree with that factual conclusion, since the signals sent from the computer were pseudo-random numbers and the responses sent by the lock did not differ (so long as the lock was in place) from the predicted responses computed by Widget C, let us assume that Northrop, J., had correctly concluded that the communications between the computer and the lock constituted instructions. If that were so, then Kelly's oscilloscopic investigation certainly gave him access to those instructions, and his Auto-Key lock clearly reproduced bit for bit the "instructions" sent by the

AutoCAD lock. Under any reading of the copyright law, the literal duplication of a set of instructions is infringement, so long as what is duplicated is a quantitatively or qualitatively substantial portion of the target work. Though the "instructions" sent by the lock were not quantitatively substantial, they were unquestionably qualitatively substantial, since AutoCAD would simply not operate without receiving them. Accordingly, on this view, finding the defendants liable for copyright infringement would be a simple and straightforward application of traditional copyright principles. Although the factual error made by the judge in concluding that the stimuli and responses were instructions disqualified his opinion from complete redemption, the notion that the infringement consisted of copying instructions being sent back and forth through the serial port and not copying the device itself at least consigned it to a purgatory from which the Federal Court of Appeal might save it.

The Federal Court rendered its judgment on September 14, 1990. Each of the three judges who had heard the appeal gave a different reason for reaching their common result: the vacating of Judge Northrop's injunction and the vindication of the Dyasons and Kelly. Mr. Justice Lockhart felt that Kelly had copied only the function of the AutoCAD lock and WIDGET C, not their expression. Mr. Justice Sheppard concluded that Autodesk had in fact authorized users to make copies of AutoCAD on floppy disk and on hard disk. Nothing in Autodesk's contracts prohibited a user from running such copies on personal computers not fitted with the AutoCAD lock, and although users who ran multiple copies of AutoCAD at the same time would be breaching their contracts with Autodesk, that issue—whether the defendants had induced users to breach those contracts—had not been presented on appeal. Mr. Justice Beaumont decided that Kelly had not produced a version of WIDGET C, which was the only computer program he felt to be at issue, the AutoCAD lock neither being nor containing a program. Autodesk was ordered to pay the defendants' cost of appealing. Not content to leave matters there, Autodesk appealed to the Australia's highest court.

The High Court disagreed with the Federal Court, and ruled that the Auto-Key was a copyright infringement. The High Court did not adopt Judge Northrop's reasoning; indeed, the justices felt that there was "some confusion in the reasoning employed by Northrop J." In rejecting Judge Northrop's reasoning that the copying of function could constitute copyright infringement, the High Court cited two leading American cases: *Whelan v. Jaslow* and *Baker v. Selden*. The court's conclusion that infringement had occurred focused on the one element on WIDGET C that was clearly copied by Kelly: the look-up table containing the sequence of bits that Widget C caused the computer to compare to the message received from the AutoCAD lock. Kelly copied that table indirectly, the court said, by copying the message sent by the AutoCad lock. Although the table was not in itself a "set of instructions," it was certainly a substantial part of Widget C. In addition to its protectability as part of WIDGET C, the look-up table was independently protectable as a compilation. The High Court's approach to the case had the merit of returning the inquiry to the mainstream of copyright infringement law. No new rule was created, and the analysis was simple and straightforward. Although it is not clear that the High Court considered carefully enough the nature of the look-up table—in particular whether its contents were a permanent aspect of WIDGET C or only a transient aspect— the ultimate resolution of the *Autodesk* case drew on long-standing tradition in order to protect the innovator's rights.

For the sake of completeness, and to illustrate that major software suppliers favor balanced copyright protection, neither extremely strong nor extremely weak, I should briefly mention the two *amicus curiae* arguments of IBM Australia in the Federal Court of Appeal. One argument went to explaining the adverse consequences to the industry of a holding that a work that copies only the function of another work can be held to have infringed the copyright in the original work. The next argument suggested that the court decide the appeal in a fashion that would confine the result to the peculiar facts of the case, rather than using the *Autodesk* case as a platform from which to pronounce sweeping principles as to whether hardware devices can constitute computer programs. There was some feeling as we entered the courtroom on that March day that the appeals court was more likely to affirm Judge Northrop's decision than to reverse it, and IBM hoped to convince the appellate judges, in that event, not to make the case a major precedent. Autodesk, of course, vigorously opposed IBM's appearance. After listening to the reasons why IBM wished to be heard, listening to Autodesk's objections to that appearance and reading IBM's submissions (solely, the court emphasized, for purposes of deciding whether to grant IBM's request to appear), the court rejected IBM's application. Frustrated, I went off with my wife to Heron Island on the Great Barrier Reef where, due to prolonged high winds, the water was unusually murky. In the event, though, the murkiness on the legal front dissipated. The High Court issued a ruling that in fact satisfied both of the concerns that IBM had expressed in the intermediate court.

# 11

## The Sun Also Rises: *Microsoft Corp. v. Shuuwa System Trading K.K.*

I scored the next great triumph for science myself: to wit, how the milk gets into the cow.... One night as I lay musing, and looking at the stars, a grand idea flashed through my head, and I saw my way!...

The moment the first pale streak of dawn appeared I flitted stealthily away; and deep in the woods I chose a grassy spot and wattled it in, making a secure pen; then I enclosed a cow in it. I milked her dry, then left her there, a prisoner. There was nothing there to drink—she must get milk by her secret alchemy or stay dry....

Toward sunset...I stole away to my cow.... Two gallons. Two gallons, and nothing to make it out of. I knew at once the explanation: the milk was not taken in by the mouth, it was condensed from the atmosphere through the cow's hair. I ran and told Adam, and his happiness was as great as mine, and his pride in me inexpressible.
      —Mark Twain, *Extract from Eve's Autobiography* (1904)

Was Eve the first reverse engineer? Her procedures had much in common with those of modern day reverse engineers. Notice her establishment of a secure facility in order to isolate her subject from outside influences. (Notice, too, the imperfect nature of that isolation, which is also a problem with the clean rooms of today.) See, too, how she sets the parameters of her experiment so as to preclude any change in the subject except the change as to which she is interested in determining the cause. Milking the cow and depriving her of water is similar to Peter Kelly's writing a program to exercise the AutoCAD lock. Finally, observe the grossly erroneous assumption to which she leaps on the basis of her initial observations. That is a typical risk of the reverse engineer. The question, "Have I got it right," is always uppermost when one is attempting to reproduce what was first done by another without knowing at the outset how it was done. The uncertainty about getting it right has in case after case led reverse engineers to stray into shady practices in order to verify their hypotheses; practices such as hiring away employees of the supplier of the target product in order to learn that supplier's trade secrets or, in the case of software, obtaining illicit copies of the target program. If she had wanted to be sure of her conclusion, Eve would have returned the cow to its pen—shorn of all its hair—for a series of more refined experiments to test her hypothesis. Instead, the Bible tells us, she succumbed to temptation and took a short cut by tasting the fruit of the Tree of Knowledge.

The Japanese have been reverse engineering Western technology for several centuries. *Sayonara Michelangelo* describes the birth of this tradition:

In 1543 a storm careering through the China Sea blew a Portuguese vessel bound north for Macao eastward instead, to a small island called Tanegashima off the southern tip of a landmass known as Kyushu. The Portuguese wanderers were well received by the locals, who saw the storm that brought these impressively large foreigners to their shores as a divine wind, or, in their own language, a *kamikaze*. The islanders were particularly excited by the firearms that the Portuguese adventurers carried with them. These were christened *tanegashima teppo*—"iron rods". It was not long before the locals began to manufacture the miraculous iron rods for themselves. The Japanese economic miracle had begun.

Conventional wisdom attributes the perpetuation of that miracle to the carefully orchestrated behavior of major industrial organizations and government agencies in Japan aimed at turning reverse-engineered technologies into superior products. Professor Robert Sobol has described the conventional view as a four-phase process, which he says is now underway in the computer industry. The strategy, as sketched by Sobol, sounds more inexorable than it is in fact:

First of all, the Japanese come to the United States to study techniques, make contacts, become aware of marketing problems, and uncover weaknesses. The second stage is marked by a return home to train workforces in the foreign ways, all the while adapting native Japanese practices to the new technologies and techniques and simultaneously entering into licensing agreements with the Americans.... Occasionally, the Japanese firms will imitate without agreements, or—in the view of the Americans—violate patents.

It is during this phase, Sobol believes, that the Japanese implement tariff and quota barriers to trade. If geopolitical considerations prevent the erection of such formal barriers, Sobol finds that the Japanese create informal barriers to the import of foreign goods. Then,

[d]uring the third phase, the Japanese unite, usually behind their Ministry of International Trade and Industry, and with that agency's assistance, make the initial foray into the American markets. They do so with superior goods priced as low as possible without incurring the wrath of the American companies or being charged with dumping. In addition, the Japanese establish superior sales and service networks and employ large-scale American-style advertising.

In the third phase, too, Sobol claims, the Japanese suppliers sell exported goods at low prices that are subsidized by higher prices maintained on the same goods sold in Japan.

The goal, of course, is market share. And when this is achieved, the Japanese businesses enter the fourth phase, that of upgrading and turning out new models while increasing prices, so that what in the beginning was a high quality, low priced unit is replaced by one that is upgraded but much higher priced.

Sobol concludes that the four-phase process used successfully by Japanese suppliers of automobiles, consumer electronics, and steel might not work as well in high-technology industries. He gives two views of that subject:

Ernest von Simpson of the Research Board put it this way when comparing the computer experience with that in automobiles: "I don't think the Japanese are in the same game this time. The computer industry is much less monolithic, because it's all those guys in the garages that push the industry." Professor Tohru Moto-oka of Tokyo University believes otherwise. "In the United States individuals are very strong, but some new scientific fields have become very complex. To create new breakthroughs, the cooperation of a group is needed. One person alone cannot change these fields very much anymore."

The first real Japanese industrial policy directed at the computer industry was indeed based largely on reverse engineering. In a strategy closely coordinated by the government's Ministry of International Trade and Industry (MITI), the major Nipponese electronics firms were assigned American targets in the early 1970s, and thereafter pursued those targets with a single-mindedness and enthusiasm that virtually guaranteed success. Through MITI, the Japanese government provided half of the R&D cost of research associations established by industry. The earliest of these (1972–76), the Technology Research Association of Advanced Computer Series, was aimed at developing mainframe processors. The work was divided among Fujitsu, Hitachi, Mitsubishi, OKI, NEC, and Toshiba, the six firms being subdivided into three groups with different missions. Hitachi and Fujitsu were given the biggest challenge: to develop and market replacements for the IBM mainframe processors and associated software that had achieved the greatest success in the Japanese market. In pursuit of that goal, and in pursuit of the business strategies that followed, the Japanese companies adopted numerous reverse-engineering techniques, some of which involved not the application of intellect but the application of industrial espionage.

The second research association, the VLSI Research Association (1976–79), laid the foundation for the phenomenal success of the Japanese suppliers in developing and producing integrated circuits. The third, the Computer Basic Technology Research Association (1979–83), concentrated on software and peripheral equipment. The focus on software arose because of MITI's recognition that software had become the most critical component of computer systems, and that there was a need to raise the level of Japanese software technology. A group including Fujitsu, Hitachi, NEC, Mitsubishi, and Toshiba was established to develop new operating systems. Fujitsu and Hitachi developed clone software for IBM mainframe systems environments using methods that were ultimately challenged by IBM. Since those challenges, Hitachi has kept a low profile in the softwars, preferring to concentrate on product development and strategic alliances and to leave the legal debates to others. The Hitachi shibboleth today is not "IBM compatibility," but "IBM culture": IBM's customers will feel "comfortable" in a Hitachi mainframe environment, though their programs may not necessarily run without modification. Hitachi's major thrust into non-Japanese markets began in 1989 with the acquisition of 80 percent of NAS, the American supplier of IBM-compatible mainframes, which may give Hitachi a ready platform for its "IBM-culture" software. While recognized as significant by the industry, the acquisition raised little controversy in the United States.

Fujitsu has taken a different course. It has vigorously contested IBM's legal challenge, and loudly proclaimed its commitment to IBM compatibility. (Indeed, from the outset, Fujitsu offered a greater degree of IBM compatibility—particularly software compatibility—than Hitachi, and its business strategy was focused on replacement of IBM systems, whereas Hitachi's business strategy was aimed at upgrading customers for earlier Hitachi systems.) Its representatives have been very visible at software law seminars around the world. In the European copyright debate, the eurocrats saw far more of Fujitsu's lobbyists than of the lobbyists for other computer firms. In 1990, Fujitsu acquired the British computer manufacturer ICL, a move that generated extensive controversy in the U.K. and in Europe, since it represented the manifest triumph of Japanese industrial policy over European industrial policy. (As the U.S. government does not have official industrial policies, Americans are not as conscious of the ebbs and flows of international competition, but in countries where the government has established stated industrial goals, the public failure to achieve those goals does not go unnoticed.) Whether Fujitsu's more assertive public posture and Hitachi's more passive public posture have been part of a MITI-coordinated "bad cop, good cop" strategy or is simply a reflection of corporate attitude is not clear. At the heart of Fujitsu's campaign, though, is the principle that all types of "reverse engineering" of software, including reverse compilation, should be permitted.

In support of its position on reverse compilation, Fujitsu argued that Japanese law does not prohibit reverse compilation. The status of reverse compilation under Japanese law was of considerable importance to the Europeans, as they wanted to assure that the EC copyright directive was reasonably aligned with American and Japanese software copyright protection. Had they looked into the question of reverse compilation in Japan independently of what they were being told by Fujitsu, the eurocrats would have discovered the case of *Microsoft v. Shuuwa Trading*, a case that represented a major setback for the antiprotectionist forces.

In 1979, the Nihon Electric Company (NEC) engaged Microsoft Corporation, then a very small software developer in the state of Washington concentrating on systems software for the emerging new market of personal computers, to write a BASIC interpreter for the NEC PC–8001. (A BASIC interpreter is a program that translates instructions written in the BASIC language into machine language instructions, which are executed as each instruction is translated.) The NEC machine was based on the Zilog Z–80 microprocessor, and the interpreter was written in Z–80 assembler language. The work of writing the interpreter consumed about eight months' time, at the end of which Microsoft delivered the program to NEC in Japan stored on floppy disks. NEC reproduced the interpreter on read-only memory chips (ROMs) and incorporated the chips into the PC–8001. When running, the interpreter caused the phrase, "Copyright 1979 © by Microsoft" to appear on the computer's screen.

Shuuwa System Trading K.K. was a company in the business of marketing published materials relating to computers. Deciding that there was a market for a source code listing of the BASIC interpreter used on the PC–8001, and apparently in utter disregard of Microsoft's intellectual property rights, Shuuwa decided to prepare and market such a listing. Pursuant to that decision, Shuuwa took four steps. First, it translated the binary object code of two existing versions of the BASIC assembler contained in the PC–8001 into hexadecimal form, which Microsoft claimed was an infringement of its copyright. Then it reverse assembled the hexadecimal listings and interpreted them, an act that Microsoft claimed was also copyright infringement. Next, it engaged a printing company, Tokyo Sugaki Printing K.K.—also named a defendant—to create copies of the reverse-assembled listing in the form of a book entitled *PC–8001 Basic Source Program Listings: The Whole Analysis of Ver. 1.0 and 1.1*. Finally, Shuuwa itself distributed copies of the book. The latter two steps were obviously also claimed to be copyright infringement.

Although the reverse assembly undertaken by Shuuwa was not performed for purposes of creating a "compatible" program, it was undertaken for purposes of commercial gain, and of course provided a useful tool for others who wished to create such a program. Microsoft sued in Tokyo District Court. The suit was filed before the Japanese copyright law was amended to state unequivocally that computer programs were protected subject matter. Shuuwa argued that the BASIC interpreter was an operating system, not an application program, and therefore could not be regarded as the creative expression of thoughts and emotions, the principal criterion for protection under Japanese law. Operating systems, Shuuwa argued, have the purpose of managing data efficiently and quickly, and therefore are products of logic, not thought or emotion. Further, Shuuwa argued, the published source listings were the results of its study of the Microsoft interpreter, and were independent creative works, not reproductions of the Microsoft programs. In this regard, I should remind the reader that reverse assembly cannot precisely reproduce the original source code, any more than a retranslation into French of an English translation from the original French of *Le Tentation de Saint Antoine* will reproduce Flaubert's original text. In the case of Microsoft BASIC, Shuuwa's translation of the object code from the NEC chip contained a different scheme of naming and labeling of program elements, made up by Shuuwa because Microsoft's original names and labels were "lost in the translation" from the original Microsoft source code into object code. Shuuwa's translation also contained comments inserted by Shuuwa's staff that were not a part of the original Microsoft program. Comments, too, are among the items normally "lost in the translation" from source code to object code. Thus, for example, the line "JP L003B" in the reverse-assembled Microsoft source code is rendered as "JP WAMCHK; CHECK COLD START OR WARM START" in the Shuuwa book. The label "WAMCHK" is simply a mnemonic for the routine that begins at memory location "003B", and the phrase following the semicolon is a comment describing the purpose of the "JP", or jump (branch) to that location.

Shuuwa also argued that in order effectively to use the NEC personal computer, users had to understand the substance of its operating system, and that since neither NEC nor Microsoft had made that information available to users, Shuuwa's act was a great benefit to the 200,000 users of PC–8001s and was therefore appropriate behavior. That argument echoes the assertions made in Fujitsu's Eurobit papers to the effect that it is not unlawful to study a copyrighted work, and therefore it should not be unlawful to translate the work into a language that is easier for a competitor to study.

The case was heard in the Tokyo District Court, Twenty-ninth Civil Division, Chief Judge Shin Motoki presiding, with the able assistance of judges Toshiaki Iimura and Eiji Tomioka. Before we assess the outcome, let's look briefly at the role of the judiciary in Japanese society, because that role will tell us a good deal about the importance of the *Microsoft* case.

Under the Japanese constitution, the judiciary is an independent branch of government, much as it is under American law. Litigation, however, has traditionally been frowned on in Japan as a way of resolving disputes. Although many Japanese collegiates take degrees in law, and there is a special course of study in college for those who wish to become judges, most law students do not become practicing lawyers and only a small number of judicial administration graduates are produced each year. The amount of litigation that takes place in Japan is proportionately far less than (perhaps a twentieth, per capita, of) the amount of litigation that occurs in the United States. Is the predisposition against litigation a cause of the lack of practicing lawyers, or is it an effect? The reader has no doubt heard the old story about the small-town lawyer whose practice languished until a second lawyer moved into town. In his excellent—though in Japan highly controversial—study of the Japanese political system, *The Enigma of Japanese Power*, Dutch journalist Karel van Wolferen suggests that the lack of litigation is due not to the paucity of lawyers and judges, but to very deep institutional and psychological factors in Japanese society, stemming from the reign of the Tokugawa *shoguns*, during which period citizens were forced to settle their disputes by conciliation rather than litigation.

The Tokugawa dynasty established the first national government in Japan in the seventeenth century, subjugating the feudal lords, or *daimyo*, closing Japan to foreigners and foreign influences, and establishing (through the use of considerable force at times) a period of domestic peace, prosperity and cultural outpouring that lasted for two centuries. In this environment of enforced tranquility, litigation—a process that produced winners and losers—was destructive of *wa*, or civil harmony, and, according to van Wolferen, was suppressed. In the post-Tokugawa period, he suggests, the number of lawyers and judges has been kept artificially low in order to prevent an independent judiciary from undermining the other institutions of government and the status quo generally. The conservatism of the judiciary and the subjugation of the bar has been assured by (1) careful filtration during the centrally controlled education process (only 2 percent of the applicants to the Legal Training and Research Institute, through which all judges and lawyers must pass, are admitted); (2) the selection process (the Japanese population has tripled since 1890, but the number of judges has not even doubled); (3) a strong centrally controlled court administrative structure (so strong, indeed, that the Japanese Supreme Court sometimes instructs the lower courts in advance as to the types of decisions it expects them to make); and (4) the reappointment process (Japanese judges are not appointed for life, as are American federal judges). As a result, judicial decisions tend to follow the policies of the bureaucracy. Although van Wolferen's analysis tends to simplify a very complex subject, there is no question that the number of judges in Japan is too low to process on an expeditious basis the number of disputes that arise in that country, and that the makeup of the judiciary is less politically heterogeneous than has historically been the case in common-law countries. With that perspective in mind, we can return to the Tokyo District Court, Twenty-ninth Civil Division.

The three-judge court listened to a good deal of technical evidence about the logic, structure, and flow of the Microsoft BASIC interpreter, and indeed included a great deal of that evidence in their opinion. Like American and Canadian courts that have dealt with evidence as to the nature of computer programs, Judge Motoki and his colleagues concluded that generally it is possible to choose among a variety of solutions to accomplish a particular programming function. In the case of a BASIC interpreter, they decided, none of the solutions chosen by Microsoft was the only way to accomplish the interpreter's purpose. The routines written by Microsoft's programmers reflected the authors' personalities and thought processes, and the court found that there was value in encouraging that individuality of expression. It concluded as well that there was no difference in that regard between a game program, an application program, or an operating system. In these conclusions, the Tokyo court aligned itself, without saying so and undoubtedly without specifically intended to, with the major American legal opinion on copyright protection for operating systems, *Apple v. Franklin*.

The court found that the writer of an operating system exercises originality and ingenuity in creating the overall structure of the program, the structure of the individual routines that comprise the program, the selection and organization of subroutines, and the collection of individual commands and data that are composed in order fully to utilize the capabilities of the hardware architecture that the operating system is intended to exploit. In finding that creativity exists in the nonliteral elements of computer programs, the court was (again, probably without specifically intending to do so) aligning itself with the principal American case on protection of nonliteral expressive elements in software, *Whelan v. Jaslow*.

I put forward the foregoing observations on the commonality between the views of judges Motoki, Iimura, and Tomioka and the views of the *Apple* and *Whelan* courts in order to draw the reader's attention to the characteristics of international predictability that inhere in copyright protection. Given similar sets of facts, one can usually anticipate the result that will be reached, because copyright law is based on a similar, well-known set of principles throughout the developed world.

Having concluded, even absent a specific enabling provision in Japanese copyright law, that Microsoft's BASIC interpreter was protected, the court turned to the question whether the defendants activities infringed Microsoft's copyright. Considering first the translation from the binary object code in the NEC chip to a hexadecimal listing, the court said that that act constituted the creation of a copy of the object code. Regarding the reverse assembly of the hexadecimal listing, the court observed that there were differences between the text published by Shuuwa and the listing produced by running the Microsoft object code through a disassembler program. (Why did the court compare the Shuuwa textbook with a disassembled listing rather than with Microsoft's original source code or object code? It appears that Microsoft chose not to put its source code onto the public record. Further, comparing the Shuuwa text, which was based on reverse-assembled object code, with that object code itself would have been unnecessarily difficult. Since the court found that running Microsoft's object code through a disassembler program produced a mechanical translation that was a copy of the object code, which was in turn a copy of Microsoft's source code, the comparison that it made was a sensible surrogate for the weeks of expert testimony that would have been required to interpret the Microsoft object code and compare it to the Shuuwa text.)

The differences between Shuuwa's text and the reverse-assembled object code related only to the substitution of alphabetic labels for the object code's hexadecimal identification of memory locations, and to the adding of textual comments. The court held that those enhancements, however creative they might have been, had no bearing on the question whether the copyright in the original work had been infringed.

That is a very important ruling. In Brussels, the trade association ECIS' lobbyists had argued most vociferously that intermediate copying done in the course of creating a substitute program should not be considered at all in determining whether or not the resulting product was infringing. If the finished clone product was not substantially similar to the original (except, of course, in those aspects that users could see, which "had to be" substantially similar and were therefore, according to the clones, "ideas" and not "expression"), it shouldn't matter whether a clone had engaged in intermediate copying, translating, or other activity normally considered infringement when undertaken in connection with other kinds of literary works. That does not appear to be the law in Japan. Judges Motoki, Iimura, and Tomioka ruled that translating the Microsoft object code into hexadecimal form was a separate act of infringement, even though the "hex" listing was not published. They also ruled that reverse assembling the hex listing was a separate act of infringement despite changes and additions made to the resulting source-like code by Shuuwa. Finally, the judges ruled that since Microsoft clearly chose not to publish its source code, Shuuwa's act of doing so in violation of the wishes of the author couldn't be justified on the basis that publication was in the interest of users.

In the process of ruling that reverse assembly constituted copyright infringement, the court considered in detail the text of two routines out of the two hundred twenty-nine routines in the Microsoft interpreter. One of the routines was part of the interface between the processor and the cassette, and the other was part of the interface between the processor and the keyboard. Although it appears that Shuuwa did not raise the Fujitsu argument that interfaces are not protectable because they are "ideas," the court nonetheless considered whether those interface routines evoked the authors' creativity, ingenuity, thought, personality, and individuality, the essential tests for protectable expression under Japanese copyright law. As a result of the court's analysis, those routines and the rest of the program were held protected by copyright. Although the Japanese copyright statute has since been amended to exclude "rules," "algorithms," and "programming languages" from protection, the *Shuuwa* court's approach suggests that in Japan, as in the United States, the question whether interfaces are protected or not will be determined not doctrinally but on the basis of a case-by-case analysis of the nature of the interfaces in particular programs.

Given the cultural and institutional conservatism of the Japanese judiciary, the paucity of legal precedent generally, and the nexus in Japan between government policy and judicial decision making, the *Microsoft* case is clearly an important precedent. Shuuwa and its printer were not, of course, suppliers of clone software, and one could argue that the result would be different in a case involving a software clone, where the excuse that copying of interfaces is necessary in order to achieve compatibility could be fully articulated. There are two problems with that argument, though. For one thing, "necessity" was an element of Shuuwa's business strategy, too. In order to write a text fully elucidating Microsoft's source code, it was necessary to copy that code. For another, it is illogical to suggest that a given program element is protected against copying by publishers but not protected against copying by clones. In the end, *Microsoft* must be seen as a strategic victory for the forces of the software innovators. Look at it this way: If the reader were a Japanese lawyer advising a client whether to engage in reverse compilation of someone else's program in the course of developing a program of the client's own, what advice would the reader give in light of *Microsoft v. Shuuwa*?

# 12

# "Been Down So Long It Looks Like Up to Me": *IBM v. AMI*

"A woman like myself knows nothing of the Art of War, but from watching you tonight, I have the terrible feeling I've seen a man who was about to be cut down. Somehow there's the shadow of death about you. Is that really safe for a warrior who may at any minute have to face dozens of swords?..."

"...[I] would be interested in knowing why you think I act like a man who's about to be killed...."

"All right.... Were you listening when I played the lute?..."

Breaking off, she went and got the lute from the next room. Once reseated, she held the instrument by the neck and stood it up in front of him....

Taking a fine, keen knife in her lithe hand, she brought it down quickly and sharply on the pear-shaped back of the lute. Three or four deft strokes and the work was done, so quickly and decisively that Musashi half expected to see blood spurt from the instrument.... "As you can see," she said, "the inside of the lute is almost completely hollow. All the variations come from this single crosspiece near the middle.... If it were absolutely straight and rigid, the sound would be monotonous, but in fact it has been shaped into a curved shape. This alone would not create the lute's infinite variety. That comes from leaving the crosspiece a certain amount of leeway to vibrate at either end. To put it another way, the tonal richness comes from there being a certain freedom of movement, a certain relaxation, at the ends of the core.

"It's the same with people. In life, we must have flexibility. Our spirits must be able to move freely. To be too stiff and rigid is to be brittle and lacking in responsiveness."

—Eiji Yoshikawa, *Miyamoto Musashi*
(1971)(Charles S. Terry, Tr.)

Flexibility is a *sine qua non* of success in the kaleidoscopically changing computer industry. Long-term success—indeed, even long-term viability—tends to elude those who cannot adapt. For example, a firm whose only business was repair of the 1970s-vintage Apple II would certainly have had "the shadow of death" around it long ago, if it had not already expired. What follows is the unremittingly sad story of a firm that clung too long, too hard to an obsolescent business, to the point of infringing copyrights in order to keep the business going.

Allen-Myland, Inc. (AMI) was a small Pennsylvania company that had made a substantial amount of money in the business of upgrading and reconfiguring IBM mainframes. AMI's principal customers were leasing companies, which engaged AMI to adjust the amount of memory and other hardware that comprised large IBM CPUs when the CPUs were being shipped from one lessee to another lessee whose requirements were different. Upgrading and downgrading IBM mainframe CPUs was at one time an interesting business. The principal requirement was the ability to use a calculator. The large IBM CPUs were offered in a graduated family of models that were technologically related, and differed from one another largely in terms both of the amount of "main memory" that they contained and of the speed-related hardware, including microcode, that they contained. The more memory the CPU contained and the faster it performed, the higher its price. AMI's business opportunity was created by those very differences in prices; in particular, the differences in the prices among the models of IBM's 303x product line. From the start, therefore, AMI had chosen a precarious business to pursue. Its opportunity was vulnerable not only to technological change but also to a single company's pricing considerations.

The calculator was the key to AMI's business because, in addition to its range of CPUs, IBM also sold the parts needed to maintain and even upgrade those CPUs. Therefore, AMI could readily calculate—based on the price difference between two models, the cost of the parts necessary to upgrade from one model to the other, the value of the parts left over after the alteration, and the amount of labor time needed to perform the alteration—which upgrades and downgrades were most profitable for it to perform. AMI was, in short, a kind of arbitrageur.

An arbitrageur exploits price differentials. The arbitrage business is ephemeral. Normally, price differentials cannot exist for long periods of time unless there are severe structural imperfections in the markets in question. The arbitrageur moves quickly, before the differential closes, and once a particular differential closes, the successful arbitrageur has already moved on to other exploitable market differentials. The difference between the spot price of oil and the 90-day futures price, the difference between the price of a stock and the price of a bond convertible into that stock, the difference between the price of carbon steel in Tokyo and the price of carbon steel in São Paulo may all create temporal opportunities for arbitrage. Those opportunities differ substantially from the arbitrage opportunity that AMI sought to exploit, in that price differences among IBM models and between models and parts are not differences that arise through macro-economic market forces. There are differences that arise through the efforts of a single firm to price its products so as to be competitive and obtain a return on investment. AMI's attempts at arbitrage threatened that return on investment by reducing IBM's revenues from selling models as opposed to parts kits. For every unit that AMI upgraded, IBM received only the parts price differential rather than the model differential, which posed a potentially serious impediment to recovery of IBM's investment in its mainframe CPU business.

For upgrades and downgrades to the 303x series, labor was a significant cost factor. The time of the customer engineer was measured in hours, even days. When the 303x series was superceded by the 308x series in the early 1980s, that situation changed dramatically. The 308x series was based on a new component packaging technology called "thermal conduction modules," or "TCMs." A major design objective for the new technology was to enable alterations to 308x processors to be performed far more quickly than were alterations to the 303x series. That objective was achieved. Roughly speaking, upgrades and downgrades of 308x processors took 5 percent as long as upgrades and downgrades of 303x processors, and the value of the labor required to make the changes averaged well under 2 percent of the price IBM charged for the service, the rest representing the value of the parts. Moreover, because of the exceedingly high value and short supply of TCMs, IBM priced its upgrade and downgrade service on the basis that any TCMs removed from the 308x CPU be returned to IBM. The value of the returned TCMs to IBM was taken into account in computing the net upgrade or downgrade price, resulting in a lower charge for the service than would otherwise have obtained. Finally, for companies that wished to buy parts from IBM in order to perform their own upgrade services, IBM charged prices for those parts such that the aggregate price of the parts equalled or exceeded IBM's price for the upgrade, and the upgrade prices themselves were set equal to the price differentials between 308x models. In short, IBM had sought to remove the opportunity for others to jeopardize IBM's return on investment by attacking IBM's price lists with a calculator or sharp pencil.

The result of these changes in technology and pricing was the breakup of the arbitrage game on which AMI's existence was based. AMI sued IBM in federal district court in Philadelphia for violating the antitrust laws. The courthouse was the same as that in which *Apple v. Franklin* and *Whelan v. Jaslow* were tried, and AMI's Philadelphia lawyers were from the firm that represented the unsuccessful defendant in the *Whelan* case. (Unnoticed but, for AMI, ominous bits of trivia, as it developed.) After a full trial before Judge Thomas O'Neill of the principal antitrust issues, judgment was rendered in favor of IBM. The judge found that IBM did not have monopoly power, in part because minicomputers, used computers, peripheral equipment, and even software were effective competitive alternatives to upgrading or reconfiguring IBM mainframe computers. He held that because of the introduction of the new technology, there was no longer a viable separate business for the supply of upgrade or downgrade labor, and even if there were, AMI was not entitled as a matter of law to have IBM parts prices and upgrade prices set in such a way that profits to AMI were guaranteed. He found that

The . . . dramatic decline in the amount and value of labor required to perform 308x upgrades has redefined the niche in the computer market occupied by AMI. This decline has eliminated business opportunities once available. By itself, such a result does not offend the antitrust laws. The antitrust laws were enacted for "the protection of competition, not competitors."

Given the expense of antitrust litigation, the manifest health and growth of the computer industry, and the rampant movement toward distributed processing, it is a wonder that the AMI lawsuit was brought at all. AMI was encouraged and supported in that action by some of its major leasing company customers, particularly Comdisco, which apparently did not want IBM personnel to be upgrading or downgrading the IBM processors owned by the leasing company, even in cases where it was not economically viable for anyone else to do so. AMI was also motivated by the chilling fact that it was out of business unless someone or something intervened to create an artificial price differential in IBM's parts business into which AMI could slip the point of its sharp pencil. The cheerleading from the leasing companies and the prospect of corporate demise served to obscure for AMI the fatal flaws in its case. Judge O'Neill made those weaknesses perfectly clear:

The evidence compellingly showed that technological advances incorporated in the 308x computer system have reduced the amount of labor involved in performing 308x MIPs upgrades to an amount which is insignificant and de minimus for antitrust purposes. [Footnote omitted]

There is insufficient evidence of demand for upgrade labor at prices AMI would have to charge to support a conclusion that a competitive market for 308x upgrade labor does or could exist.

AMI has failed to establish the "adverse impact on competition" with which the antitrust laws are concerned "because no portion of the market which would otherwise have been available to other sellers has been foreclosed" by IBM. [Citation omitted.]

Given the existence of legitimate reasons for net pricing, and the fact that its procompetitive effects outweigh its virtually nonexistent anticompetitive impact, I conclude that AMI's rule of reason challenge to net pricing [i.e., that net pricing imposed unreasonable restraints on competition] fails.

AMI's antitrust case was an utter and dismal failure, but that was not the worst of it. This book is not about antitrust law, and the discussion of the *AMI* case would not appear here unless significant software protection issues were raised therein. Here, the issues related to the copying of microcode.

It is not a good idea to take on the mantle of antitrust crusader if one has something to hide. Antitrust cases are generally broad economic and behavioral inquiries into the business of the plaintiff as well as that of the defendant. Under the pretrial discovery provisions of the Federal Rules of Civil Procedure, the opposing parties may demand to see documents or question employees under oath not just on relevant subjects, but on any subject that *may* lead to the discovery of admissible evidence. For that reason, when a firm sues a competitor for allegedly violating the antitrust laws, the defendant often finds during the discovery phase of the case that the plaintiff itself has engaged in what appear to be unlawful activities. Frequently, the result is a dramatic role reversal in the litigation. I will give two examples from personal experience. In the late 1960s, the Control Data Corporation (CDC) sued IBM for monopolizing the computer industry. During the discovery phase of the case, IBM found that CDC has engaged in precisely the same acts that it claimed to be illegal. IBM countersued Control Data, on CDC's own legal theory, for monopolizing the supercomputer industry. Both cases were ultimately settled. In 1970, the Telex Corporation sued IBM for monopolizing the market for computer peripheral equipment, seeking damages of hundreds of millions of dollars. In discovery, IBM learned that Telex had misappropriated valuable IBM confidential information, and sued Telex for theft of trade secrets. When the dust settled, Telex had lost both the antitrust case and the trade secret case, and ended up owing IBM some $18 million in damages.

Likewise, in the *AMI* case discovery brought to light a particularly cavalier disregard on AMI's part for IBM's intellectual property rights. Indications of that unfortunate behavior turned up when IBM came across evidence that AMI had provided a customer with an unauthorized adaptation of the microcode in a 309x processor in connection with a reconfiguration of that 309x. This evidence provoked a copyright counterclaim against AMI. As discovery in the copyright case unfolded, it became clear that AMI was maintaining a library full of unauthorized copies and adaptations of IBM copyrighted microcode.

The 309x line—successor, as the reader may already have concluded, to the 308x series—was introduced by IBM in 1985. A 309x processor complex consisted of the processor itself plus one or two 3097 power and cooling distribution units, a 3092 processor controller, two 3370 disk drives attached to the 3092, and operator and service consoles. The 309x was available in both single processor ("uniprocessor") configurations and multiple processor ("multiprocessor") configurations. Multiprocessors had the capability to run in "partitioned mode," in which each half of the processor ran its own operating system. On the disk drives attached to the 3092 was the 309x microcode. Each disk contained a copy of that program, which consisted of a modified version of IBM's VM operating system for mainframes as well as various application programs that provided processor control facilities as well as facilities for storing information about the configuration of the processor complex. One copy of the 309x microcode was a backup copy in uniprocessor configurations, but in multiprocessor configurations, both copies of the microcode were actively used by the service processors. In addition, IBM provided each customer with an archival copy on a storage medium such as magnetic tape.

IBM protected the 309x microcode by copyright. After mid-1987, IBM also saw to it that the archival copies of the microcode, although on customer premises, were kept securely under the control of IBM customer engineers. A year later, in order to provide additional protection against loss of the asset value of its microcode, IBM also introduced changes to its purchase agreement. Those provisions (called "licensed internal code" provisions, or "LIC") prohibited copying, adapting, displaying, modifying, or distributing the microcode except in connection with running or maintaining the hardware or in order to make an archival copy if IBM did not provide one. The LIC provisions explicitly prohibited reverse compilation. They also prohibited transfer of the microcode other than in connection with the transfer of the hardware.

Despite IBM's copyright notices and despite the LIC, AMI freely copied, adapted, modified, and distributed the 309x microcode. Each reconfiguration of the 309x necessitated a change in the accompanying microcode. In addition, certain kinds of reconfigurations, called "splits," necessitated creating new copies of that microcode. A split was simply the separating of a large processor into two smaller processors. To support its reconfiguration activities, AMI created a library of 309x microcode tapes, some of which were unaltered copies of the originals and some of which were modified. Sometimes, AMI made the copies for its library using the microcode that accompanied processors sent to AMI for reconfiguration. In other cases, AMI copied microcode sent to it separately, without a processor, by Comdisco, its largest leasing company customer. Judge O'Neill found that

When using its library to provide 3090 microcode for a reconfiguration, AMI typically made at least five copies of a portion or of an entire copy of the 3090 microcode: the original IBM 3090 microcode was copied into the library; AMI modified the original tape and copied the modified 3090 microcode into its library; the modified 3090 microcode was copied onto tape to load the microcode on the reconfigured 3090 and to serve as backup; and the modified 3090 microcode was copied onto each of the two 3370s for the reconfigured machine.

In about forty instances, AMI created what came to be called "rainbow tapes," by combining portions of tapes from several different 309x processors.

At trial, AMI's president Larry Allen conceded that he did not view the copies made for AMI's library or in the course of its reconfiguration activity as authorized by IBM. Nonetheless, when AMI shipped the copied or altered microcode to customers, the copies bore labels virtually identical to those that IBM had placed on the originals. According to Allen, AMI "intentionally attempted to duplicate that label as IBM would have produced it." (Is there any doubt in the reader's mind how this story will end?)

What on earth were AMI and its leasing company customers hoping to accomplish by defending these unambiguously unlawful activities? What on earth were AMI's lawyers saying about the legitimacy of AMI's actions? In court, AMI's defense was nothing but the last, valiant battle cry of a doomed army that technology had left behind. Centuries earlier, in the year 1450, an army of English invaders armed principally with longbows and swords was soundly defeated at Formigny by the forces of Charles VII of France, which used the new (to Europe) technology of gunpowder. Firing light, long-barrelled cannon called "culverins," the French artillery cut to pieces the archers from across the channel. AMI's defenses to the infringement charge were as the English arrows to the French cannonballs: numerous, but ineffective. Here they are.

1. *IBM's microcode was not copyrightable.* Although AMI conceded that the 3090 microcode contained some protectable material, it argued that Tape 2 (one of the five magnetic tapes on which the archival copy of the microcode was delivered to customers) contained only a parts list in digital code and was therefore neither sufficiently original to be copyrightable nor intelligible by human beings; further, that unless it could make an exact copy of the contents of Tape 2, it could not engage in the reconfiguration business; thus prohibition of reproduction of Tape 2 would extend protection not just to the expression but to the idea of the 309x microcode. Judge O'Neill found that Tape 2 in fact contained instructions, software tools, and data. In his opinion, the separation of the 309x microcode into five tapes was a matter of convenience, which did not alter the fact that the program was an integral work. Since infringement analysis requires that the works be compared as a whole, not component by component, he found the

contents of Tape 2 to be a "substantial, necessary portion of a single work" that was protectable. As to the necessity to copy, the court found that the 309x microcode could have been written in a number of ways other than the particular expression selected by IBM. To the argument that AMI could not economically write a replacement for the million lines of instructions in the 309x microcode, Judge O'Neill said

Whether it would be economically feasible for AMI to write its own program to perform the 3092 processor controller functions without copying any of the 3090 microcode is not relevant to the idea/expression distinction. Otherwise, a computer program so complex that vast expenditures of time and money would be required to develop a different program expressing the same idea would not be protected, even if innumerable different programs expressing that idea could be written, while a simpler program requiring less expenditures of time and money might be protected. So long as other expressions of this idea are possible, a particular expression of the idea can enjoy copyright protection, regardless of whether a copying party possesses the resources to write a different expression of the idea. [Footnotes omitted.]

Amplifying on the latter thought, the judge also rehearsed the famous warning from *Apple v. Franklin*:

If other methods of expressing [an] idea are not foreclosed as a practical matter, then there is no merger [of idea and expression]. Franklin may wish to achieve total compatibility with independently developed application programs written for the Apple II, but that is a commercial and competitive objective which does not enter into the somewhat metaphysical issue of whether particular ideas and expressions have merged.

In other words, though AMI might want to be in a business that required copying the 309x microcode, the question whether that microcode was protectable subject matter did not depend in any way on AMI's business objective. It depended only on the nature of IBM's original work.

At bottom, AMI's argument was no different from the argument of an imaginary record producer whose "business" is overlaying voice tracks—without authorization—over the jazz recordings of the Marsalis brothers. Copying the instrumental tracks may very well be indispensable to that "business," but that indispensability does not make the copying lawful.

2. *AMI's copying constituted a "fair use" of IBM's microcode.* The Copyright Act provides that copying for uses such as criticism, comment, news reporting, teaching, scholarship, or research may be fair use, not infringement. AMI's lawyer put forward, with a straight face, the argument that AMI's copying of the 309x microcode was educational in nature. Its library was constructed, the argument went, so that AMI could learn how to use the 309x processors and to support different configurations of the 309x.

Its copying was therefore a form of reverse engineering. (Note again the resemblance to Fujitsu's reverse-compilation argument.)

The assertion was a gross perversion of the "fair use" section of the copyright statute, and Judge O'Neill dispatched it with a few deft strokes. The statute requires the court to consider the purpose and character of the use (e.g., whether commercial or nonprofit), the nature of the original work, the amount and substantiality of the portion copied, and the effect of the copying on the potential market for or value of the original work. Six years earlier, the judge pointed out, the United States Supreme Court had established the ground rule that every commercial use of copyrighted material by someone other than the copyright owner is presumed to be an unfair exploitation of the owner's rights. AMI's use, however educational it might have been, was not academically oriented, but was undertaken in aid of AMI's commercial business purposes. The 309x microcode, though in part informational in content, was as a whole imaginative and original in nature and the result of substantial creative effort. AMI in many cases made and distributed complete copies of the microcode, and the making of complete copies militates against a finding of fair use; even in those cases where only Tape 2 was copied, the material reproduced was an essential and substantial part of the microcode. AMI's activities could not, in the court's view, be considered "reverse engineering, because they consisted simply of determining what patterns of copying would produce 309x microcode that would operate in various 309x configurations." Finally, since AMI's copying was undertaken for commercial purposes and its distribution of copied code stood in the place of distribution by IBM, there was clearly harm to the potential market for or value of the original work.

3. *AMI's copies were made for operational or archival purposes.* AMI's first two arguments were half-hearted attempts to fight again battles that had long ago been lost. Its third argument was a new offensive. Section 117 of the copyright statute permits the owner of a copy of a program to make an additional copy or even an adaptation of that program either (1) when such acts comprise an essential step in utilizing the program in conjunction with a machine or (2) for archival purposes, provided that any archival copy is destroyed when possession of the original program is no longer rightful. Prior to the *AMI* case, there had been little judicial interpretation of the meaning of the phrases "essential to its utilization" or "archival purposes." Leaping into this exegetic vacuum, AMI argued that its library was both "essential to [the] utilization" of the 309x microcode and a set of "archival copies" of that microcode. In order to cloak that self-serving argument in a robe of intellectual respectability, AMI hired as co-counsel Edmund Kitch, a noted intellectual property law professor from NYU, and hired as an expert witness a noted writer on the subject of why the copyright law should not protect computer programs. (The expert witness' role in the *AMI* case is discussed in Chapter 13.)

The august presence of Professor Kitch failed to persuade Judge O'Neill. Section 117 had been made part of the copyright law in 1980 on the recommendation of CONTU. In order to focus the court's attention on the reasons for CONTU's recommendation, IBM hired as its expert witness Professor Arthur Miller from the Harvard Law School. The American reader may know Professor Miller (electronically) from his numerous appearances as legal analyst on "Good Morning America" or from his own PBS television series on major legal issues of the day. Copyright afficionados know him as well as a key member of CONTU, a man well placed to explain the purpose of Section 117. After considering the CONTU evidence, Judge O'Neill found that copies "essential to the utilization" were those made in the course of loading the program into the computer. He quoted from the CONTU Final Report:

Because the placement of a work into a computer is the preparation of a copy, the law should provide that persons in rightful possession of copies of programs be able to use them freely without fear of exposure to copyright liability.

Neither the copies nor the adaptations that AMI made for its library or for reconfigured systems were permitted by Section 117, the judge ruled. The copies were not essential to the use of the microcode in a computer, since the computer was already supplied with copies of the microcode by IBM; and AMI's adaptations were merely assemblages of partial copies of the microcode.

Nor were AMI's copies and adaptations legitimate archival copies. An archival copy "merely protects against the risk of loss of a program due to mechanical or electrical failure or some other form of destruction," the judge found, whereas AMI's copies were intended to perform functions in addition to archival functions, such as operating the 309x systems or serving as an active library for the production of additional copies.

Because of the foregoing findings, Judge O'Neill did not need to reach the question whether AMI was in fact the "owner of a copy" of the 309x code. IBM's view, as the LIC made clear, was that its customers were only licensed to use the copies of the microcode they received, but that ownership of those copies remained with IBM. Section 117 arguably did not apply at all, because it only applies where ownership has passed to the user. That argument is no mere technicality; it appears to reflect the intent of Congress. CONTU's recommendation to Congress was that Section 117 allow "rightful possessors" of copies to make operational and archival copies. In the process of adopting the CONTU recommendation as an amendment to the Copyright Act, however, Congress changed the term "rightful possessor" to "owner," a significant distinction in an industry where products containing intellectual property are licensed as well as sold.

4. *IBM's right to control AMI's distribution of the 309x microcode was "exhausted."* Ownership of the code was implicated in this argument as well. Under the law, once a product containing intellectual property is sold to a customer, the copyright owner cannot control further distribution *of that copy* by the customer. The copyright owner's right to control distribution is said to be "exhausted" by the sale. Once again, however, the judge didn't need to decide whether IBM had "sold" copies of the 309x microcode or only licensed them. Since none of the microcode that AMI distributed was that which it had received from IBM, but rather copies of that IBM microcode, the exhaustion doctrine simply didn't apply.

5. *IBM is "estopped" by its prior acquiescence in AMI's behavior.* To a lawyer, "estopped" is a wonderful word: at once a link to the ancient past, a reminder that the profession speaks a secret language only dimly understood by the unanointed (indeed, not all that well understood by many of the anointed), and a prime example of the "fuzzy logic" that guides the law. Reaching forward, the etymologists speculate, from the ancient Sanskrit *stuka* (tuft of hair) through the Greek *styphein* (to be astringent), with a jump through *styppe* to the Latin *stupa* or *stuppa* (the coarse part of flax), thence more surely to the vulgar Latin (not the pornographic graffiti scrawled on the walls at Pompeii, but rather the spoken Latin of the Roman middle class that is the direct foundation of modern Romance languages) *stupare*, which became the Middle French *estoper* (stop up) and the Middle English *estoppen*, the word "estop" reeks of history, yet its meaning is not clear to most of us despite its age. To lawyers, it means—figuratively—that a suitor's mouth is stopped or closed by virtue of an action the suitor has taken that makes it improper or unfair to hear the suit. The notion of equity that underlies the estoppel defense makes it a fuzzy defense, not sharply outlined and highly dependent on the facts of particular cases. In its case, AMI argued that because IBM had never complained about AMI's copying of the microcode in the predecessor 308x processors, of which it had knowledge at the time, IBM was estopped from complaining about AMI's copying of the 309x microcode.

There were two problems with that argument. First, the predecessor microcode had not been copyrighted. Second, even if it had, authors have every right to enforce some of their copyrights but not others. Failure to enforce some rights implies nothing with respect to the enforceability of others. That principle is so clear that, with an eminent copyright scholar as its co-counsel, AMI couldn't even dispute it as a general proposition. Instead, AMI asserted that computer programs are different from ordinary literary works, and therefore the general proposition should not apply. How are programs different? Programs are "functional," AMI said in its brief, and "utilitarian," and therefore estoppel should apply in this case although it would not apply in the case of other kinds of literary works. In addition to leaning on a fairly shopworn and discredited distinction, AMI's argument was a complete *non sequitur*. Judge O'Neill held that "[n]either the Copyright Act nor any case law supports the distinction AMI suggests."

(He also mentioned in passing that aesthetic works also perform a "function," suggesting that two plays could be seen to perform the same entertainment "function." He might also have said that all commercially produced literary works are designed to perform the function of causing consumers to reach into their wallets, extract legal tender, and hand it over.)

6. *AMI engaged in legitimate self-help*. Here, the theory was that after IBM announced it would keep archival copies of the 309x in the possession of the IBM customer engineers (in effect) even when the code was installed at customer premises, AMI had to copy the tapes in order to prepare for the time when it would no longer have access to them. A significant difficulty with that theory was that it didn't fit the facts. AMI's copying activities had commenced well before IBM announced the new practice, and they continued long after the new practice went into effect, when AMI supposedly could not access the tapes. Accordingly, AMI's self-help defense was dismissed without even reaching the question whether self-help is even in theory a defense to copyright infringement.

7. *IBM's infringement claim is barred by "unclean hands."* Like "estoppel," the term "unclean hands" is a favorite of lawyers. It refers to a way of putting a plaintiff on the defensive, by accusations of acts of fraud, deceit, unconscionability, or bad faith related to the subject matter of the lawsuit, which acts injured the defendant and make it inequitable to allow the lawsuit to be prosecuted. Unfortunately for AMI, none of the acts in which IBM had engaged was fraudulent, deceptive, unconscionable, or taken in bad faith. Each one was simply an action taken to enforce IBM's copyrights and protect its intellectual property.

8. *Miscellaneous defenses*. With excessive *chutzpah*, given the outcome of its antitrust suit, AMI argued that IBM had misused its copyright by violating the antitrust laws; also that its copying was implicitly or explicitly licensed by IBM, that the 309x microcode was in the public domain, and that IBM's claim was barred by the statute of limitations. The judge gave each of those feeble efforts the brief attention it deserved, and dismissed them all.

9. *IBM's claim is estopped by IBM's violation of its 1956 Consent Decree.* This defense, far more esoteric than the others, achieved a degree of success with the trial court, though that success did not matter to the outcome of the case. Thirty-four years earlier IBM had settled a lawsuit brought by the Justice Department by entering into an agreement with the Department that was filed with the court in order to give the court continuing jurisdiction over the settlement. Given the monumental changes in the computer industry, that agreement, called a "consent decree" (as was the much later

agreement between the Justice Department and Borland International), has little relevance to the modern world, but it is still on the books at this writing. Though the consent decree serves today as nothing more than a hobble to a firm that is competing with numerous large multinationals that do not have such hobbles, IBM remains obligated to comply with its terms. One of those terms prevents IBM from "prohibiting, or in any way subjecting to IBM control or approval, alterations in or attachments to [punch card tabulating or electronic data processing] machines." Private parties like AMI cannot sue IBM if they think IBM is violating the decree; only the Justice Department can do that. However, AMI argued that it could assert a violation of the decree as a *defense* to a suit by IBM for copyright infringement. In order to make that assertion stick, AMI had to prove that IBM had violated the decree in a way that had "caused or brought about" AMI's infringement, an argument known in other circles as "the devil made me do it."

In preparing to demonstrate that IBM had violated the decree, AMI's lawyers went to Washington to try to convince the Justice Department that IBM's practices in respect of the 309x microcode had the effect of prohibiting alterations to 309x processors. Not only did AMI fail to succeed with the Justice Department, but it received for its efforts a letter from the Department indicating that agency's view that IBM's actions did not violate the decree, which letter was entered into evidence at trial.

Now, IBM certainly did not think that its actions violated its agreement with the Justice Department, and if the Justice Department did not think so either, then as far as the parties to the 1956 agreement were concerned, there was no violation and that should have ended the matter. For reasons that he did not explain, however, Judge O'Neill chose to ignore the Justice Department letter. "I have not relied in any way on the Department's letter," he wrote, "in reaching my conclusions concerning the Consent Decree." Instead, he interpreted the agreement without reference to the interpretation put forward by both parties who signed it. In terms of AMI's reconfiguration activity other than splits, he found that AMI could readily have obtained from IBM copies of the necessary microcode for reconfigured machines, at prices from $420 to $2100, and therefore that IBM had not "caused and brought about" the copying in which AMI engaged. As to certain of the splits that AMI had performed, however, the judge ruled that they were "alterations" (though they clearly are not intended to be anything other than the production of unaltered smaller IBM processors) and that pricing the necessary microcode at levels designed to reduce arbitrage— the very practice he had found perfectly lawful in the earlier antitrust case— in effect prohibited those alterations by removing the economic incentive to perform them. He indicated that if IBM had proved to his satisfaction that pricing to reduce arbitrage was necessary in order to recover its investment in the 309x, his decision might have been different.

Although Judge O'Neill's ruling on certain splits deprived IBM of a clean sweep, it did not affect the outcome of the case. AMI ended up with a substantial liability to IBM for copyright infringement and an obligation to destroy all of its microcode library save that portion necessary to perform splits of one 3090 model. Even as to those splits, the judge ruled that consent decree violations were no defense to breach of contract suits. Since AMI's copying violated the LIC clause in IBM's purchase contracts, IBM had recourse against such copying as a breach of contract despite Judge O'Neill's ruling that it could not enforce its copyright against AMI. AMI asked Judge O'Neill to reconsider his ruling in light of the *Feist* decision, which the Supreme Court handed down subsequent to the *AMI* copyright ruling, but the judge had little difficulty in differentiating a compilation of preexisting facts from a tape containing "instructions, software, tools and data" all of which were created by IBM.

The *AMI* case was, as noted above, the third offense on software copyright protection mounted in the federal courthouse in Philadelphia. Like the two earlier cases, it was a case in which the best defense—indeed, the only defense—was an offense. There was no question that copying had occurred, so the only refuge lay in attacking the law to the extent that it protected the things copied. The judicial terrain in Pennsylvania seems somehow inhospitable to such defensive strategies, as defendants who have adopted them have repeatedly withdrawn from the fray bloodied and broken, and the law has emerged more clearly and more vigorously stated after each engagement. Though by the time you read these words the case may be on appeal, or through the appeal, to the Third Circuit Court of Appeals (also in Philadelphia, and also the venue for the appeals in *Apple v. Franklin* and *Whelan v. Jaslow*), the result is not likely to change markedly. The *AMI* case was an important battle in the softwars for two reasons. First, it adds a strong precedent to the fairly small body of case law extending copyright protection to microcode. Though there is no reason to have expected microcode to be treated any differently from other software in that regard, until courts confirmed that fact the clones could argue to the contrary— and indeed have been doing so. Second, the case reiterates in a new context the principle that business strategy is no defense to copyright infringement. Just as *Apple v. Franklin* teaches that a desire to be compatible does not excuse copying, and *Whelan v. Jaslow* teaches that a desire on the part of a copier to extend a copyright holder's business into a market not being addressed by the copyright holder does not excuse copying, *IBM v. AMI* teaches that a desire to continue an obsolescent business in the face of new technology does not excuse copying. A general principle can be seen in this line of cases. One who is intentionally copying software of another should not be deluded into thinking that the copying will be excused on the grounds that the business being pursued could not succeed without copying.

# 13

# The Lady Vanishes: An Academic Ventures into the Real World and Retreats in Dismay

"Oh, Toto. I don't think we're in Kansas anymore."
—Dorothy, *The Wizard of Oz*

While those of us following the softwars were waiting for Judge Keeton to decide the *Lotus* case, I got a call from Dan Charles, a fortunate young man in two respects: first, he was recipient of a journalism fellowship from MIT, and second, he already had a journalistic outlet for his craft, the British magazine *New Scientist*. His commentaries are now occasionally heard on National Public Radio in the United States. Someone had given Mr. Charles my name in connection with an article he was writing on "look and feel" issues. We had two or three pleasant discussions on the subject, and I sent him some materials. After the *Lotus* decision was published he gave me his interpretation of Judge Keeton's ruling. The judge, Charles had concluded, was practically begging Congress to change the law. Predictably, his article when it appeared took little advantage of the valuable insights I had given him.

In our last conversation, Charles asked me whether I really believed that the academic critics of copyright protection for software are twentieth-century Luddites, as I seemed to suggest—as, indeed, I do suggest—in some of my writings. The simple answer is that I do believe technophobia underlies much of the academic criticism. I have formed that judgment as a result of appearances before groups of law professors whose rejection of the very idea that software should invade the domain of copyright law was so energetic and adamant as to appear to be based on an unwillingness to learn anything at all about software rather than a professional assessment based on a knowledge of the nature of the software-writing process. Luddism, however, is too simple an answer to encompass the complex forces that drive the academic mind. Since the views of respected law teachers can strongly influence the course of the law, and therefore the course of the softwars, it is worthwhile to consider how those views are shaped.

One shaping force of academic thought is the premise that intellectual prowess can—and therefore should—always invent improvements on the existing order of things. That premise is debatable, it may fairly be said, but its corollary—that inventions of intellectual prowess *are* always improvements on the order of things—is demonstrably false. Yet many academics subscribe to the corollary as well, and pass that view on to their students. A lawyer just beginning practice, who had worked for me as a summer student, wrote a law review article proposing that copyright law be abandoned as a form of protection for software, in favor of a system of his own design. The cover letter to the copy he sent me said that he was hoping to specialize in computer law. In reply, I told him not to worry, the industry would forgive him for recommending chaos, as he had not yet had sufficient experience to be able to tell that chaos would be the sure result of a sudden, radical, and unpredictable change in the order of rights and responsibilities of software authors. The student article was only one among a large number of suggestions by professors of law, in scholarly journals and in the trade press, that copyright be thrown out in favor of a *sui generis* statute protecting computer programs.

Another force driving academic criticism is the need to write. Soldiers fight or perish. College professors publish or perish. In either case the will to survive impels the actor forward. It is obvious that an academic the body of whose writings simply conveys the message that the law is working quite well in a particular area will not attract much attention or provoke much thought, and therefore will not gain respect in university circles. Therefore, academics criticize. That is as it should be, and much good comes of it. But not everything that comes of the publication imperative is good.

An additional force behind the academic criticism of copyright protection for software, a darker force, is consultancy. Consultancy is the principal fashion by which eminent professors enhance the meager six-figure salaries paid to them by their schools. This force is darker because it is harder for the public to perceive, and because it distorts the assumed intellectual purity of the opinions that teachers express in their classes and in their writings. When I go to Washington or to Brussels to discuss software legal issues, the interests that I represent are on my sleeve. Likewise, the reader of these words knows that the writer represents a leading producer of original software, and that he is not likely to write anything that will get him fired. (Hopefully, the reader can take some comfort from the fact that large producers of original software cannot survive overprotection of intellectual property any better than they can survive underprotection. Overprotection subjects them to litigation at the instigation of others claiming infringement; underprotection puts their own investments at risk. I have, in fact, seen both sides of the courtroom.) On the other hand, when an eminent law professor from a leading American law school travels to Brussels to talk to government representatives about software legal issues or serves on an advisory board to a government agency concerned with software protection, or when his treatise on copyright law lumps software with maps, charts, and other works in which the range of expression is quite narrow and therefore the protection afforded by copyright quite thin, does his audience know that he is also associated with a law firm that represents a major supplier of clone software and hardware? In order that readers may understand why it is necessary to view much of the academic writing and speaking on the subject of software copyrights as "junk science," we will examine in this chapter one academic's contribution to a particular softwar, the conflict described in the previous chapter.

In Hitchcock's movie, *The Lady Vanishes*, there is a character who leads a double life as a governess and a spy, and whose disappearance is at the heart of the plot. Her name is Miss Froy. Since the story of the copyright expert hired by AMI also involves a disappearance, I will refer to that person as Professor Froy.

Professor Froy teaches at a large American university, and has expressed abundantly, in writings and speeches, strong negative feelings about the leading cases extending traditional copyright protection to computer programs. After the landmark *Apple v. Franklin* decision held that programs stored in ROM were eligible for copyright protection, the professor wrote a lengthy law review article arguing that it was a mistake to have ruled that object code was protected by copyright. After the equally important decision in *Whelan v. Jaslow* held that the detailed design of software was protected subject matter, Froy called the decision an "abomination" and the court that decided it "ignorant" and "obstinate." After the first round of "screen interface" cases was decided in favor of the protectability of screen displays, Froy published an article explaining why the look and feel of software user interfaces should not be protected by copyright. In general, Professor Froy believes that copyright law should be replaced by some other mechanism of protection as far as software is concerned. In general, too, this teacher's positions have consistently run diametrically counter to the direction in which the law has moved both before and since those opinions were expressed. Even though the professor's views of the existing state of the law are so critical that they put Froy outside the middle range of commentators whose work explains and rationalizes copyright law, a legal theorist of such pronounced persuasions would obviously enjoy favorable attention from the copyist forces in the softwars.

And indeed it came to pass that, in the spring of 1989, Professor Froy received a phone call from one Paul Fish, a lawyer in Chicago. Fish was then general counsel to the leasing company Comdisco, which had been profoundly interested in aiding AMI in its disastrous antitrust suit and then-pending copyright suit with IBM. Fish had read an article that the professor had written, putting forward the idea that it would be wise to change the copyright law to permit third parties to do whatever was necessary to modify programs written by others. He told Professor Froy that Comdisco and the Computer Dealers and Lessors Association (CDLA) were planning to visit the Justice Department in connection with the issues at play in the *AMI* case. The issues, as Mr. Fish described them, were whether customers who bought IBM machines were free to make changes to the microcode in the machines they had bought in order to make those machines more useful for the customers' purposes, and whether such customers could split IBM processors they had bought into smaller processors without violating the copyright law, an act that Fish described as simply doing physically what the processors already do logically when they are partitioned internally by software into two smaller processors. From the outset, in other words, the true nature of AMI's activities—and indeed of Comdisco's, since Comdisco had its own library of unauthorized 3090 microcode tapes—was hidden from the professor. Or perhaps Froy failed to ask the right questions. In a subsequent phone call to Froy, for example, a Comdisco representative said that that IBM's consent decree with the government prohibited IBM from preventing Comdisco and other CDLA members from making alterations or attachments to purchased IBM processors, but Professor Froy doesn't remember asking any questions of the persons who made those representations. At any rate, Mr. Fish asked Professor Froy to participate in the meeting with the Justice Department, and the professor agreed.

The meeting with the Justice Department took place late in April 1989. Professor Froy flew into Washington the night before and had dinner with the CDLA lawyers and spokespersons. There was further discussion of the then-pending *AMI* case, the importance to the leasing company business of being able to modify IBM equipment, and the arguments as to why IBM should not be able to prevent such modification. Apparently, little attention was paid to what AMI and Comdisco were actually doing with the copyrighted IBM microcode. The next day, the entourage went to the Justice Department offices and met with agency personnel for not more than an hour. At that meeting, the leasing company representatives made the presentation they had planned, during the course of which Professor Froy proselytized for the first time on behalf of the CDLA. On the basis of the grossly inaccurate rendition the professor had been given as to what AMI personnel were actually doing with the 3090 microcode, Froy told the Justice Department representatives that Section 117 of the Copyright Act gave customers the right to make reasonable modifications to a program in order to make the program useful for their purposes, that changing the configuration data on Tape 2 was the same as crossing out a superceded number in a phone book and writing in the new number, and that splits of large processors were lawful because they simply perfected a division already made possible in partitioned mode. In connection with splits, Froy was just parroting what Mr. Fish and other leasing company representatives had said. Professor Froy was not herself familiar with the 309x microcode or with the 309x hardware, and would later repeatedly admit, "I'm not a technical person."

Whether the professor was too busy to investigate the nature of the reconfiguration activity sought to be defended, or simply did not understand the subject matter, or had intentionally remained ignorant of the facts (not likely in Froy's case), makes little difference to the interests that were being served and those being disserved by rendering these apparently thoughtful but actually ill-considered opinions to persons wielding the power of the federal government. It is most probable, of course, that Professor Froy simply took on faith what most of us usually take on faith: that we are being told the truth. Based on that faith, Froy was willing to lend the considerable weight of a respectable academic presence to the oral petition of a group seeking Justice Department intervention in support of activity that was later judged to be unlawful, and fairly obviously so. At the time, Froy had no appreciation at all for the true nature of the activity for which Comdisco had sought support. That is the dark side of consultancy: the willingness of many academics to augment their incomes or visibility by appearing, like move stars at political rallies, to declaim on behalf of causes they have not sufficiently investigated. If the illusion of mastery of the subject matter works, the appearance may have caused harm to persons who, in a proper view of the social order, should not be harmed, and may have advantaged those who should not be advantaged. In the case at hand, of course, the person to be harmed was IBM, which is an organization large enough to defend its interests. That is not always the circumstance, though. There is a small group of academic mercenaries prowling the fringes of the softwars who often speak against the interests of software authors who do not have the wherewithal to protect themselves. (Fortunately, it is not the case that most academics are willing to sell off their prestige in this fashion; quite the contrary. Academic integrity is a very real notion—as we will see, it appears to have redeemed Professor Froy in the end—and most professors whom I have encountered in a litigation context have insisted, as a condition of engagement, on being thoroughly briefed as to the subject matter on which they are being asked to testify, even at the risk of developing opinions contrary to the interests of the client.)

In the course of pretrial discovery on the copyright issues in the IBM/

AMI case, Professor Froy gave a deposition under oath. During that deposition, the teacher was repeatedly put in the uncomfortable position of having to take refuge in a lack of understanding of the facts of the case:

"Again, it depends on a technical subject that I'm not competent to speak on."

"But, again, I'm not a technical person and I haven't reviewed all of the facts in the record."

"I don't know specifically the content of [AMI's] database."

"I haven't been told anything that causes me to believe otherwise." (This in response to a question whether she believed AMI's copies of 309x microcode were used for backup purposes.)

"Again, I'm not a technical person." (When asked how many copies of 309x microcode were stored on disk files in the case of an unsplit multiprocessor.)

"Again, I'm not a technical person, and that seems to be the crux of the matter, whether there are two copies or one copy."

"I don't know. I'm not a technical person." (In response to a request to list archival functions for computer programs.)

These were obviously instantiations of the "any shelter from the storm" adage. For a nontechnical person, Professor Froy had not in the past been shy about publishing views as to the nature of computer programs and the reasons why that nature should deprive programs of traditional copyright protection, and was not thereafter shy about joining the group of law professors—all but one of them even less "technical" than Froy—who filed an *amicus curiae* brief on behalf of Borland International in its lawsuit with Lotus.

During the months following the Justice Department meeting, Professor Froy was contacted again by leasing company representatives, this time about contributing to a position paper that was planned, and about visiting the Justice Department again. In connection with the position paper, Froy forwarded to the CDLA lawyers some materials prepared by the eminent legal scholar mentioned earlier in this chapter, whose trips to Brussels on behalf of a major software clone are said to have scandalized the eurocrats, who in the Continental tradition expect opinions expressed by law professors to be—or at least appear to be—as independent and objective as judicial opinion. For the Justice Department meeting, which took place in November 1989, the professor rearranged a "very, very busy" schedule in order to attend. Once again, there was a preparatory meeting, and once again, incredibly, the question of how reconfigurations were actually being done was never discussed. The ensuing presentation to the government attempted to persuade the enforcement agents that it would be a violation of the consent decree if IBM were allowed to prevent "alteration and modification of machines and programs." The senior Justice Department official at the meeting told the visitors that IBM had represented to the Department that when splits were performed, extra copies of the microcode were being created. One of the CDLA representatives denied that extra copies were being created in that process, and in support of that denial described the ability of 309x processors to operate in partitioned mode. Professor Froy again gave her interpretation of Section 117 of the Copyright Act, despite (or perhaps because of) not knowing "anything more about what AMI actually does" than at the earlier meeting with the government. The state of Froy's belief at the time, according to the transcript of the deposition, was that copying was certainly *not* being done in order to accomplish reconfigurations other than splits. Though Froy's testimony is confused as to splits, it seems to indicate a belief that no copying was being done by AMI in connection with splits, either.

After that meeting, at the request of the CDLA, Professor Froy began to take a greater interest in the AMI case. The CDLA was preparing to file a brief *amicus curiae* with Judge O'Neill, and wanted Froy's comments on their draft, which were willingly supplied. Froy also provided the CDLA with an outline of arguments it might make in support of AMI's business. Paramount among these was that IBM was "trying unlawfully to extend its copyright monopoly, and through this unlawful extension of its monopoly, to move back to a 'lease only' policy and to eliminate the competitive market for the leasing and resale of IBM machines." In support of that thesis, Professor Froy proposed that the CDLA analogize AMI's activities to "scratching out the telephone number in telephone book when operator tells you the number has been changed" and to separating "Siamese twins—born connected together; yet capable of being physically separated and existing as separate entities; not making two persons where there was once only one." Both these analogies, as the reader will appreciate, are wildly dissonant with AMI's actual behavior, which entailed creating a library of unauthorized copies of IBM microcode from which further copies were made in connection with splits and other reconfigurations. Was the consultant suggesting that the CDLA simply paper over the unsavory aspects of the AMI reconfiguration process, or did Froy truly have an abysmally erroneous understanding of that process? The latter seems clearly to have been the case. Nonetheless, the reader may again wish to consider whether, in terms of real world consequences, it matters what the answer to that question is.

In any event, in February 1990, Professor Froy was asked to appear as an expert witness on copyright law at the *AMI* trial. The request came not from AMI but from Comdisco's lawyer, Mr. Fish, and was later repeated by AMI's co-counsel, Professor Kitch. At Professor Kitch's request, Froy called Larry Allen, President of AMI, not to discuss the reconfiguration process but to discuss the matter of a retainer. The trial was already in progress, but Froy had not read the transcripts of the proceedings, or looked at any of the evidence before testifying. Nor had Judge O'Neill's 1988 antitrust opinion, in which the subject of IBM's lack of monopoly power was thoroughly addressed, passed beneath the professor's gaze. Of greater significance, Froy had not questioned Larry Allen or any other AMI employee or Comdisco employee about what sort of copying was actually being done in the course of their reconfiguration work. The only information on which Froy based an "expert" opinion as to that subject was the abbreviated and distorted description previously advanced by the Comdisco and CDLA lawyers. Yet Professor Froy agreed to testify that AMI's use of 309x microcode in connection with its reconfiguration business was consistent with the copyright law, and as a consequence this noted academic was required to appear before testifying in the Baltimore office of AMI's lawyers, to be deposed by IBM's trial counsel, Evan Chesler of the New York firm Cravath, Swaine & Moore. Under the Federal Rules of Civil Procedure, an expert may be questioned by opposing counsel before taking the stand about the relevant opinions held by the expert and the facts on which those opinions are based.

Chesler knew that AMI's expert witness had an attitude problem when it came to copyright and computer programs. He had collected all of Professor Froy's writings on the subject; there was no question how the professor felt:

—it was wrong for the copyright law to protect object code;

—the state of American copyright law is so unpredictable that teaching it is difficult;

—the *Whelan* decision was seriously flawed and could stifle progress in software engineering;

—copyright law should permit third parties to offer modifications to copyrighted software;

—the look and feel of user interfaces should not be protected by copyright.

Here, Chesler knew, was a teacher with a mission. For some reason, Professor Froy was spending valuable "publish or perish" time railing against the natural consequences of copyright protection for software. Did we have here a clandestine operative in the softwars, or a teacher whose mind had closed like an oyster shell around the brittle pearl of a personal ideology. For one reason or another, Professor Froy had become an articulate champion of software copyists, and IBM would have to defend itself vigorously against such "expert testimony."

IBM's defense took two forms. First, as mentioned in the last chapter, IBM engaged Professor Arthur Miller of Harvard as its own expert. As a member of CONTU, Professor Miller was far better placed than Professor Froy to explain the purpose of Section 117, which CONTU had drafted. He was also a copyright teacher of long standing. Though a student of the late Ben Kaplan (an advocate of the view that copyright should not be taken too seriously as a form of intellectual property protection), and not a strong protectionist himself, Miller would be faced in AMI's case with such blatant copying that Chesler was sure his testimony would be devastating.

The second line of defense, of course, would be the cross-examination of Professor Froy in the flesh. Good cross-examination at trial is a defense in the nature of an offense, or, perhaps better put, an offense disguised as a defense. The Baltimore deposition of Professor Froy was designed to pave the way for that cross-examination by doing four things: (1) confirming that Froy's views about copyright remained so extreme as to be inconsistent with existing law (a task easily accomplished, as the professor readily admitted to believing that existing law was wrong); (2) demonstrating that Froy was put up to her testimony by the CDLA (also easily done); (3) establishing that Froy either did not know the facts or didn't care what the facts were (which can be seen from the repeated disclaimers of knowledge or expertise quoted above); and (4) establishing that, on the facts of the AMI case, this copyright expert simply could not deny the existence of copyright infringement. In the latter connection, sitting across the table from Professor Froy at the deposition, Chesler asked whether the act of copying and inserting into split machines microcode from a library of tapes that were themselves made by copying microcode in systems owned by IBM would constitute infringement. The professor conceded that it could. Chesler asked whether a third party modifying microcode on the authorization of the owner of a copy of the microcode, but for use on a processor not owned by the authorizer, would be committing copyright infringement. Professor Froy replied that it might, depending on the nature of the industry and the uses which were being made of the original microcode. The consultant also admitted to lack of sufficient knowledge about the computer industry or about the 309x reconfiguration business to be able to say whether such copying was infringement or not, but agreed that there were no copyright cases holding that such copying was lawful. Chesler asked whether reverse engineering a copyrighted work in order to create a direct copy of that work was copyright infringement. Professor Froy said that it was. IBM's lawyer then asked whether Froy understood that AMI had used copies it had made of the IBM microcode in order to generate additional copies for machines other than those from which the microcode originally came. The professor had not known about such copying. At that stage, a little more than halfway through the deposition, Professor Froy was undoubtedly beginning to doubt the wisdom of having become involved with the CDLA and AMI.

Now, Chesler forced the deponent to contemplate that which had theretofore evaded contemplation: the precise series of steps through which AMI went in reconfiguring an IBM multiprocessor. He asked Froy to assume that, in splitting a 3090 model 400 into two models 200s, AMI took one of the two on-line copies of the microcode on the disk drives attached to the 3092 controller—specifically, the copy that would take over in the event the primary copy failed—and installed it on one of the model 200s, and then made a backup copy to use on the same machine. Based on that assumption, he solicited Froy's opinion as to whether making the additional copy would constitute permissible use of an archival copy under Section 117. At first, the scholar resisted the hypothetical on the grounds that it assumed facts on which the parties did not agree. As an expert witness, however, Froy was obligated to answer hypothetical questions posed by IBM's counsel, and, ultimately, was impelled to admit that such copying was not consistent with Section 117.

Under further questioning, Professor Froy testified to being unaware that evidence already admitted at the trial demonstrated that AMI's copying extended even to a serialization number inserted by IBM in the 309x microcode for the very purpose of detecting copying and transfer of the microcode among systems. Chesler elicited agreement from the deponent that, in a patent context, if it were necessary to create a second 3092 controller device in the process of creating a split, and IBM held a patent on the 3092, AMI would not be entitled to manufacture the second 3092 without a license from IBM; that the 309x microcode was much easier to copy than was the 3092 hardware; and that the easier it was to copy a work, the greater was the need for copyright protection. Froy claimed not to have seen the testimony demonstrating that AMI put labels on its "rainbow tapes" intended to look exactly like IBM's labels, and that customers in fact thought the "rainbow tapes" were supplied by IBM. In addition, the scholar admitted to having no idea how the configuration data on microcode Tape 2 had been selected, arranged, or organized by IBM, conceded that the protectability of the data on Tape 2 depended on its selection, arrangement and organization and agreed that in any case if the microcode was a combination of copyrightable and noncopyrightable subject matter there would be infringement unless the copying were privileged for some reason.

The deposition of Professor Froy ended with a series of questions about the academic's writings on the subject of Section 117; questions that—had Froy not previously considered the effect of those writings on the expert testimony AMI was expecting at trial—would have led to the realization that the "publish or perish" record would force her to testify that under facts such as those underlying the questions Chesler had earlier asked her, Section 117 did not protect AMI.

Professor Froy was to testify at trial shortly after the deposition. On the first trial day of the week in question, Froy appeared in the court room for the first time to await the inevitable turn in the witness box. This gave the expert witness an opportunity to observe the direct examination of AMI's witnesses by AMI's lawyer and, more importantly, the cross-examination of those witnesses by Chesler. The clock on the courtroom wall ticked, bringing the moment of truth inexorably nearer. A second trial day passed, with more grilling of other witnesses. AMI's copyright witness was hearing for the first time facts that the people who were paying for that copyright expertise had theretofore hidden, and that Froy had not taken the time to ferret out; facts, unfortunately, that matched Chesler's hypothetical questions. At one point in the exposition of those facts, Professor Froy and AMI's lawyers were seen engaged in intense conversation during a break. The fateful day arrived. Professor Froy was not in the courtroom. On the eve of testifying, the expert had vanished.

AMI's lawyer rose to address the court. His witness, he said, had run out of time. Froy's schedule was too crowded to permit testimony now or at any later time in the trial. Instead of her testimony, AMI would offer her deposition into evidence. The lawyer didn't say so, but the turn of events was disastrous for AMI. It had been at the initiative of AMI's counsel that Judge O'Neill had agreed to accept expert testimony on the copyright law in the first place. Now, all that AMI had to offer was the dry transcript of a deposition in which every single question was asked by IBM's lawyer; a deposition, in other words, consisting entirely of cross-examination. (In the ultimate, it was IBM, not AMI, that offered the Froy deposition in evidence.) Meantime, because of AMI's counsel's initiative, IBM had engaged a renowned law professor, TV personality, and most significantly co-author of Section 117, on which provision AMI's defense principally rested. When it was his turn on the witness stand, Arthur Miller testified without equivocation that the same reconfiguration practices described to Professor Froy in her deposition constituted copyright infringement. On cross-examination, he was asked whether, if IBM refused to give AMI access to the microcode tapes or a license to modify them, AMI could legitimately engage in copying of customers' tapes as a form of self-help. Miller's answer: "there's no notion of a right to self help by infringement.... [T]here's nothing in the Copyright Act entitling anyone to say, you got something I want, and I'm going to steal it from you ... because you won't give it to me."

Why had Professor Froy abandoned AMI? Had the pace of the trial that week in fact been so slow that the teacher's academic calendar had caught up with AMI? Possibly, but in most cases an accommodation can be found to such a problem by rearranging the order of witnesses, or even interrupting the testimony of other witnesses. That is particularly common in cases tried to a judge without a jury, as the *AMI* case was. Had Froy claimed not to be a "technical person" once too often for the taste of AMI's counsel? Maybe, but AMI had obviously never asked Professor Froy to testify about the technical activities involved in reconfiguration. Had Evan Chesler's relentless questioning in the deposition convinced the academic that any copyright expert who attempted to support AMI's case would be made to look a fool? That, I think, is getting closer to the truth, but if so, it is as much a compliment to the witness as to the lawyer. Put more positively from the scholar's viewpoint, what probably happened was this: as a result of the deposition, Froy learned that the client of this particular consultancy had not told the truth about its activities, and had allowed its "expert" to develop opinions based on a false view of those activities—and to state those opinions to the Justice Department. In the end, it seems likely, Froy decided that AMI had broken the law and that in good conscience a copyright expert could not be associated with an obvious infringer.

What does this experience teach those of us who constitute the audience for academic opinions about the softwars? Should there be a rule that academics who moonlight as experts must subject themselves to rigorous cross-examination before appearing as a spokesperson or oath helper for private interests, in order to assure that professors who wish to serve in the softwars, understand the facts before they speak? Felicitous though such a rule might be, it is an unrealistic goal. An objective more likely to be achieved would be full disclosure in connection with writings and appearances: the listing by academics—and all private consultants and lawyers, for that matter—of the private sponsors whose views they are promoting. Thus, for example: "This article funded by the Taiwanese Computer Industry Association," or "Consultant to the following software clones:..." Or, for that matter: "Sponsored by IBM." (Which this book is not, by the way.) A full disclosure requirement would not have a chilling effect on academic speech, since it would affect only sponsored speech, and the sponsors need only pay enough to overcome whatever shyness such disclosure might engender. Without some such rule, academics and private consultants are free to work the margins of the softwars, like propagandists, sowing disinformation and dissension masked as dispassionate commentary.

Centuries ago in Japan, a samurai visited a zen master for a lesson. The zen master gave him this koan: "You are going into the bathtub, stark naked, without a stitch on. Now a hundred enemies in armor, with bows and swords, appear all around you. How will you meet them? Will you crawl before them and beg for mercy? Will you show your warrior birth by dying in combat, or does a man of the Way get some special holy grace?" The samurai's reply was: "Let me win without either surrendering or fighting."

Professor Froy's answer seems to have been: "That is why the lady vanished."

# Part IV

## Thinking about the Unthinkable: Lasers, Hackers, Nightmare Scenarios, and Truces

Herein, we explore the nether regions the battleground, areas in which there abound dragons, bugbears, and other monsters of the id.

# 14

# Circuit Theory: Nonliteral Copying by Any Other Name...

We don't want to kill anymore. But the others are treacherous and cannot be trusted.
> —Yanomamo saying (Amazonia), quoted in Myriam Miedzian,
> *Boys Will Be Boys* (1991)

Up to this point in our tour of the battlefields, we have been concerned with the mainstream issues of the softwars: conflicts over the nature and scope of intellectual property protection for computer programs, and the relative strengths and weaknesses of the innovative and imitative forces as a result of those conflicts. In Part 3, we are going to step outside the mainstream to walk along—and in some cases beyond—the fringe of the disputed territory. This will give us a perspective from which to view the gross shape of that territory. Like viewing the Grand Canyon from the rim, one might say, rather than from the riverbed.

Guiding us on the first leg of our stroll will be the Honorable George C. Pratt, judge of the United States Court of Appeals for the Second Circuit. The federal appellate court system is divided into eleven geographic "circuits" (so named from the days when judges rode on horseback from one major city within their jurisdiction to another in order to hold court). There is also one nongeographic circuit that deals primarily with appeals in patent cases. The Second Circuit encompasses New York, New Jersey, and Connecticut, and once in a while its judges help out the federal trial court judges in those states by taking over cases at the trial level. Judge Pratt did just that in a case called *Computer Associates, Inc. v. Altai, Inc.*, picking up the lawsuit as pretrial preparation was being completed.

The changing of horses in midstream is no more felicitous a practice in software-related litigation than it is in any other field of human endeavor. Because of the arcana in which software development is steeped, it is much better for a single judge to keep the case from inception through the pretrial jockeying and into and out the other end of the trial. Doing so gives a jurist ample opportunity to profit from the educational efforts of the parties, as each side tries to explain what its program consists of, how it was written, what range of expression was available to its authors, and so forth. More importantly, because of the powerful assimilation experience of learning by doing, a judge can actually acquire a reasonable facility in the terms of programming art by deciding the motions by which the parties attempt to shape and focus (or blur) the issues that must go to trial. At the same time, a theory of the case has the opportunity to evolve in the mind of the jurist, and to be tested against the politely critical judgments of each party's counsel.

In the *Apple/Microsoft* litigation, for example, Judge Walker, as the third judge to handle the suit, was bequeathed a theory of the case with which he was initially not comfortable and which, when he applied it, caused him to count "trees" and ignore the "forest": the notion that only the elements of the Macintosh user interface that had not been licensed to Microsoft could be compared with elements of the Windows user interface in assessing substantial similarity. More than just a theory of the case, that notion had become embodied in a ruling by one of Judge Walker's predecessors, a ruling on which subsequent activities in the case had been based and which Judge Walker was not free simply to jettison. His own ruling on the "originality" of the Macintosh interface, which we perused in Chapter 6, reflects his unease with the inherited theory, his attempt to harmonize it with his own views as to how the lawsuit before him should be resolved, and the ultimate, confused result.

In the *Computer Associates* case, which by agreement of the parties was being tried to the court without a jury, Judge Pratt apparently felt that the technical aspects of the case would be beyond his comprehension as a latecomer, and appointed a technical expert to help him interpret the evidence and weigh the testimony of the parties' expert witnesses. That action put the *Computer Associates* case into a somewhat unique category, as most judges have not found it necessary or desirable to cede to others the responsibility for interpreting technical evidence in software infringement cases. As the court's expert, Judge Pratt appointed Professor Randall Davis of MIT's Artificial Intelligence Laboratory. In Randy Davis, the jurist had found an intelligent, articulate, and interested computer scientist. Davis had participated in important privately and publicly sponsored forums on the subject of software protection. He is known as a moderate, not an extremist either for or against protecting computer programs. He thinks of software as "this wondrous stuff," "the ultimate creative medium," "a tangible form of dreams and imagination," but at the same time feels that "we need to be willing to question some of the most fundamental assumptions" of intellectual property law as they apply to software. On the whole, therefore, Davis was about as neutral an expert as the court could have found.

As I mentioned at the outset, however, no one active on the software protection lecture circuit is neutral. Everyone has a bias, and Davis is no exception. His bias is not that of the partisan, but rather that of the skeptic, as reflected in the notion, just mentioned, that fundamental assumptions of intellectual property law are open to question in the case of software. In October 1990, Davis moderated a panel discussion entitled "Intellectual Property in Computing: (How) Should Software Be Protected? An Industry Perspective." The purpose of the discussion, which was conceived and in major part organized by Mike Ernst, who is associated both with MIT and with the League for Programming Freedom, was to "help shape the future of intellectual property and the software industry." In his introductory remarks, Davis set out his view that software (not just computer programs, but all digital software) is a different kind of property from any other that has ever existed; that the "old ways of doing business and the old ways of thinking may simply not work any more"; and that the challenge for the panelists and the audience was to "design the future of the industry." Just as there are people biased in favor of retaining existing modes of intellectual property protection for software, there are people biased in favor of questioning existing modes of intellectual property protection for software, and Davis is among the latter. That kind of bias, which might be called either the bias of an open mind or the bias of the tinkerer (depending on one's own biases), is not as hurtful to the role of independent advisor to the court as, say, Professor Froy's might have been. Nonetheless, it did sway the outcome of Computer Associates' case, as we shall see.

When parties to a lawsuit put forward experts of their own, as had AMI and IBM, the result is sometimes mutual neutralization: the opposing opinions simply cancel one another out, and the judge or jury is left to sort out the facts without effective expert help. More often, the expert for one of the parties will give more cogent testimony than his opposite, or will strike the judge or jury as more believable, and the interpretation of the facts offered by that expert will be credited by the trier of fact. Either way, each party has had the ability to challenge the biases, knowledge base, and assumptions of the other party's expert, through pretrial deposition, as was done in the case of Professor Froy, and then through cross-examination in the courtroom. That crucible is not available in the case of court-appointed experts. Davis' job was to evaluate for Judge Pratt the facts of the case and the expert testimony propounded on behalf of Computer Associates and Altai. His own testimony was not subject to the same kind of evaluation. Although he was made available for questioning at trial, the attorneys for both parties felt they had to treat him fairly gingerly. Plaintiff's counsel, for example, expressed uncertainty as to whether he should approach the questioning of Professor Davis as though it were direct examination or as though it were cross-examination. As a consequence of the diffidence of the parties' counsel in questioning the court-appointed expert, it is likely that Judge Pratt did not appreciate the significance of his technical assistant's inclination toward questioning the fundamental premises of intellectual property law, a predisposition that, while reasonable enough in the context of a panel discussion or letter to the editor, unduly influenced Judge Pratt, whose role as a jurist was to *apply* the fundamental premises of intellectual property law to the case before him, not to question those premises.

The case over which Judge Pratt, with Davis' assistance, presided in a Long Island courtroom was interesting both for the range of issues it presented and for the way Judge Pratt, guided by Davis, handled those issues. It involved computer programs with the user-friendly names ZEKE, ZACK, and OSCAR, among others, that ran on the IBM System/370 family of mainframe computers. For that hardware family, IBM provided three operating systems: DOS/VSE, MVS, and VM/CMS. (There is actually a fourth: AIX/370, a UNIX variant, but it was not on the market during the relevant time period.) Those operating systems provided disparate programming interfaces for use by authors of application programs, and in consequence an application program written to run on one operating system generally would not run without modification on one of the other operating systems unless the portions of the application program that called on the services of the operating system were rewritten. In order to reach the broadest base of customers at the lowest cost, it behooved Computer Associates (CA) to write its application programs in such fashion that modification of system calls to accommodate the three IBM operating systems was not a difficult process. To that end, CA organized its application programs into two components. One component contained all of the application-specific modules of the program; the other contained the modules of the program that intermediated between the first component and the operating system. That second component was called by Judge Pratt the "interface." Calls for operating system functions written by the authors of application-specific modules were issued not to the operating system itself but to the "interface." The "interface" translated those internal calls into the proper external calls to one of the three IBM operating systems. By writing three different "interfaces," CA was able to provide DOS/VSE, MVS, and VM/CMS versions of its application programs without having to engage in wholesale rewriting or restructuring of those programs.

The tale of infringement begins with CA-SCHEDULER, a CA program written in the fashion just described. Its "interface" component was called "ADAPTER." ADAPTER had been in use by CA since 1979, and had been enhanced many times between 1979 and 1990. One of the programmers who worked on those enhancements, in relation to the DOS/VSE version of ADAPTER, was Claude Arney. A five year veteran of CA, Arney quit the company in January 1984, to got to work for Altai, a company founded by James Williams, a former product manager at CA. Williams had told Arney that his first job would be to write the MVS version of the Altai program ZEKE. Arney had no experience, however, in writing an MVS "interface." Why, the reader might consider, did Williams hire a programmer with no MVS experience to write a program that interfaces with MVS? There are a number of possible answers to that question. They are all colored, however, by the fact that before he left CA, Arney appropriated copies of the source code of the DOS/VSE and MVS versions of ADAPTER and removed them from the premises, in violation of his employment agreement and of the law of trade secrets. He brought those copies to Altai and kept them in his desk while he worked on the ZEKE project.

ZEKE was a program that accomplished job scheduling on IBM main-frames. Job scheduling, simplistically put, is the task of sequencing programs for execution in the computer. ZEKE was a direct competitor to CA-SCHED-ULER, which performed the same function. Williams had developed ZEKE in 1981–82 for DOS/VSE environments. He was unfamiliar with the way CA-SCHEDULER was organized however, and not sufficiently perspicacious to recognize on his own that bifurcating the program would facilitate port-ability. Arney recognized the benefits of bifurcation, however, as a result of his knowledge of CA's design, and he convinced Williams to restructure ZEKE so that it would issue calls to an interface component. That compo-nent, which Arney apparently wrote single-handed, was called OSCAR. Arney developed OSCAR/VSE first. That project took him three months. Then he wrote the MVS version, which required another month. The speed with which both tasks were accomplished was admirable, particularly in com-parison to the development schedule for CA's ADAPTER, which was on the order of five person-years. Unfortunately, though, almost a third of the source code of OSCAR was copied from the purloined ADAPTER source code. In addition, it appears that there were strong structural and organizational similarities between the two programs.

These latter unfortunate facts were unknown to anyone else at Altai at the time, according to evidence submitted by Altai at trial. Judge Pratt seems to have accepted Altai's assertion, despite the evidence that Williams knew he was asking Arney to write interface code of the same type as the latter had written at CA. According to the facts as found by the court, then, Altai's first clue as to the true provenance of its OSCAR programs came in the form of the complaint served on Altai by CA in 1989. By then, OSCAR had been in the market for three years. The then-current release level of Altai's interface program was designated OSCAR 3.4.

As soon as the complaint was served, Williams called Arney to account and Arney confessed the error of his ways. The defrocked infringer identified to Williams which modules of OSCAR had been copied from ADAPTER and

which had been, in the court's words, "separately devcloped either from
ZEKE or independently." Williams then called his lawyer. He wanted advice
as to how to rewrite OSCAR as quickly as possible without ending up with
an infringing product. To the extent that his subsequent actions mirror the
advice he was given, it was not overly conservative advice. The ADAPTER
source code was placed in a locked receptacle. (Why wasn't it returned to
CA, whose property it was?) Arney was "excluded entirely from the rewriting process." (Why wasn't he fired?) Williams prepared the specifications of the systems calls that the new OSCAR was to recognize, "primarily,"
according to Judge Pratt, by looking at ZEKE (apparently in the form in
which it existed prior to Arney's arrival), rather than at OSCAR 3.4. OSCAR
3.4 was reviewed during the rewrite process, though, ostensibly to ascertain
which elements had been copied from ADAPTER. (Why look at OSCAR 3.4
*at all*? Why not toss it out and start over again?) For reasons only partly
explained in his opinion, Judge Pratt did not find it relevant to consider the
nature of the rewriting process in any detail.

All of Altai's programmers except Arney went to work on the project.
There were eight of them in all, and in their efforts they were forbidden
access to OSCAR 3.4 and also to Arney. It took them six "work-months,"
by which I assume the judge meant "person-months" rather than elapsed
time, to complete the job. (In its subsequent brief to Judge Pratt's colleagues
on the Court of Appeals, CA pegged the elapsed time to rewrite OSCAR at
a thousand hours.) It is not clear why the substantially longer time to
complete the rewrite wasn't recognized in and of itself as evidence that
Altai should have realized Arney's transgression early on because of the
inordinately rapid pace of his development work. Perhaps Dr. Davis gave
Altai the benefit of the "mythical man-month" theory, as expounded by
Professor Frederick P. Brooks:

I vividly recall the night we decided how to organize the actual writing of external
specifications for OS/360. The manager of architecture, the manager of control
program implementation, and I were threshing out the plan, schedule, and division
of responsibilities.

The architecture manager had 10 good men. He asserted that they could write the
specifications and do it right. It would take ten months, three months more than
the schedule allowed.

The control program manager had 150 men. He asserted that they could prepare
the specifications, with the architecture team coordinating; it would be well-done
and practical, and he could do it on schedule. Furthermore, if the architecture team
did it, his 150 men would sit twiddling their thumbs for ten months.

To this the architecture manager responded that if I gave the control program team
the responsibility, the result would *not* in fact be on time, but would also be three
months late, and of much lower quality. I did, and it was.

Whatever the reason for overlooking Arney's rapid development schedule of OSCAR 3.4, the rewritten product of Altai's authorial octet began shipping to customers as OSCAR 3.5 in November 1989. CA claimed that it, too, represented both a copyright infringement and a misappropriation of CA's trade secrets.

The opinion of the district court on those claims was issued on August 12, 1991, after a full trial. Dealing first with the copyright question, the judge found Altai's admission that 30 percent of OSCAR 3.4 was copied directly from the source code of ADAPTER to be an admission of infringement, and awarded CA $501,934.04, a figure that included damages plus interest. As to OSCAR 3.5, there was no direct evidence of copying, so the judge was required to rely on the standard two-fold copyright test for infringement: access plus substantial similarity. "Access," he wrote, "is not seriously disputed in this case." Altai had, after all, retained copies of ADAPTER on its premises while the rewrite was taking place. Too, portions of ADAPTER were contained in OSCAR 3.4, which was also available on Altai's premises during the rewrite. The question, though, was not whether access was possible but whether access was had. (Though unsaid by the judge, the level of similarity of the resulting program affects the nature of proof of access required to establish infringement in a copyright case. The less strikingly similar two programs are, the more direct evidence of actual access will be required. OSCAR 3.5 was in most respects, apparently, not strikingly similar to ADAPTER.) Regarding actual access, the parties differed. Altai claimed that the precautions it had taken prevented the use by its programming octet either of ADAPTER or of OSCAR 3.4. CA claimed that the ADAPTER code was available to Williams indirectly through his conversations with Arney, "particularly at the time that Williams set up the parameter lists for the new OSCAR." The court sided with Altai, finding its efforts to isolate the octet from the source code of the target program to be sufficient to prevent functional access to that code.

The important issue, then, was substantial similarity. It was in connection with this issue that Judge Pratt relied heavily on Randy Davis' opinions, and where Dr. Davis took the opportunity to call into question some of the fundamental assumptions of copyright law as it is applied to computer programs. The judge began his revisionist analysis of the substantial similarity test by saying that "[i]n the context of computer programs, many of the familiar tests for similarity prove to be inadequate, for they were developed historically in the context of artistic and literary, rather than utilitarian, works." That assertion was questionable on two counts. First, the most familiar test for similarity—the principle that similarities in idea rather than expression do not constitute infringement—was developed in a case involving utilitarian works; specifically, accounting forms. That case resulted in the Supreme Court opinion known as *Baker v. Selden*, perhaps the single most important copyright case ever decided. Further, numerous important

cases involving utilitarian writings other than computer programs have contributed to the evolution of the substantial similarity test. Second, utilitarian
or not, programs are works of imagination, not works of fact, and the range
of expression available to authors of original programs can clearly be as
broad as that available to authors of artistic and literary works. Where the
range of potential expression is broad, the "familiar test" of substantial
similarity is quite appropriate to establish a *prima facie* case of copying,
thereby shifting the burden to the defendant to defend the similarities.

From his shaky premise, Judge Pratt leapt to the even more tenuous
conclusion that the *Whelan* case, without question one of the most important software copyright cases decided to date, was "inadequate," "inaccurate," "simplistic," and "fundamentally flawed." The *Whelan* case, which
held the detailed structure, sequence, and organization of a program to be
an aspect of its expression, was decided by the United States Court of Appeals
for the Third Circuit. Although acting in this case as a trial judge, Judge
Pratt was a member of the Court of Appeals for the Second Circuit, and
was not, even at the trial level, bound to follow precedent established in
another circuit. The Second Circuit has a long tradition of being a strong
copyright circuit as a result of New York's history as a center of the publishing industry, and is justifiably proud of that tradition. Accidents of programming history, however, had conspired to cause the important software
copyright cases to be brought in circuits other than the Second Circuit. Just
as Judge Pratt could ignore legal precedents, such as *Whelan*, from other
federal judicial circuits, those other circuits were not required to follow
Second Circuit precedents either, and Second Circuit copyright methodol-
ogies had at the time of the *CA* case not yet been adapted to software
contexts. Judge Pratt seemed to be seizing the moment to correct that
imbalance. In reaching to do so, he was not as careful as he might have
been.

He articulated three reasons for criticizing *Whelan*. One of these was the
assertion that *Whelan* holds that there can be only a single idea in a program,
and everything else is expression. That is very much a misreading of the
case, which the judge adopts from Professor Nimmer's famous treatise on
copyright law. The Professor Nimmer who penned that critique, however,
was not the Professor Melville Nimmer who made the treatise famous, but
the son of that great personage, who has been updating that seminal work
since his father's death. Nimmer *pere* and Nimmer *fils* did not see eye to
eye on the subject of scope of protection for computer programs. The former
believed that a program's structure, logic, and flow could indeed be part of
its expression; that the traditional copyright tests for protection of nonliteral
elements of copyrighted works were applicable to computer programs.

In addition to walking unawares into an interfamilial dispute over copyright theory, Judge Pratt's first critique was in itself inaccurate and simplistic.
Though there is a sentence in the *Whelan* opinion which, if taken completely

out of context, could lead one to conclude that the rule of the case excludes from protection only a single, generalized idea about what a program's purpose is, when that language is read in the context of the rest of the opinion, and in light of the kinds of similarities that the *Whelan* court found to be infringing—for example, detailed data structures and logic flows—it is clear the court was saying no more than this: neither the overarching purpose of a program nor anything necessary to accomplish that purpose are normally part of the program's expression, but the detailed design of the program is normally part of the program's expression.

Judge Pratt's second criticism of *Whelan* came directly from Professor Davis, who pointed out that a computer program is comprised of "sub-programs and sub-sub-programs, and so on," and at each level those programs can be said to have at least one idea. Some of those programs might be separately copyrightable, others might be standard or routine in nature and not eligible for copyright protection. The implication was that *Whelan* does not allow for a sufficient level of analytic granularity. Again, however, such an interpretation of *Whelan* is forced rather than natural. Certainly, a single software product may be composed of a number of separate or separable programs, and each program may have one or more ideas, and may be analyzed individually for copyright purposes. But this does not mean that the detailed structure, logic, or flow of the program should be considered unprotectable, any more than the structure, logic, or flow of a novel should be considered unprotectable because each chapter, each paragraph, each sentence, or each word contains at least one idea.

The court's third objection to *Whelan* also was credited to Professor Davis. Computer programs, the computer scientist observed, have both a textual nature and a behavioral nature; that is, they have a static form (the written code) and a dynamic form (the sequence of execution of that code in a computer). In Davis' view, there was no necessary relationship between the two manifestations of a program. Therefore, he concluded, "it makes no technical sense to talk simply about the 'structure' of a program, because the term is ambiguous and the distinction [between dynamic structure and static structure] matters." Thus, when the *Whelan* court said that "structure, sequence and organization" are really synonymous terms referring to the same nonliteral elements of a program, that conclusion was "exactly wrong technically; it is precisely because a program is not only text, but also behaves, that these terms (in all their meanings) are not synonymous. The problem is thus compounded: where [prior to Whelan] the terms were merely ambiguous, they have now been declared equivalent when they are not." (It is not clear why the court emphasized this aspect of Dr. Davis' testimony, since *Whelan* was concerned both with similarities in static structures [data files] and with dynamic structures [program logic and flow].)

In emphasizing that software has both static and dynamic structures, Randy Davis was merely attempting to point out that the *Whelan* court did not seem to understand that it was dealing with both static and dynamic attributes, and that sound copyright analysis should be based on an understanding of that distinction. Judge Pratt clearly made more of the point than was intended or even appropriate. While the distinction between static and dynamic structures is real, and is meaningful from a technical point of view, it is not a distinction that makes a difference for copyright purposes. If it did, the law would be different for a number of more traditional types of works of authorship which also have static and dynamic structures. For example:

—A movie on laserdisk or on videotape has a static structure, an organized sequence of optical bits or magnetic codings on, respectively, the disk or tape. The two static structures, if examined microscopically, would seem to be highly dissimilar, even though both derive from the same static structure created at an earlier point in the filmmaking process: the screenplay. The movie also has a dynamic structure: a complex combination of picture tube element movements, phosphorescent screen element illuminations, and loudspeaker vibrations that, when viewed from the comfort of your sofa, tell the story of Bill and Ted's Excellent Adventure or *Saalam* Bombay or whatever movie you have rented. The separate static structures of visual track and soundtrack are combined in the processing hardware to create a single audiovisual structure. Today, a computer *could* provide the necessary processing hardware to play a movie; tomorrow, when computers and televisions are a single "information appliance," it *will* do so.

—A musical score has static structures, the organized sequences of notes, bars, rests, signatures, and other musical notations written by the composer. It also has dynamic structures, in the form of the physical motion of the musicians and their instruments and the overall auditory structures perceived by the audience. The orchestra members each process their particular static structures in coordinated fashion to create the dynamic auditory structures heard by the listeners. Today, the musicians can be replaced by a computer that directly converts the score into its dynamic form. Indeed, I have a program on my desk that allows me to write in musical notation and plays back the score through my computer and stereo system. If you visit my home, I'd be happy to "process" through that hardware the static structure of a blues suite I have written, so that you may experience its dynamic form.

—A hologram has a static structure in the organized pattern of developed chemical particles on the holographic film and a dynamic structure in the form of the image that appears when the proper form of light is shone on the film, and in the perceived movement of that image as the viewer perambulates the hologram. Today, a computer can be used to generate a hologram. Tomorrow, a computer may be able to display a hologram.

In all three of the foregoing cases, copyright protection is available for both the static structures and the dynamic structures, and in all three cases that protection extends to the nonliteral, expressive elements of those struc-tures. Indeed, Professor Davis' criticism of the "structure, sequence, and organization" formulation ends with a listing of the terms that he proposes for use in assessing evidence of nonliteral infringement of copyright in computer programs: control structure, logic structure, data structure, con-trol flow, and data flow. Davis' listing, while not identical to the description of static and dynamic nonliteral elements given in Chapter 1, is certainly highly evocative of that description and makes it clear that the scientist was not criticizing the *Whelan* court for having held such elements protectable, but rather for imprecision of technical thought and explication.

After Judge Pratt misused Randy Davis' static/dynamic analysis to put *Whelan* to one side, he set about to explain what the proper test for assessing similarity between two programs was. Not surprisingly, it was a homegrown substitute: the widely adopted Second Circuit test propounded in 1930 by Judge Learned Hand in *Nichols v. Universal Pictures Corp.*, a case involving a screenplay for a motion picture. This test is known as the "patterns test" or the "abstractions test." It reads as follows:

Upon any work . . . a great number of patterns of increasing generality will fit equally well, as more and more of the incident is left out. The last may perhaps be no more than the most general statement of what the [work] is about and at times might consist only of its title; but there is a point in this series of abstractions where they are no longer protected, since otherwise the [author] could prevent the use of his "ideas" to which, apart from their expression, his property is never extended.

Was the whole point of the rejection of the *Whelan* analysis to promulgate a Second Circuit test for nonliteral infringement instead of a Third Circuit test, a kind of Not-Invented-Here reaction? Perhaps. In any case, the *Com-puter Associates* case gives both weak protectionists and strong protec-tionists something to trumpet. The weak protectionists can point to the opinion of an eminent computer scientist that the *Whelan* court was wrong. The strong protectionists can point to the suggestion that while the title and the most general statement of what a program is about are not protected, everything else is. Both assertions would be erroneous, but both are to be expected.

Traditionalists like myself take a middle view of Judge Pratt's handiwork. What I would draw to the reader's attention is the following. It is of critical importance to recognize that the jurist reached into the rich history of copyright for a famous test of substantial similarity to apply to the case before him. The Third Circuit had done the same thing, casting back into the last century for *Baker v. Selden*. The precedent for which Judge Pratt reached was less hoary, perhaps, but in fact the "patterns test" is only a twentieth-century restatement of the *Selden* test. The judicial methodology used by Judge Pratt and by the Third Circuit was the same, and the general area of law from which the courts sought guidance was the same: the wellspring of presoftware precedents dealing with the idea/expression dichotomy. In addition, both the Second Circuit "patterns" test and the Third Circuit "purpose" test contemplate that nonliteral similarities may be evidence of infringement. In *Nichols*, the Second Circuit held that copyright protection "cannot be limited literally to the text, else a plagiarist would escape by immaterial variations." In *Whelan*, the Third Circuit held that copyrights in computer programs "can be infringed even absent copying of the literal elements of the program."

Finally, I would ask the reader to consider what the essential differences are between the two tests. According to the *Whelan* test, the programs purposes, everything essential to those purposes, and in appropriate cases the particular way the program accomplishes its purposes are unprotectable idea, while everything else is protectable expression (subject, of course, to defenses such as merger, fair use, nonsubstantial copying, etc.). According to the *Nichols* test, patterns of increasing abstraction may be identified for a computer program, and at an appropriately high level of abstraction, a line is crossed from protectable expression to unprotectable idea. The only real differences between the two approaches are that *Whelan* provides a top-down test, while *Nichols* provides a bottom-up test, and that *Whelan* gives explicit guidance while *Nichols* leaves it to the discretion of the court to pick the level of abstraction which is no longer protectable. In picking that level, judges looking for further guidance are all bound by and drawn back to the Supreme Court opinion in *Baker v. Selden*, which says, as to accounting forms:

[W]here the art it teaches cannot be used without employing the methods and diagrams used to illustrate the book, or such as are similar to them, such methods and diagrams are to be considered as necessary incidents to the art and given to the public.

At the heart of the idea/expression dichotomy in both circuits, in other words, lies the concept that aspects of a work that must unavoidably be present because they are necessary to the elucidation of its ideas are not protectable, while aspects of a work that are arbitrary choices among many ways of elucidating the work's ideas are protectable. For those arbitrary modes of expression, both *Whelan* and *Nichols* recognize that protection extends to nonliteral elements.

Having adopted the "patterns" test for purposes of assessing infringement, Judge Pratt turned to the evidence. The evidence presented by CA as to similarity between OSCAR 3.5 and ADAPTER, the judge said, fell into five categories: object code, source code, parameter lists, macros, and "high-level structure." Unfortunately, Judge Pratt's opinion is quite cryptic in describing the nature of that evidence. As to the first two categories, it says only that "there remained virtually no lines of code that were identical to ADAPTER." If there remained *some* lines of code that were identical, however, and particularly if other portions of the code, while not identical, were highly similar, the presumption that there had been no functional access to ADAPTER in rewriting OSCAR would have been called into question. For purposes of posterity (as well as the inevitable appeal), the judge should have elaborated on the presence or absence of patterns of similarity in the code.

Regarding the parameter lists and macros, the court found sufficient evidence of similarity from which to infer copying, but also found that many of the similarities were dictated by the functions of the program. Some similarities were engendered by the need to conform to the IBM operating system calls. Other similarities were engendered by calls from the application-specific modules of the CA programs or the Altai programs. (The court's discussion of the latter similarities is quite opaque. Since there is no necessity for the Altai application-specific module to use the same calls to OSCAR as the CA application-specific modules used in calling the services of ADAPTER, one would not expect any particular level of similarity to exist in the parameters and macros used to express those calls. The court seems to have concluded that unless CA had also sued for infringement of the similarities in the calling portions of its application-specific modules, it could not claim infringement for the called portions of ADAPTER. That is not the law.) In all events, Dr. Davis could not determine from the evidence whether the parameter lists and macros were copied "to any significant extent" from ADAPTER or not, and asked the parties to supply further evidence. None was forthcoming before Professor Davis left the witness stand, and in assessing the supplemental evidence on his own, Judge Pratt concluded that CA had not met its burden of proving substantial similarity. Here again, since the lists and macros were apparently copied at least to *some* extent, the court should have revisited the question of access, since the conclusion that there was at least some copying is flatly inconsistent with the presumption that there was no access of a type that would have permitted copying.

Next, the court considered the similarities in two kinds of high level structural elements. These were: (1) the list of the services provided by ADAPTER and OSCAR, as to which "there was considerable overlap, but a great deal of that was required by demands of functionality and was not attributed by Dr. Davis, nor is it by the court, to direct copying" and (2) the "organization chart" of the programs' structure, which the expert and the court found to be too simple and obvious to be "important." Once again, the court failed to confront the fact that if there was some evidence of direct copying, the presumption of lack of access was invalid, and if so CA's burden of demonstrating similarity of expression was lower. Ultimately, the court seems to have been swayed by its expert's conclusion that Altai had engaged in a "good faith effort to correct something that was wrong." That is certainly a factor to be weighed in apportioning the benefit of the doubt in gray-area cases, but it is not a sufficient factor to relieve the defendant of the burden of defending itself by showing that the similarities are explained by reasons other than copying.

Turning to CA's trade secret claims, the court noted that Altai had agreed not to dispute those claims insofar as they arose from the use of the ADAPTER code brought to Altai by Arney. Nonetheless, Judge Pratt rejected CA's claims on the ground that they were preempted by copyright law. The federal Copyright Act explicitly preempts any state laws that provide rights equivalent to copyright. While trade secret protection provides numerous rights not equivalent to copyright, CA's complaint was that the "incorporation into its ZEKE, ZACK and ZEBB programs of the various elements contained in the ADAPTER component of [CA's] CA-SCHEDULER program . . . constitutes the willful misappropriation of the proprietary property and trade secrets of plaintiff." The court held that the trade secret claim was nothing more than a claim that Altai had copied ADAPTER, a claim that the copyright law preempted. A more sophisticated analysis than that was required to reach a conclusion on the trade secret claim, however. The judge should have considered that trade secret law protects secret ideas as well as secret expression, and also protects expression that is "dictated by functionality" and even a selection of expressions that are in the public domain, so long as the particular selection chosen by the author is kept secret. The right to protect such ideas and expression is not equivalent to the rights granted by copyright. While one might argue that the preemption clause in the copyright act promulgates a negative preemption as well, so that elements of a literary work that are not protected by copyright cannot be protected against copying by trade secret law, that argument would run counter to the principles expressed in the *Kewanee* Supreme Court case discussed in Chapter 9. It seems to me that Judge Pratt should not have rejected CA's misappropriation claims without addressing these points, but of course it was up to CA's counsel to present the court with that imperative in a manner the court could not ignore.

CA appealed without success. Not surprisingly, Judge Pratt's brethren upheld his ruling. In the appellate court, two *amicus curiae* briefs were filed. One, filed on behalf of the Software Protection Association, the leading software antipiracy group in the United States, supported CA's position; the other, filed by an organization called the American Committee for Interoperable Systems, supported Altai's position. The composition of these two groups was roughly similar to that of the two software industry associations formed in Europe to lobby the European Community institutions concerning the European software copyright directive. (See note 14.5 for commentary on the appellate decision.)

The use of a court-appointed expert in the *CA v. Altai* litigation did not, in my view, have a positive effect on the process of judicial decision making. This was true despite the unquestioned competence of the expert chosen and the technical solidity of the expert's opinion. The insertion of an "official" expert between the facts and the ultimate finder of fact insulated the court from the necessity to understand the works at issue and the nature of the elements being compared in the substantial similarity test. As a result, the court either failed to grasp the significance of some of the expert's findings or substituted the expert's judgment as to the legal significance of those findings for its own. In contrast, in the Apple/Microsoft/H-P litigation, the late-coming Judge Walker directed the parties to provide him with the necessary hardware and software to allow him to familiarize himself with the programs at issue, and the requisite instruction in the use of that hardware and software. With several months before trial in which to accomplish his purpose, Judge Walker intended to put himself in a position from which to assess both factual and expert testimony at the trial and to draw the appropriate legal conclusions without the need for an intermediary. Though the particular path chosen by Judge Walker will not suit every judge or every case, the perils inherent in the use of a court-appointed expert should not be ignored. In *CA v. Altai*, the lack of separation between the role of the judge and the role of the expert triggered a kind of "friendly fire" that worked to the advantage of the extreme forces in the softwars.

# 15

# The Outer Limits: *Lasercomb v. Reynolds*

As the sick man that in his sleep doth see
some ugly dream, or some chimera new,
though he suspect, or half persuaded be,
it is an idle dream, no monster true,
yet still he fears, he quakes and strives to flee,
so fearful is that wondrous form to view;
so feared the knight, yet he both knew and thought
all were illusions false by witchcraft wrought.
                    —Torquato Tasso, *Gerusalemme Liberata* (1581)

I was standing in a hearing room, about to counter the argument of opposing counsel to the effect that accepting a position that I had earlier espoused would unleash a series of unforeseeable but surely dire consequences that would reveal—too late to do anything about it—my client's supposed hidden agenda. As the room was provided with an overhead projector and a screen, I riffled through my papers looking for the transparency on which I had recorded, in anticipation of just such a fright-wig appeal, the above quotation from the crowning work of the greatest Italian poet of the late Renaissance and the personage after whom the locus of the hearing was named. *Accidente!* The transparency was MIA. It failed to manifest itself among my otherwise impeccably organized, though outwardly disheveled-looking, materials. Since fumbling through one's papers is not generally thought to be an effective approach to oral argument, I moved directly into

the substance of my response, letting pass the opportunity to enrich culturally the lives of my opposing counsel and the decision makers.

Not one to waste a good quote, I have presumed to bestow the culturally
enriching Tuscan tidbit on the reader, by way of introducing a chapter that
I hope will help dispel false monsters that followers of the trade press may
have come to fear. The monsters are those of impending monopolization
through control of seminal copyrights, the conjuring up of which gives rise
to fears that competition in programs of particular types will be stifled.
Copyright itself does not confer a monopoly, as we've already seen. The
right to produce a similar or even identical work by independent creation,
and the right to copy the ideas in copyrighted works, both serve to prevent
the mere exercise of copyrights from leading to monopoly. One can imagine,
however, ways in which a copyright owner may use a copyright to obtain,
or attempt to obtain, a monopoly.

Happily, though, we need not fear that such situations will occur, because
copyright protection is not a particularly powerful offensive weapon in the
softwars. It is in fact a better shield than a sword. Owners of a software
copyrights can only protect the intellectual turf covered by their copyright
against those who infringe its territory. They cannot skewer those who
independently create the same intellectual property. Developers who have
not had access to that software may obtain equally valid copyrights to exactly
the same property. If in fact the copyright owner attempts to use the copyright to gain additional turf not covered by the copyright—for example, to
prevent others from copying unprotected material, such as ideas, or to
threaten competitors who are not engaged in plagiarism—the law no longer
smiles on the copyright owner. In the ultimate, the right provided by law
may be taken away. A misused copyright, in their words, may be unenforce-
able.

Such was the lesson learned by Lasercomb of America, Inc. The *Lasercomb*
case demonstrates as starkly as possible—perhaps a little too starkly—the
unhappy fate of a copyright owner found to have misused a lawfully obtained
copyright.

Lasercomb was in the business of manufacturing steel rule dies that are
used in cutting and scoring cardboard and paper stock preparatory to folding
it into boxes or cartons. In order to automate its operations, Lasercomb
developed a computer program, called "Interact," that allowed a designer
to create on a display screen a template for a cutout. Once the template
was complete, Interact provided for the automatic cutting of the steel rule
die that would be used in the actual scoring of a piece of cardboard or
paper cut in the shape of the template. Interact, in other words, was a
"computer-aided design/computer-aided manufacturing" ("CAD/CAM")
program.

Normally, programs such as Interact, created in-house to give a manufacturer a competitive edge (if the reader will entertain a small pun), are

treated as trade secrets and in particularly are not shared with competitors. Sometimes, though, the allure of financial return on the programming investment cannot be resisted. Lasercomb succumbed to the temptation, and decided to market Interact to other manufacturers. That decision having been taken, it followed that prerelease versions of Interact would be installed with other die manufacturers. Prerelease installations are the software industry's way of letting a few lucky customers debug suppliers' products free of charge. In the case of Interact, any candidate for prerelease installation would of course be another manufacturer of steel rule dies or, in other words, a competitor of Lasercomb.

The Holiday Steel Rule Die Corporation was such a competitor. Holiday was willing to install and even pay for four prerelease copies of Interact, though it was apparently unwilling to sign Lasercomb's license agreement and never in fact did so (the significance of that omission will be considered shortly). For its part, Lasercomb was willing to provide its competitor with four prerelease copies of Interact, and apparently did not care terribly that its license agreement was never signed. Lasercomb did, however, care about preventing unauthorized copying of Interact, for it provided Holiday with a hardware device, called a "chronoguard." Reminiscent of the AutoCAD lock, the chronoguard had to be used with Holiday's computers in order for Interact to function. Holiday received one chronoguard for each copy of Interact delivered to it, and Lasercomb repeatedly inquired of Holiday whether the chronoguard was in use.

What happened next is not very pretty, and the morally squeamish reader may want to skip this paragraph. Holiday's staff figured out how to circumvent the chronoguards and run the Interact software without them. They created and used three illicit copies of Interact for Holiday's internal use. This they did while representing to Lasercomb that the chronoguards were being used. Not content with the modest windfall represented by the additional copies of Interact that its personnel were using, Holiday's president decided to extend the scope of his company's competition with Lasercomb from the field of steel rule dies to the field of computer programs. In order to implement this diversification plan, a Holiday programmer created a program called "PDS–1000," which was almost entirely a direct copy of Interact. Seeking to disguise that copying, the Holiday programmer attempted to modify PDS–1000 so that it would produce output differing in appearance from that produced by Lasercomb's program. Bluntly put, Holiday had not only engaged in bald-faced copyright infringement, for its internal consumption, but had sought to deprive Lasercomb of customers through the marketing of an infringing program. That kind of behavior is, of course, the abiding fear of the software author.

Lasercomb sued Holiday, its president, and its programmer, all of whom were separately liable under the copyright law. At the trial level, the suit succeeded. Holiday and the individual defendants were enjoined from publishing and marketing PDS–1000, and were ordered to pay Lasercomb $120,000 in damages. The case, at that stage, was unremarkable.

For reasons perhaps unconnected with the judgment against it (the court's opinion doesn't say), Holiday went into bankruptcy. The individual defendants, however, appealed the judgment against them. They raised a number of arguments in their defense, only one of which had any effect on the outcome of the case: the defense of copyright misuse. The defendant-appellants argued that Lasercomb misused its copyright in Interact by supplying it only pursuant to a restrictive license agreement that exacted the licensee's promise not to "write, develop, produce or sell computer assisted die making software" for the succeeding ninety-nine years. The reader will have still in mind the fact that Holiday did not sign Lasercomb's license agreement. That fact weighed against the defendants at the trial level. The trial court had found that since Holiday had not subjected itself to the restrictive license, it was not in a position to claim that the license constituted misuse. It also found that the clause was reasonable, and in addition that the so-called defense of misuse might not in fact exist in the copyright law.

The three-judge panel of the Court of Appeals for the Fourth Circuit took a very different view of the matter than had the trial court. Dealing first with the question whether there was in fact a defense of copyright misuse, the appellate court conceded that the question was beset by uncertainty. The misuse defense, common and well established in the case of patents, had never been clearly articulated in the case of copyright. In only a small number of cases had the issue whether there was in fact such a defense ever been considered. Opinion in those cases was split as to whether copyright misuse was a valid defense or not. The Fourth Circuit law clerks, who researched the question no doubt by diligently interrogating case law data bases from their personal computers, had managed to find only one case in which a defendant had actually succeeded in fending off a claim of infringement using the defense of copyright misuse. It was a trial court opinion from another circuit, and therefore not necessarily a precedent that the Fourth Circuit judges were bound to follow.

There is nothing an appellate court loves so much as *tabula rasa*: the blank slate, the open field, an area of the law in which the significant issues have not been settled. Trial judges, on the other hand, detest such territory, because trial judges do not like to see their decisions reversed, and if they are making new law their decisions are more likely to be reversed than if they are (or at least seem to be) simply applying existing statutes and precedents to the facts before them. Appeals court judges—particularly those whose decisions are not susceptible to still further appeal, as for example the justices of the United States Supreme Court or, in many cases, judges of the highest state courts—see the unsettled question as an opportunity to be creative, to consider broad questions of legal and social policy, to make history. The blank slate, in short, is a power trip. The law, Holmes said, is what courts will do in fact, and on the open field courts will do as they please.

It pleased the Fourth Circuit to take its judicial time machine back to sixteenth century England, back to the roots of what has become American intellectual property law. Let us take our own time machine back to that period, in order to expand slightly on the genesis described by Judge Sprouse, the author of the Fourth Circuit's *Lasercomb* opinion. What we learn is as follows.

The sixteenth century was the century of the Tudors, dominated by the reign of one of England's most powerful (and most frequently married) monarchs, Henry VIII, and the reign of one of England's greatest (and unmarried) monarchs, his daughter Elizabeth I. Intellectual property in that time and place was basically a means of regal fund raising and regal censorship. The crown granted "letters patent" for a fee to private parties. At first, patent monopolies were granted for all manner of items, novel or commonplace, and wealthy individuals were able to corner the market on staple goods of many sorts. In reaction to the economic dislocations caused by this practice, and after the throne had passed from the Tudors to the unloved Stuarts, Parliament managed early in the seventeenth century to limit the patent grant so that it did not apply to staple goods and was available only to creators of new inventions. At the same time, Parliament provided for expiration of a patent's monopoly after fourteen years. The notion of a exclusive patent rights limited in time has endured to this day, forcing patent owners to attempt to obtain a return on their investment within the term of their patents, and freeing the invention for unlimited use by others thereafter.

As to copyrights, the Tudor practice had been to grant exclusive rights to publishers, not authors, of new works. Again a fee was paid to the crown for the privilege of publication. By the middle of the sixteenth century, the publication rights were being granted exclusively to members of the Stationers' Company, whose subservience to the monarchy guaranteed that seditious material would not emanate from the Company's printing presses. This powerful form of censorship was eliminated a century later, along with the monarchy itself, during the Puritan Revolution led by Oliver Cromwell. In 1649, the year in which the head of the Stuart king Charles I was separated from its body, the publishing monopoly was eliminated. A chaotic period ensued, in which published works were freely pirated and, incidentally, the monarchy was restored. After the Glorious Revolution established the dominance of Parliament over the reinstated crown in 1689, the old Stationers' Company petitioned Parliament to recognize again the rights of its members, whose revenues had suffered mightily at the hands of the copyists. Instead of giving the power back to the publishers, Parliament gave it to authors. The Statute of Anne, named after the last of the Stuart monarchs, gave

exclusive rights of publication to authors, and was the progenitor of all
Western copyright legislation. As in the case of patents, the term of copyright
exclusivity was limited, the Statute of Anne having imposed a twenty-eight
year period of exclusivity.

Both patent and copyright, as established under English law, were imported into American law through the Constitution of the United States
which, as we already know, gave Congress the power

To promote the Progress of Science and the useful Arts, by securing for limited
Times to Authors and Inventors the exclusive Rights to their respective Writings
and Discoveries.

Consistent with Madison's observation that the public good fully coincides
in the case both of writings and of discoveries with the claims of individuals,
Judge Sprouse concluded that the same public policy underlay both forms
of intellectual property protection and brought his time machine back to
the present.

The perceived coincidence of public policies as between patent and
copyright allowed the Fourth Circuit to import patent principles into the
copyright law; specifically the principles relating to patent misuse. Patent
misuse is a well-established defense to a patent infringement charge. The
paradigmatic case of patent misuse is one in which a patent holder attempts
to take advantage of the monopoly grant to force licensees to purchase
goods or services not covered by the patent. In the *Morton Salt* case, for
instance, a salt company sued a competitor for infringement of its patent
not on salt—a staple—but on machinery for depositing salt during the food
canning process. The Supreme Court, to which the case ultimately found
its way, held that the court system should make itself unavailable to help
Morton Salt enforce its patent, because Morton was using its patent in a
manner contrary to public policy. Specifically, Morton was requiring licensees of its hardware patent to use only Morton's salt in their depositing
machines. To the Supreme Court, the attempt to protect items not covered
by the patent was completely contrary to the policy underlying the patent
law, and the appropriate remedy for such transgressions was to decline to
aid the patentee in its pursuit of infringers.

Analysis of "public policy" is a highly subjective exercise, as to which
only a court whose decision is not subject to further appeal can be sure of
being right. Judge Sprouse's views might well be considered by the Supreme
Court at some point. Accordingly, the jurist's description of the public policy
underlying copyright misuse was reasonably conservative. First, he observed, history shows that the policies underlying the patent law and the
copyright law are highly similar. Second, both laws seek to increase human
knowledge by rewarding authors and inventors with exclusive rights. Finally,
both patent and copyright grants are limited to the subject matter covered,

respectively, by a patent or a copyright, and do not extend to property not covered by the grant. Therefore, the judge concluded, copyright misuse is a valid defense in copyright infringement litigation.

Conservative though it is, the Fourth Circuit's public policy analysis has certain weaknesses. Paramount among these is the lack of recognition of the substantial differences between the extent and strength of the patent grant and the copyright grant. The patentee may exclude anyone else from using the patented invention in any way. The copyright owner may only prevent copying of the particular expression protected by the copyright, not the use of ideas contained in that expression or materials not contained in the copyrighted work. Whether copyright actually puts a rights holder in a position of sufficient power to extend the protection of the copyright to subject matter not covered by the grant is therefore substantially open to question. Nonetheless, it is likely that, in cases where the equities weigh heavily against the copyright owner because of the owner's egregious over-reaching, a misuse defense will receive serious consideration by the courts. That egregious overreaching will typically be a violation of the antitrust laws as well; an attempt to monopolize or extend a monopoly to a part of commerce not governed by the statutory grant. Judge Sprouse, though, felt that copyright misuse could exist even if the conduct in question did not amount to an antitrust violation. That conclusion, too, is open to question. (A bill introduced in the Senate, but rejected in the 1990 Congress, would have made it clear that, in the case of patents, at least, no conduct that is not also an antitrust violation would constitute misuse. Since copyright protection is weaker than patent protection, the same rule should apply to copyrights.)

In any case, having accepted the notion that a defense of misuse could be interposed in a case of copyright infringement, Judge Sprouse went on to assess whether the terms of Lasercomb's license agreement constituted misuse or not. He found that the terms prohibited licensees not just from copying but from developing any kind of computer-assisted die-making software at all; that by the contract's terms the benefit of the creative talents of Lasercomb's licensees was withdrawn from the public for a period far longer than the life of the copyright; and ultimately, that Lasercomb's attempt to use its copyright in Interact to control competition "in an area outside the copyright, *i.e.*, the idea of computer-assisted die manufacture," constituted misuse. Little or no attempt was made by the court to assess whether Lasercomb's practices would have the actual effect of controlling competition. Frankly, with thousands of commercial CAD/CAM programs then available on the U.S. market alone, such a prospect was remote, at best. Along with the question of competitive effect, the court seemed to consider the fact that Holiday was not bound by Lasercomb's license agreement to be irrelevant as well. Until Lasercomb "purged itself of the misuse," or in other words stopped using the offending license agreement and maybe even released existing licensees from its onerous terms, the court system would simply refuse to enforce the copyright in Interact against anyone.

Lasercomb's surprise at this sudden reversal of fortunes must have been akin to that of Brigadier General Edwin H. Stoughton, who awoke early on the morning of March 9, 1863, to find that a completely unexpected, embarrassing, and debilitating shift in the fortunes of war had occurred. As told by Jeffry Wert, in his book, *Mosby's Rangers*, the story is as follows:

In January, 1863 Confederate Major General J. E. B. Stuart, with the approval of General Robert E. Lee, detailed one of Stuart's best scouts, John Singleton Mosby, and fifteen men to operate within Union lines in northern Virginia. From this original nucleus, the unit evolved into the 43rd Battalion of Virginia Cavalry or Mosby's Partisan Rangers. During a span of roughly twenty-eight months, the 43rd Battalion was a matchless body of guerillas, in turn becoming probably the most renowned combat unit of the Civil War.

Early on the morning of March 9, 1863, Mosby's Rangers, having slipped through Union lines, entered the town of Fairfax, where General Stoughton, commander of the Vermont infantry brigade, was headquartered in a private home. After capturing the stables, cutting the telegraph wires and quietly taking prisoners, Mosby and three subordinates walked to the house and forced their way in.

The four raiders found the general asleep in bed. Mosby, according to his memoirs, removed the bedcovers, lifted Stoughton's nightshirt and unceremoniously spanked his bare behind. Other accounts, however, have Mosby shaking the young Vermonter. Regardless, Stoughton groggily asked who was present.

"General, did you ever hear of Mosby" asked the Confederate lieutenant.
"Yes, have you caught him?"
"I am Mosby," came the reply. "Stuart's cavalry has possession of the Court House; be quick and dress."

As stunned as General Stoughton, Lasercomb first petitioned the Court of Appeals for a rehearing, claiming that the court overlooked a crucial distinction between patents and copyrights—to wit, that copyright does not protect against independent development, and is therefore a far weaker bundle of rights than patents, and far less exclusionary of competition— and that the only use of the offending terms established at trial was in a highly unusual source code license to a single company. The court was unmoved. Lasercomb's only recourse, if any, was to the U.S. Supreme Court.

Here, then, is a line in the sand, to borrow a term from a more recent war. When a copyright owner attempts to use the exclusive rights granted by law to achieve an end other than that envisioned in the copyright law, any attempt to enforce the copyright in question against even a shameless, prevaricating infringer will be turned aside. This harsh consequence is intended to serve as a warning to copyright holders not to push their privileges too far.

It must be said, however, that there is a problem with this particular line in the sand. The problem is that the sand is shifting. The line is blurred in some places, and broken in other places. It may in due course be seen not to be a line at all, but just a Spike Lee-type exhortation to "do the right thing." For example, the general rule is that antitrust allegations are not a defense to copyright infringement actions. Yet in *Lasercomb*, proof of exclusionary conduct that may not even have arisen to the level of an antitrust violation was considered to be a very effective defense to a copyright infringement action. Further, the analogous but more generic defense of "unclean hands," which we first encountered in our analysis of the IBM/AMI conflict, applies only where the "uncleanliness"—the unconscionable conduct of the plaintiff—is directly related to the matter on which the plaintiff is suing. In *Lasercomb*, though, there was no disputing the lack of a direct relationship: Holiday had not signed the offending license agreement. It appears, therefore, that the Fourth Circuit has upheld an equitable defense on less direct evidence than "unclean hands" would have required. The intellectually unsatisfying dichotomy thus presented calls into question the solidity of the *Lasercomb* rule. Too, it can be argued that Lasercomb had two kinds of property rights in Interact, copyrights and trade secrets, and that to the extent that its restrictive license went beyond the boundaries of its copyright, the extension was necessary in order to protect trade secrets. In my view, that is not a good argument, because Lasercomb's terms also went beyond what was reasonably necessary to protect its trade secrets; but the general proposition that a contract may bind a licensee both to refrain from infringing copyrights and to refrain from misappropriating trade secrets is quite sound. Finally, the doctrine of copyright misuse has so little case law behind it that it can hardly be called a doctrine. The Fourth Circuit law clerks found only one prior case, a trial court opinion more than forty years old, in which a court declined to enforce a copyright because it had been misused.

Despite the indistinctness of the line in the sand, there is no doubt that sufficiently egregious conduct aimed at diminishing competition will cause a court to refrain from aiding a copyright plaintiff. Whether *Lasercomb* presented such a case can be debated. What does not seem open to debate, however, is that where the conduct consists only of exercising rights that the copyright law provides, such as the exclusive right to reproduce and distribute the protected expression in the copyrighted work, a misuse defense will not succeed even though competition is diminished thereby. On the other hand, where the conduct goes beyond the mere exercise of copyright and attempts to preclude competition in areas not protected by the copyright, in at least some cases the copyright holder will be held to

have exceeded the outer limits of permissible conduct. The potential availability and grave consequences of a copyright misuse defense, even if ill-
defined, is a powerful deterrent to overreaching conduct on the part of
copyright owners. It is the softwar equivalent of a ban on the use of certain
types of weapons.

# 16

# Revenge of the Nerds: Guerrillas, Terrorists, Peaceniks, and the Legion of Doom

When he returned to the white breakfast table, he carried a shallow square black tray with a number of tiny controls arranged along one side. He placed it on a table and touched one of the minute switches. A cubical halo display blinked on above the projector: the neon grids of cyberspace, ranged with the bright shapes, both simple and complex, that represented vast accumulations of stored data. "That's all your standard big sh-ts. Corporations. Very much a fixed landscape, you might say. Sometimes one of 'em 'll grow an annex, or you'll see a takeover and two of them merge. But you aren't likely to see a *new* one, not on that scale. They start small and grow, merge with other small formations. ..." He reached out to touch another switch. "About four hours ago"— and a plain white vertical column appeared in the exact center of the display—"this popped up. Or in." The colored cubes, spheres, and pyramids had rearranged themselves instantly to allow for the round white upright; it dwarfed them entirely, its upper end cut off smoothly by the vertical limit of the display. "Bastard's bigger than anything," Tick said with a certain satisfaction, "and nobody knows what it is or who it belongs to."

—William Gibson, *Mona Lisa Overdrive* (1988)

Cyberspace. The final frontier, in the minds of a small but growing class of computer users. Clever, amoral, mischievous, sometimes malicious, sometimes bent on crime, these computer adventurers stalk the fabricated territory inside the electronic mind, raiding data structures and intruding on the logic of stored programs, taking what they wish and leaving behind the tell-tale traces of the cyberpunk: grafitti, worms, and viruses. In the worst case, valuable government or industrial secrets are compromised, and time bombs that tick with each clocking cycle of the invaded systems explode in cascading, cancerous code that brings down entire networks of computers. With honorable intentions, high-minded techno-junkies organize like futuristic Guardian Angels with the stated aim of bringing a kind of justice to what they call the "electronic frontier," although justice in their minds seems to be equated in most cases with freeing the cyberpunks from the clutches of the law. Meanwhile, a long-haired revolutionary, at once the Albert Einstein of software development and the Che Guevera of software protection, spends his time "fighting for the freedom to write software" by preaching the abolition of intellectual property rights. With the exception of the do-gooders, these marginal figures represent a fifth column, attempting to subvert the forces of industrial innovation through acts of sabotage, espionage, and propagandizing. In fact, though, their efforts are having effects entirely contrary to those sought by these self-styled freedom-fighters, as we shall see after examining the nature of the marginalists' efforts.

We begin with the terrorists. Some of them are organized into groups. The nuPrometheus League, named after the Titan who stole fire from the gods and gave it to mankind, steals portions of the source code for the Apple Macintosh operating system and sends them to unappreciative computer industry notables or to the trade press. The Legion of Doom, a loosely-knit coalition of computer buffs who have taken their name from the comic books, hack their way into public and private computer networks and exchange information on how they have done so and what they have found inside those networks. On a certain morning in 1991, the tabloid-style headlines screamed out the evidence of the shadowy activities of a similar European group from page one:

**Dutch Computer Rogues Infiltrate American Systems with Impunity.**

Underneath, the lengthy article began with a breathless lead-in:

Beyond the reach of American law, a group of Dutch computer intruders have been openly defying United States military, space and intelligence authorities for almost six months. Recently they broke into a United States military computer while being filmed by a Dutch television station.

This was not the *National Enquirer*. It was not *Star Magazine* or *Marvel Comics*. It was the *New York Times* for Sunday, April 21, 1991, and in addition to reporting on the escapades of the Low Country hackers, the paper devoted a chunk of its vaunted magazine section to a cowboy, lyricist for the Grateful Dead, and computer enthusiast who is about as close as cyberspace gets to a civilizing force. Hackers, then, are big news, as a result of a few notorious cases, of which the most notorious is the case of the young man who called himself Hunter.

In August, 1986, a junior astronomer at Berkeley, down on his luck, astronomically speaking, was assigned part-time to work on computer-related projects for the Lawrence Berkeley Laboratory. Four and a half years later, he was a best-selling author, star of a PBS docudrama, and widely sought-after speaker in computer circles. He owed it all to Hunter, an East German hacker.

The astronomer was Cliff Stoll. Among other stops for him on the lecture circuit after he became famous was the IBM Thomas J. Watson Research Laboratory in Yorktown Heights, New York. On January 15, 1991, Stoll told his story there, in an auditorium walled with cut stone and rich wood panelling. He dressed for the occasion, in a green flannel shirt, yellow tie, baggy pants, and sneakers. Stoll captivated a mixed audience of scientists, businesspeople, and students by pacing the stage in a Groucho-like stoop, flinging his hands about as though he were trying to separate them from his forearms, spilling his transparencies all over the floor and walking on them, tilting the podium back and forth so that bonbons provided for him rattled to the floor, giving out his favorite milkshake recipe, leaving the auditorium so that the disembodied voice broadcast from his wireless lapel microphone floated over the audience from elsewhere in the building, racing up and down the aisles to hand copies of one of his articles to those who asked "good questions," and all the while spinning out a mesmerizing tale of intrigue and computer espionage.

It began with a seventy-five cent error in the accounting records for computer usage for the laboratory. At Lawrence, computers supplied by IBM, Digital, Apple, and others were linked together locally in an Ethernet network, and also linked to the outside world through Internet, a nationwide network of university systems that is in turn linked to Milnet, a network of unsecure and therefore unclassified military computer systems. The accounting program that kept track of time used on the Lawrence systems had been written at Berkeley, and Stoll, attempting to resolve the seventy-five cent discrepancy, assumed that the program contained a bug that was the cause of the error. A review of the code told him that his assumption had been wrong, however, and with that tenacity that is the hallmark of good science, he dug deeper and deeper into this seemingly trivial anomaly until he found the source of the problem: an unauthorized user with the ID "Hunter" had used time on one of the UNIX systems, time that could not be billed because Hunter was not listed as billable. Curious as to how Hunter could use a system for which he did not have authorization, Stoll looked at the UNIX software itself, and discovered that Hunter had changed it to give himself "superuser powers": the ability to survey all other activity on the multiuser system and the ability to modify the operating system. It would have been easy to change UNIX so as to bar Hunter from the system,

but the perceptive astronomer concluded that Hunter was a phenomenon
that warranted study. Like an ethnobiologist setting up a blind from which
to study an animal population, Stoll arranged an essentially passive study
environment. He noted that Hunter's access to the system had been through
one of the processor's serial communication ports. He therefore set about
to scrounge fifty printers from elsewhere in the lab, filling up a pushcart
with the devices after hours, on the theory that it was easier to apologize
than to ask permission, and attached one printer to each serial port. He
then found sufficient bubble-pack to make a bed, brought in his sleeping
bag and settled in to wait for his subject to reappear.

Eventually, Hunter did reappear, activating one of the printers. Every
move Hunter made on the system was recorded on fan-fold paper, almost
fifty feet of it on this first occasion. Stoll saw how Hunter had accessed the
UNIX system, how he arranged to become a superuser, how he turned off
the accounting program, and how he then got down to business. Hunter's
business consisted of using the UNIX system as a gateway to Internet. Stoll
watched Hunter use the UNIX system to dial into Milnet and access a
computer at an Air Force base in Anniston, Alabama. He watched Hunter
copy information that was contained on that Air Force computer. Over the
following year, the scientist monitored Hunter's attempted break-ins of over
450 military computer systems, of which approximately fifty were successful. Early on during that year, Stoll attempted to involve a number of federal
agencies, with limited success. The Department of Energy, which funded
the Lawrence laboratory, was not interested in pursuing the matter. In Stoll's
view, DOEs disinterest was due to a fear that the situation, besides being
embarrassing, could affect DOE funding. The FBI lost interest quickly because the only amounts of money at issue, the modest Lawrence computer
usage billings that Hunter was stealing, were not high enough to meet its
threshold of action. The National Computer Security Center was interested
in hearing whatever Stoll had to tell them, but not interested in giving him
any advice. The Air Force computer security experts were very interested,
but said they lacked jurisdiction. In general, military computer experts were
more interested in closing the security gaps in their systems than in finding
out who was breaking in.

It didn't make any difference that government support was not forthcoming. Stoll was hooked. Here was a problem worthy of the scientific method,
and thrilling to boot: unmask Hunter. He appropriated a beeper and rigged
up the printers so that when any of them started printing out the hacker's
incursions, the beeper sounded, allowing Stoll (whose world apparently did
not extend far beyond the laboratory) quickly to return to the lab to observe
Hunter's forays through Milnet and Internet. In one of those moments to
which anyone who has made extended use of beepers can relate, Stoll was
showering with his girlfriend when the device summoned him. Like any
good scientist, he opted to respond to the call of the lab, dressed quickly

and bicycled full tilt down to his stake-out, only to discover that Hunter had disconnected after only two minutes on the network.

Based on his rudimentary knowledge of what military data might be sensitive, Stoll worked out a method for depriving Hunter of any information of consequence without raising the intruder's suspicions. Hunter tended to search for files containing terms like "Star Wars" or "SDI." Whenever the hacker tried to read a file about which Stoll felt uncomfortable, Stoll took out his keychain and jangled the keys against the serial port connector, creating "noise on the line" that interfered with the readability of the file to such a degree that Hunter usually became frustrated and hung up. Hunter's interest in Star Wars is what led to his undoing. In order to make the tracing of his calls difficult, Hunter used numerous different communications paths to call into the Berkeley lab. To trace the calls back to their source, Stoll needed some way of keeping Hunter's interest, without compromising national security, long enough to call the agencies that could perform the traces. The amount of time thought to be necessary lengthened when it was discovered that Hunter's calls were coming from Germany, so that the cooperation of the German phone utility would be required. Stoll's girlfriend came up with the idea of creating bogus files with enticing titles and extensive contents. Thus was born "SDInet," a fictitious electronic bulletin board containing "information" about Star Wars projects. The "information" was created by Stoll and his girlfriend, and for the most part consisted of bureaucratic correspondence concerning meeting schedules, available publications, and similar matters. In a clever attempt to open a second front, the couple included on SDInet a note giving an address to which to write for copies of papers referred to in the files. (A response was received from one Laslo J. Baylo of Pittsburgh. What a name for a spy! Or is it otherwise, that a spy would never use such an evocative name? Or perhaps it's a double blind: a name redolent of espionage, chosen by a spy because others would conclude that a spy would never use such a name. Or...In any case, Stoll called the FBI, who told him—too late, obviously—not to touch the letter but instead to send it by express mail to Washington. He did so, and never heard further about Baylo.)

Hunter was captivated by SDInet. He began browsing at length through its contents, and his sessions were long enough for the international line trace to be carried out. The calls were traced across the Atlantic to Hannover, and from Hannover to the University of Bremen, where a DEC microVAX was being used as a gateway to the public switched data network. Unfortunately for the college, the microcomputer was programmed so as to allow unlimited, unmonitored outgoing calls. Hunter's activities were costing the school tens of thousands of dollars. Until SDInet snared him.

His name was Marcus Hesse. He was twenty-seven years old, a UNIX programmer, but no genius. Logging on to Internet was not difficult. Breaking into the Berkeley system, and other Internet or Milnet systems was not difficult. Hesse used the brute force method of presenting likely passwords until one afforded him access. Not to give aid to hackers, but to illustrate how poorly protected these systems were, I will tell you that one of the most serviceable passwords for Hesse was "GUEST." Once into a system, especially a UNIX system, it was not difficult for Hesse to take it over, for reasons that we will consider momentarily, setting up an account for Hunter, disabling software that might alert others to his activities and trolling through other people's files. Stoll considered Hesse and the four other programmers caught with him to be "semi-pros." Still, they were good enough for the KGB, which had them under oral contract to provide military secrets and the source code for Western operating systems. The five hackers received from $10,000 to $30,000 per drop. Good money. It sparked their entrepreneurial spirits, and at the time of their arrest they were negotiating with the KGB to hold a series of seminars in the USSR on the subject of breaking in to American computer networks.

Stoll and Hesse met at the latter's trial in Germany. Stoll, the liberal, hippyesque free-spirited academic, was a witness for the prosecution. His friends at Berkeley were surprised, and in some cases dismayed, at the "political incorrectness" of his pursuit of Hunter. They identified with Hesse, the anti-establishment spoiler striving to bring down the capitalist system. They could not understand Stoll's view that he was "doing science," and science, as is well known, is morally neutral. Hesse was convicted of espionage, but received only a suspended sentence and did not go to prison. Stoll memorialized his adventure in a book, *The Cuckoo's Egg*, which was a wildly successful report on one counterespionage effort in the softwars. It described the military secrets that Hunter was seeking, but did not say a great deal about the commercial software secrets that the East German hacker had targeted. He had, in fact, also broken into systems owned by the Stanford Research Institute, the MITRE Corporation, and Unisys, three organizations engaged in the design of high-security computer systems.

The KGB is no more, but it is likely that if they still have funding its remnants in the former Soviet states continue to try to steal American source code. The ending of the Cold War and the reconstitution of the Soviet Union into a confederation has not led to a revival of their economies, and *glasnost* has only given unemployed and underfed citizens a political voice. The desire to catch up with the West economically and the lessening of the strategic imperative for military espionage has freed former KGB agents to pursue the trade secrets of American high-tech companies. The KGB initiative with Hunter was softwar in the ultimate: direct action by government agencies to usurp the key intellectual properties of successful innovators. Stoll, in a sense, was the Paul Revere of the information age.

The Soviet Union, it turns out, was not alone in turning to hackers to advance the national cause. Intelligence agencies of major Western nations as well have turned to "collecting data" on one anothers' industries. The tapping of phone lines and electronic mail lines of foreign subsidiaries of large software and hardware companies is endemic. In the most dramatic example of direct action to date, hackers working for the American military are reported to have infected the Iraqi command and control system with a virus some three weeks before the start of the Persian Gulf War. The virus caused information displayed on the system's monitors to disappear without warning.

As for the "Dutch computer rogues," at this writing not enough has been publicized about the targets of their hacking activities or the ultimate destination of the information they purloin to be able to say what their purpose is. They have tapped into computers at the Kennedy Space Center, the Pacific Fleet Command, Livermore National Laboratory, and Stanford University. All the systems were connected to Internet, and all were repositories for "unclassified" data only. Still, a Dutch television crew filmed one of the hackers, a student at the University of Utrecht, accessing missile test information on an American military computer. And during April and May of 1991, the Dutch hackers accessed, modified, and copied information relating to the movements of troops and equipment during the Persian Gulf war. For the moment, though, what is more interesting about the Dutch situation than the targets of the hackers is the hackers' methodology. They do not appear to be employing any advanced computer science techniques. One person who saw printouts of incursions made by "Adrian," the account name used by one of the hackers, said "You could tell that the guy wasn't conversant with the computer he was on. It looked like he had a cookbook sitting next to him telling him what to do next at each step." The cookbook reference suggests that a collection of descriptions of methods for breaking into American computer networks that has appeared on numerous electronic bulletin boards in this country has found its way to Europe.

Which takes us to the case of Robert Morris, the first convicted computer hacker. Morris, whose father is an expert on computer security, was a student at Cornell in 1988 when he decided to take advantage of the vulnerabilities of Internet. On November 2, 1988, he slipped a "worm" onto Internet: a program he had written that, he thought, would replicate itself only a few times on each Internet computer to which it was sent. Unfortunately, there was a bug in Morris' program (a "bug" in the "worm"?), and instead of entering each Internet computer to which it was sent and sitting quietly, the worm reproduced itself incessantly on each computer, ultimately bringing over 6,000 academic and military computers to a halt. Morris was the first person prosecuted successfully under the Computer Fraud and Abuse Act of 1986, and his conviction in January 1990 was widely publicized. The youthful defendant claimed that his program was an academic experiment gone awry. The purpose of his schoolboy prank, he said, was to publicize the lack of security in the country's computer networks. If so, his actions were successful beyond his expectations, at the personal cost—after the Supreme Court declined to hear his appeal—of a $10,000 fine, three years' probation, and 400 hours of community service. Illustrating the adage that the worm turns, however, Morris has been since early 1991 employed as a programmer by a software company in Cambridge, Massachusetts.

Although Morris' escapade did serve to raise the security consciousness of operators and users of computer networks, and presumably also to warn hackers that they risk criminal penalties if they attempt to injure the integrity of such networks, change has been slow in coming. The federal government attempted to attack the problem with a massive Secret Service offensive called Operation Sun Devil, a Phoenix-based task force that by mid-1990 had served some twenty-eight search warrants in fourteen cities, appeared with guns drawn on residential doorsteps, confiscated some 23,000 diskettes and over forty computers. Operation Sun Devil was up against the "Legion of Doom," a cabal of "phone phreaks" who exchanged information on how to make free use of telecommunications lines and perhaps also stole credit card and phone card information. There was tremendous concern among telephone companies that the phreaks would damage or disable the country's phone system, a paranoia that arose, no doubt, because of the insecurity engendered by the thought of teen-aged vandals roaming at will through the electronic corridors of the public networks, and by the ominous sound of the group's name, which in fact was taken from the world of comic books. Robert Morris' prank, too, was a scarifying event: it did not take much imagination to envision the phone companies' computers clogged to the point of incapacity with self-reproducing viruses.

The Sun Devil investigators, unfortunately, were able to absorb only a rudimentary understanding of the technology they were trying to protect before it was time to act. To an outsider, it seems that their highly publicized program of searches and seizures was intended more to shock a generation of "computer geeks" out of some potentially dangerous behavior than to achieve successful prosecutions. The Legion of Doom, it developed, was almost without exception a bunch of kids. As a result of Operation Sun Devil, though, they were kids whose parents, according to newspaper accounts, answered knocks at the door and found themselves staring down the barrels of government-issue shotguns, and whose families' home computers, answering machines, and even telephones were confiscated. The Sun Devil team's most notorious misstep was the arrest and prosecution of college student and electronic newsletter publisher Craig Neidorf, who obtained from a member of the Legion of Doom, who called himself "the Prophet," material on the organization of Bell South's 911 emergency system. Neidorf then disseminated that information on an electronic bulletin board, in an electronic periodical called Phrack of which he was publisher. Neidorf's indictment also included charges that he published tutorials on breaking into computer systems. One such article was called "Basic Concepts of Translation." Authorship of that article was attributed to a group of cyberpunks named "The Dead Lord and the Chief Executive Officers." During the course of Neidorf's trial, it came to light that the information Neidorf had published was not confidential; indeed, Bell South made much of it available to the public in booklets. As soon as that fact was introduced into evidence, during cross-examination of the government's witnesses, the prosecutors called in the defense and asked for a review of the defendant's evidence as to the public nature of the information stolen by the Prophet. As a result of that review, the prosecution dismissed its own case.

The fact that saved Neidorf was supplied by the Electronic Frontier Foundation (EFF), an organization founded by, among others, Mitch Kapor, whose future was secured by the proprietary software known as Lotus 1–2–3, and Steve Wosniak, co-developer of the proprietary computer known as the Apple II. These industry legends joined John Barlow, whose intellectual property rights arise not from computer programs but from having penned such Grateful Dead tunes as "Mexicali Blues" and "I Need a Miracle," in forming a foundation for the purpose of promoting "the public interest in the development of computer-based communication technology." The Electronic Frontier Foundation's "mission statement" spells out the following objectives:

Engage in and support educational activities which increase popular understanding of the opportunities and challenges posed by developments in computing and telecommunications.

Develop among policy-makers a better understanding of the issues underlying free and open telecommunications, and support the creation of legal and structural approaches which will ease the assimilation of these new technologies by society.

Raise public awareness about civil liberties issues arising from the rapid advancement in the area of new computer-based communications media. Support litigation in the public interest to preserve, protect and extend First Amendment rights within the realm of computing and telecommunications technology.

Encourage and support the development of new tools which will endow non-technical users with full and easy access to computer-based telecommunication.

These lofty-sounding goals are actually so ambiguous that they can only be given meaning by the activities of the group in furtherance of them. Contributing to Craig Neidorf's defense was one such activity. Because of the EFF's intervention, the government decided that the Neidorf case was not a good test of the computer crime law even though the young hacker had published information obtained by the Prophet's invasion of a network into which he was not invited, and had published instructions for committing criminal trespass on computer networks. Was that a desirable result? Was Neidorf exercising his First Amendment rights by distributing information obtained by breaking into the Bell South network? The judge who presided over his trial felt that the First Amendment did not protect criminal activity that entailed communication, but the dismissal of the case meant that the issue would not be decided.

Another of the EFF's "litigation in the public interest" activities was the filing of an *amicus curiae* brief in the case of *United States of America v. Leonard Rose*. Rose was a computer consultant from Baltimore who was being prosecuted for computer crimes in connection with the transmission of source code of AT&T's UNIX operating system. Basically what Rose—whose hacking monicker was "Terminus"—had done was to modify the UNIX log-in routine by inserting a "Trojan Horse" program that collected authorized passwords from the system being "hacked" and stored those passwords in a file from which they could be retrieved by the hacker. Terminus then sent the modified source code to other hackers, including Knight Lightning (a.k.a. Craig Neidorf). Among the statutes that Rose was charged with violating was one that prohibited the communication, with intent to defraud, of "information through which a computer may be accessed without authorization." The EFF brief urged the court to dismiss that part of the indictment on the ground that the quoted language was unconstitutionally vague. It would, the Foundation's brief said, prohibit speeches or articles containing information that someone might use to gain unauthorized entry, prohibit programmers from discussing programs designed to test computer security, prohibit exchange of "constitutionally protected" information about computer security over electronic bulletin boards, and prohibit journalists from publishing articles reporting on security deficiencies in government security systems (citing, as one such journalist whose free speech was chilled to absolute zero by the statute in question, Craig Neidorf, who had suspended publication of Phrack). The statutory requirement of intent to defraud, the EFF brief said, was insufficient to render the law constitutional because Congress can only prevent such communications if they amount to "advocacy . . . directed to inciting or producing imminent lawless action" and are "likely to incite or produce such action." The statute "hangs over citizens 'like a sword of Damocles,'" the brief concludes.

Vague though the statute may have been in other circumstances, it fairly clearly covered what Rose had done, but the trial court never had to deal with the question. Leonard Rose copped a plea. Terminus pleaded guilty to wire fraud charges both in Baltimore and in Chicago, and received a one-year jail sentence.

The EFF is looking for other defendants to assist. According to its electronic newsletter (release #1.00), it is "continuing to investigate legal opportunities for helping to establish the First and Fourth Amendment rights [i.e., free speech and privacy] of computer users and sysops," the latter being the people who create and manage electronic bulletin boards. Electronic bulletin boards may indeed become the town meetings of the future, the nerve system of the global village. It is also the case, however, that they have been the medium through which much information on cracking the security of computer networks has been circulated. Are the members of the EFF the Guardian Angels of the electronic frontier, protecting innocent computer users against government excesses, or are they, in the words of the Cowboy Junkies' song, "misguided angels," defending acts of intellectual property vandalism and theft because they have assumed that, since they, the EFF, have good intentions, *any* deeds they do are good deeds. Time will tell, and time has a way of tempering radical positions by applying to them the ravages of entropy. In the case of the EFF, entropy intruded in July 1991 in the form of Mycroft, a hacker who had adopted the name of Sherlock Holmes' brother. Mycroft broke into the system at the EFF, which is connected to Internet. Although the hacker did not damage any files, and apparently didn't leave any worms behind, Mitch Kapor—who likes to refer to cyberspace as a kind of "neighborhood"—admitted to the *New York Times* that the 'hood had become unsafe.

The best defense against hackers lies not in prosecution but in shoring up weaknesses in the networks into which they are trying to break. There is a lesson that students of the softwars can learn by considering the sources of one of those weaknesses. Cliff Stoll's nemesis, Hunter, was able to forage through Internet because of a particular infirmity in the UNIX system being used at Berkeley. The infirmity was amplified by the use of an editor called EMACS on that system. EMACS is freeware, a computer program distributed by the Richard Stallman's Free Software Foundation. Stallman is a brilliant programmer, a visionary revered by many in his profession, a recipient of the MacArthur Foundation "genius" award. He has been called "the greatest programmer that ever lived." He writes terrific software, and gives it away. Moreover, he believes that all other software authors should give away their software as well, and in the fervor with which he proselytizes that belief, Stallman has moved out of the realm of software engineering and into the realm of social engineering, a realm in which his reputation is rather less secure. We saw in Chapter 4 the shrill singlemindedness, the "Support Mental Health or I'll Kill You" intensity, with which the League for Programming Freedom—of which Stallman is a principal—has attacked patent and copyright protection for computer programs. Underneath the purple prose, there lurks an even deeper problem with Stallman's philosophy: free software cannot replace commercial software as the programming support for American commerce and industry because it cannot be relied on. The League's agenda is thus an unintentional assault on the industrial infrastructure of the computerized world.

That is not to say that free software is junk, or technically inferior; in point of fact, some free software is superior to comparable commercial software. EMACS is widely felt to be a superior UNIX editor. It is to say, however, that distributors and customers cannot rely on free software, for three reasons. First, free software tends to be less robust. Commercial software incurs more testing before it is distributed; freeware or shareware tends to be tested by users after they have installed it. EMACS allowed Hunter, or anyone else who was able to access a UNIX system of which EMACS was a part, to become a system programmer having complete control of the operating system, with the ability to set up new accounts, monitor the activity of other users, and modify the operating system itself. That loophole in the Berkeley system must, in hindsight, be viewed as a design problem. Was the problem in EMACS, or was it an inherent characteristic of UNIX, which EMACS merely passed along? If the problem was inherent in UNIX, should EMACS have been designed so as not to allow that problem to destroy the security of users' systems? If the Free Software Foundation had explained that its editor would allow people like Hunter to do the thinks that Hunter did, would EMACS have been installed as widely as it has been? In any system for which security, or even usage accounting, is important, that design characteristic was quite harmful. Yet it was discovered at Berkeley, for example, only after the program was installed and running, and then only by the happy accident of Cliff Stoll's unusual interest in a $.75 accounting anomaly.

Second, free software tends to be of uncertain provenance. One can find in the source code for popular free software the copyrights of several different individuals. It may be that, in principle, the agreement of those people to distribution of their contributions has been obtained, but if it were important to be sure that those other authors agreed to that distribution (as it would be to a commercial or industrial user who cannot afford to have the software impounded as infringing, or to a software author who wishes to incorporate free software into another program and redistribute the combination), could those authors be found today? The answer, according to one who has tried, is "not easily." Even more serious, as of 1990 there was at least one important free software package to which a commercial company, the name of which does *not* appear in the code, claimed copyright and demanded licenses from those who sought to redistribute the program. Free software is not alone, of course, in attracting claims of infringement, but suppliers of commercial software tend to be more securely capitalized than suppliers of free software, and can both verify originality more completely and provide meaningful indemnities against infringement suits.

Third, free software comes without warranty, or at least without a financially reliable warranty. If freeware users who suffered economic injury because of errors in free software were to seek recompense for their damages, for example, to whom would they look, and what guaranty do they have that recompense would be forthcoming?

There is certainly a place for free software in users' libraries; in some cases an important place. But in a world where computers are the pace-makers of the industrial infrastructure, it is understatement to point out that not all software should be free. Stallman the revolutionist is not the visionary that Stallman the programmer is. In truth, he is hawking not revolution but counterrevolution; not vision but nostalgia. Once upon a time, all software *was* free. In the first two decades of the computer industry, computer manufacturers distributed operating systems without separate charge, and customers passed application programs around through user groups and other informal channels. Users were large institutions that could afford to hire armies of programmers to debug, enhance, and adapt that free software so that it would work reliably in the users' particular operating environments. Was that utopia, a state of grace, Eden before the fall? Perhaps; but it was also a time of shaggy, unreliable, inefficient, and non-user-friendly software. If we reverted to that epoch today we would find ourselves very quickly in an electronic stone age. Yes, programmers in the 1950s and 1960s did not have to worry about intellectual property laws; but worrying about intellectual property laws is a small price to pay for the richness, diversity, and ease of use of modern software. It is a price, by the way, paid by suppliers of all other types of products in commerce around the world. Programmers are not high priests of human thought, eligible for exemption from laws that apply to everyone else.

Wittingly or unwittingly, hackers and phreaks are altering the course of the softwars. They are forcing suppliers of commercial computer programs to be innovative in a particular direction, a direction that has considerable significance to the course of the global campaign for software leadership: *security*. In the ultimate, these electronic adventurers are not doing would-be clones any favors, although in the short run the situation may seem otherwise. Hackers and phreaks take on, unsolicited, the task of cracking the security of computer systems, computer networks, and computer programs. Like disease vectors invading a host organism, they seek out the vulnerabilities, the exposures, the nonrobust aspects of a program, and attack them. They defeat copy protection mechanisms, laying commercial software open to the cancerous, unrestrained reproduction of offshore pirates. They modify other authors' programs, often in harmful ways. They log onto networks that they have no right to access. (In June 1991, Mitsubishi International sued AT&T for selling a private branch exchange [PBX] that was insecure, allowing phreaks to run up $430,000 in unauthorized phone charges by manipulating a feature that allowed Mitsubishi employees anywhere in the country to charge calls using a personal access code. Another company lost $1.4 million to PBX phreaks over a four-day holiday weekend. In what must be a supreme irony, hackers—including, apparently, some "Dutch computer rogues"—have so bedeviled the Free Software Foundation's system, destroying files and using its systems as an entree into Internet, that in mid-1991 the FSF reportedly decided to disconnect from

Internet.) Creators of software likely to be the target of such vectors must attempt to prevent infection. Preventive medicine is called for, in the form of more secure code, to reduce the likelihood of intrusion, and antiviral medicine in the form of diagnostic and eradication code in the event an intrusion does occur. In a kind of Darwinian economic dance, less penetrable code evolves and is naturally selected by the marketplace. A significant byproduct of that process, of course, is the propagation of software that is more difficult to reverse engineer. Reverse engineering is a favored tool not only of the hacker but also of the software clone, as we have seen.

The historian Arthur Toynbee believed that the genesis of civilizations lay in adversity, that in responding to severe environmental challenges, populations developed the intellectual depth to form culture out of custom. Today, though his writings seem quaint, his methods less than scientific, one still senses a germ of truth in his theory. Hackers and phreaks engaging in their private wars against computer systems will produce a software industry that is stronger than it would have been without them. In the words of the historian: "it was only *after* Adam and Eve had been expelled from their Eden Lotus-land that their descendants set about inventing agriculture, metallurgy and musical instruments."

# 17

# "All That Glisters": *Nintendo v. Atari*, the Nightmare Scenario

'Twas on a lofty vase's side,
Where China's gayest art had dyed
  The azure flowers that blow;
Demurest of the tabby kind,
The pensive Selima, reclined,
  Gazed on the lake below.

Her conscious tail her joy declared;
The fair round face, the snowy beard,
  The velvet of her paws,
Her coat, that with the tortoise vies,
Her ears of jet, and emerald eyes,
  She saw; and purred applause.

Still had she gazed; but 'midst the tide
Two angel forms were seen to glide,
  The genii of the stream:
Their scaly armor's Tyrian hue
Through richest purple to the view
  Betrayed a golden gleam.

The hapless nymph with wonder saw:
A whisker first and then a claw,
  With many an ardent wish,
She stretched in vain to reach the prize.
What female heart can gold despise?
  What cat's averse to fish?

Presumptuous maid! with looks intent,
Again she stretched, again she bent,
   Nor knew the gulf between.
(Malignant fate sat by and smiled)
The slippery verge her feet beguiled,
   She tumbled headlong in.

Eight times emerging from the flood
She mewed to every watery god,
   Some speedy aid to send.
No dolphin came, no Nereid stirred;
Nor cruel Tom, nor Susan heard;
   A favorite has no friend!

From hence, ye beauties, undeceived,
Know, one false step is ne'er retrieved,
   And be with caution bold.
Not all that tempts your wandering eyes
And heedless hearts is lawful prize;
   Nor all that glisters, gold.
              —Thomas Gray, "Ode on the death of a favorite cat,
                     drowned in a tub of goldfish" (1748)

The cat of poetic memory overcame its abiding fear of water in order to scoop up a forbidden prize, and found that the fear suppressed was not irrational, but was rather a survival imperative. The software clone overcomes its fear of drowning in litigation in order to seize the prize of a proven market and a proven design. The worst nightmare of the software clone is that by some means the supplier of a target program will manage lawfully to preclude such competition; that by judicious use of technology and intellectual property rights, such a supplier will be able to prevent compatibility without running the risk of a misuse charge. This chapter is about that nightmare come true.

To some extent, Apple Computer accomplished a preclusive interlink between technology and intellectual property rights by providing, in the Macintosh operating system, facilities to generate an elaborate user interface, and by not offering the operating system separately from the hardware. To clone the Mac, one was therefore required either to develop an entire operating system with a Mac user interface or to develop a "Mac user interface" shell for an existing operating system. In either case, the product would be likely to infringe the copyright in the Mac operating system (unless the copying was licensed by Apple) because the Mac operating system, including its user interface, unquestionably contains some protected expression. Did the proprietary product strategy work to Apple's advantage? It has been argued that had the Mac been a more "open" (i.e., clonable) system, it would have achieved greater and more accelerated popularity. That argument, as we saw in Chapter 6, seems to have had some effect at Apple recently. On the other hand, Apple's gross profit margins have been relatively high for a supplier of personal computers, and a business strategy that sacrifices market share in favor of profit, if that is the strategy Apple has had in the past, is certainly a legitimate option.

The strongest anticlone interlink between technology and intellectual property rights seen so far in the software industry was forged by a company that in the end avoided sacrificing either market share or profit. As the 1990s opened, Nintendo controlled almost all of the market for video game consoles in the United States, and by virtue of a copyright-protected and patent-protected interface between the consoles and the games that ran on the consoles, Nintendo controlled almost all of the game market, too. The technology in question consisted of patented computer chip, one of which (the "master" or "lock") resided in the console and the other of which (the "slave" or "key") resided in each game cartridge, together with a copyrighted program (called "10NES") contained on the chips, which caused the cartridge and the console to communicate with one another. That communication was prerequisite to the running of the game in the console. One is put in mind immediately of the AutoCAD lock, except that the metaphysical questions concerning whether the lock contained a computer program do not arise in Nintendo's case, since 10NES was indisputably a computer program, and except for the fact that Nintendo's security chip was protected by a patent.

Nintendo could have utilized those intellectual property rights, assuming that they were valid, in any number of ways. At one end of the spectrum, it could have excluded everyone else from making games that ran on the Nintendo consoles. As well, it could have excluded everyone else from making Nintendo-compatible consoles. With such a strategy, it would have been the sole supplier of Nintendo games and consoles, but would it have come to dominate the video game market? Likely not. There were other suppliers of noncompatible consoles and games, and Nintendo itself could not have written a sufficient variety of attractive games for its own consoles to eliminate those other suppliers. At the other end of the spectrum, Nintendo could have licensed all comers to its copyright and patent at reasonable royalty rates, so that anyone who wished to could develop Nintendo-compatible games or cartridges. Would an open licensing strategy have propelled Nintendo to dominance of the video game market? Again, not likely. Though the Nintendo interface architecture may have come to dominate the market, the number of alternate suppliers for the hardware and software would have assured plenty of competition for Nintendo, whose presence in the market would have become, over time, more thematic than physical, like the Cheshire cat's grin. (Nintendo, of course, would have had, in that case, the royalty checks from its licensees with which to console itself over its loss of market share. The level of consolation those checks would provide would depend entirely on whether the royalty rate approximated the profit that Nintendo would have earned on each system it would otherwise have sold.)

In actuality, Nintendo chose a middle course. It did not license the production of compatible consoles, but did license the development of compatible games. This strategy was designed to increase the variety of games available for its consoles. Nintendo's license agreement, however, stipulated that Nintendo would manufacture the cartridges containing games developed by the licensee; it also contained a two-year exclusivity clause: for a period of two years after the game was put on the market, the licensee agreed not to adapt it to run on other video game systems. At the time when it adopted the described licensing strategy, Nintendo did not dominate the video game market. Was its licensing strategy the instrument of Nintendo's subsequent dominance, and if so, why?

Atari Games Corporation (a company separate from the eponymous video console manufacturer) set itself on a course to find out. An Atari unit had been a Nintendo licensee, but Atari was not pleased with Nintendo's license terms. Atari decided it would manufacture and sell Nintendo-compatible games without having a license from Nintendo. It first attempted to do various "soft" analyses of the Nintendo security system to see what elements needed to be reproduced in order to allow Atari's game programs to run on Nintendo consoles. Those analyses did not produce useful results, and the responsible engineer recommended that "[u]nless there is a specific profit motivation, or there is a hacker available with nothing to do," the project be dropped. (Note here an instance of the direct link between hackers and clones described in the last chapter.) The court—naturally, this matter ended up in court—found that Atari did indeed have a specific profit motivation.

Next, Atari tried to shave the Nintendo chips in order to decipher the object code of 10NES. Though its engineer was able through that process to read the object code, he could not determine how the code worked. At that point, Atari capitulated and became a Nintendo licensee.

Here, we must pause to weight the equities of the situation, for after we take the next step across this particular mine field, objectivity about the equities will be lost. Consider, first, Atari Games Corporation. Its business was developing video games. Its revenues per game were maximized by maximizing the number of installed consoles on which those games will run. Particularly in the time period well before Nintendo had captured over ninety percent of those installations, an agreement to offer games on the consoles of only a single supplier for an extended period was very much against Atari's economic interests. Nintendo's license terms were, in other words, unreasonable from Atari's perspective. Indeed, they were a restraint of trade, since absent such terms Atari would offer its games on the consoles of Nintendo's competitors as well as on Nintendo's consoles. Further, Nintendo's patent was not clearly valid. (After all, very few patents, software-related or otherwise, are *clearly* valid.) Its copyright, while more likely to be held valid, might not have to be infringed in order to create a compatible game. It was simply a matter of good business judgment to decide to investigate unlicensed compatibility. The emphasis here is on the term "investigate." Whether subsequent *investment* in unlicensed compatibility was a matter of good business judgment or not is a separate question.

Now, consider Nintendo. At the time it determined how it would exploit its intellectual property rights, Nintendo was not a dominant supplier by any means. It faced substantial competition from other console suppliers. In the video game business, as in the computer business generally, the software is what sells the hardware. If Nintendo could offer a broader range of better games for its consoles than those available for other suppliers' systems, it would achieve greater success than its competitors. Nintendo could not itself write all the game programs needed to achieve that end, however, and in any case there was no assurance that it could write the best game programs. To achieve its purpose, Nintendo needed to attract and work with outstanding game developers. It chose game developers carefully, made investments in development of the games it wanted for its consoles, controlled the quality of cartridges by manufacturing them itself and actively promoted the games that issued for Nintendo systems. Through the security system invented by its engineers, Nintendo assured that game programs that did not meet its quality standards would not run on its consoles. In exchange for its development assistance and promotional activities, Nintendo exacted what it thought was agreement to a reasonable lead time in the marketplace: the two-year exclusivity. Entrée to the Nintendo consoles required Nintendo's patented chips and copyrighted program. Game developers were free agents. Those that did not like Nintendo's terms had other outlets for their games. No one was forced to write for the Nintendo consoles, but those who did were—if Nintendo's strategy worked—joining an elite circle.

In sum, both sides of the argument are respectable. Atari's position, favoring as it does free competition, is psychologically more attractive than Nintendo's, which—though it is also rationalized on a procompetitive basis, that is, the "better mousetrap" theory—has overtones of artificial constraint. Further, the greater success Nintendo achieved in the market, the less compelling the justification for continuing to use the exclusivity clause. At the time of Atari's capitulation, then, both sides had reasonable arguments regarding the exclusivity clause, but Atari's argument was intuitively easier to accept.

Bad facts can destroy the best theory, though, and at this point bad facts intrude on what would otherwise have been an interesting theoretical debate, irreparably skewing the equities of the situation. A month after be-

coming a Nintendo licensee, in December 1988, Atari resumed its efforts
to crack Nintendo's security system. In order to register its copyright, Nintendo had deposited 10NES or portions thereof with the copyright office.
Atari's lawyer applied to the copyright office to obtain a copy of 10NES,
stating that Atari was a defendant in infringement litigation in California,
and needed the code for use "only in connection with the specified litigation." That statement was untrue. No infringement action was filed until
1989. Moreover, the code was not used by Atari's lawyers; it was used by
Atari's engineers to supplement its reverse engineering of Nintendo's security chip. From the copyright office materials, Atari learned which microprocessor Nintendo was using, and also found that some of the
information it had deduced from the shaved chips was erroneous. Based on
all of its efforts, in the laboratory and with the fraudulently obtained hard
copy from Washington, Atari was able to write a program, called "Rabbit,"
which when used with a microprocessor chip in an Atari game cartridge
allowed Atari game programs to run on Nintendo consoles. By the end of
December 1988, Atari had breached its licensing agreement with Nintendo
and filed suit seeking to have the agreement declared unlawful on antitrust
grounds.

The purity of Atari's free-competition argument thus corrupted by distinctly impure behavior, the issue of technological/intellectual property
interlock was thrown into the courts. Nintendo countersued for infringement in November 1989. Before the case reached the trial stage, both parties
filed motions designed to solidify their respective positions. Atari moved
for summary judgment that Nintendo had misused its intellectual property
rights and was therefore prohibited from enforcing its patent and copyright.
In addition, it asked the court to hold that Atari was the beneficiary of an
implied license from Nintendo to purchasers of its consoles that permitted
those purchasers to use any game they wanted on Nintendo consoles. Finally,
Atari sought, on antitrust grounds, an injunction preventing Nintendo from
coercing retailers to stop doing business with Atari. For its part, Nintendo
simply moved for a preliminary injunction barring Atari from copying, selling, or using in any way either 10NES or the Rabbit program; a simple tactic,
but, if it succeeded, devastating.

Atari's decision in December 1988 was in many ways analogous to Kim
Il-Sung's decision in June 1950. The reader may recall that, after the Soviet
Union made a late, token entrance into the war against Japan in August
1945, the terms of the Japanese surrender required capitulation to the
United States below the thirty-eighth parallel in Korea and to the Soviet
Union thereabove. Separate governments formed in the two zones, and each
government armed itself. The thirty-eighth parallel became a line of confrontation. On June 25, 1950, the army of the north invaded the territory
of the south, touching off a three-year conflict that resulted in almost four
million casualties, mostly civilian, destruction of over 40 percent of the

Koreas' industrial capacity and 30 percent of the homes in the two states. When the war ended in July 1953, the border between the two Koreas lay, for the most part, where it had been before the North Korean invasion: slightly north of the thirty-eighth parallel.

The *Nintendo/Atari* cases were assigned to Judge Fern Smith of the federal court for the Northern District of California. In March, 1991, she ruled on all the motions. She observed that Atari's motions raised basically a single issue: "whether Nintendo has a right to restrict which games are played on its NES consoles, and whether it has the right to restrict where else those games are played (via the two-year exclusive licensing provision)." She ruled that Atari was more likely to succeed on those issues, if at all, as antitrust issues rather than patent or copyright issues. She was not impressed with Atari's misuse arguments. The patent law, she said, expressly permits patent holders the right to exclude others from supplying "nonstaple" products used substantially only with the patent holder's invention. The Supreme Court had found that provision of the patent law to be "a manifestation of Congressional intent to balance the important policy of free competition against the equally valid and important policy of stimulating invention and rewarding creativity." (Contrast the treatment of "nonstaples" with the treatment of the staple product, salt, involved in the *Morton Salt* case discussed in Chapter 15.) The Nintendo video game cartridges, Judge Smith had no problem in determining, were nonstaples.

Atari argued that whatever treatment nonstaples had under the patent law, they could not be restricted under copyright law, since there was no equivalent provision in the Copyright Act and, moreover, *Lasercomb* had held that any exclusivity requirement as a condition of a copyright license constituted misuse of the copyright. The judge did not agree. The same public policy underlay the protection of both patents and copyrights, she found. Among other things, this meant that the same concerns about abuse of the patent misuse defense that underlay the patent rule permitting restrictions on nonstaples also underlay the copyright law, whether or not there was a specific statutory provision. Insofar as *Lasercomb*, a case from a different federal circuit, suggested otherwise, Judge Smith declined to follow it. Further, she found a vast difference between the restrictions in *Lasercomb* and the restrictions she was asked to judge. Lasercomb exacted ninety-nine year noncompete clauses as to *any* software in the area of the license. Nintendo exacted a two-year exclusivity and only as to the specific games developed for Nintendo consoles. Since Nintendo licensees were free to develop other games for other consoles, there was no proof that the creativity of those licensees, which the patent and copyright laws were designed to promote, had been restrained by the license restrictions. Atari's motion for summary judgment on patent and copyright misuse grounds was therefore denied. (Denial of that motion did not serve as a definitive finding that Nintendo was innocent of misuse of its intellectual property rights.

Rather it meant only that Atari had failed to show that the misuse issue could be resolved without a trial.)

Atari had been charged with *contributory* infringement—providing customers with the means to infringe Nintendo's patent. Its second ground for summary judgment was that Nintendo's customers had under law an implied license to run whatever game programs they wanted on Nintendo's consoles. There is a line of cases—unfortunately for Atari, a fairly short line of cases—holding that a patent licensee who has an *explicit* license to practice the patented invention by manufacturing goods incorporating the invention also has an *implied* license both to use materials supplied by persons other than the patent holder in the manufacturing process, where the patent itself does not cover such materials, and to set whatever prices the licensee chooses to set for the finished product. Judge Smith could not accept that those cases applied to Atari's situation. For one thing, Nintendo's customers did not manufacture anything; they bought finished consoles and plugged them into television sets. For another, Nintendo customers did not have explicit patent licenses. Ultimately, the Judge felt, the implicit license cases dealt with the situation in which the patent holder was attempting to get value out of a patent beyond the value inherent in the invention. In Nintendo's case, the value of the invention extended to the game cartridge itself, which incorporated elements of the invention, to wit the slave chip. Since Nintendo derives revenues from the sale of patented game cartridges as well as consoles, imputing to customers the implied license that Atari proposed would undercut the value of Nintendo's patent. Result: no summary judgment here, either.

Atari's request for a preliminary injunction barring Nintendo from inducing retailers not to deal in Atari's games was a somewhat impolitic tactic. An earlier Atari motion had sought to prevent Nintendo from suing Atari's dealers or users for patent infringement. Judge Smith had granted that motion. Unfortunately, her decision had been reversed by the court of appeals, which held that she had abused her discretion by granting the motion without supporting her decision with explicit factual findings. When an injunction relates to the interplay between the patent law, with its grant of legitimate exclusive rights, and the antitrust laws, with their emphasis on free competition, preliminary injunctions should not be granted without a careful analysis of the facts. To the court of appeals, the restrictions in Nintendo's license agreement were not *per se* unlawful. In other words, whether they were unlawful or not depended on the circumstances, and the circumstances can only be ascertained by an examination of the facts. Duly chastened, Judge Smith gave short shrift to Atari's request, on the basis that once again an insufficient factual demonstration had been made. As if to signal her displeasure with Atari for attempting to lead her down that unpleasant trail a second time, Judge Smith quoted the appellate court's "abuse of discretion" language in denying the injunction.

Of greater interest for our purposes was the jurist's treatment of Nintendo's preliminary injunction motion. In desired effect, it was exactly the opposite of Atari's motions. Whereas Atari had asked the court, in essence, to dismiss all or a substantial part of Nintendo's case without even letting it go to trial, Nintendo was asking the court to grant it in advance much of the relief to which it would be entitled if it ultimately won at trial. In order to obtain that relief, including an injunction preventing Atari under threat of contempt of court from continuing to develop or market Nintendo-compatible games, Nintendo had to show either

—that it was probably going to prevail at trial and that monetary damages would not be sufficient to repair the harm visited on Nintendo by Atari's continued development and marketing efforts, or

—that serious questions going to the merits of the case existed and the hardship to it resulting from Atari's continued development and marketing of such games was sharply higher than the hardship to Atari that would result from an injunction.

Judge Smith did not expend much effort balancing the hardships (though as we shall see one element of that balancing exercise was psychologically of profound importance). Instead, she focused on the question whether Nintendo was likely to succeed in proving its case at trial. That question led her first to consider the similarities between the 10NES program and the Rabbit program. In that regard, she relied on the expert testimony submitted by both sides. Nintendo's expert had testified that the two programs were "remarkably similar" in structure, sequence, and organization. Protection of such nonliteral elements was of course one of the basic contributions to U.S. law of the *Whelan* case. Without citing *Whelan* for the proposition, Judge Smith concluded that the copied elements were protectable. Atari's principle arguments against protectability were the familiar twofold assault: first, that the idea of 10NES merged with its expression and, second, that what was copied, from 10NES was only its functionality. In the words of Atari's expert, his Nintendo counterpart had failed to examine "*why* the similarities exist"; to wit, that they were "due to either (1) the requirement of functional indistinguishability, or (2) the use of standard programming techniques."

Atari's approach to the functionality question was to set up *Whelan* as a kind of bugbear. The case, Atari argued, described the idea of the Whelan program as "the efficient organization of a dental laboratory," and everything else in the program was held to be expression. In fact, as discussed in Chapter 16, that is not at all what *Whelan* stands for, but Judge Smith was willing to accept Atari's reading of the case, and also willing to accept that a *Whelan*-comparable statement of the idea of Nintendo's program (say, the provision of quality control for a computer) would be too broad and too protective. Atari suggested that if the idea of 10NES were more specifically stated, it could be seen that there was only one way of expressing that idea. The idea of 10NES, Atari proposed, was to restrict games that would play on Nintendo consoles to cartridges containing the 10NES program (or any future variations of 10NES). Atari explained further that the similarities between Rabbit and 10NES were "absolutely necessary to [Rabbit's] intended purpose of rendering the Atari Games' slave chip functionally indistinguishable from the Nintendo slave chip," and argued that the decoding of the master chip could not be prohibited. Further, Atari claimed that certain of the programming techniques adopted by the Nintendo programmers, although they had concededly had been arbitrary when they were adopted, should now be considered functional because the Rabbit program could not depart from them and remain compatible. By extension of these principles, Atari argued, Nintendo could not prohibit Atari from copying elements of 10NES that were not presently parts of the master-slave interface but might become part of the interface in the future.

As the decision on Nintendo's motion turned on resolution of the latter argument, it is helpful to consider how it arose. The 10NES program contained both "master" and "slave" code. There was no dispute over that fact, or over the fact that game cartridges did not utilize the "master" code at all; that is, that it was not necessary to copy the "lock" portions of 10NES in order to create a compatible game cartridge. Atari, however, had done so. In particular, Atari had programmed its game cartridges to issue Nintendo's "master message," so that when the copy of 10NES in the console compared the message from the Atari cartridge with its own message, it would find sequences within that message to be identical to the slave sequences expected by the master code. The parties had adopted the convention of referring to the communications between the lock and the key as "songs" having "verses," "notes," and "rests." That convention tended to favor Nintendo, of course, because it emphasizes the arbitrary or creative aspects of interface design. It is reminiscent of the thought experiment discussed in Chapter 4, wherein we toyed with the idea of substituting Beatles' lyrics for the Lotus 1–2–3 menu prompts. Judge Smith found the music analogy helpful, and adopted it in her opinion. Atari, she said, had copied the entire "song" from 10NES, even though only a small portion of that song had any function. Although the game cartridge played verses during the entire time it was mounted on the console, the console did not listen to those verses most of the time. Every so often, the console payed attention to the cartridge's song, and at those times, the cartridge needed to be playing the proper series of notes and rests, or the game would terminate. The fact that at other times the cartrige could be playing anything at all meant that there were an infinite number of songs (actually, the judge, a master of understatement in things mathematical, found that there were "billions" of such songs). Atari explained the extent of its copying on the basis that 10NES could be modified in the future to allow the "slave" to issue some or all portions of the master message that at present were not part of the "slave" message, and conceded that it could have obtained a currently functioning "key" program by copying less of 10NES.

In certain respects, then, the clones' arguments have not changed very much over the course of the softwars. The argument that the idea of the Nintendo program was to allow games to run on consoles in which that program was resident is precisely the same as Franklin Computer Corporation had made a decade earlier in attempting to convince one of Judge Smith's confreres in Philadelphia that the expression in the Apple II operating system had merged with the idea of that system. (Recall that Franklin had described the "idea" of the Apple operating system as being to run application programs written for the Apple II.) And Judge Smith reacted to that argument exactly as had Judge Sloviter, who decided the ultimate appeal of the Apple case in 1983:

Atari's conception of the "idea" of the 10NES program would eviscerate copyright protection for computer programs. This perspective would turn both equity and copyright law upside-down. In essence, Atari would have the Court give the would-be infringer the right to determine what is important in a copyrighted work, and thereby bestow the right to copy whatever the infringer thinks is worth having.

Atari is free to develop a lockout program for its own video game machines. Nintendo cannot copyright that idea. By contrast, Atari is not free to appropriate Nintendo's specific technique for "locking" its own game console. More important, Atari cannot identify changes that it fears Nintendo could make to its copyrighted program; then redefine those features as functional and unprotected. Things that are admittedly non-functional at the time of copying are not made functional by the infringer's efforts to preempt reactions to its infringement.

In the *Apple* case, the court had phrased the same idea in a slightly different expression:

Franklin claims that whether or not the programs can be rewritten, there are a limited "number of ways to arrange operating systems to enable a computer to run the vast body of Apple-compatible software." ... This claim has no pertinence to either the idea/expression dichotomy or merger. The idea which may merge with the expression, thus making copyright unavailable, is the idea which is the subject of the expression. The idea of one of the operating system programs is, for example, how to translate source code into object code. If other methods of expressing that idea are not foreclosed as a practical matter, then there is no merger.

Franklin may wish to achieve total compatibility with independently developed application programs written for the Apple II, but that is a commercial and competitive decision that does not enter into the somewhat metaphysical issue of whether particular ideas and expressions have merged.

It is not clear why Atari thought that recycling the Franklin argument would work to its advantage. *Apple v. Franklin* is a precedent both well established and well reasoned.

As one would expect, therefore, Judge Smith adopted the analytical approach of the *Apple* court. She held that "the 'purpose' of being indistinguishable from a copyrighted item is not one recognized in law." (In that quote lies the heart of the problem with cloning: "goodness," in the cloning world, consists of indistinguishability, but that kind of "goodness" is in legal terms "badness.") While a broad view of the idea of 10NES—for example, a view that the idea was to assure quality control for computers—would protect elements of 10NES that the copyright law should not protect, a view of 10NES' idea narrow enough for Atari to succeed in establishing noninfringement—"restriction of game play to cartridges containing the 10NES program or any future variation on it"—was equally unacceptable. It was not necessary to adopt a broad view of a program's idea to find a lack of merger between the expression in 10NES and its idea, Judge Smith felt.

Nor was it necessary to decide whether copying those notes and rests of the 1ONES song that *were* necessary to be reproduced in order to achieve compatibility constituted infringement or not. Atari had admittedly copied more than what was necessary. (Here, we see a second recurrent problem for the clone: courts have never been forced to decide the hard question whether copying limited to minimal programming interface elements constituted infringement, since the defendants are always found to have copied something more. Some years ago, I had the opportunity to cross-examine a clone programmer about why he had copied elements of a program that he had admitted were not part of the program's interface. He answered that, as to some of the elements, when they were creating their clone program he and his colleagues had not been sure whether those elements were part of the interface or not, and as to other elements they suspected that while the elements were not then part of the interface, they might be at some future time.)

For the foregoing reasons, Judge Smith found that Nintendo was likely to succeed at trial. The second part of the preliminary injunction standard, injury not reparable later on by an award of monetary damages, was dealt with summarily by the court. Under traditional copyright principles, copyright owners who show that they are likely to be able to prove infringement at trial are presumed to be suffering irreparable injury. They therefore are not required to offer any proof of what that injury might be. Rather, it is the putative infringer's burden to prove that irreparable injury is not occurring, a task that the reader may fairly compare to the old cross-examiner's saw, "When did you stop beating your wife." In that regard, Atari had not offered any evidence to rebut the presumption of irreparable harm except, apparently, evidence of Nintendo's size and success. Consequently, Nintendo was deemed to have satisfied this part of the test as well.

Though it was not necessary to her decision, Judge Smith returned in her opinion to the subject of Atari's behavior before the copyright office. That behavior, the judge said, consisted of lying and deception. Atari's argument that its behavior was justified by the fact that Nintendo had, after the fact, sued for infringement, thereby turning lie into truth, was given a very cold judicial shoulder. Also rejected was Atari's argument that by the time it used the information from the copyright office, its programmers had already copied the object code of 10NES from the shaved chips. The court said that although it was not necessary to reach the question whether the balance of hardship tipped decidedly in favor of withholding an injunction, Atari's conduct at the copyright office did not enhance its position in that regard.

Judge Smith concluded that a preliminary injunction was appropriate in the circumstances. She issued an order containing such an injunction, and what an order it was! Take a look:

It is therefore ORDERED that Atari Games Corp. and Tengen, Inc., their officers, directors, employees, and agents, and all persons in active concert and participation with them who receive actual notice of this order by personal service or otherwise, are enjoined and restrained from manufacturing, converting, copying, making any derivative of, producing, promoting, marketing, distributing, offering for sale, or selling either Nintendo's program, or Atari's Rabbit program contained in its NES-compatible home video game cartridge, or any copy or derivative of either program, or anything substantially similar to either program.

Upon further Order of this Court, Atari Games and/or Tengen shall give written notice of this Order to all persons or entities to whom Atari Games or Tengen has distributed the Rabbit program or Nintendo's 10NES program, or any derivative or copy of either, including any NES-compatible video game cartridge containing the Rabbit program or derivative thereof. Atari shall request that they immediately halt any further marketing, distribution, or sale of said cartridges or other copies in any form in their possession or control.

This was the clones' worst nightmare made real. Atari's investment in the Rabbit program had been made, and cartridges produced containing the Rabbit. The cartridges were circulating in commerce through a network of dealers that Atari had cultivated. Judge Smith had shut down a thriving business without even giving Atari's defenses the full hearing that a trial would allow, just because Atari—having embarked on its compatible game strategy—had tried to protect itself against exceedingly simple but strategic changes that Nintendo could make in its cartridge-to-console interface.

As debilitating as Judge Smith's order was to the revenue stream created by virtue of the Rabbit program, there lurked in that order an even more ominous prohibition. One of the footnotes omitted from the above-quoted order read as follows:

The prohibition on copying does not apply to reverse engineering by counsel and independent experts for purposes of this litigation.

Implicit in that footnote was the ultimate nightmare: except for litigation counsel and their consultants, Atari was prohibited from making intermediate copies of 10NES in the course of reverse engineering that program. Thus, if Nintendo made any changes to the master-slave "song," Atari was not in a position to copy 10NES to study those changes in order to prepare itself for remarketing of its cartridges should Judge Smith's opinion change after trial or should she be reversed on appeal. There had been a general debate in the industry over intermediate copying as a step in reverse engineering. Reverse compilation, for example, would produce such intermediate copies. The Copyright Act does not permit such activity. No American court had held that intermediate copying is lawful. The most that can be said for Atari's position is that some courts, faced with evidence of such copying, have not held it unlawful, which gave the clones hope. There is a California case, *See v. Durang*, which holds that intermediate copies of a screenplay could not be used as proof that the final version of a second screenplay was infringing. Intermediate copying became the largest issue in the European copyright debate and, as we shall see, significantly shaped the final form of the EC copyright directive. It is a subject worthy of more than a footnote, and in fact Judge Smith gave it more extensive treatment in the body of the opinion that preceded her order. She relied on an earlier software copyright case, *SAS Institute, Inc. v. S&H Computer Systems, Inc.*, in which the court had considered whether intermediate copying of a computer program constituted infringement in its own right, and had found such copying to be unlawful.

Atari asked the judge to modify her opinion by eliminating what it described as the "perhaps unintended" prohibition on intermediate copying. "It is Atari Games's constitutional right," the defendants' lawyers said, "to express the 10NES program's ideas," and that right could not be exercised without copying 10NES:

To read the program contained in the lock-out chip, the chip's contents must be painstakingly and microscopically analyzed.

First, the rows and columns of binary "1's" and "0's" which are visible physically in the ROM must be recorded (*i.e.*, copied) as they are arranged in the ROM. Then, because their physical arrangement in the ROM is scrambled from their logical sequence as its [sic] exists in the actual program as written by its author, they must be laboriously rearranged and reorganized (*i.e.*, copied again). (To illustrate the scrambled physical arrangement, if a single command in the program consists of eight 1's and 0's in sequence—comprising one 8-bit number—the first digit might be located in the center of the rectangular ROM, the second in the upper right, the third in the lower middle and so on.)

Second, these logically arranged thousands of "1's" and "0's" must be disassembled—translated to human-readable pseudo-source code which consists typically of words and mnemonic abbreviations (*i.e.*, copied again). Only then can the ideas in the program begin to be perceived. In source code version, the analysis of the program often involves "direct, one-to-one" annotation of instructions (*i.e.*, copies). [Citation omitted.] Typically, a reverse engineer also enters the code into a computer (*i.e.*, copies it again) and "runs the program" to see how it operates, to understand fully how it works and what it does. There is virtually no other way to understand a program stored in a ROM such as this.

Atari's reargument moved the jurist only to the point of saying that she was not relying on the evidence of intermediate copying as the basis for her order.

Has Nintendo broken the code: Has this purveyor of pixel-lated diversions discovered the key (and lock) to using the intellectual property laws to exclude compatible competition? Is that why Nintendo's founder has become one of the world's richest men?

Let us not leap to conclusions. It may be that Nintendo has achieved its success by doing no more than exercising its exclusive rights under the patent and copyright laws. If so, the law says *mazel tov*. If the master-slave song or the hardware and software that generates it qualify for patent and copyright protection, then it was well within Nintendo's rights to prevent others from making the chip or copying the program. That is not a guaranteed key to riches, though. Keeping the interface proprietary rather than "open" was a business decision that could have led to limited customer acceptance of Nintendo consoles, as a similar decision is thought to have done in the case of the Macintosh computer. Conversely, it could have increased Nintendo's popularity over time. There was no way of knowing in advance what the future would hold for such a strategy, but the strategy itself, if limited to exercising statutory rights, was legitimate. On the other hand, if Nintendo had reached beyond the bounds of the statutory grant to protect things not a part of the patent or the copyright, another body of law may come to Atari's rescue; a body of law that prohibits unreasonable restraints of trade and tying the purchase of one product to the purchase of another. "Atari's remedy, if any," Judge Smith mused, "more likely lies in antitrust law than in patent or copyright." (As to the likelihood that Atari's antitrust arguments would succeed, however, Judge Smith indicated her doubts by denying Atari's motion to enjoin Nintendo's efforts to exclude Atari from the Nintendo-compatible game business. [Note 17.4 describes Nintendo's success on appeal.])

# 18

## Some Animals Are More Equal Than Others: "Open Systems," Truce or Consequences?

When Saul Kent had the suspension team at the Alcor Life Extension Foundation in Riverside, California, surgically remove the head of Dora Kent, Saul's mother, from her body, his hope was that she could eventually be restored to life and health, probably even youth. The *last* thing on his mind was that they'd all wind up being investigated for murder. Murder! The thought was entirely ludicrous—not, indeed, that any of them had given even a moment's consideration to that possibility at the time of the event. After all, the two classic signs of life, respiration and heartbeat, had vanished minutes before, and so Dora Kent, at age eighty-three, was for all intents and purposes now legally dead. The hope of the surgical team was that at some point in the distant future a fresh, new body could be cloned for Dora Kent from one of her old cells. Her old brain would then be placed inside the head of the new body, after which her brain would be revived and the patient would come back to life just as if she had been awakened from a very long sleep.

—Ed Regis, *Great Mambo Chicken and the Transhuman Condition* (1990)

Wet work gone amock. The cryonicists are obviously on the wrong track. Anything as gruesome as calling in the surgeons to decapitate one's mother at the moment of her death has *got* to be the wrong track. Does computer science have a better solution to the problem of mortality (if "problem" it is)? Hans Moravec of Carnegie Mellon thinks so. It's called "downloading." A process well known to users of networked computers, downloading is simply the reading into one computer's memory of the contents of another computer's memory. On the premise that the human mind is just (!) a collection of programs and data, Moravec envisions a day when we will be able to download to disk the contents of our minds, and live on as computers forever (or at least until someone accidentally reformats us). Moravec's proposed solution has the advantage of being no more improbable and yet far more socially acceptable than that of the cryonicists. It raises a number of interesting questions, however. Some of them are rather removed from the subject of the present discourse. Are free will or personal morality susceptible of being downloaded along with the algorithm for tying shoe-laces, for example? If so, how could those higher-level abstractions be exercised by a computer? Readers who believe in the existence of an immortal soul may wonder whether the soul would follow the bitstream and become, if you will, the soul of a new computer, whether it would stay with its biochemical host, or whether it would decide that in the face of such messin' with God's work the best course is to abandon both receptacles.

Along with such metaphysical questions, considerations more relevant to the issue of software protection arise in connection with Moravec's idea. Would it be permissible to reverse engineer the digitized brain? A scientist whose life's work involved studying Einstein's undigitized brain was unable to find any particular difference between it and the brain of your average cadaver. However, if the genius's brain had been digitized, its bit patterns could be unscrambled and disassembled into pseudo-source code almost like that written by the original author. (The Almighty? Mother Nature? Our alien progenitors?) Would such activity be lawful? What about cloning the digitized form of Einstein's brain? Why not make Einstein an open system, so everybody can have one?

These questions depend on whether the mind can be copyrighted or not. That in turn depends on whether it is an original work of authorship. If it is the work of Mother Nature, that work would not qualify as authorship, I'm afraid, because it would lack the requisite intentionality. If it is the work of the Almighty, I would be the last to deny copyrightability on authorship grounds (or on any other grounds, for that matter), though the Almighty is not likely to be concerned with commercializing the product. If it is the work of aliens, one could lawfully attribute authorship to such beings, but it might be commercially prudent to condition the recognition of their copyrights on the reciprocal recognition of earthling copyrights on their planet.

Assume for the moment that *you* were entitled to hold a copyright on the contents of your own brain. Suppose further that the rest of humanity had come to realize, to a much greater extent than you may feel they now do, that yours is one of the most unique and valuable minds extant today, that no one thinks as lucidly as you do, and that the way your mind works gives you a substantial edge over your competitors. How would you respond to demands to put your mind through Moravec's downloading machine so as to create digitized copies of your "program"? What about requests to license that program, or to clone it, or to create second sources for it? What would you say to a proposal to make it an industry standard?

Welcome to the peculiar world of "open systems." It is a world in which suppliers say things that they do not mean, do things that they do not like to do, and still smile a great deal. "Openness" is said to be the answer to the welter of competing software and hardware architectures that crowd the marketplace today, confusing customers and locking them in to the systems of particular vendors once they have made a choice. "Openness" is a movement said to be driven by customers, a bandwagon onto which suppliers must jump or find their products spurned by users. Open systems is an idea, the trade press seems to believe, whose time has come.

Is it? To answer that question, it would be helpful at the outset to have some understanding of what the term "open systems" means. Helpful as that might be, though, there is no agreed definition of the term. Indeed, the publicity and marketing hype for open systems has become so superheated that attempting to define open systems with reference to each system that a supplier describes as "open" leads quickly into a semantic quagmire reminiscent of that which resulted from the orange juice industry's overuse of the term "fresh" to describe liquids other than fresh-squeezed juice. Worse, the term has become a shibboleth in the softwars, a form of newspeak that provides legitimate cover for shady activities: companies wishing to provide close copies of innovative software refer to themselves as purveyors of "open systems." Suppliers of innovative software who sue to preserve their intellectual property are accused of favoring "closed systems."

Writing in *Computerworld* for May 13, 1991, Bill Gates of Microsoft asserted that "open systems" has a very simple definition: customer choice. In other words, Gates wrote, "[c]ustomers are able to choose their products and solutions from a host of hardware and software vendors." Yet freedom of choice among a broad range of hardware and software alternatives was a hallmark of the industry long before the movement toward open systems arose. What, then, is new? According to Gates, what is new is that customers "do not want to be locked in." They want "standards." They want the economics of quantity purchasing. They no longer want operating systems unique to a particular supplier's hardware. One might conclude from that description that users want to be able to buy the same operating system from a number of suppliers, but Gates' conclusion was that customers want Microsoft's DOS, a proprietary operating system, rather than UNIX, a (theoretically) standardized operating system with numerous sources of supply.

A second opinion as to the meaning of the term "open systems" is offered by Scott McNealy, CEO of Sun Microsystems. In the same issue of *Computerworld,* McNealy says that the term "open systems" refers to interfaces that are "written down for the world to see and use." Open systems, in

McNealy's opinion, refer to sets of interfaces that are *published, well-written* (i.e., implementable), *inexpensive or free, legally usable by multiple suppliers,* implemented in a *reference implementation* and preferably supported by a *branding* or *compatibility testing organization.* Not coincidentally, McNealy's particular "checklist of criteria for openness" is drawn closely around Sun's SPARC microprocessor chip architecture and the UNIX efforts of the industry group UNIX International, of which Sun is a prominent member. McNealy says that DOS is not truly an open system, despite its popularity, because Microsoft controls its evolution. In response, Gates argues that SPARC is not truly an open system because Sun has historically not freely licensed the latest releases of its operating system to other suppliers of SPARC hardware, and has discouraged Sun dealers from offering the SPARC computers manufactured by Sun's competitors.

There is a germ of commonality in these competing statements of self-interest. That germ is the notion of multiple sources of supply of goods that are similar in some important respects. In Gates' dream world, those goods are hardware platforms on which his company's operating system will run without substantial modification. In McNealy's dream world, those goods are operating systems that conform to standards his company plays a leadership role in setting. Other suppliers live in dream worlds somewhat different from either Gates' or McNealy's. In all of these dream worlds, however, we are likely to find a common attribute: a declared neutral zone. Declaring a neutral zone, or in other words a domain in which competition through innovation will not take place, is the only way for a high-tech industry to provide customers with multiple sources of supply of goods that are, in ways customers consider important (often, either "look and feel" or programming interfaces), the same. In the neutral zone, a truce is declared in the softwars. The combatants continue to engage in innovation battles outside the neutral zone, but within there is peace and stability. Intellectual property is not an issue here, as the intellectual property that defines the neutral zone is, like Central Park, freely accessible to everyone. To the extent of the neutral zone, the products for which such a truce is declared are essentially commodities, not unique in character. If the neutral zone is large enough, competition among products tends to be price competition, not competition on the basis of function or innovation.

"Open systems," in other words, is a way of legitimizing cloning within the neutral zones. If we step back from the buzzwords of the moment, and consider for what range of activities the computer industry has to date created neutral zones for cloning and why, we find that there has in fact been quite a variety of such activities over the years. One important type of neutral zone created decades ago was the standardization of high-level programming languages. In theory, that standardization permitted the writing of compilers for multifarious operating systems that would translate customers' application programs written in high-level languages so that they could be "ported" from one operating system to another. In practice, what happened was that suppliers of compilers, who were often also suppliers of operating systems and hardware, could not resist putting unique and innovative extensions into their compilers. Those extensions could generally be ignored by customers who wished to remain within the bounds of the standard, but the benefits the extensions offered were often so significant that the temptation to use them in writing applications—thereby rendering the applications less "portable" because other suppliers' compilers did not offer those extensions—was too great to resist.

A more recent standardization activity of considerable significance is the International Standards Organization's "Open Systems Interconnect" (OSI). OSI is a comprehensive standard for communication protocols designed to promote data communications among computer networks having internally disparate designs. By the end of the 1980s, the standard had been articulated in such detail that it could serve both as a design architecture for software interconnecting otherwise incompatible networks and as an internal design architecture for computer networks themselves. If all network vendors adopted the OSI architecture, either for interconnect programs or for their internal network designs, there would be little difficulty in communication among networks of different suppliers. Yet suppliers of network hardware and software have not been aggressively moving to implement OSI. In part, this is because enough information has been available about the major proprietary communications architectures, such as IBM's Systems Network Architecture and Digital's Digital Communications Architecture, to allow a wide variety of interconnection hardware and software programs to be written by numerous suppliers. In part, vendor lethargy has been caused by the fact that the standard has been slow in arriving, so that proprietary architectures have outpaced it technologically. And in part, it is because customers don't seem to want standardization for its own sake. What they want, according to OSI Network Management Forum's Director of Operations Beth Adams, are the kinds of benefits that standardization offers; in particular, product stability, longevity, and the ability to support the existing variety of network products. In effect, those benefits are already available within the context of proprietary architectures.

The activity of standards organizations—of which there is a great deal in respect of computer hardware and software (someone counted over 1000 computer-related standards in 1989)—is but one way in which the industry has created neutral zones. Another way, historically as important as, if not more important than, national or international standards bodies, is the relaxation of control over a portion of its intellectual property by a company holding copyrights, patents, or trade secrets. In 1964, for example, IBM introduced a family of computers called the IBM System/360, that covered a performance range theretofore only available from computers of differing and incompatible types. The System/360 family provided compatibility from the smallest processor to the largest, and became a huge success. IBM published the instruction set for that family of computers, and also published interface information that facilitated attachment of peripheral products such as disk and tape drives to System/360 processors. System/360 was a huge success. It was called a standard, but here the word had a different meaning. System/360 was a standard in the same sense that "As Time Goes By" is a standard. It consisted in major part of unique intellectual property that remained extremely popular over a long period of time. It has served as the template for systems developed by Amdahl, Fujitsu, Hitachi, and others. Those systems conform to the IBM instruction set; however, some of them offer proprietary embellishments that depart from the IBM architecture.

More recently, one could point to Microsoft's flagship product DOS as the same kind of standard: a highly popular product that accommodates attachment of hardware and software from numerous other suppliers and has demonstrated stability and longevity. Proprietary technologies offer the advantage over official standards of not requiring the agreement of all and sundry in the industry before they can evolve. The supplier who controls the technology can adapt it as the competitive environment dictates. That is also the disadvantage of proprietary technologies: they may change or not, and indeed the amount of information made available about them may change or not, to suit the competitive needs of the owning supplier. On the whole, however, proprietary technologies have evolved much more rapidly than official standards, and have been the principal source of innovative hardware and software in the industry.

Supporting Microsoft's revenue stream are the armies of IBM-compatible personal computer suppliers, whose presence has made the instruction set of the IBM PC a kind of proprietary open system. It might be expected that those clone suppliers would be the leading proponents of standardization. Now, however, some of those suppliers are, as *Computerworld* puts it, "step[ping] out of the clone zone." Here is Gary Stimac, senior vice-president of systems engineering at Compaq: "If I just copied IBM's hardware, then I could be no better than IBM. That wasn't our intention at all." *Computerworld's* analysis of the effect of this divergence is interesting.

For users, the divergence between IBM and PC clone vendors may mean more choices and greater innovation. But it also injects a good deal of confusion into the once simple universe of the IBM PC compatible.

That is a succinct statement of the relative merit of proprietary systems and open systems, to which we shall return at the end of the chapter.

Between standardization and voluntary openness lies a third mechanism for creating neutral zones, one which is often thought of as a hybrid of standardization and technology sharing: the consortium. Consortia are groups of like-minded suppliers each of whose best interests are served by agreeing with others in the group to conform to a common set of interfaces. UNIX International and the Open Software Foundation are two such consortia, each devoted to promulgating a variant of UNIX. ACE (Advanced Computing Environment) and SPARC (Scalable Processor ARChitecture) are two more, each aimed at promulgating a type of Reduced Instruction Set Computer (RISC) chip. Consortia are often likened to standards bodies, and indeed they frequently try to look and act like standards bodies, but in truth they are more like the individual companies that have from time to time found it advantageous to relax control of certain of their intellectual property. Consider, for example, the strange case of UNIX. UNIX is an operating system designed to run on multiple, otherwise incompatible lines of computers. It is AT&T's principal contribution to the computer industry since the transistor. UNIX is and has for some years been available to anyone who wanted it, on a royalty-bearing license basis. Although from time to time, AT&T seems to have been tempted to keep its own enhancements to UNIX proprietary, on the whole the company has treated its asset as one to be shared with others for a fee that many, at least, would describe as reasonable. Indeed, together with Sun Microsystems, AT&T founded UNIX International in December 1988 to lay the mantle of "vendor independence" over its operating system. UNIX International is self-described as a "nonprofit organization responsible for directing the evolution of UNIX System V, the industry-standard open operating system for multiuser computing." Membership in UNIX International (UI) is open to users, software vendors, computer manufacturers, system integrators, value-added resellers, industry standards bodies, academic and research institutions, and government agencies. Formation of UI was a way of demonstrating that control of enhancements to the UNIX operating system was being relinquished by AT&T to a quasi-public group. (A contraindication is provided by the limitation of UI's scope to UNIX System *V*. Who is in charge of UNIX System *VI*?)

Before the formation of UI, there had been great concern in the industry that AT&T and Sun Microsystems, with which AT&T had close business ties, would between them control the development direction of and the access to UNIX, giving themselves the advantage of lead time in the marketplace. That concern had led in May 1988 to the formation of the Open Software Foundation (OSF) by Digital Equipment, Hewlett-Packard, IBM, Hitachi, Bull, Siemens/Nixdorf, and Philips. OSF is also an open-membership, nonprofit organization dedicated to developing enhancements to UNIX and allied products. The motivations of the sponsors were not altruistic. In part, they were defensive, but in part they were also offensive, in the sense that some of the sponsors already had UNIX implementations or enhancements of their own, which they were hopeful that OSF would adopt. OSF's first operating system, however, aptly called OSF/1, is an enhanced UNIX that is neither the same as UI's UNIX nor the same as the UNIX implementations of any of its sponsors. Application programs written to run on UNIX System

V will not necessarily run without modification or recompilation on OSF/1, and vice versa. (In addition to these two incompatible UNIXes [UNICES?] there are a large number of UNIX implementations by individual suppliers, including, obviously, the separate UNIX implementations of the OSF sponsors.) OSF/1 was, however, the product of a vendor-independent organization, and the prospect of such a product finding greater favor with customers than UNIX Version V led to the formation of UI and the surrendering by AT&T of Version V enhancement rights to UI.

Does this sound like standardization to you? Does it sound like a description of a neutral zone? It is not, for two good reasons. Number one: UNIX, the UNIX-compatible application programs, and the processors on which they run compete with traditional operating systems, their application programs, and processors on which *they* run. Thus, this headline from *Electronic News*: "Battles Lines Shaping in $30B OLTP Market." The associated article reported on the assault by UNIX software and workstations on the customer base for on-line transaction processing systems (e.g., banks), a customer base now served by IBM, DEC, NCR, Unisys, Tandem, ICL, and others with non-UNIX, proprietary systems and data base software. Number two: the software industry is highly competitive, and competition through innovation is the principle form of that competition. In truth most software suppliers do not even know how to compete without creating some form of product differentiation, some feature or features that make their programs more attractive than their competitors'. Consortia to establish neutral zones and truces may make for good marketing themes, but they run counter to the life force of the industry. Consortia members are constantly looking for some competitive advantage outside the consortium's neutral zone. Thus, DEC was a founding sponsor of OSF in 1988. Yet in 1991 it helped found ACE, which, along with its effort to establish the RISC chip set of MIPS Computer Systems, Inc.—on which DEC's RISC workstations are based—as the leading RISC architecture, is also attempting to establish a new UNIX standard based only in part on OSF/1. In part, the new standard will also be based on DEC's own "Ultrix" implementation of UNIX, *and* on a new *non-UNIX* operating system standard based on Microsoft's OS/2 Version 3.0. IBM was a founder of OSF, but is joining with Apple to promote multiplatform operating systems based on IBM's own UNIX implementation, AIX, and Apple's Macintosh operating system. Unisys was a prominent member of UNIX International, but is developing another version of UNIX with a company called Chorus Systems.

The uneasy alliances to promote common architectures, the international standardization activities on top of which proprietary accretions keep appearing, the unilateral (and usually partial) "opening" of proprietary architectures are all said to be driven by customer demand. But how real is that demand? A DMR Group study of companies that had bought or were in the process of buying open systems indicated that 15 percent of those companies were in fact considering active use of open systems. Why were the other 85 percent motivated to buy those systems if not for "active use"? The study doesn't say, but suggests that the purpose was to study the economic and technical merits of those systems. In general, the study shows, customers have not justified open systems expenditures with cost analyses, but with a sort of "bandwagon" analysis. The report quotes Bob Dylan to explain customers' actions: "You don't need a weatherman to know which way the wind blows." Not a particularly flattering description of the customer decision process, or one that suggests conviction that open systems are better than proprietary systems. Indeed, in 1989 DMR had found that only 30 percent of the users it surveyed could describe the benefits of open systems, and hardly any of them could put a value on those benefits. When users are forced to sharpen their pencils, however, as they have been by the recession of the early 1990s, they do not find open systems more cost-effective than proprietary systems, particularly since their installations at present consist almost entirely of proprietary systems, and changing to open systems would require conversion of installed programs. Moreover, users seem to recognize that open systems present something of a risk, and the more closely they look at the unease of their vendors at playing in the neutral zone the more they will realize the nature of that risk. On the one hand, customers may want their procurement decisions to be more commodity-like and price sensitive; on the other, however, the computers and software they acquire can make those customers more or less competitive against their own competitors, and if a customer's competitors might choose software with proprietary accretions that make their operations more efficient, that customer may be impelled to do the same. Finally, of course, there is the fact that proprietary systems always reach the market earlier, so that by the time an open system arrives there is already a base of applications running on competing proprietary systems, which makes the latter more attractive.

The principal desire of customers appears to be the ability to run applications they have written or purchased, without modification, on systems and networks of differing architectures. If that were possible, then customers could readily change hardware and software platforms as technology advances were offered by different vendors, in the same way that you and I can change our old CD players for new ones having greater oversampling rates. That desire is not something new; customers have been wanting such freedom since the early days of the industry, though they have generally been unwilling to pay the price for that freedom. As noted above, writing applications in standard programming languages, and forbearing the use of proprietary accretions on the standard languages offered in commercially available compilers, has assured that kind of portability for decades. Customers are schizophrenic about open systems, however, just as vendors are.

There is another aspect of open systems that customers tend to ignore, but that in the long run they may not find to their liking. The teachings of the dismal scientists suggest that the consequences of declaring neutral zones through creation of open systems will be no different from the consequences of declaring neutral zones by holding some or all elements of computer programs to be unprotected by intellectual property laws. Removing the opportunity to innovate is no different in effect from removing the incentive to innovate. If customers resolutely insist that suppliers not differentiate their user interfaces, programming interfaces, or the other design elements that customers may use as interfaces (recall Franklin's argument that customers of the Apple II had used or could have used all parts of that computer's operating system as interfaces for their application programs), investment in the innovation that creates meaningful differentiation will dry up as assuredly as if those interfaces were declared by the courts to be unprotectable. The innovation in programming have in major part come from programmers applying their imaginations to the task of anticipating the conversations that customers would want to have with them if they, the program authors, rather than their programs, were delivered to the customers to provide services. Those anticipated conversations are structured into interfaces and services in the course of writing the program. The open systems peace activists are signaling to programmers that they do not want those conversations to differ from program to program. The wider the neutral zone created by that movement, the more the software industry will resemble—indeed will be—a commodity industry.

The consequences of open systems on innovation can be seen quite clearly on the eastern landfall of the Atlantic, where, according to an ICL executive, "Europe is moving to open systems very much more rapidly than America. We don't think it's a minority sport." According to *Datamation*'s July 1991 report on the top twenty-five European firms in information technology (of which two-thirds were software suppliers and a quarter supplied only software and services), firms that had been "supporting fat staffs with the sizable income made on proprietary equipment felt the pinch of skimpier profit margins for items like PCs and UNIX-based systems that look more like commodities. In response, staff reductions were widespread." Not specified in the *Datamation* article is the fact that, in an industry where annual investments of between 5 and 15 percent of gross income in research and development are the norm, the "fat staffs" to which the report uncharitably referred were in substantial measure computer scientists, engineers, and programmers. For observers of the softwars, it is interesting to note that in order to return to the profitability necessary to support innovation, these European firms appear to be looking to proprietary software. The most successful of the top twenty-five European computer companies during the recession year 1990 were "those with solid offerings in software and services," and almost all of the top twenty-five "went roving the Continent and the United States in search of software acquisitions with which to enter the software market or solidify their positions there."

A month earlier, *Datamation* had published an article with a similar theme:

More and more workstations made in Europe are complying with standards. That's great, say users, but how do you tell them apart?

Do they want to be told apart, or are European workstation suppliers content to compete as suppliers of mere commodities?

[A]s more and more vendors claim their products promote software portability and seamless interoperability, workstation purveyors are looking increasingly alike. And, in this commodity market, it's difficult for European vendors to compete, as their labor costs and the current devaluation of the dollar and the yen make U.S. and Japanese-manufactured goods cheaper in Europe.

At Siemens-Nixdorf, Philips, Groupe Bull, Olivetti, Acorn, and other major European suppliers of workstations, there is substantial effort aimed at differentiating UNIX workstations. How? By offering unique and valuable software aimed at specific, high-volume applications, and in many cases "bundling" or packaging those applications with the otherwise undifferentiated hardware and systems software. One might well wonder what the open systems movement has accomplished in Europe, other than (1) to weaken European systems suppliers by giving the edge to non-European suppliers having a comparative advantage in the technologies of low-cost production and (2) to induce European systems suppliers to "bundle" systems software and application software thereby changing the terms of engagement in proprietary software from the level of systems software provided by a number of firms to the level of applications software provided by the same firms.

American suppliers appear to be reluctant to narrow the terms of engagement as much as European suppliers have done. For instance, the multiplicity of UNIX implementations, and the resolve of the major UNIX suppliers who also supply hardware to continue to offer UNIX enhancements that give their systems an edge in the market, indicate a desire to keep the neutral zone relatively narrow. The divergence of the PC clones from IBM architectures is a similar indicator. So is the flurry of strategic alliances between systems suppliers and software houses. The American software industry is fundamentally antientropic and fiercely competitive in spirit. Innovation is an irrepressable attribute of competition in that industry, and the open systems movement is not likely soon to overcome it.

So, what is the upshot of the customer-driven movement to establish neutral zone in the softwars? The upshot is confusion. Indeed, the open systems hype has caused so much confusion as to warrant a lengthy cover feature story in *Business Week* in mid-1991. The customer decision-making process has become more complex, not less, and identifying the hardware and software architectures that will prevail in the future has become more difficult, not easier. Proprietary systems have not disappeared; instead they are finding new vitality. At this writing, Microsoft's Windows 3.0 and DOS 5.0 have given the somewhat hoary DOS a new lease on life. IBM's OS/2 2.0 has brought the full potential of the highly functional but underinstalled OS/2 operating system to the fore, and IBM's OS/400 operating system has fueled the signal success of the IBM AS/400 mid-range computer systems. Apple has finally delivered the long-delayed System 7 version of the Macintosh operating system, to favorable reviews, and there has been considerable publicity over the new, object-oriented operating system on which it has been working and which is involved in the alliance with IBM. The proliferation of open systems alternatives, therefore, represents to customers an additive layer to the already challenging process of choosing the software systems on which to base one's business.

Adding that layer would not be a terrible burden if the result of the open systems movement had been simply to add one open system alternative to each of the major software types acquired by customers; but that is not what happened. Instead, because software suppliers cannot resist differentiating their products, because differentiating software is fairly easy once the creative spark is ignited (no retooling of production lines is required), and because—in the end—customers are attracted to the features that make one program better than another, a number of open system alternatives are becoming available for each of the major software types that most customers utilize. The *Business Week* article began with a hypothetical conversation between a customer and some industry gurus about what should be a fairly simple decision: choosing new personal computers for a business.

"First," says one, "you've got to pick your hardware—CISC or RISC? If you go with the IBM PC standard—that's CISC—you'll also have to choose between EISA or MCA. With RISC, there's ACE, along with SPARC, RS/6000, PA, the Motorola 88000, and . . . "

"No," another expert chimes in. "You should really pick your basic software first. Do you want MS-DOS 4.0 or OS/2 Release 1.0? Of course, there's UNIX, too, but which flavor? Xenix, Ultrix, Dynix, AIX, AUX, Berkeley 4.0, System 5? Each one's different, you know."

"But what about the GUI?" asks yet another. "There's Motif, New Wave, Presentation Manager, Windows 3.0, Open-Look, Desqview. . . . And don't forget networks: SNA or OSI? EtherNet or Token Ring? LU 6.2 or TCP/IP? What'll it be?"

It is a hallmark of a healthy industry, of course, that there is such a cornucopia of options, but the presence of that very abundance can slow customer decision making, and there is some indication that the open systems movement has done just that. If so, the movement can only be described as a major evolutionary thrust that has been essentially counterproductive, both for suppliers and for customers.

There is, it seems, a need for customers and their suppliers to return to first principles, to consider what the impetus for the open systems movement was instead of what the sloganeering and politicking of today's movement is producing, before the second law of thermodynamics plunges the industry into chaos. The reason for the movement was that customers were spending an inordinate amount of time and money attempting to make heterogeneous, noncompatible systems work together. That is why the movement is more advanced in Europe. There, government pressures and national pride have assured indigenous computer suppliers a significant share of customer installations in each European country, but superior technology has also assured foreign suppliers a substantial position as well. A customer might have found Macintosh computers attractive, in terms of intrinsic capabilities, for departments producing brochures and other customer literature, Siemens computers attractive for home-office processing, and IBM mid-range computers attractive for regional office work. However, unless those disparate systems could communicate with one another, exchanging data and messages accurately and efficiently, the whole system would be unsatisfactorily less than the sum of its parts. That problem, which first became critical in Europe, is now felt globally. We are in an age where the world's major industries transmit and receive data from outlying offices electronically, enter into contracts electronically, issue purchase orders and specifications to their suppliers electronically, move funds electronically, and in general use computers to communicate electronically much of what used to be communicated in writing or by phone. Since the companies involved in this global telecommunication web do not all use the same types of computers, the need for a digital *lingua franca* is profound.

The things that must be done, and in fact are being done, to satisfy that need are not things that encourage technological sameness and thereby drive the industry into repeated price wars that sap its ability to fund research and development. Just as one can speak Esperanto as well as French, the *lingua franca* of computer interoperability can be an additional feature of an otherwise differentiated system. Suppliers of software have lived comfortably with that notion for some years. The aspect of the open systems ground swell that is both unnatural and destructive of innovation is the insistence of some adherents on the availability of multiple sources for what is in effect the same product. The demand for an identical second source, which may be of real importance in government contracting for custom systems, where there is no marketplace to test the reasonableness of prices

quoted by contractors, is overkill in a market where there is strong competition that assures reasonable prices. The standardization process, no matter how it is accomplished, lays well below the envelope of the technology
curve. By the time the suppliers agree on what the standard will be, and
then implement that standard, new technologies will be available from one
or more of them that go beyond what the standard can offer—provided
those suppliers are earning enough profit out of which to fund further R&D.
One user quoted in *Business Week* observed that open systems standards
"give vendors an excuse to be mediocre." Worse yet, they may *force* vendors
to be mediocre, in the same way that repealing intellectual property protection for software would do. There is no prospect of such repeal occurring,
of course. Signs of recognition of that essential fact are becoming apparent.
"I've detected a major shift in the meaning of open systems," Berl Hartman,
an executive at the software company Sybase is quoted as saying. "Open
systems used to be synonymous with UNIX. Now, it's coming to mean
interoperability between systems." It would be constructive for all involved
to recognize that there is no prospect of enforced mediocrity occurring
either, since software suppliers *will* continue to differentiate their products
so long as they can profitably do so. That recognition, while an invitation
to continue the softwars, would also be an invitation to continue the dynamic progress in software that has been experienced around the world
over the last four decades.

# Part V

Conclusion... For Now

Wherein, Janus-like, we look both back and ahead with the eyes of combat journalists.

# 19

## "The One Who Controls the Software...": A Meditation on the Future of the Softwars

"Goodbye, my book! Like mortal eyes, imagined ones must close some day. Onegin from his knees will rise—but his creator strolls away. And yet the ear cannot right now part with the music and allow the tale to fade; the chords of fate itself continue to vibrate; and no obstruction for the sage exists where I have put The End: the shadows of my world extend beyond the skyline of the page, blue as tomorrow's morning haze—nor does this terminate the phrase."
—Vladimir Nabokov, *The Gift* (1963)

"Darling," replied Valentine, "has not the count just told us that all human wisdom is summed up in two words?—*'Wait and hope.'*"
—Alexandre Dumas, *The Count of Monte Christo* (1894)

For a number of reasons, it is less risky to be an historian writing about a war from a safe temporal distance than a war correspondent reporting on battles in progress and attempting to predict an outcome not yet consummated. This collection of reports from the front must necessarily end with the wars' shadows extending beyond the skyline of the page. The reporter in such circumstances feels an irresistable urge to prognosticate. It would be quite appropriate for the reader to take a grain of salt with such prognostications, as they cannot be pinned to any authority other than the author's belief system. Nonetheless, readers find comfort in writers' predictions, reliable or not, because they attempt to explain the unknown (else why would newspapers and magazines devote valuable space to horoscopes). If readers feels a prediction is reliable, they can adjust their behavior accordingly. Even if they feel a prediction is unreliable, though, they can use it as a foil for improving their own views of the future. Make of what follows, then, what you will.

After my name appeared on a list of top high-tech intellectual property lawyers in 1991, the headhunters began to call. What they were hunting was someone to build an intellectual property litigation group for one or another major law firm. Those firms, like many others, had come to the conclusion that intellectual property litigation was destined to be a "hot" area of legal practice during the 1990s. There is no doubt that they are right. In a way, of course, a flood of lawyers into the field of high-tech intellectual property litigation would tend to make that conclusion a self-fulfilling prophecy. Yet whether or not the number of attorneys specializing in the field increases, there are certain technological, economic, and moral forces that seem to assure patents, copyrights, and trade secrets a place at the forefront of technology-based industrial disputes for the next several years. While intellectual property disputes will occur in a number of high-tech areas during that period, software will be a particularly fertile source for litigation and alternate dispute resolution.

Software is hard to write, can be highly valuable when written, and yet is easy to copy. Popular software can have millions of users, can sell billions of dollars' worth of hardware, and can spawn large markets for ancillary products. Progress in software functions, features, "look and feel," and other attributes tends to be rapid, in large measure because no factories are necessary in order to enter the software business and no retooling is necessary in order to create new versions of a software product. These attributes have made and will continue to make it attractive for an enterprise to enter into or expand within a product area by copying as closely as possible computer programs written by others. As copyists test the legal boundaries of the phrase "as closely as possible" and innovators attempt to protect their turf, disputes are inevitable. The two decades of software-specific legal precedents on the books in the United States (even less history in other countries) have not yet staked out those boundaries fully. Though the legal regimes that define those boundaries have centuries of development that can guide companies in determining right from wrong, there is an unshakeable tendency in the industry simply to ignore precedent that doesn't specifically involve software. As a result, many copyists and commentators have convinced one another that the well-known, stable regimes of intellectual property protection are highly unpredictable from the point of view of software developers. True or not (and my view, as you have gathered, is that it is not true), that conviction, too, is a guaranty of continuing litigation.

In addition, there is the prospect of a fusing of computer software and other types of software during the 1990s. Some anonymous etymological terrorist has dubbed this phenomenon "infotainment." Less radical word-benders refer to it simply but ungrammatically as "multi-media." Call it what you will, traditional aesthetic arts are going digital with a vengeance. The reader undoubtedly has a library of music delivered in object code form on compact disk. Digital movies on laserdisk are also now available. Digital TV and radio broadcasts are on the horizon. Digital books are even closer to hand. Computer programs will be the glue that holds the object code forms of these works of authorship together, melds them into data bases, and makes them accessible to users. The movie industry, publishing industry, broadcast industry, and music industry are each more litigious than the software industry insofar as intellectual property disputes are concerned, and therefore the evolutionary confluence of the former industries and the latter is bound to increase the number of software-related cases on court calendars everywhere.

Finally, of course, the struggle for economic dominance of the software industry is far from over. Indeed, it is just now entering a superheated phase, in which hardware know-how—absent major new breakthroughs that give leading-edge suppliers a clear and dramatic advantage—has proliferated around the globe. Exascerbating that problem is the fact that the "infotainment" movement will lead to a merger of computer hardware and entertainment hardware, and entertainment hardware know-how is ubiquitous. Thus software will from here forward be absolutely indispensable to success in the computer industry.

So the softwars will continue unabated. You want to know, I suppose, who will win. The answer is complex, depending as it does on the varying comparative advantages of suppliers in different parts of the world and on the evolution of the rules of war in the major countries. Let's begin with Europe where, as the 1990s opened, a major reexamination of those rules was underway.

Free-market economics tends to be viewed as a curious and somewhat suspect notion by the eurocrats. Natural selection through the interplay of market forces sounds to them like rolling dice, rather than managing orderly, effective, and balanced industrial sectors. Competition is a kind of rough-and-tumble economic activity that cries out for regulation. Too much of it is as bad as too little. Sitting at lunch with a European official one day during the EC copyright debate, I remarked that the eagerness with which the Poles were embracing free-market principles suggested that before long Poland would be a more openly competitive market than the European Community. "Oh, no," the official replied in all seriousness. "Our representatives have already begun to meet with the Poles, to explain to them how to regulate competition."

Regulating competition in the EC takes two principal forms: industrial policy and competition policy. Industrial policy has consisted of a combination of subsidies, coordination of R&D, jawboning, and other bureaucratic efforts aimed at strengthening European industry. Competition policy is aimed at correcting "distortions" in the European market. A market can be "distorted" by the abusive or collusive behavior of large numbers of European suppliers and foreign suppliers, and the eurocrats are often forced to make an example of a particular wrongdoer rather than pursuing all wrongdoers. In the computer industry, the attention of the competition regulators has tended thus far to focus on large American suppliers, particularly IBM.

In recent years, European industrial policy has suffered substantial reversals. Like dominoes, European computer suppliers fell from their independent status as the 1990s opened, and were acquired in whole or in part predominantly by their Japanese competitors. The takeover of the U.K.'s flagship computer company ICL by the premier Japanese computer company Fujitsu in late 1990, though widely seen in Europe as a harbinger of apocalypse for the European computer industry, was accepted by the eurocracy as the only alternative to bankruptcy for the U.K. company. The Fujitsu move followed an earlier absorption of Apricot Computers, Ltd., once the number one compatible PC supplier in the U.K., by Mitsubishi. NEC's 1991 acquisition of a 15 percent stake in the leading French computer supplier Groupe Bull, initially opposed with unsubtle vigor by Prime Minister Edith Cresson, was ultimately accepted after the realities of Bull's situation became understood. Also in 1991, the major Dutch computer firm Philips, sold all of its computer business save its IBM-compatible PC activity to DEC, marking yet another sign of defeat for EC industrial policy. In truth, the economic forces at play in the industry, paramount among which was the fact that the European computer suppliers had not developed strong followings outside their home countries and therefore could not achieve the economies of scale of their global rivals, were probably too strong to be deflected by EC industrial policy initiatives, no matter what those initiatives were. Nonetheless, it cannot be denied that—for whatever reason—EC industrial policy in the computer sector has failed to preserve the position of European systems suppliers. Indeed, to the extent that EC policies have attempted to counter the product differentiation of U.S. suppliers and encourage open systems, they may be said to have promoted competition on terms that did not favor the comparative economic advantages of European firms at all.

Now that the hope of European computer suppliers is that the availability of attractive software will cause their products to stand out from the pack of commodity hardware systems, now that the software sector looms as the most promising area for European revitalization in the computer industry, now that Europe has become—in the words of Bull CEO Francis Lorentz— "the major battlefield in our industry," it is interesting to reflect on the nature of European industrial policy for software. That meditation must center on the EC copyright directive. Within the European Commission, the draft directive had been the product of an energetic negotiation among, on the one hand, its drafters whose purpose was to harmonize the member states' copyright laws as they apply to computer programs, and, on the other, representatives of the industrial policy and competition directorates whose purpose at the time was to promote the creation of clone software. The inevitable tension that those different and substantially conflicting objectives created in the draft document were most readily apparent in the declarations that on the one hand computer programs should be protected as "literary works," a term that invoked traditional principles of copyright, and on the other that certain major attributes of computer programs, in particular "interfaces" and "logic," should not be protected whatever their definition.

During the deliberations in the European Parliament, the Commission and the Council of Ministers' working group, nervous industry representatives lobbied the eurocrats in numbers previously unseen in EC lobbying history. Like Fujitsu, other ECIS members had studied the draft directive and realized that it contained a trap for suppliers of compatible software: it prohibited interim copying, just as Judge Smith had in the *Nintendo* litigation. Accordingly, in addition to supporting notions of nonprotectability of interfaces and of structure, sequence, and organization, ECIS lobbied for a specific readout of reverse compilation from the acts prohibited by copyright law. In its lobbying literature, ECIS recommended that the final directive provide for

1. protection of computer programs against "piracy" [i.e., mechanical reproduction], and

2. encouragement of "interoperability" and "open systems" by

   a. exempting interface specifications from copyright protection, and

   b. permitting those "research and analysis techniques" required to produce "interoperable products".

ECIS defined "interoperable products" as

products that are interchangeable and can function together as part of the same system, despite their being produced by different manufacturers. Car tyres are a good example of interoperability.

Users may, for a variety of reasons, prefer to purchase central hardware produced by one manufacturer and peripheral equipment produced by others. For such a system to work, hardware, software and peripherals must, like tyres and wheel rims, fit together. They must be "interoperable".

That definition failed to capture the essence of the ECIS motivations, though, which were to legitimize cloning. One does not have to reverse engineer the car in order to make a replacement tire. The ECIS agenda was more candidly set out in its description of "research and analysis."

It is quite often necessary to engage in some form of reverse analysis to determine and confirm the specifications of interfaces to ensure that a new product being developed will in fact work with *or in place of* the existing product being analyzed. [Emphasis added.]

The principal "reverse analysis" technique for which ECIS was lobbying was reverse compilation. ECIS justified reverse compilation on the basis that it was a necessary step in studying a target program's ideas. Many software innovators, however, knew from bitter experience that reverse compilation was a handy way of creating a source-code-like translation of a target program, which can then be manipulated to disguise its source and even enhanced to improve on the target program's performance. Their lobbying group SAGE's approach, accordingly, was to lobby to replace the interface exclusion with a statement to the effect that copyright protects only a program's expression, not its underlying ideas and principles:

We support "interoperability", but we believe that it is unnecessary and inappropriate to carve out an exception to copyright for this objective. The necessary ideas and principles are already available for achieving interoperability and open systems, i.e., systems open to one another for exchanging information by their mutual use of applicable standards.

Such ideas and principles may be obtained through manuals and other technical information and support provided by program vendors and standards bodies. Furthermore, they can also be obtained through observing, studying, or testing the functioning of the program while loading, displaying, running, transmitting or storing the program without unauthorized reproduction or adaptation of the program.

The SAGE position on disassembly, strongly negative at first, evolved into highly qualified acceptance as the political realities became manifest. Sage proposed the following language for the directive:

1. It shall not be a copyright infringement if it is established that the owner of a lawfully made and acquired copy of a program has engaged in [otherwise infringing acts] as part of the development of a new program solely in order to allow it to interoperate *at a supported point of attachment* of the original program and to function *as part of an open system standard,* as long as such acts are *consistent with fair practice* and *neither impair the actual or potential market for or value of the program, nor conflict with a normal exploitation of the work or unreasonably prejudice the legitimate interests of the right holder.*

2. The provisions of section 1 of this Article shall not apply unless the acts are performed only on an *insubstantial part of the original program* and only to the extent *essential to develop an interoperable product,* and are performed only *after the owner of the copy has exhausted all non-infringing means* of obtaining information *essential for the new program to interoperate* with the original program, without achieving such operation.

3. The provisions of section 1 of this Article *shall not permit* the performance of [otherwise infringing acts] for the purpose of *developing a substitute or replacement product* for the original program, and shall not permit any communication, distribution, or commercialization of the original program's expression, nor the sharing with any third party of any information obtained. [Emphasis added.]

The pain and internal torment underlying this concession to the realities of European industrial policy are almost palpable. The realities were that, with powerful European suppliers on both sides of the debate, the EC was inexorably drawn down the middle, politically impelled to satisfy both sides to some extent.

SAGE's position was grudging, but had the virtue of being consistent with the attitudes of the group's members toward their own intellectual property. There was a curious elasticity in the ECIS members' views, however, which seemed to be different for their own software than it was for the software of others. The two major American ECIS members, NCR and Unisys, seemed to have felt that the exemption of software interfaces of others from copyright protection would not threaten their own interfaces because clones would likely not attempt to copy NCR or Unisys interfaces in the foreseeable future. Fujitsu, the major Japanese member of ECIS, engaged in a multimillion dollar lobbying campaign to legalize reverse compilation while at the same time prohibiting reverse compilation of its own programs through the terms of its license agreement:

The Customer shall not reverse assemble or reverse compile or cause or permit any other person to reverse assemble or reverse compile any licensed program product in whole or in part.

Similarly with Sun Microsystems, champion of "open systems," whose U.K. legal counsel seemed unaware of his client's contract practices when he published an article scathingly critical of efforts to prevent reverse compilation during the debate over the EC software directive:

Customer may not modify, translate, adapt, reverse engineer, decompile, disassemble, or create derivative works based on the documentation without the prior written consent of Tops, a Sun Microsystems Company.

(Note that the phrase "or create derivative works from the documentation" appears aimed at preventing a clone even from using the customer manuals for Sun programs to create, without looking at the Sun code at all, a competing product.)

The Plasticman award for elasticity, however, must go to Groupe Bull, which with its European face urged the French government to press the EC for a liberalizing of interface exclusions to copyright and of reverse compilation privileges in aid of creating substitute products, while with its

American face, it was suing in federal court to prevent copying of its own interfaces. The lawsuit, against software house TSR and its customer, American Express, sought damages for the creation by TSR of an emulator program that allowed programs written in Bull's SCREENWRITE language to run unmodified on IBM mainframes with IBM's VM/CMS operating system resident on them. Basically, the emulator accepted commands in the SCREENWRITE language as input and produced VM/CMS commands as output. It was, conceptually, very much like the CA APAPTER code discussed in Chapter 14. Bull claimed protection in the SCREENWRITE commands and in the functions of its operating system.

SAGE members did not suffer from such attacks of terminal inconsistency, but neither was their position in the EC copyright debate above criticism. The weakness of the SAGE position was that it advocated a scope of legal protection that in some respects was stronger than that available under existing law. Their justification for such overzealousness was that statutory ambiguities such as those with which they were happy to live under U.S. law, where the long tradition of caselaw precedent served to fill in the legislative ellipses, could not be allowed to exist in the statutes of Continental countries, where judges are not bound to follow case law precedent. By way of example, the U.S. copyright statute provides that copying for research purposes is lawful so long as the nature of the copying is "fair" under the circumstances. "Fairness" is obviously an ambiguous standard, but judicial decisions have made it clear that copying in order to create a competitive product is hardly ever "fair." (We will see momentarily, however, that recent judicial decisions in the U.S. have blown through "fair use" territory like Hurricane Andrew blew through South Florida.) Many SAGE members insisted that the EC directive must explicitly indicate that copying in order to create a substitute product is never fair, a rather stronger statement. What they feared was that a fairness standard would be too large a loophole if judges were free to ignore earlier cases. Without precedent to constrain them, continental judges might view *each* case that came before them involving copying for competitive purposes as one of those rare, "fair" cases. That concern forced SAGE into a position too rigid for the highly politicized, highly public European debate.

On the path to Europe 1992, no issue was more heavily lobbied than the software copyright issue. At first bemused, then annoyed, and finally swamped by the endless parade of industry representatives prattling in cyberbabble about arcana beyond their comprehension, the eurocrats pleaded with the lobbyists to work out a common industry solution to the interface and reverse-compilation questions. Attempts were made by company representatives, but all of them foundered on a fundamental, irreconcilable difference: ECIS insisted on language that would permit an argument that interim copying to create a substitute product was lawful, and SAGE insisted that there be no such language. Ultimately, the eurocrats could wait no longer. The Europe 1992 countdown forced a resolution. The directive issued in May 1991. On the interface issue, the exclusion favored by ECIS had been deleted. The final directive provided only that ideas and principles in computer programs—including those contained in interfaces—were not protected by copyright. As to reverse compilation, the directive provided a heavily circumscribed right: where information necessary for interoperability was otherwise unavailable, reverse compilation limited to those portions of an original program necessary to achieving interoperability is permitted (whether or not a supplier's contract provides to the contrary) so long as it does not interfere with a normal exploitation of the original program or unreasonably prejudice the rights of the original program's author. The program resulting from such reverse compilation and subsequent activity is not permitted to be substantially similar to the original program.

What does the directive suggest about the course of the softwars? First, it seems to adopt the view of interfaces reflected in American case law: interfaces may contain, but not be limited to, ideas and principles. To some extent, therefore, they may be protected by copyright. While that view is consistent with the urgings of SAGE and inconsistent with those of ECIS, it represents in fact a balancing of the interests of innovators and followers of a sort traditional in copyright law. The reverse-compilation provision, too, balances the interests of innovators and followers, but in a negative way. It is equally ominous for both sides. For innovators, the provision permits copying without compensation for purposes of creating a replacement product, a notion completely antithetical to the basic principle of copyright. What the courts will make of that basic contradiction cannot be predicted. Also, the term "interoperability" is not defined in the directive, and until it is defined by someone, perhaps a judge, the proportion of a program that may be reverse compiled is uncertain. Further, since continental judges are not bound by precedent, the term could be redefined in every lawsuit. And finally, the directive's suggestion that contractual provisions prohibiting reverse compilation may not be enforced is a manifest threat to trade secret protection for software in Europe.

For followers, the requirement not to reverse compile more of the program than is necessary for interoperability is far from a model of clarity, both because "interoperability" is not defined and because to a court what is "necessary" may not depend on a follower's particular business strategy, but rather on whether there are technological imperatives that dictate the scope of reverse compilation. Also, the requirement that the resulting program not be substantially similar to the original appears to carry over the American rule that a business objective of "compatibility" will not in itself be a defense to an infringement action.

What the directive will mean in practice cannot be determined because it is not in itself a copyright law. Rather, it is a mandate to the EC member states to conform *their* copyright laws to its terms. For those countries that change their laws in order to achieve conformance, interpretation will only begin after those changes are made, litigated, and—more importantly in Continental law—opined on by copyright scholars. For those countries that consider their laws already compliant and therefore make no changes—a great temptation in the short time given to implement the large number of EC 1992 directives on various subjects—interpretation will be a process of recasting existing legal principles in ways that do them no great violence while at the same time making them appear consistent with the directive. How that process will take place is presently unclear.

It can be said, though, that currently, European public policy is more favorable to clones than is American public policy. Whether the directive changes that direction at all depends very much on how it is interpreted by the member state governments. In an article in *Frankfurter Allgemeine Zeitung,* law professor Ulrich Immenga of Goettingen University issued the following warning about adoption of a reverse-compilation right:

The effect of a directive which rolls back copyright protection can be forecast, namely, that the economic advantages would be transferred from the program developers to the copiers ["Nachahmer"]. European firms are among the most successful creators of original programs. They have the incentive to invest ideas and capital.... The right to copy will redound to the benefit of computer firms which have not historically invested in development of new programs; firms which for the most part have their headquarters in non-European countries. Competition from these program copyists would lead to a reduction in the commercial success of European suppliers. A shrinking of economic growth can also be expected as a result of the general reduction in innovation.

Shortly after the final software directive was promulgated by the EC Council of Ministers, the European Court of First Instance ruled that British TV networks could not use their copyrights to prevent copyright infringement of their programming guides by an independent publisher of such guides, because EC competition law overrides national copyright law, and the networks monopolized the market for their own program guides. What, if anything, distinguishes program guides from other sorts of copyrighted works, so that each author of a copyrighted work will not be held a monopolist of the market for that work, was not clearly articulated by the court. However, the EC Competition Directorate immediately hailed the ruling as having significance for the software industry. If those rulings are taken to mean that every software firm doing business in Europe is prevented by competition law from protecting the aspects of its programs that are uniquely attractive to customers, then victory in the softwars in Europe will go to firms whose expertise lies in the art of reproduction, not in the art of innovation. As professor Immenga suggests, those firms tend to be non-European. That fact cannot be lost on the eurocrats, though, and it is even less likely to be lost on the governments of the member states, which are more responsive to constituent pressures than is the overarching EC bureaucracy. Given that the prevalence in any one region of the developed world of a substantially lower degree of intellectual property protection than that prevailing in other strong trading areas works to the long-term disadvantage of the suppliers based in that region, the safest bet is that European law will maintain a rough parity with U.S. and Japanese law insofar as software protection is concerned.

The major clone suppliers have indeed recognized that parity will probably be maintained, and so they have set about to lower the level of protection for software in comparable fashion everywhere. In Australia, where the government undertook a major review of software protection beginning in 1990, there was a virtual replay of the European debate, with the same lineup of global industry players making the same arguments. This time, however, industry bore the burden of demonstrating that the European solution, which the Australian commission investigating the matter knew to have been a heavily worked compromise, was inappropriate for Australia. (The outcome of the Australian reexamination is unknown at the time of this writing.) In the United States, clone suppliers have begun to lobby within the major trade associations for positions that would weaken intellectual property protection for computer programs, and a Congressional committee will be considering the question whether current levels of protection are appropriate. As mentioned earlier, trade groups are beginning to submit *amicus* briefs in important cases. In two major multilateral negotiations, the GATT Uruguay Round and the World Intellectual Property Organization's multiyear effort to develop a model copyright law, the scope of protection for computer programs has been an important issue. The American delegations have generally favored traditional protection. The Europeans tended to keep their powder dry until after the EC copyright directive was adopted. Thereafter, they put that directive forward in international negotiations as the preferred balancing of interests, in part to solve a treaty problem: the directive may not comply with the Berne copyright convention, to which all member states have subscribed.

The Japanese delegations to these international negotiations have tended to favor protection, but of a more limited sort. In support of the Japanese delegations, which do not have direct private sector representation, the Japan Electronic Industry Development Association has widely distributed a pamphlet called "Computer Programs and Intellectual Property Rights." The tenor of the pamphlet is conveyed in the following description of the nature of computer programs:

A computer program is a utilitarian and functional work. Moreover, the ways of expressing a computer program are extremely limited. To create a program which performs the same or similar function as another, the "ideas" for the two will necessarily be alike or very similar.

Unlike cultural works, the languages used in computer programs have very small vocabularies in comparison with natural languages, and since computer programs are technical and functional industrial products, the grammatical systems of the languages are also much more restrictive. It must be remembered that individualistic expression which is important to artistic works is, in creating a computer program, preferably left out, and the latest programming techniques are used to create the most functional, high-performance, effective product possible. Programs with expression "similar" to other programs are thus to be expected.

Transparent as a piece of window glass, the notion that the range of expression available to program authors is limited because programs are "functional," "technical," or "industrial" is violently out of line with the findings of objective observers who have examined the question. CONTU concluded that for software, "availability of alternative noninfringing language is the rule rather than the exception." Judges in software protection cases having reached conclusions such as these:

(a) "Throughout the preparation of a complicated computer program . . . , the author is faced with a virtually endless series of decisions as to how to carry out the assigned task . . . At every level, the process is characterized by choice, often made arbitrarily, and only occasionally guided by necessity."

(b) "There is no doubt that computer programs are highly individualistic in nature and contain a form of expression personal to the programmer. No two programmers would ever write a program in exactly the same way (except perhaps in the case of the most simple program). Even the same programmer, after writing a program and leaving it for some time, would not write the program the same way on a second occasion."

(c) "In the computer field, '[t]here exists a virtually unlimited number of instruction sequences that would enable a programmer to construct a program which performs even the more basic algorithmic or mathematical procedures.' "

And the reader will recall the numerous descriptions of the creative nature of the software writing process with which our excursion began.

The Japanese government in 1985 had amended its copyright law to exempt from protection "programming languages," "rules," and "algorithms." There has not been much case law interpreting those exemptions, but a 1991 decision has given the term "algorithm" a liberal interpretation, suggesting narrow protection for structural and organizational elements of programs in Japan. In general, it is to be expected that the law in Japan is more likely than the law in Europe to develop broadly in accordance with the short-term interests of the indigenous industry. What would lead to that expectation? For one thing, the more up-front role of industrial policy in shaping legislation. In the case of the EC copyright directive, for example, the industrial policy directorate inserted its interests into the debate largely by internal politicking within the Commission and other Community institutions, and by sponsoring papers written without identifying the sponsors, whereas in connection with the 1985 Japanese copyright law amendments, MITI quite publicly inserted its interests into the debate by drafting and promoting its own amendments in competition with those of the cultural agency responsible for copyright matters. For another, the closer cooperation of industry and government in Japan, the phenomenon that has long been known as "Japan, Inc.," has been instrumental in development of government-sponsored programs and associated legislation that historically have been seen as contributing materially to the manifest success of Japanese computer suppliers on the world market. Finally, there are the institutional factors, discussed in Chapter 11, which tend to incline the judiciary toward stated government policies.

That is not to say that Japanese suppliers will achieve the same successes in the softwars that they have achieved in the "hardwars." The past is only prologue, not *denouement*. There are serious long-term impediments to achievement of control of the software industry by the Japanese. The most significant of these are:

—Language barriers. The *lingua franca* of the software industry is not and will never be Japanese. It is English. Programs with English-language user interfaces and manuals, while not fully salable in countries where English is not the first language, are more salable than programs with Japanese language user interfaces and manuals. This gives American suppliers, and European suppliers with English language facility (which means most European suppliers, particularly as the EC sees to the free movement of workers among EC countries), a slight but permanent edge in the marketplace. Add to this the fact that for computer programs, user manuals and on-line help screens are more important to the proper use of the product by the end-user than they are for hardware, and manual-writing in languages other than Japanese is a particular weakness of Japanese suppliers. And finally—for whatever it's worth—the essence of Japanese expression is subtlety and indirection, while the essence of English expression, especially in America is blunt directness. The latter is characteristic also of programming languages.

—Nonbusiness attitudes. Japanese systems suppliers are two decades behind Western suppliers in treating software as a business. In 1990, Fujitsu achieved considerable notoriety in Japan for bidding on a multimillion yen software contract for the city of Hiroshima at a price of one yen. More symbolic than substantive, the famous one-yen bid is indicative of the attitude that achieving a return on investment in software is less important than using software as a vehicle for selling hardware. "Offering to do the works for one yen," conceded a Fujitsu official, "is tantamount to admitting that software is something to be provided free of charge." Those who do not read history are doomed to repeat it. Historically, until American industry set about to make a business of marketing software, the software written in the United States was not of superior quality, nor was it designed to meet customers' software requirements.

—Cultural factors. Creativity, in the sense of individual expression, is said not to be valued in Japanese society. Programming, however, is a form of self-expression. The best programs reflect creativity on the part of the author or authors. Many commentators have attributed the inability of the Japanese to achieve prominence in the software industry to the Japanese notion that "the nail that sticks up gets hit." Certainly, the coordinated efforts of Japan, Inc., to leapfrog Western software technology, most notably the Sigma project to develop software tools and reusable code and the Fifth Generation Computer project to develop knowledge-based, easy-to-use systems, have been significant labors that have not met their initial objectives. A principal technological focus in Japan at this time is on "software factories," where computer programs can be mass-produced by assembling standard routines, modules, or other elements into complete systems. This, it seems to me, is the programming equivalent of moving from the animation techniques that produced *Fantasia* to the animation techniques that produced *Yogi Bear*. The result will undoubtedly be software produced quickly and cheaply, but not likely software that is innovative.

—Government interference. Computer hardware is procured by customers for the sole purpose of running computer programs. MITI's orchestration of the Japanese assault on the global hardware industry, which must be viewed as an industrial policy success, was therefore aimed at a submerged aspect of customer demand, an element where price, speed, and capacity were the principal aspects of competition. Competition in the software industry has more to do with communicating with users, either through programs or through program manuals, in order to meet their operational requirements. Government institutions, including MITI, are— to put it mildly—not best placed to identify and assess how to satisfy sophisticated private sector demand.

—Impediments to acquisition. In fields other than computers where software is important and Japanese software suppliers are not significant factors on the world market, Japanese hardware manufacturers have gone on the acquisition trail. Sony acquired CBS Records and Columbia Pictures, and the Asahi *Evening News* speculated that Sony's Beta format for VCRs might have prevailed over Matsushita's VHS if Sony had owned Columbia when the Beta format first came out. Matsushita acquired MCA at a price of $7 billion, and the same newspaper reported that the acquisition gave Matsushita movies, TV shows, and recordings that assured it a "ready supply of programming compatible with any technological improvements that emerge." Japanese computer companies have considered acquiring major American software houses, but have foreborn action for fear of attracting the same sort of adverse public and governmental reaction that greeted Fujitsu's proposal to acquire Fairchild Semiconductor.

—External Pressures. Japanese law cannot move so far away from international norms as to be the handmaiden of Japanese industry. Two or three decades ago, that might have been possible, but today the spotlight shines too brightly on Japan. The pressure to open its domestic markets to foreign suppliers has, as an essential component, the pressure to afford intellectual property protection that conforms to international standards. The emphasis in the GATT negotiations on adequate intellectual property rights, though aimed primarily at third world countries, assures that none of the developed countries can stray too far from the norm either.

The reader may by now have concluded that, having painted problematic scenarios for European and Japanese contenders in the softwars, this American author is about to predict victory for suppliers marching under the Stars and Stripes. Far from it. American suppliers do dominate the industry today, but their current position does not give them a lock on tomorrow. Software "technology," at bottom, is the "technology" of writing things down. Though I have done so from time to time, and it is a widespread convention in industry and academia to do so, it is incorrect to refer to computer programming as a technology at all. Certainly, one can study programming as a science, just as one can study human languages as a science, but a computer scientist is no more guaranteed to be an innovative programmer than a linguistics professor is guaranteed to be a good novelist. Advances in the technology/art of writing things down diffuse very rapidly, so that there is no technological barrier to the narrowing, and even ultimate usurpation of, the U.S.' lead in the software industry.

Too, the United States has developed a fascination with automating the writing of programs. CASE (computer-assisted software engineering) has become as much of a buzzword as "open systems," and CASE tools are pouring onto the market, giving the promise of increased mechanization of software production. One thing CASE tools have not yet been taught to do, however, is innovate, and without wishing to open up at this late point in the narrative a debate on the limits of artificial intelligence, I will suggest to the reader that CASE tools will never be able to innovate. New ways of communicating with users, novel approaches to coding, innovative structural organization or logic flow should not be expected to be the products of CASE tools. In the world of fiction, CASE technology has recently allowed the automation of the writing of novels in the style of Jacqueline Susanne. We should have no higher level of expectation in the world of programming. If U.S. suppliers move too far in the direction of "software factories," they too will be ceding territory to suppliers in countries that have a comparative advantage in manufacturing.

Another factor that may weaken the U.S. industry is the current fascination with "alliances." The term "alliances" covers a broad and amorphous range of business relationships, including joint development agreements, distribution agreements, joint ventures, partial or complete mergers or acquisitions, and consortia. There is nothing inherently wrong with alliances; indeed they have brought much good to the industry and its customers. What is wrong is the current penchant for creating alliances for their own sake. Invariably, a lash-up with another company entails a rechannelling of energies—whether financial, developmental, or marketing—away from internal growth. Among other things, that may mean a redirecting of funds or personnel-hours away from projects as to which the intellectual property rights would be exclusively owned in favor of expending those funds or personnel-hours on projects as to which the intellectual property rights will be shared with the new-found ally. Since in the software business, almost any ally is also a potential competitor, the sharing of rights has a bittersweet aftertaste in many cases. Investments that result in shared rights only make sense (1) where either the resulting product could not have been timely produced by the investing firm acting alone, (2) where the partial rights obtained are expected to return more on the amounts invested than would rights in an internally developed product, or (3) where the investing firm hopes to learn something of long-term value by exposure to the particular skills or talents of its ally. Alliances that do not have those characteristics will tend to weaken both (or all) partners as against competition. Too many American firms are treating alliances like designer dresses, making investments for the purpose of being fashionable in external development efforts rather than building internal development skills. The great (and only) redeeming value of designer dresses is that, once the purchaser has made the initial investment, the dress may be either worn, mothballed, or discarded without further consequence. A business relationship, however, is an intermediate-term to long-term committment that requires constant care and feeding whether or not it eventually bears fruit. More importantly, in an industry whose product is pure intellectual property, such that success depends heavily on ownership of rights, the decision to develop products in a shared-rights environment should not be taken lightly.

Yet another enemy of the American software industry is Wall Street. Of all the major equity markets in the world, the American stock market is the most fickle. Its motto seems to be, "What have you done for me lately?" The focus on short-term results and circumstances has become so intense that American companies live from quarter to quarter, unable to pursue long-term business strategies that require the sacrifice of immediate profit. The well-known and much discussed fact that Wall Street's mercurial character disadvantages American firms vis-à-vis their foreign competitors— particularly the Japanese, since Japan's equity markets demand neither substantial profitability nor short-term success—strikes with a vengeance at the software industry. That is because the software business is characterized by up-front investment. Money is sunk into designing programs, then writing and testing them, then rewriting and retesting, well before revenues are received from those programs. Access to equity investors to fund such development is important to program authors. Yet, particularly since the 1987 stock market debacle, equity investors have not been a reliable source of capital. Indeed, in the late 1980s and early 1990s, institutional investors in particular avoided high-tech stocks because their short-term earnings results were unpredictable. Firms have had more than ever to look to profits or, where available, borrowings as the only sources of capital for research and development. In addition, venture capital—the seed money once freely available in Silicon Valley and elsewhere to new and promising software companies—had dried up, relatively speaking, for the computer industry by 1990, attenuating the flow of new entrepreneurs into the software business. An army travels on its stomach, and the food that companies thrive on is called capital. At the moment, the American capital markets are not provisioning the combatants in the softwars adequately for victory.

"The ultimate unhorsing of the U.S. advantage in software development may prove to come from the American judiciary, which seems recently to have lost sight of its heavy responsibility to provide an orderly regime of protection for the "almost pure thought-stuff," these "tangible forms of dreams and imagination" on which one of the world's most important industries is based. (See note 19.10.)

In the end, victory in the softwars should go to those firms that are capable of sustained, solid innovation of computer programs that meet customers' needs and provide them ways of using computers that reduce their operating costs and make them more competitive. Whatever role macroeconomic, cultural, governmental, or market factors may play in fostering that sort of innovation, one thing is certain: leadership in the software industry will come from countries with large internal markets where the laws protect the fragile intellectual property that is software—works that Fred Brooks called "only slightly removed from pure thought-stuff"—from being appropriated with such ease as to deprive innovators of returns on investment sufficient to fund future research and development. The attack on such laws, which continues apace throughout the developed world, cannot succeed in weakening patent, copyright, and trade secret protection for software sufficiently to achieve that deprivation without threatening those three legal regimes generally for all industries; and a general assault on intellectual property laws would attract defenders from outside the software industry in such numbers as to preclude its success. Stripped naked, as all philosophies can be if challenged sufficiently, the clones find themselves in the fundamentally unsupportable position of arguing that original software should not be afforded traditional copyright protection because it is "functional," should not be afforded patent protection either, because it is nonfunctional (i.e., it is purely algorithmic), and should not be accorded trade secret protection because otherwise it cannot be "studied." In countries where the institutions of government recognize the strategic importance of software not only to the computer industry but to the industrial infrastructure generally, that argument is untenable. The intellectual property laws already accommodate competition by imitation, of which there is plenty even in the United States where during the twentieth century the intellectual property laws have been the strongest, and wise legislators will conclude, as did a participant in the National Research Council's 1990 workshop on software protection, who improved on an old military injunction by advising, "If it ain't broke, don't break it."

As for the industry itself, it behooves those who run its corporations, those who write its software, those who report on the ebb and flow of the competitive clashes, and those who buy its products to return to first principles. It is innovation that makes the computer industry exciting, challenging, nerve-wracking, spooky, and fun, all the while producing products that by enhancing human intellect are allowing the world's people to weave together a global village of democratized knowledge, rapidly disseminated ideas and vastly improved management of businesses, industrial processes, financial markets, health care, and the environmental effects of human activity. That which makes the industry innovative is important to preserve. There is a familiar story about Benjamin Franklin who, as he left the debates over the constitution of the new national government for the rebellious former British colonies, was asked by an elderly woman what form of government the delegates had given the people. "A republic," he replied, "if you can keep it." The partisans in the softwars would do well to remember that war is too costly if it destroys the prize being fought for. Were such a partisan to ask me what kind of industry the softwars have given us, my reply would be as cautionary as Franklin's. "A high-tech industry," I would say, "if you can keep it."

# Notes and References

Regarding the annotation convention below, see the last paragraph of the Preface.

## PREFACE

0.1. For a brief history of medieval forms of justice, see Dick Hamilton, *Lawyers and Lawbreakers* (New York: Dorset Press, 1979) pp. 1–12.

0.2. The view that the software industry is litigious is expressed, e.g., in Sam Whitmore, "Litigious Software Industry Needs Training," *PC Week,* July 16, 1990, p. 55.

## CHAPTER ONE

1.1. The suggestion that Western computer manufacturers should give up the hardware business: Andrew S. Rappaport and Shmuel Haleri, "The Computerless Computer Co.," *Harv. Bus. Rev.,* July/August 1991, p. 301.

1.2. The ACM user interface questionnaire is described in Pamela Samuelson and Robert Glushko, "Comparing the Views of Lawyers and User Interface Designers on the Software Copyright 'Look and Feel' " Lawsuits, 30 *Jurimetrics* 121 (Fall 1989). The unscientific "survey" straw polling process was repeated at the ACM graphics conference in 1991, with equally unenlightened results. See, Pamela Samuelson, Michel Denber and Robert Glushko, "Developments on the Intellectual Property Front," *Communications of the ACM,* June, 1992, p. 33.

1.3. "[T]he ability to make a business out of software depends heavily on the existence of intellectual property rights in that software...." National Research Council, *Intellectual Property Issues in Software* (Washington, D.C.; National Academy Press 1991) (hereinafter "NRC Report") p. 8; Ken Wasch, "Soft Focus: Competitiveness: A View From Washington", *Computer Reseller News,* June 29, 1992, p. 65.

1.4. Shrink-wrap licenses as an example of the law needing to catch up with technology: *Note: The Enforceability of State 'Shrink-Wrap' License Statutes in Light of Vault Corp. v. Quaid Software, Ltd.,* 74 Cornell L. Rev. 222 (November, 1988).

1.5. American software suppliers dominate the world market: U.S. Congress, Office of Technology Assessment, *Finding a Balance: Computer Software, Intellectual Property and the Challenge of Technological Change,* (Washington, D.C.; U.S. Government Printing Office, 1992) (Hereinafter, "OTA Report") pp. 94–96, *See,* Russell Glitman, "Top 3 Software Houses Finding Profits Overseas, Say Market Analysts," *PC Week,* July 1, 1986, p.109; Carol Ellison, "Why Japan Can't Write Software", *PC-Computing,* December, 1988, p. 110; Glenn Rifkin, "Software Is the Next Target," *New York Times,* October 15, 1989, Section 3, p. 2.

1.6. Japanese suppliers' cloning strategies are described in Chapter 11, *infra.*

1.7. European industrial chauvinism led to the need for connectivity between European hardware/software and foreign hardware/software: *See,* Gary H. Anthes, "Quota Imposed by Trade Group," *Computerworld,* May 7, 1990, p. 91; Michael Faden, "UNIX, Europe and a Continental System," *UNIX Review,* December, 1988, p. 16; Jack Robertson, "(GATT)-ling Gun," *Electronic News,* November 12, 1990, p. 12; Simon Collin, "The Unseen Standard," *PC User,* April 25, 1989, p. 60.

1.8. Programming as "pure thought-stuff": Frederick P. Brooks, *The Mythical Man-Month* (Reading Mass.: Addison-Wesley, 1975) p. 7.

1.9. Programming described by Randy Davis as the "ultimate creative medium: *NRC Report,* supra, note. 1.3, p. 48.

1.10. Lammers' interviews on the nature of programming: Susan Lammers, "Programmers at Work," *PC World,* September 1986, p. 187.

1.11. The Leathrum quote is from J. F. Leathrum, *Foundations of Software Design,* (Reston, VA.: Reston Publ. Co., 1983) p. 11.

1.12. The difficulty of managing programmers because of the creative process in which they are engaged: Patricia Keefe, "The Art of Managing Programmers," *Computerworld,* November 12, 1990, p. 87.

1.13. Instruction sets of computers are a vocabulary for programmers: *See,* Harry L. Helms, *The McGraw-Hill Computer Handbook,* (New York: McGraw-Hill Book Co., 1987) §6.16.

1.14. Hierarchy of programming languages: Marilyn Bohl, *Information Processing,* 4th Ed. (Chicago: Science Research Associates, 1984) pp. 192–93, 365–68, 370–91.

1.15. The discussion of the elements of a computer program's design are taken from Anthony Lawrence Clapes, *Software, Copyright, and Competition: The "Look and Feel" of the Law* (Westport, CT.: Quorum Books, 1989) (hereinafter, *"Soft/Copy"*) pp. 69–110.

1.16. The description of the process of writing microcode is found in Tracy Kidder, *The Soul of a New Machine,* (Boston; Little, Brown & Co., 1981) pp. 101–2.

1.17. The author's credo is abstracted from *Soft/Copy, supra,* note 1.15, *passim.*

1.18. "I confess at the outset that this book made me angry." M. C. Gemignani, "Clapes, Anthony L., *Software, Copyright, and Competition,*" *Computing Reviews,* March, 1990, pp. 147–48.

1.19. "Elsewhere, he has passionately argued that computer programs should not be protected by copyright law at all." M. C. Gemignani, *Legal Protection for Computer Software: The View from 1979,* 7 Rutgers J. Computers, Tech. & L. 269, 278–21 (1980).

## CHAPTER 2

2.1. The full citation to the *Whelan* case is: *Whelan Associates, Inc. v. Jaslow Dental Laboratories, Inc.,* 797 F. 2d 1222, (3rd Cir.) *cert. denied,* 479 U.S. 1031 (1987).

2.2. Rules against copying dictate the boundaries of the software business: *See,* Deborah G. Johnson, *Computer Ethics* (Englewood Cliffs, N.J.; Prentice-Hall, Inc., 1985) pp. 87–103; "Lotus Lowdown," *ComputerWorld,* February 4, 1991, p. 6. ("Lotus' franchise is in trouble if Borland has created the perception that the spreadsheet is a commodity.")

2.3. Apple IIe, MS-DOS, Lotus 1–2–3 and dBase lose position to newcomers. Kathleen K. Wiegner, "Taking the High Road," Forbes, September 13, 1982, p. 214; Paul M. Leghart, "Day of Reckoning Looms for Desktop OS Winners," Software Magazine, November 15, 1991, p. 68; Michael Ellis, "Microsoft [MSFT.0] Takes Aim at Spreadsheet Market," *Reuters,* March 23, 1992; "Product Milestones—Ashton-Tate's High Water Mark—dBase III," *Computer Reseller News,* June 22, 1992, p. 56.

2.4. James Madison on copyright and patent: "The Federalist No. 43," *The Federalist,* (New York: The Modern Library) p. 279. Brief histories of patent and copyright laws can be found in S. Rep. No. 1979, 82d Cong. 2d Sess. 1–4 (1952) (patent law); 1 *Lipscomb's Walker on Patents,* Sec. 1.6 (3rd Ed. 1984); B. Bugbee, *The Genesis of American Patent and Copyright Law* (1967); B. Kaplan, *An Unhurried View of Copyright* (1967); E. Ploman and L. Hamilton, *Copyright: Intellectual Property in the Information Age,* 14–17, 19 (1980).

2.5. Protection of functional works by the first copyright act: *Goldstein v. California,* 412 U.S. 546, 555 (1973). ("The first congressional copyright statute, passed in 1790, governed only maps, charts and books.")

2.6. Commercialization of computers depended on the quality diversity and availability of programs: *See, Soft/Copy, supra,* note 1.15, p. 19 and endnotes 2.1, 2.2.

2.7. As to copyright registration of computer programs under the "rule of doubt", 17 U.S.C. Sec. 401(a) requires the Register of Copyrights to examine claims to copyright and to ascertain that material deposited for copyright registration constitutes copyrightable subject matter. Where the Register cannot tell from the deposited materials whether the work deposited contains copyrightable subject matter, the work may nonetheless be registered if the applicant confirms in writing that the work as deposited does contain such subject matter. "Rule of doubt" registration is still being used in cases where an applicant deposits object code rather than source code. Dorothy Schrader, "Copyright Office practices and Pending Rulemaking," *Computer Software 1988: Protection and Marketing* (Practicing Law Inst., 1988) p. 347, 364, 366.

2.8. Early video game copyright cases establishing the protectability of software. E.g., *Stern Electronics, Inc. v. Kaufman,* 669 F. 2d 852 (2d Cir. 1982); *Williams Electronics, Inc. v. Artic Int'l., Inc.,* 685 F. 2d 870 (3d Cir. 1982); *Atari, Inc. v. North*

*American Philips Consumer Electronics Corp.,* 672 F. 2d 607 (7th Cir.), *cert. denied,* 459 U.S. 880 (1982).

2.9. CONTU's report: Final Report of the National Commission on New Technological uses of Copyright Works (Washington, D.C.: U.S. Government Printing Office, July 31, 1978) (hereinafter, "CONTU Report").

2.10. The *Synercom* case, *Synercom Technology, Inc. v. University Computing Co.,* 462 F. Supp. 1003 (N.D. Tex 1978), often cited by weak protectionists as precedent for unprotectability of nonliteral elements of computer programs (because it is one of the few cases so holding) was decided before Congress had legislated the protectability of software as literary works, and is not consistent with the current state of the law.

2.11. The Gottschalk case: *Gottschalk v. Benson,* 409 U.S. 63 (1972).

2.12. Patent law does not preempt trade secret law: *Kewanee Oil Co. v. Bicron Corp.,* 416 U.S. 470 (1974).

2.13. A comparison of patent, copyright and trade secret protection may be found in Stephen J. Davidson, "Reverse Engineering and the Development of Compatible and Competitve Products under United States Law," 5 *Computer and High Technology Law Journal* 399 (1989).

2.14. Software plagiarism and software litigation phenomena during the 1980's: *See,* OTA Report, *supra,* note 1.5, pp. 97–103.

2.15. The discussion of *Apple v. Franklin* is taken from the reported decisions: *Apple Computer Inc. v. Franklin Computer Co.,* 545 F. Supp. 812 (E.D. Pa. 1982), *aff'd* 714 F. 2d 1240 (3d Cir. 1983), *cert. dismissed,* 464 U.S. 1033 (1984).

2.16. An accounting program for dental laboratories makes legal history: the *Whelan* case, *supra,* note 2.1.

2.17. The "open systems" movement is discussed in Chapter 18.

2.18. Post-*Whelan* cases: *Plains Cotton Cooperative Assoc. v. Goodpasture Computer Serv., Inc.* 807 F. 2d 1256 (5th Cir.), *cert. denied,* 484 U.S. 821 (1987); *Digital Communications Assoc., Inc. v. Softklone Distr. Corp.,* 659 F. Supp. 449 (N.D. Ga. 1987); *Frybarger v. International Business Machines Corp.,* 812 F. 2d 525 (9th Cir. 1987); *Data East USA, Inc. v. Epyx, Inc.,* 862 F. 2d 204 (9th Cir. 1988).

2.19. The discussion of *Diamond v. Diehr* is taken from the Supreme Court opinion: *Diamond v. Diehr,* 450 U.S. 175 (1981).

2.20. Computer programs can constitute trade secrets: *See,* e.g., *Telex Corp. v. International Business Machines Corp.* 367 F. Supp. 258 (N.D. Okla. 1973), *rev'd in part* (on antitrust issues), *aff'd in part* (on trade secret issues), 510 F. 2d 894 (10th Cir.), *cert. dismissed,* 423 U.S. 802 (1975); Davidson, *supra,* note 2.13.

2.21. International patent and copyright protection for computer programs: Michael S. Keplinger, "International Protection for Computer Programs," *Computer Software 1988, Protection and Marketing* (Practicing Law Inst. 1988) p. 423.

2.22. The similarities between the films *Battlestar Galactica* and *Star Wars* resulted in a lawsuit: *Twentieth Century-Fox Film Corp. v. MCA, Inc.,* 715 F.2d 1327 (9th Cir. 1983).

2.23. America is the dominant source of writers and publishers of software: *See,* note 1.5, supra.

## CHAPTER 3

3.1. The author's predictions as to the outcome of *Lotus v. Paperback* were published in *Soft/Copy, supra,* note 2.15, pp. 199–200. They apply equally to the outcome of Lotus' lawsuit against Borland International.

3.2. The description of Lotus 1–2–3 and Judge Keeton's opinion comes from the opinion itself: *Lotus Development Corp. v. Paperback Software, Int'l,* 740 F. Supp 37 (D. Mass. 1990).

3.3. The "gang of ten" were Ralph Brown and Stephen Carter of Yale, Rochelle Dreyfus of NYU, Peter Jaszi of American University, Dennis Karjala of Arizona State, David Lange of Duke, Peter Menell, Acting Professor of Law at Boalt Hall, L. Ray Patterson of Georgia, Jerome Reichmann of Vanderbilt and Pamela Samuelson of Pittsburgh. *Lotus Development Corp. v. Borland Int'l, Inc.,* Civ. No. 90–11662-K (D. Mass), Brief Amicus Curice of Copyright Law Professors, October 27, 1991. Of these anti-software-copyright activists, we will encounter the most vociferous in Chapter 13, *infra.* The brief of the gang of ten is an object lesson in how *not* to write a "friend of the court" brief. It begins by telling Judge Keeton that his lengthy and carefully-reasoned opinion in *Lotus v. Paperback,* which examined in detail the language and history of the copyright statute and caselaw, and articulated the basic principles of copyright and their applicability to computer programs, was in the professors' view "inconsistent with the copyright statute, the copyright caselaw, and traditional principles of copyright law." It suggests that the judge (who described in detail the factual basis for his conclusions and insisted that the parties install copies of their respective products on computers available to him so that he could become familiar with them) did not make appropriate factual inquiries in the *Paperback* case. It accuses the judge of failing to "follow through" on his observation that copyright does not protect "function", and of "losing sight of" the legislative history of the copyright statute (two matters which Judge Keeton in fact treated comprehensively in *Lotus v. Paperback*). The professors' brief is an exercise in academic *hauteur* that may have satisfied its authors but was in no way designed to elicit a sympathetic response from the court. Nor did it. On July 31, 1992, Judge Keeton ruled that the Lotus-compatible mode in Borland's Quattro Pro spreadsheet program unlawfully copied the menu hierarchy of Lotus 1–2–3. The jurist concluded that the expression in the Lotus menu hierarchy was not substantially constrained by its functionality, and therefore was protected by copyright. Opinion and Order, *Lotus Development Corp. v. Borland Int'l, Inc.,* Civ. No. 90–11662-K (D. Mass., July 31, 1992). Remaining issues in the case were scheduled for trial while this book was in the final stages of production, but the July 31, 1992, ruling basically determined the outcome of the case.

3.4. "They cited in that regard the conclusions of a group of ten American law professors...." This is not a reference to the "gang of ten", but to the Last Frontier conference, a deeply-flawed experiment conducted at Arizona State University, in which three of the nonprotectionist "gang of ten" (Samuelson, Menell and Karjala) were constituted as a "steering committee". The three then chose a panel of academic "experts" to consider software copyright questions, chose the people who would make presentations to those experts, chose the guests who would listen to and comment on those presentations, and after the presentations were made drafted the "consensus report" for the panel of "experts". Not surprisingly the "consensus report" of this conference, and its operating procedures, were broadly criticized by a substantial segment of the software industry. The Last Frontier "consensus report", together with a summary of the controversy surrounding the conference and most of the presentation made at the conference, appears in *Jurimetrics* V.30 No. 1 (Fall, 1989). The Jurimetrics volume compounds the bias in the "consensus report" by omitting a presentation that expressed satisfaction with the way copyright law was being applied to user interfaces and substituting instead a paper co-authored by a member of the steering committee, critical of copyright protection for user interfaces, that was not even presented at the conference.

3.5. The Principles for Software Clones were first published in *Soft/Copy, supra,* note 2.15, pp. 200–201.

## Chapter 3: Endnote

3.E.1. Microsoft is facing the struggle of its corporate life: Paul M. Leghart, *supra,* note 2.3; Paul Lavin, "Aiming High: Alliance Between Apple, IBM and Motorola Looks Set to Change the Shape of Desktop Computing," *Which Computer?,* April, 1992, p. 114.

3.E.2. Sun Microsystems has been forced to offer its UNIX-based operating system on Intel-based processors: Barbara Jarvie, "SunSoft Taps Partners: Solaris 2.0 Goes to Vendors for Adoption," *Computer Reseller News,* July 13, 1992, p. 55.

3.E.3. PCs and workstations compete against mainframe and midrange computers: David Kirkpatrick, "Breaking up IBM," *Fortune,* July 27, 1992, p. 41; "IBM Had $2.8 Billion Loss—Its First—in '91," *Washington Post,* January 18, 1992, p. C1; "Mainframes Lag, but Workstations and PCs Are Rising," *Electronics,* September, 1991, p. 61.

3.E.4. The software industry is highly competitive: Heather Clancy, "Industry's Competitive Environment Stunts Innovation," *Computer Reseller News,* April 6, 1992, p. 113; "U.S. Software Industry Urges Government to Foster International Competitiveness", *EDGE: Work-Group Computing Report,* November 18, 1991.

3.E.5. Émile Zola, quoted in Robert Darnton, *The Kiss of Lamourette.* (New York: W. W. Norton, 1990) p. 298.

3.E.6. Interview with T. J. Rogers: Michael S. Malone, "The Great Patent War," *Upside,* January, 1991, p. 33.

3.E.7. 1964 U.N. study lamenting the lack of economic analysis of the technology/economics interface: *The Role of Patents in the Transfer of Technology to Developing Countries,* (New York, United Nations, 1964).

3.E.8. The observation that intellectual property has not been a focus of economists is from Robert Sherwood, *Intellectual Property and Economic Development* (Boulder, Co.: Westview Press, 1990) pp. 67–81. *See also,* OTA Report, *supra,* note 1–5, p. 183.

## CHAPTER 4

4.1. Background on Lotus Development Corporation's lawsuits against Borland and Santa Cruz Operations: Michael Domingo, "1991 in Review: The Top Stories,"

*Data Based Advisor,* December 1991, p. 132; "Lotus seeks coup de grace in suit against Borland," *PC Week,* May 13, 1991, p. 141; Esther Dyson, "Lotus lawsuit leaves a gloomy lesson," *PC Computing,* October 1990, p. 21.

4.2.  A law professor advises that the *Paperback* judgment would be appealed: Pamela Samuelson, "How to Interpret the Lotus Decision; and How Not to," *Communications of the ACM,* November, 1990, p. 27. See, Patricia Keefe, "Paperback Pulls Spreadsheet, Won't Appeal Lotus Victory," *ComputerWorld,* October 22, 1990, p. 7.

4.3.  The League for Programming Freedom pickets Lotus: "Freedom Chant," *Communications of the ACM,* October 1990, p. 9. The picketers' chant was written by Richard Stallman: "1–2–3–4, kick the lawsuits out the door/5–6–7–8, innovate, don't litigate/9-A-B-C-, interfaces should be free/D-E-F-O, look and feel has got to go."

4.4  A lawyer with clients at risk comments adversely on the *Paperback* case: G. Gervaise Davis in "Airing Both Sides of the 'Look and Feel' Debate," *Computerworld,* August 13, 1990, p. 21.

4.5.  The writer of critical commentary on the *Paperback* case in the Communications of the ACM: Samuelson, *supra,* note 4–2.

4.6.  A New York lawyer criticizes Judge Keeton's treatment of the utilitarian aspects of software: Ronald Abramson, "Why Lotus-Paperback Uses the Wrong Test and What the New Software Protection Legislation Should Look Like," *The Computer Lawyer,* December, 1990, p. 39.

4.7.  The Lennon-McCartney discussion leads to a fundamental question: Why is it that functional articles are said to be only "thinly" protected by copyright? The answer is that everyone ought to be able to duplicate the functionality of an article, if it is not patented, and since functionality is thought to limit the range of expression, the expression should be free to be copied, too. When the article under scrutiny is, say, a hammer, that answer is easy to understand. Most of the hammer's contours are dictated by its functionality. Where the article is a text, however, the fact that the text may have functionality (or, more properly put, may cause a computer to produce a result in the real world) does not add much to the copyright inquiry. After all, a laserdisk causes a television to produce a result in the real world; Rachel Carson's *Silent Spring* produced a result (*i.e.,* pesticide bans) in the real world. The question is whether the functionality does in fact dictate the expression, and the answer, in the case of computer programs, is that it does not. Were it otherwise, how could programming be spoken of as "the ultimate creative medium", as we saw in Chapter 1? For the reader who is not proficient at computer programming, I suggest experimenting with other types of literary works that have functionality, to see whether functionality tends substantially to constrain expression or not. As I write this note, I have in front of me four cookbooks, each opened to the recipe for chocolate truffles (a recipe selected because of my addiction, not by searching for recipes that prove my point). The shortest recipe consumes five lines of text; the longest, four pages of text and photographs. Two of the recipes call for semisweet chocolate, a third calls for bittersweet and the fourth for sweet. One calls for butter, a second for milk, a third for heavy cream and the last for very heavy cream. One has four briefly described steps; another, thirteen amply described steps. The result produced by following each recipe is a chocolate truffle, though the four recipes produce chocolate truffles that taste rather different. The only sense in which any one of those recipes can be said to consist of expression constrained by its functionality is if a second comer were to say, for example, "I wish to write a chocolate truffle recipe that will produce results identical to Jacques Pepin's recipe in *La Methode*". That would be the gustatory equivalent of saying, "I want to write a program that produces results identical to Lotus 1–2–3." Since a program's results are communications (on the screen, on the hard disk or on the printer or through the loudspeaker), such a statement describes a desire not to perform a like function, but to perform a like function using identical expression, as Borland International discovered. For fellow chocaholics, the four cookbooks are: Paul Bocuse, *French Cooking* (New York, Pantheon, 1977), Craig Claiborne, *The New York Times Cookbook* (New York, Times Books, 1980), Jacque Pepin, *La Methode* (New York, Times Books, 1979), and Julee Rosso and Sheila Lukins, *The Silver Palate Cookbook* (New York, Workman Publishing, 1982).

4.8. The League for Programming Freedom's article arguing against copyright protection for user interfaces: Richard Stallman and Simson Garfinkel, "Viewpoint: Against User Interface Copyright," *Communications of the ACM,* November, 1990, p. 15.

4.9. New Age software concepts such as "shareware" are dealt with in Chapter 16.

4.10. The copyright lawsuit against rap singer Biz Markie: *Grand Upright Music Ltd. v. Warner Bros. Records, Inc.,* 780 F. Supp. 182 (S.D.N.Y. 1991).

### Chapter 4: Endnote

4.E.1. The work of economists Solow, Denison and Mansfield: *See,* Robert Solow, "Technical Changes and Aggregate Production Function," *Review of Economics and Statistics* (1957); E. Denison, *Accounting for Slower Economic Growth* (Washington, D.C.: Brookings Inst., 1979); Edward Mansfield, et al., "Social and Private Rates of Return from Industrial Innovations," *Quarterly Journal of Economics,* May, 1977; Sherwood, supra, note 3.E.8. pp. 75–84.

4.E.2. Products rich in intellectual property, including software, are critical to American export trade: Congressional Economic Leadership Institute, *Intellectual Property at the Crossroads.*

4.E.3. Intellectual property as a public good: Wendy J. Gordon, *Fair Use as Market Failure: A Structural and Economic Analysis of the Betamax Case and Its Predecessors,* 82 Colum. L. Rev. 1600, 1610 (December, 1982); Linda J. Lacey, *Of Bread and Roses and Copyrights,* 1989 Duke L. J. 1532 (*passim*).

### CHAPTER 5

5.1. Computer programs and data bases compared to compilations for copyright purposes: J. H. Reichman, "Review Essay: Goldstein on Copyright Law: A Realist's Approach to a Technological Age," 43 *Stan. L. Rev.* 943, 955, (April 1991); Note: "Copyright and Computer Data bases; Is Traditional Compilation Law Adequate?" 65 *Tex. L. Rev.* 993 (April, 1987).

5.2. The discussion of the *Feist* case is based on the Supreme Court opinion: *Feist Publications, Inc. v. Rural Tel. Serv. Co.,* 111 S. Ct. 1282.

5.3. Weak-protectionists attempt to bootstrap *Feist* into an argument against copyright protection for software: *See, e.g.,* "Note: Sui Generis Intellectual Property Protection for Computer Software," 60 *Geo. Wash. L. Rev.* 997, 998–99, (April, 1992); Pamela Samuelson, "Copyright Law and Electronic Compilations of Data"; Communications of the ACM, February, 1992, p. 27.

The most egregious case of such bootstrapping is the U.S. Court of Appeals opinion in *Computer Associates, Inc. v. Altai, Inc.,* Docket Nos. 91–7893, 91–7895 (2d Cir., 1992), in which the range of expression in computer programs is assumed, without any evidentiary basis, to be analogous to that in telephone directory white pages. Slip op. at pp. 40–41. See Chapter 14, *infra.*

5.4. The baseball rating forms case: *Kregos v. Associated Press,* 937 F. 2d 700 (2d Cir. 1991).

## Chapter 5: Endnote

5.E.1. Robert Benko's views on intellectual property as public goods are memorialized in Robert Benko, *Protecting Intellectual Property Rights: Issues and Controversies* (1987).

5.E.2. Mansfield's findings concerning imitation of new products are summarized in Edward Mansfield, "Technical Change and Economic Growth," *Intellectual Property Rights and Capital Formation in the Next Decade* (C. E. Walker and M. A. Bloomfield, eds.) (Lanham: University Press of America (1988); Edward Mansfield "How Rapidly Does New Industrial Technology Leak Out," *34 J. Indus. Econ.* 217 (1985).

5.E.3. Judge Easterbrook's observations on imitation and innovation appear in Easterbrook, "Intellectual Property Is Still Property," 13 Harv. J. L. & Pub. Pol. 99 (1990).

5.E.4. A nightclub full of Beatles imitators: Waldemar Januszczak, *Sayonara Michelangelo* (Reading, Ma.: Addison-Wesley, 1990), p. 92.

5.E.5. Mansfield's conclusions as to private rate of return and social rate of return from new technologies: Edward Mansfield, *et al.,* "Social and Private Rates of Return from Industrial Innovations," supra, note 4.E.1.

## CHAPTER 6

6.1. The Bauersfeld-Slater paper on the use of color in computer-human interfaces: Penny F. Bauersfeld and Jodi L. Slater, "User-Oriented Color Interface Design: Direct Manipulation of Color in Context," in Scott P. Robertson, Gary M. Olson, and Judityh S. Olson, eds., *Reaching Through Technology: CHI '91 Conference Proceedings* (Reading, Ma.: Addison-Wesley, 1991) (hereinafter, "CHI '91") p. 417.

6.2. The discussion of *Apple v. Microsoft* is based on the court papers in *Apple Computer, Inc. v. Microsoft Corp.,* No. C–88–20149 VRW (N.D. Ca.), as well as on discussions with counsel for both Apple and Microsoft.

6.3. "The Beatles were pursuing Apple." *See,* "Apple Settles Beatle Suit," *MacUser,* February, 1992, p. 45; "Apple Makes Peace with the Beatles," *Business Week,* October 28, 1991, p. 45.

6.4. "The jurist concluded that he should not exclude the unprotected elements of the Macintosh interface...." In what seemed to be a radical retrenchment from that conclusion, Judge Walker decided on April 14, 1992 that he would dissect the Macintosh user interface into its constituent elements, decide which of the elements were individually unprotectable and compare the remainder, if any, with Windows and New Wave. That exercise was of course substantially more favorable to the defendants. Opinion and Order, *Apple Computer Corp. v. Microsoft*, 1992 U.S. Dist. LEXIS 5986 (N.D. Cal., April 14, 1992). The judge seemed in part to be reacting to a just-decided case in the Court of Appeals for the 9th Circuit—the court that would hear any appeals from his ruling in *Apple v. Microsoft*. The new case, *Brown Bag Software v. Symantic Corp.*, 960 F. 2d 1465 (9th Cir. 1992), stressed the importance of analytic dissection of original works and element-by-element comparison. In the *Brown Bag* case, however, the Court of Appeals did *not* say that analytical dissection was to be performed to the exclusion of a comparison of the works as a whole. That is a point with which either Judge Walker or ultimately the Court of Appeals itself will have to contend in *Apple/Microsoft*.

6.5. Xerox's abortive lawsuit against Apple: *Xerox Corp. v. Apple Computer, Inc.*, 734 F. Supp. 1542 (N.D. Cal. 1990).

6.6. IBM/Apple/Motorola joint ventures: Neal Boudette, Robert Scheier, "IBM, Apple Seek a Brave New World," *PC Week*, July 8, 1991, p. 1; Steward Alsop, "Apple, IBM Duo Would Be Boon to PCs", *InfoWorld*, July 1, 1991, p. 81.

6.7. The discussion of Ashton-Tate v. Fox is drawn from the court papers in *Ashton-Tate Corp. v. Fox Software, Inc.*, CV No. 88–6837 TJH (Tx) (C.D. Cal.).

6.8. Judge Hatter's unexplained rulings both appear in *Ashton-Tate Corp. v. Fox Software, Inc.*, 760 F. Supp. 831 (C.D. Cal. 1990).

6.9. Borland's acquisition of Ashton-Tate: John L. Hawkins, "The other shoe has dropped: Borland International acquires Ashton-Tate," *Data Base Advisor*, September, 1991, p. 10.

6.10. The consent judgment between Borland and the Justice Department is reported at *United States v. Borland, Int'l. Inc.*, 1992–1 Trade Cas. (CCH) P69,774. Ironically Fox Software, a principal beneficiary of that judgment, was subsequently acquired by Microsoft, which Justice's sister agency, the Federal Trade Commission, is investigating for alleged monopolistic practices. *See*, Karen D. Moser, "Microsoft Bids to Outfox Borland," PC Week, March 30, 1992, p. 1.; John Burgess, "Microsoft Cooperating with Probe, Gates says; Software Company Denies It Engaged in Monopolistic Practices," *Washington Post*, June 24, 1992.

6.11. The presentations at the 1991 CH1 conference are collected in *CHI '91*, supra, note 6.1.

6.12. "The moving finger writes...." Omar Khayyam, The Rubaiyat, (New York, Walter J. Black, 1942) (Edward Fitzgerald, tr.) p. 36.

6.13. Super Mario Brothers as a user interface: *See*, Lori Valigra, "Super Mario Strikes Stock Market Gold," *Computerworld*, July 15, 1991, p. 6. ("Since 1987, the mustachioed Super Mario character has been dancing across the screens of Japanese television sets as the system automatically logs on to a value-added network run by Nomura Securities Co., the top Japanese securities broker.")

## Chapter 6: Endnote

6.E.1. Twenty-five centuries of technological advance, chronicled in Joel Mokyr, *The Lever of Riches: Technological Creativity and Economic Progress* (New York: Oxford University Press, 1990).

6.E.2. Intellectual property rights as a precondition to progress: David Landes' comment is from Sherwood, *supra,* note 3.8, p. 90.

6.E.3. Sherwood's and Mansfield's criticism of tax incentives for research instead of intellectual property laws for the fruits of that research: Sherwood, *supra,* note 3.E.8., p. 136.

6.E.4. Proposal that software suppliers obtain revenues, if any, only from service and support: G. Pascal Zachary, "Free for all: Richard Stallman Is Consumed by the Fight to End Copyrighting of Software," *Wall Street Journal,* May 20, 1991, pp. R23, R24.

6.E.5. Analogizing intellectual property rights to commonly-owned resources: Richard T. Rapp and Richard P. Rozek, *Benefits and Costs of Intellectual Property Protection in Developing Countries,* (White Plains: National Economic Research Associates, Inc., 1990) pp. 4–5.

6.E.6. The ability of an author to earn money depends on intellectual property laws: William M. Landes and Richard A. Posner, "An Economic Analysis of Copyright Law," 18 Journal of Leg. Studies 325, 326 (1989).

6.E.7. Invention of the chronometer would have happened sooner had there been a system of intellectual property rights. D. North and R. Thomas, *The Rise of the Western World: A New Economic History* (Cambridge, Cambridge University Press, 1973) p. 3.

6.E.8. The comments of John Shoch are reported in NRC Report, *supra,* note 1.3, p. 8.


## CHAPTER 7

7.1. The League for Programming Freedom opposes software patents: Richard Stallman and Simson Garfinkle, "Viewpoint: Against Software Patents," *Communications of the ACM,* January, 1992.

7.2. "Software Developers Who Understand the Impact of Patents Are Demoralized.": Brian Kahin, "The Software Patent Crisis," *Technology Review,* April 1990, p. 55, 58.

7.3. Professor Samuelson on software patents: Pamela Samuelson, "Benson Revisited: The Case Against Patent Protection for Algorithms and Other Computer Program-Related Inventions," 39 Emory L. J. 1025, 1031.

7.4. Mitch Kapor's description of software patents as "toxic waste" was uttered during a panel discussion at the Licensing Executives Society meeting in Boston on June 28, 1991, in which the author also participated.

7.5. Equivalence of hardware and software. See Randall Davis, "The Nature of Software and Its Consequences for Establishing and Evaluating Similarity," 5 Software L. J. 299, 315 (1992).

7.6. Patents have played only a minor role in the computer industry: Robert P. Merges and Richard R. Nelson, "On the Complex Economics of Patent Scope," 90 Columbia L. J. 839, 894 (1990).

7.7. U.S. patent examination process is imperfect. *See,* Malone, supra, note 3.E.6., pp. 46–48; Kahin, *supra,* note 7.2, p. 55. See also, *Request for Comments for the Advisory Commission on Patent Law Reform,* 56 Fed. Reg. 22, 702 (May 16, 1991).

7.8. Professor Galler's efforts to improve the software patenting process: Torsten Busse, "Software Floods the Patent Office," *Infoworld,* September 30, 1991, p. 35.

7.9. The draft recommendations of the Patent Commissioner's Advisory Commission regarding software-related patents were that no change in the current protection regime be made, and no special test of patentability be applied to such patents, that the U.S. government encourage other countries that do not recognize the patentability of software-related inventions to change their laws, that recruiting and training of patent examiners emphasize software experience, and that access to prior software art be improved. "Advisory Commission Reviews Draft Recommendations on Patent Law Reforms," *43 BNA Patent, Trademark and Copyright Journal* 383 (March 5, 1992).

7.10. PTO article on standards of review for software patents. Fred E. McKelvey, *PTO Report on Patentable Subject Matter: Mathematical Algorithms and Computer Programs, BNA's Patent, Trademark & Copyright Journal,* September 21, 1989, p. 563.

7.11. Etymology of the word "algorithm": See, Owen Gingerich, "Islamic Astronomy," *Scientific American,* April, 1986, p. 74.

7.12. Citations to the cases discussed in this chapter: *In re Abele,* 684 F. 2d 902 (1982); *In re Meyer,* 688 F. 2d 789 (C.C.P.A. 1982); *Paine, Webber, Jackson & Curtis, Inc. v. Merrill Lynch; Pierce, Fenner & Smith, Inc.,* 4564 F. Supp. 1358, (D. Del. 1983); *In re Pardo,* 684 F. 2d 912 (C.C.P.A. 1982); *Polaroid Corp. v. Eastman Kodak Co.,* 789 F. 2d 1556 (Fed. Cir. 1986); *Polaroid Corp. v. Eastman Kodak Co.,* 16 U.S.P.Q. 2d (BNA) 1481 (D. Mass. 1991).

### Chapter 7: Endnote

7.E.1. Fritz Machlup's criticism of the patent system: Fritz Machlup, "An Economic Review of the Patent System," *Subcommittee on Patents, Trademarks and Copyrights, Committee on the Judiciary, U.S. Senate, 85th Congress, 2d Session,* 1958.

7.E.2. "Software Patents: a Horrible Mistake?" *See,* Michael Murie, "Developers, law experts decry patents," *MacWeek,* April 18, 1989, p. 59.

7.E.3. The law professor's view that patents seem likely to increase barriers to entry: Samuelson, *supra,* note 7.3 at 1135, 1136, 1137.

7.E.4. The economist's view that patents seem unlikely to increase barriers to entry: Mansfield, supra, note 5.E.2.: See also Rapp and Rozek, *supra,* note 6.E.5. at 25.

7.E.5. Licensing and disclosure as ways of proliferating technology: See, R. Levin, A. Klevorick, R. Nelson and S. Winter, "Appropriating The Returns from Industrial R & D," *Brookings Papers on Economic Activity* 3 (1987) 783–831.

7.E.6. The use of blocking patents by the Japanese: Malone, *supra,* note 3.E.6. at 39.

7.E.7. Correlation between strength of patent systems and rate of economic development: Rapp and Rozek, *supra,* note 6.E.5. at 7–10.

7.E.8. Judge Easterbrook's view that patents do not accord monopolies: Easterbrook, *supra,* note 5.E.3.

### CHAPTER 8

8.1. This chapter is based on personal experience and on the following papers submitted to the 3000 member user group Eurobit by or on behalf of Fujitsu Limited during 1989: "Executive Summary of Fujitsu Limited's Comments on Section 5 of the Commission's Green Paper on Copyright and the Challenge of Technology (undated);" "Memorandum on Proposed EC Directive (undated)."

## Chapter 8: Endnote

8.E.1. This endnote is based on Landes and Posner, *supra,* note 6.E.6.

## CHAPTER 9

9.1. This chapter is based on the Supreme Court opinion, *Bonito Boats, Inc. v. Thunder Craft Boats, Inc.,* 109 S. Ct. 971 (1989).

9.2. "Copyleft" distribution of Free Software Foundation programs: Zachary, *supra,* note 6.E.4. at p. R24.

9.3. How software acquires trade secret protection: L. J. Kutten, "Software Developers Must Take Steps to Protect Own Secrets," *Computerworld,* August 25, 1986, p. 86.

9.4. The *Compco* case: *Compco Corp. v. Day-Brite Lighting, Inc.* 376 U.S. 234 (1964).

9.5. Cryptanalysis examples are from Hamilton Nickels, *Codemaster: Secrets of Making and Breaking Codes* (Boulder, Co.: Paladin Press, 1990).

9.6. The argument that in the case of computer programs, neither copyright law nor trade secret law should be permitted to protect source code for programs published in object code form: See, *Comment: Improving the International Framework for the Protection of Computer Software,* 48 U. Pitt. L. Rev. 1151, 1163–64.

## Chapter 9: Endnote

9.E.1. In the most notorious case of alleged employee misuse of software trade secrets, police raided the offices and homes of Gordon Eubanks, head of Symantec, and Eugene Wang, a former Borland executive hired by Symantec. Wang was said to have sent Borland trade secrets by E-mail to Eubanks just before he quit Borland. The trade secrets were said to include marketing strategies, potential business relationships, new product development, potential recruiting prostpects and Borland's business strategies vis à vis Symantec. EDGE: Work Group Computing Report, September 21, 1992.

9.E.2. Lack of dispersion of technology in countries that do not protect trade secrets: Sherwood, *supra,* note 3.E.8 at 115–129.

## CHAPTER 10

10.1. The story of the *Autodesk* case is based on the opinions of the trial court, intermediate court and high court, *Autodesk, Inc. and ANOR v. Martin Peter Dyason and ORS* (1989) 15 IPR 1, *appeal allowed,* No. VG 300 (September 14, 1990), *appeal dismissed,* No. 92/001 (February 12, 1992) and on personal experience.

10.2. IBM's System/360 was microcoded to achieve compatibility: Richard A. Shaffer, "Innovation at Apple and IBM," *Personal Computing,* September 1989, p. 45.

10.3. At last report, Peter Kelly was in the process of petitioning High Court for a rehearing on grounds that the Court's judgment was based on reasoning different from that raised by the parties; reasoning which he had had no opportunity to rebut. The beat goes on.

## CHAPTER 11

11.1. The beginning of the Japanese economic miracle: *Sayonara Michelangelo, supra,* note 5.E.4., at p. 65.

11.2. Japanese export strategy is described in Robert Sobel, *IBM v. Japan, Inc.,* (New York: Stein and Day, 1986) p. 149–150.

11.3. Japanese industrial policy toward the computer industry: Sobel, *supra,* pp. 157–159; H. J. Welke, *Data Processing in Japan,* (New York: North Holland Publishing, 1982) pp. 22–24, 39, 58–61, 115–123. *See,* Tateishi, "Japan/U.S.—The Final Round," *Bungei Shunju,* July, 1992.

11.4. Hitachi's "IBM culture" and acquisition of NAS: Jean S. Boeman and Lori Valigra, "Japan's Mainframes: Long-Term Global Strategies Unfold," *Computerworld,* November 26, 1990, p. 1; Jean S. Bozman and Lori Valegra, "Unix Evens Odds for Japanese," *Computerworld,* November 26, 1990, p. 102; Jean S. Bozman, "Amdahl and HDS Hold Allies in Separate Light," *Computerworld,* November 26, 1990, p. 101.

11.5. Fujitsu's aggressive cloning strategy and acquisition of ICL: Michael Cross, "Fujitsu Duels for the Crown," *Business* (U.K.), May, 1991, p. 76; Amiel Kornel and Nell Margolis, "Fujitsu Aiming to Purchase ICL," *Computerworld,* July 23, 1990, p. 116.

11.6. The Microsoft/Shuuwa lawsuit in Japan: *Microsoft Corp. v. Shuuwa System Trading, K.K.,* 1219 Hanrei Jihoo 48 (Tokyo D. Ct. 1987).

## CHAPTER 12

12.1. The description of the litigation process and court papers in the IBM/AMI litigation is taken predominately from Judge O'Neill's antitrust opinion, *Allen-Myland Inc. v. International Business Machines Corp.,* 693 F. Supp. 262 (E.D. Pa. 1988), and his copyright opinion, *Allen-Myland, Inc. v. International Business Machines Corp.,* 746 F. Supp. 520 (E.D. Pa. 1990).

12.2. "A desire to continue an obsolescent business in the face of new technology does not excuse copying." It doesn't excuse trademark infringement, either. In June, 1992, IBM filed a trademark infringement lawsuit against AMI, as a result of AMI's practice—apparently begun in an earlier technological generation—of unsoldering memory modules from certain 309X memory cards, resoldering the modules onto other IBM 309X memory cards and selling the end-product, or conspiring with others to sell it, as authentic IBM memory. Complaint, *International Business Machines Corporation v. Allen-Myland, Inc.,* Civ. No. 92-C2896. Why bother subjecting IBM memory modules to this heating/reheating, contamination-prone process just to move them from one IBM memory card to another? Arbitrage again. Market demand for authentic cards with different numbers of modules on them varies over time. If modules can be removed from less-popular cards in order to fabricate more popular cards which are then marketed as IBM factory-made, the arbitraguer can make a profit. The illegality here lies not in the resoldering, but in misusing the IBM trademark. IBM memory cards are manufactured in a special reduced heat, float-solder, hermetic environment to assure longevity. Whatever process AMI uses to cobble together its cards, those cards should be marketed under AMI's trademark, not IBM's.

## CHAPTER 13

13.1. Elsewhere I have suggested that much of the academic criticism of copyright protection for software derived from technophobia. *See, Softcopy,* pp. 46–47.

13.2. A law student invents his own system at protection for software: "Comment: The Incompatibility of Copyright and Computer Software: An Economic Evaluation and a Proposal for a Marketplace Solution," 66 N.C. L. Rev. 977 (June, 1988).

13.3. A sampling of academic proposals to discard traditional copyright protection for software in favor of *sui generis* legislation: Pamela Samuelson, "CONTU Revisited: The Case Against Copyright Protection for Computer Programs in Machine-Readable Form," 1984 Duke L.J. 663 (September, 1984); Pamela Samuelson, "Benson Revisited: The Case Against Patent Protection for Algorithms and Other Computer Program-Related Inventions," supra, note 7.3; "Note: Sui Generis Intellectual Property Protection for Computer Software," 60 Geo. Wash. L. Rev. 997 (April, 1992). A catalog of early articles of this type may be found in Leo J. Raskind, "The Uncertain Case for Special Legislation Protecting Computer Software," 47 U. Pitt. L. Rev. 1131 (Summer, 1986).

13.4. The eminent law professor who writes and speaks in favor of "thin" copyright protection for software is Paul Goldstein of Stanford, a courtly, urbane and intelligent man whose opinions about copyright law principles, which were most likely arrived at irrespective of the software-clone client base of his law firms, are entitled to great respect. His opinions as to the range of software expression are another thing altogether. As to whether writing computer programs is like map-making or chart making, or is "the ultimate creative medium", builds "castles in air" and "gratifies creative longings", it would be best for the reader to credit the views of the computer scientists and computer programmers quoted in Chapter 1 than to rely on the opinion of a law professor.

13.5 Professor Froy's identity is of course a matter of public record. The description of Professor Froy's participation in the IBM/AMI litigation is taken from the deposition of Professor Pamela Samuelson in that case.

13.6. Professor Samuelson's anti-copyright articles (a sampling only): "CONTU Revisited: The Case Against Copyright Protection for Computer Programs in Machine Readable Form," 1984 Duke L. J. 663; "Creating a New Kind of Intellectual Property: Applying the Lessons of the Chip Law to Computer Programs," 70 Minn. L. Rev. 471 (1985); "Why the look and feel of software user interfaces should not be protected by copyright law," *Communications of the ACM,* May, 1989, p. 563; "Reflections on the State of American Software Copyright Law and the Perils of Teaching It," 13 Columbia - VLA J. L. & Arts 61 (1988).

13.7. The "gang of ten" law professors in the Lotus/Borland litigation, including Samuelson, became the "gang of eleven" in the case of *Sega Enterprises, Ltd. v. Accolade, Inc.,* Case No. C–91–3871; BAC (N.D. Cal. 1992), filing an *amicus curiae* brief in support of reverse compilation of computer programs by competitors. See, notes 17.3 and 19.10, infra.

13.8. The Zen koan at the end of this chapter is adapted from John Newman *Bushido: The Way of the Warrior: A New Perspective on the Japanese Military Tradition* (New York: Gallery Books, 1989).

## CHAPTER 14

14.1. The trial court opinion in *Computer Associates v. Altai* is reported in 775 F. Supp. 554 (E.D.N.Y. 1991).

14.2. The MIT panel moderated by Randy Davis was videotaped and transcribed: "Intellectual Property in Computing: (How) Should Software Be Protected? An Industry Perspective," October 30, 1991.

14.3. Fred Brooks' lesson in effective software design is from Brooks, *supra,* note 1.8.

14.4. Judge Learned Hand's "patterns of abstraction" test: *Nichols v. Universal Pictures Corp.,* 45 F. 2d 119, 121 (2d Cir. 1930).

14.5. "Not surprisingly, Judge Pratt's brethren upheld his ruling." In doing so, the Second Circuit worked serious mischief. After asserting that the nature of computer programming was "vital" to its decision, the appellate court obtained virtually all of its "facts" about the nature of computer programs from a handful of law review articles by law students and a member of the "gang of ten". Not surprisingly, the court concluded that the range of creative expression in computer programs generally is quite narrow, and that applying copyright law to computer programs was like attempting to "fit a square peg into a round hole." Ignoring the report of the court-appointed expert, the court also concluded that the only nonliteral element of a program was its structure and that the structure of a program consisted of the function of its modules and their relation to one another, its macros and the parameter lists for those macros. The court called the *Whelan* case "the most thoughtful attempt to accomplish [the separation of idea from expression in computer program]", but went on to trash the *Whelan* court's reasoning. Predictably, the court concluded that the Second Circuit's "patterns" test was a better way to accomplish that separation, but then invented a wholly novel and improper methodology for performing the "patterns" test. The new methodology involved filtering out each idea, process, efficiency-dictated element, externality-dictated element, or standard technique in *each* structural item, *before* comparing the original program with the accused program. *Computer Associates International, Inc. v. Altai, Inc.,* Docket Nos. 91–7893, 91–9935 (2d Cir., June 22, 1992). The notion of filtering out parts of an original program before comparing it to an accused problem has been called by a judge who had read Judge Pratt's opinion "wholly inconsistent with case law authorities" and having "the potential to eviscerate the application of the prevailing substantial similarity test as defined by *Whelan* and its progeny." *Gates Rubber Co. v. Bando American, Inc.* 1992 WL 152250 (D. Colo., June 24, 1992). In an absolutely masterful synthesis of *Computer Associates* with pre-existing caselaw, Judge Keeton in *Lotus v. Borland* found the underlying principles of *Computer Associates* to be (1) that nonliteral expression in computer programs is protected by copyright and (2) that a program can have more than one idea. He also found the abstraction-filtration methodology was "compatible substantively" with his own approach in *Lotus v. Paperback* but not appropriate as an analytical tool for the case before him. Memorandum and Order, Lotus Development Corp. v. Borland Int'l., Inc., Civ. No.

90–11662-K (D. Mass. July 31, 1992) pp. 19, 25–27. He opined that both *Whelan* and *Computer Associates* were instructive precedents. Id. at 26.

## CHAPTER 15

15.1. The copyright misuse case described in this chapter is *Lasercomb America, Inc. v. Reynolds,* 911 F. 2d. 970 (4th Cir. 1990).

15.2. The tying of salt-machinery patents to the use of the patent holder's salt: *Morton Salt Co. v. G.S. Suppinger Co.,* 314 U.S. 488 (1942).

15.3. The capture of General Stoughton by John Mosby: Jeffry D. Wert, *Mosby's Rangers* (New York, Simon and Schuster, 1990) pp. 19–20.

## CHAPTER 16

16.1. Theft of Apple source code by the nu-Prometheus League: Carol Said, "Apple fires two after FBI interview," *MacWeek,* March 29, 1990, p. 3; Howard Millman, "Mystery group steals Mac Source code," *PC Computing,* November, 1989, p. 62.

16.2. The hackers known as the Legion of Doom: Mark Lewyn and Even I. Schwartz, "Why the Legion of Doom has Little Fear of the Feds," *Business Week,* April 15, 1991, p. 31; Willie Schatz, "The Terminal Men; Crackdown on the 'Legion of Doom' Ends an Era for Computer Hackers," *Washington Post,* June 24, 1990, p. H9. An internal rift in the Legion of Doom has resulted in the formation of the Masters of Deception, a group of hackers with a larcenous bent. Mary B. Tabor and Anthony Ramirez, "Computer Savvy, with an Attitude," *New York Times,* July 23, 1992, p. BI.

16.3. In addition to recounting his escapades at the Thomas J. Watson Research Laboratory, Clifford Stoll has chronicled them in a best-selling book, *The Cucoo's Egg* (New York; Doubleday, 1989).

16.4. Western intelligence agencies spy on one another's industries: Mitch Betts, "CIA steps up Foreign Technology Watch," *Computerworld,* April 20, 1992, p. 121; Glenn Frankel, "British Spies Seek Meaningful Work," *Washington Post,* February 26, 1992, p. A20; Ronald Ostrow and Paul Richter, "Economic Espionage Poses Major Peril to U.S. Interests," *Los Angeles Times,* September 28, 1992, p. A1.

16.5. American hackers infected Iraqi computers with viruses before the Persian Gulf War: Michael Alexander, "Military Sees Problems, Promise in Viral Strikes," *Computerworld,* April 8, 1991, p. 97.

16.6. The story of Robert Morris: Jonathan Littman, "The Shockwave Rider; Background on Robert Morris," *PC Computing,* June, 1990, p. 142; John Burgess, "No Jail Time Imposed in Hacker Case," *Washington Post,* May 5, 1990, p. A1.

16.7. Operation Sun Devil: Johnathan Littman, "Cyberpunk meets Mr. Security," *PC Computing,* June 1992, p. 288; W. John Moore, "Taming Cyberspace," *National Journal,* March 28, 1992; Craig Bromberg, "In Defense of Hackers," *New York Times,* April 21, 1991, Magazine Section, p. 45.

16.8. Electronic Freedom Foundation: John Perry Barlow, "A Man from the FBI," *Effector,* March, 1991, p. 1; Mitchell Kapor, "Why Defend Hackers," *Effector,* March, 1991, p. 1; Mitchell Kapor and Mike Godwin, EFF News #1.00, December 10, 1990 (USENET e-mail).

16.9. The Leonard Rose saga: Mark Potts, "Hacker Pleads Guilty in AT&T Case," *Washington Post*, March 23, 1991, p. A1; Willie Schartz, *supra*, note 16.2; Mitchell Kapor and Mike Godwin, "Special Edition: Amicus Brief in Len Rose Case," EFF News #1.01, January 7, 1991 (USENET e-mail).

16.10. Richard Stallman's mission: *See*, Zachary, *supra*, note 6.E.4.

16.11. Hackers are forcing software suppliers to increase the security of their programs: *E.g.*, Michael Alexander, "Antivirus Vendors Form Consortium," *Computerworld*, August 19, 1991, p. 85.

16.12. Mitsubishi sues AT&T over insecure PBXs: Michael Alexander, "Mitsubishi Blames AT&T for Security Breach," *Computerworld*, June 24, 1991, p. 12.

16.13. Hackers bedevil the Free Software Foundation's systems: "Freedom Carries a Price," *Computerworld*, July 15, 1991, p. 82.


## CHAPTER 17

17.1. This chapter is based on the case of *Atari Games Corp. v. Nintendo of America, Inc.*, 19 U.S. P. Q. 2d (BNA) 1935 (N.D. Cal. 1991).

17.2. The effect of having a "closed" system on the success of the Macintosh is discussed in Ezra Shapiro, "Twelve All-Time Favorites," *Byte*, August, 1988, p. 21; Richard A. Danca, "Norton Looking for New Challenges as PC Matures," *Government Computer News*, May 27, 1988, p. 14.

17.3. "Atari's remedy, if any, more likely lies in antitrust law than in patent or copyright." A second California case confirms that view. *Sega v. Accolade*, supra, note 13.7, 785 F. Supp. 1392 (N.D. Cal. 1992). The game company Accolade had reverse-compiled the code of video games written by Sega International in order to determine how Accolade's games could reproduce the legend that the games produced by authorized Sega licensees displayed on TV screens when those games were running on Sega video game consoles. Accolade had inquired into the terms of an authorized license from Sega, but did not care for the terms of such licensees. Though the Accolade games were different from the Sega games that were reverse-compiled, Sega sued Accolade on grounds that the reverse-compilation itself was unauthorized copying, which of course it was. Federal Judge Barbara Caulfield awarded Sega an injunction barring further sale of Accolade games developed as a result of the reverse compilation. Like the *Nintendo* case, the *Sega* case was appealed by the defendant. Due to the pendency of the injunction, an expedited appeal was granted by the 9th Circuit Court of Appeals.

17.4. Atari had its choice of appeals courts. Geographically, the case was pending in the Ninth Circuit in California. Because Nintendo had sued for patent infringement as well as copyright infringement, however, Atari was free to appeal Judge Smith's order either to the Ninth Circuit or to the Federal Circuit Court of Appeals in Washington, D.C., which has jurisdiction over appeals in patent infringement cases. Atari chose the Federal Circuit, which ruled on its appeal on September 10, 1992, in *Atari Games Corp. v. Nintendo of America, Inc.*, No. 91–1293. (Slip op.) It was not a felicitous choice for Atari. The Federal Circuit affirmed Judge Smith's draconian order. The court took its view of the history of American copyright law from Judge Keeton's "thorough" review in *Lotus v. Paperback*. Based on that view, the Court found that it should not invent a new test for determining what is protected expression in computer programs, but employ the "tests used for other literary works."

The court held that Nintendo was likely to be able to prove at trial that 10NES program was a unique sequence of arbitrary instructions that created a "purely arbitrary data stream" and therefore that 10NES contained protected expression. Applying the "patterns" test to separate Nintendo's console program into "manageable components" (rather than into each conceivable structured element as the *Computer Associates* court recommended) the court concluded that the idea of the 10NES component was probably "the generation of a data stream to unlock a console," and that in copying the 10NES "song," Atari copied protected expression. It also held that obtaining and copying the 10NES source code from the Copyright Office constituted copyright infringement. Finally, the panel concluded that because of Atari's "unclean hands" in lying to the Copyright Office it would probably not be able to sustain its defense of copyright misuse; therefore Judge Smith had not erred in denying Atari's antitrust motion.

Along the way, the court gave lip service to the Second Circuit's "filtering methodology" (see note 14.5), but did not follow it, utilizing instead the Ninth Circuit's two-step test in which the two works are first compared objectively element by element, and then subjectively as a whole. The three-judge panel seemed to be persuaded by the evidence that Atari's Rabbit program contained similarities to 10NES that were not "necessary to embody the unprotectable idea, process or method of the 10NES program," and contained instructions equivalent to instructions that had later been deleted from 10NES and had therefore been unnecessary to copy.

The Federal Circuit opinion was sent to me by Gerry Davis, one of Atari's lawyers. Why, the reader may wonder, was a lawyer for the losing party sending me the evidence of his defeat? You will find the answer, which has to do with fair use and reverse engineering, in note 19.10, which also discusses why Accolade fared better in its Ninth Circuit appeal of the *Sega* ruling discussed in note 17.3.

## CHAPTER 18

18.1. Hans Moravec's vision of computerized minds: Ed Regis, *Great Mambo Chicken and the Transhuman Condition* (New York, Viking, 1990).

18.2. Open Systems interconnection standards: Carolyn V. Woody and Robert A. Fleck, "International Telecommunications: The current environment," *Journal of Systems Management*, December, 1991, p. 32; *see also*, articles collected in "State of the Art: Interoperability," *Byte*, November, 1991; Elisabeth Horwitt, "OSI Delays Forcing Firms to Seek Other Options," *Computerworld*, February 4, 1992, p. 91.

18.3. The IBM System/360: James Connolly and Jeffrey Beeler, "The Price of Success", *Computerworld*, November 3, 1986, p. 179.

18.4. "Stepping out of the clone zone": Richard Pastore, "IBM Compatibles step out of the Clone Zone," *Computerworld*, April 15, 1991,

18.5. UNIX and OSF: Johanna Ambrosio, "AT&T's Unix Sell-off Won't Sway OSF," *Computerworld*, April 8, 1991, p. 12; Dom Panucci, "Open to Question," *DEC User*, May 1991, p. 24; Tim Grantham, "Unix Standard Rivals Put on Competitive Face," *Computerworld*, June 4, 1990, p. 6.

18.6. The OLTP operating systems battle: Stuart Zipper, "Battle Lines Shaping in §30B OLTP Market," *Electronic News*, April 8, 1991, p. 1.

18.7. The ACE consortium is described in Maryfran Johnson and Richard Pastore,

"Compaq, DEC Lead Bid to Trump Sun with ACE," *Computerworld,* April 15, 1991, p. 1. The consortium is already beginning to fall apart due to the proprietary interests of some of its members. *See,* Paul Lavin, "A House of Cards," *Which Computer,* May, 1992, p. 52; Dom Panucci, "Compaq ditches ACE Consortium," *PC User*, May 6, 1992, p. 15.

18.8. The DMR study of use of open systems: Tim Grantham, "Open Systems Finds a Place in Users' Heart," *Computerworld,* May 27, 1991, p. 25; J. A. Savage, "Open Systems Escape Scrutiny, *Computerworld,* October 22, 1990.

18.9. Customer motivations regarding open systems: Horwith, *supra,* note 18.2.

18.10. European suppliers react to the commoditization brought about by open systems: Elaine L. Appleton, "Ouch: Europe's Biggest Suppliers Feel the Pinch," *Datamation,* July 1, 1991, p. 60; Peggy Salz Trautman, "Can You Solve the Desktop Dilemma," *Datamation,* June 1, 1991, p. 96–7.

18.11. Business Week reports that the result of open systems initiatives is customer confusion: John W. Verity, Richard Brandt, Jonathan B. Levine and Gary McWilliams, "Computer Confusion," *Business Week*, June 10, 1991, p. 72.

18.12. Open systems is coming to mean interoperability: *see,* Maryfran Johnson, "OSF Changes Emphasis to Focus on 'Middleware'," *Computerworld,* May 11, 1992, p. 1.8 ("The customer definition of open systems is interoperability over multivendor environments"). *See also,* Horwith, *supra,* note 18.2. Indeed, as strong proprietary operating systems such as OS/2 2.0 and Windows NT, the UNIX standards groups have been forced closer together. Maryfran Johnson, "Political Mine Field Could Sabotage OSF Future Plans," *Computerworld,* July 27, 1992, p. 1.

## CHAPTER 19

19.1. The fusing of computer software and other forms of expression into "multimedia" products and industries: Evan I. Schwartz, "The Lucie Show: Shaking Up a Stodgy IBM," *Business Week,* April 6, 1992, p. 64; John Gantz, "Explosion on the Desktop," *Computer Graphics World,* April, 1992, p. 27; Karen Wright, Fred Guturi and Henry Scott, "The Road to the Global Village," *Scientific American,* March, 1990, p. 83.

19.2. European Community economic policy for the computer industry seen as having failed: Louis S. Richman, Shawn Tully, Sandra L. Kirsch and Lenore Schiff, "The real danger in Europe's Slump," *Fortune,* July 1, 1991, p. 67; Jonathan B. Levine, "The Last Hurrah for European High Tech?" *Fortune,* April 1991, p. 44; Guy de Jorquieres and Alan Cane, "National Champions Become Laggards, *Financial Times,* April 29, 1991, p. 17.

19.3. "Europe has become the major battlefield in our industry." The Lorentz quote is from Richard L. Hudson, "IBM, Other U.S. Computer Makers Face Challenge from the Japanese in Europe," *Wall Street Journal,* August 13, 1990, p. B5.

19.4. The draft EC copyright directive was a compromise between harmonizing Member States' copyright laws and adopting industrial policies that promote clone software: *See,* Hilary Pierson, Clifford Miller and Nigel Turtle, "Commercial Implication of the European Software Copyright Directive," *The Computer Lawyer*, November, 1991, p. 13. The draft itself was published as Commission of the European Communities, Green Paper on Copyright and the Challenge of Technology: Copyright Issues Acquiring Immediate Action Com (88) 172, Brussels, June 7, 1988.

19.5. ECIS' position on the draft directive: European Committee for Interoperable Systems, "Introduction to the Proposed Directive on the Legal Protection of Computer Programs" (undated).

19.6. SAGE's position on the draft directive: Software Action Group For Europe, "The Decompilation Issue in the EC Directive: The Views of Industry on the Draft Text of the European Commission Services," April 25, 1990.

19.7. Fujitsu's license contract is that of Fujitsu Australia, as of this writing the only English-speaking country in which Fujitsu's software is generally available. The Fujitsu Australia and Sun Microsystems contracts are part of the author's private collection of software industry license agreements. Some people collect stamps...

19.8. The Bull case is reported as: *Bull HN Information Sys., Inc. v. American Express Bank, Ltd.,* 1990 Copyright Law, Dec. (CCH) § 26,555 (S.D.N.Y. 1987). It adopts the reasoning of *Whelan v. Jaslow* as to what constitutes expression in computer programs. *Id.* at 23,278.

19.9. SAGE's justification for advocating a European directive more protective than existing law was conveyed to the author in discussions with SAGE members. The author was also involved in negotiations between SAGE members and ECIS members to attempt to forge an industry compromise.

19.10. The straying of the American Judiciary from a long history of applying traditional principles of copyright law to computer software began with the *Computer Associates* case, and in particular with the Second Circuit's August 1992 affirmance of Judge Pratt's decision. In that affirmance, the Second Circuit evinced an animus against copyright protection for software and crafted a test for substantial similarity that, if followed literally (which no court has been willing to do as of this writing) would eviscerate the Copyright Act as a protective mechanism for software. The deterioration in the quality of judicial opinions continued later that year, when the Federal Circuit and the Ninth Circuit turned to the subject that had dominated the EC copyright debate: reverse compilation.

The Federal Circuit spoke first, in the *Nintendo/Atari* case. Although the panel of judges affirmed the injunction barring Atari from marketing Nintendo-compatible games, on its way to doing so the panel concluded that reverse-compiling the Nintendo software was "far use" because the unprotected elements of that software could not be understood without translation from object code to Source-like code. Unfortunately for Atari, "fair use" by reverse compilation did not absolve it of responsibility for the other types of copying in which it had engaged—reproducing the code wrongfully obtained from the Copyright Office and developing a substantially similar program. Unfortunately for the rest of the software industry, though, a federal appeals court had now expanded the "fair use" defense explosively in software cases, and perhaps in cases involving other types of copyrighted works which do not wear all their ideas on their sleeves.

Next, the Ninth Circuit rendered its opinion in the *Sega/Accolade* litigation. (See note 17.3, *supra.*) As in the *Nintendo* case, the video game supplier Accolade had appealed the injunction which had barred it from marketing games compatible with Sega consoles on grounds that Accolade's compatibility was achieved by reverse compiling (i.e., translating) Sega's lockout programs. The Ninth Circuit dissolved the injunction, holding that reverse compilation that did not result in a substantially similar program was fair use. In doing so, the Ninth Circuit joined the Federal Circuit in observing (erroneously) that object code cannot be read by humans, and that where there is a "good reason" for studying the unprotected aspects of a program, reverse compiling the object code of that program for such purposes is fair use. The panel assumed (erroneously) that the Sega data stream (unlike the Nintendo data stream) was unprotectable. The panel also concluded (erroneously) that if reverse compilation of object code were an unfair use, the copyright owner would gain a *de facto* monopoly over the functional aspects of its work.

Now, as we have seen, the copyright grant can in no way be likened to a monopoly. Further, unlike functional articles, the design of which is normally dictated by their function, the design of a computer program is not dictated by functionality. The Sega lockout data stream, for example, could have consisted of the binary form of a *haiku* written by a Sega in-house poet, or a few bars of music written by a Sega in-house musician, or any other arbitrary sequence of characters. *Apple v. Franklin* taught the industry a decade ago that the desire of a second comer to be compatible cannot convert protected expression into unprotected idea, and as we've seen, that teaching has been widely adopted. Finally, to worry that Sega might monopolize the "market" for Sega-compatible games is to speak from a dream world in which Sega-compatible games do not compete with games written for other consoles or for personal computers, and in which Sega is not a small competitor struggling to increase its business in the face of strong competition for console and game placements.

For now, both the *Nintendo* and the *Sega* cases must be viewed as setbacks for almost everyone in sight. For the clones, the fact that the Federal Circuit had found the reproduction of the 10NES "song" and the instructions that produced it to be infringement did not bode well. Similarly, the fact that the Ninth Circuit had found reverse compilation to be copyright infringement except in cases where the use was "fair," and suggested that if Accolade's games had competed directly with Sega's games the result would have been different, had to come as cold comfort.

For software innovators, the notion that wholesale reverse compilation could ever be fair use—a concept that goes far further than the EC directive—was shocking for reasons that by now should be obvious to the reader. In addition, the apparent about-face from the *Apple/Franklin* rule was unsettling in the extreme.

For the music industry, the movie industry, the book publishing industry and other industries that are "going digital," the two recent reverse compilation cases were a chilly welcome to the brave new world. Visions of musicians reverse-compiling compact disks into sheet-music form in order to avoid having to pay for sheet music, visions of special effects producers reverse-compiling videodisks into source-like form so that the effects could be imitated, and visions of users reverse-compiling interactive CD-ROM reference books into complete hardcopy form (all, of course, just for purposes of studying the unprotected ideas in the works) send shivers through the traditional copyright world. And in that shivering lies this author's final prediction.

19.11. The final EC copyright directive was promulgated as: *Council Directive 91/250 on the Legal Protection of Computer Programs,* 1991 O.J. (L. 122/43).

19.12. Professor Immenga's warning against adoption of a reverse-compilation right: Ulrich Immenga, "Wege Zur Software-Piraterie," *Frankfurter Allgemeine Zeitung,* November 8, 1990, p. 28.

19.13. The European litigation on enforceability of copyrights in television programming guides: British Broadcasting Corp. v. Commission of the European Communities, Case No. T–70/89; Independent Television Publications Ltd. v. Commission of the European Communities, Case No. T–76/89 (Ct. of First Inst. 7/10/91).

19.14. Australia is reexamining copyright protection for software in the wake of the EC directive: Beverley Head, "Australia: Software a New PSA Worry," *Australian Financial Review* (Reuters Textline), January 28, 1992.

19.15. GATT and WIPO software issues are described in: "Copyright Panel Reviews Bilateral and Multilateral Trade Developments," 41 *BNA Patent, Trademark and Copyright Journal* 433 (March 21, 1991).

19.16. JEIDA's paper on software protection: Japanese Electronic Industry Development Association, "Computer Programs and Intellectual Property Rights," (undated).

19.17. The judicial view that software authors have a broad range of expression:

(a) *SAS Institute, Inc. v. S&H Computer Sys.,* 605 F. Supp. 816, 825 (M.D. Tenn. 1985).

(b) *Apple Computer, Inc. v. Macintosh Computers, Ltd.,* No. T–1232–84, No. T–1235–04, slip op. at 3 (F.C. Can. April 29, 1986)

(c) *M. Kramer Mfg. Co., Inc. v. Andrews,* 783 F. 2d. 421, 436 (4th Cir. 1986)

19.18. The 1991 Japanese decision liberally interpreting the term "algorithm": Systems Science Corp. v. Toyo Sokki K.K., Tokyo Dist. Ct., March 31, 1989, *aff'd. in part, rev'd. in part,* Tokyo High Court, June 20, 1989.

19.19. A major, if openly sycophantic, study of Japanese software factories is: Michael A. Cusamano, *Japanese Software Factories: A Challenge to U.S. Management* (New York, Oxford University Press, 1991).

19.20. Japanese acquisitions of entertainment firms: See, Alan Citron, "Japan's Thirst for Hollywood Is Unquenched," *Los Angeles Times,* December 10, 1990. That software acquisitions can affect hardware sales was the theme of American VCR designer Go-Video Inc.'s lawsuit attempting to block the acquisition of entertainment giant MCA Inc. by Matsushita. "VCR Maker Challenges MCA Buyout on Antitrust Grounds," Asahi Evening News (Tokyo), December 10, 1990. ("We know that if you control the software, you control the hardware.... Except for Go-Video, they already have a monopoly on hardware. This [acquisition] is to make sure guys like us don't get in," i.e., that "Go-Video's products will not play their software, and anybody else (outside Japan) who makes HDTV won't either.") See also, Eduardo Lachica, "U.S.-Japan VCR Antitrust Suit to Start," *Wall Street Journal,* April 1, 1991, p. B1.

19.21. Japanese software developers' difficulties in succeeding on the world market: *See,* Ellison, *supra,* note 1.5; Rifkin, *supra,* note 1.5; Charles P. Lecht, "Japan's software threat: a U.S.-made paper tiger," *Computerworld,* April 8, 1991, p. 25.

19.22. For a review of the computer industry "alliance" fad: *See,* Brian Bollen, "A growing trend to word alliances," *Financial Times;* Anthony J. Michels, "Customers Drive Company Tie-ups," *Fortune,* January 27, 1992, p. 12.

19.23. Dearth of venture capital available for computer industry start-ups: Nell Margolis, "Lack of venture capital defers start-ups," *Computerworld,* August 12, 1991, p. 65.

19.24. "If it ain't broke, don't break it." Howard Figueroa of IBM, quoted in *NCR Report, supra,* note 1.3, p. 2.

# Index

**About the Author**

ANTHONY LAWRENCE CLAPES is Assistant General Counsel at IBM, responsible for managing litigation matters, including intellectual property litigation. Mr. Clapes is a frequent lecturer at seminars on intellectual property protection for software. In 1991, he was named one of the leading high-tech intellectual property lawyers in the United States by the *National Law Journal*. He is the author of a seminal book on copyright law and computer programs, *Software, Copyright, and Competition: The "Look and Feel" of the Law* (Quorum, 1989).